Apocalypses in Context

Apocalypses in Context

Apocalyptic Currents through History

Kelly J. Murphy and Justin Jeffcoat Schedtler,
editors

Fortress Press
Minneapolis

APOCALYPSES IN CONTEXT
Apocalyptic Currents through History

Cover image: Disaster City, Apocalyptic/Grandfailure/Thinkstock.com

Cover design: Rob Dewey

Library of Congress Cataloging-in-Publication Data
Print ISBN: 978-1-4514-9623-9
eBook ISBN: 978-1-5064-1685-4

The paper used in this publication meets the minimum requirements of American National Standard for Information Sciences — Permanence of Paper for Printed Library Materials, ANSI Z329.48-1984.

Manufactured in the U.S.A.

This book was produced using Pressbooks.com, and PDF rendering was done by PrinceXML.

Contents

Foreword

The apocalyptic imagination has many mothers and many children, as the far-reaching essays in this volume demonstrate. Searching for the origins of apocalyptic thought takes one back into the second millennium BCE, into the cultures of the ancient Near East and the memorable mythic narratives and images that were forged in the Bronze Age and that continued to fund the religious imaginations of peoples and cultures for many centuries after that. But even as we recognize the deep roots of many of the characters, plots, and tropes of apocalyptic literature in earlier myths and images, we also recognize that the emergence of a distinctively apocalyptic imagination represents something new, something unprecedented in the life of the cultural west.

Like all cultural births, the birth of the apocalyptic imagination is not so much a defined point in history as it is a gradual materialization of a cluster of ideas, schemata, notions of time, conceptualizations of evil, senses of the structure of history, and so forth. Scholars are divided as to when and where they would locate its origins. Most, however, would see the apocalyptic imagination as first taking shape within the cultural milieu of the Jewish diaspora that settled in Babylon and its environs after the Babylonian destruction of the kingdom of Judah and the exile of many of its leading citizens to Mesopotamia in the sixth century BCE. That context, perhaps as much by accident as by design, became an extraordinary melting pot of civilizations. Peoples from all across the Babylonian empire were relocated into villages in close proximity to one another. Many aspired to enter into the Babylonian administrative and military bureaucracies. In such contexts, cultural mixing flourished. Thus the scribal culture with its high regard for books and the written word, for knowledge that was marked as restricted and mysterious, for curiosity about heavenly mysteries, and for attempts to master the logic of political change became the province not just of Babylonian elites but also of the educated among their subject peoples, who used these new approaches toward knowledge to reflect upon their own place in history.

At this same time, a decisive new set of concepts was introduced when the Persians conquered the Babylonian empire and extended their control throughout the ancient Near East. Many scholars would identify some of the most distinctive ideas of apocalypticism—its pronounced dualism, the notion of strongly marked temporal periods culminating in the victory of good over evil—as derived from Persian Zoroastrian ideas. But although Zoroastrianism continues to this day as a small religious community in Iran and India and in diaspora, it is through the appropriation and transformation of these ideas in Judaism and then subsequently in Christianity that apocalypticism has come to be one of the most formative intellectual constructs of western thought.

But what exactly *is* the apocalyptic imagination? The problem of definition bedevils attempts to study apocalypticism. And for good reason. It is important to remember that concepts are labels of convenience that we use to organize information. They are not categories that identify unchanging essences, such as we would expect if we were asking about the chemical composition of salt or fructose. Furthermore, the use of terms changes over time. So, we have two related problems when we want to talk about "apocalypse" and "apocalypticism." First, we often form concepts by thinking of a prototype example that we use as a point of reference. Because of the dominance of Christian culture in the west and the familiarity of people with the book of Revelation in the Christian canon, the book of Revelation often serves as the prototype of what we think of as an apocalypse—a revelatory vision in which the events of the end times are described in vivid detail. These events are highly catastrophic, both politically and cosmically, and they are framed in a dualistic struggle between personified figures of evil and good. They eventuate in a definitive defeat of evil and the establishment of an eternal future of peace and well-being for a transformed elect. As most scholars of ancient Christianity and Judaism will attest, however, the book of Revelation is actually a fairly anomalous example of the genre apocalypse. In particular, its focus on visualizing destruction is far more intense than one finds in most other apocalypses. Nevertheless, one has to recognize that, culturally speaking, it has had an outsized impact on the imagination of subsequent generations within the Christian and secular West.

If the first problem is that of recognizing the impact of prototypes in shaping our sense of apocalyptic literature, the second is recognizing that changing cultural concerns undercut the normative force of earlier definitions. Especially in the modern period, some of the earlier notions that attached to the idea of apocalypse fall away. This is particularly true as apocalyptic moves from being a concept of the religious imagination to being a concept within the secular cultural imagination. No longer is the focus so much on mysteries revealed. The emphasis is more on the dualistic struggle between sharply defined good and evil and on the destruction of all that is familiar and cherished. In the contemporary imagination, "apocalypse" is almost equivalent with "disaster" or "catastrophe." This is a shift that requires some reflection. In traditional religious apocalypses, even those that are strongly dualistic, the struggle between good and evil is highly stylized. But the structure of the plot is known in advance. Good will triumph over evil. Indeed, the moral satisfaction of reading or hearing an apocalypse is the experience of feeling the danger of evil, imagining it vividly, even while knowing that it is already doomed, and that good will be established forever. In this sense, the genre of apocalypse is close to the modern genre of the thriller. In those novels and films, a dualistic struggle between good and evil takes place. It is usually between two political civilizations or cultures (e.g., Communism and the "Free World," Islamic Terrorism and the West, the Mafia and the FBI), but any strongly dualistic struggle will do. The plot is one of increasing menace, anxiety that evil will triumph, and then a decisive defeat of evil and the establishment of peace and security.

In modern contemporary culture, however, "apocalyptic" novels and films distinctively deviate from this model. That is to say, "apocalypse" has been redefined. The modern apocalyptic imagination is more focused on the destruction of those structures that constitute civilization—the climate, the infrastructure, the social bonds. The evil that provokes this collapse is of equal interest. Sometimes it is from without—aliens or objects from another planet, for example. Sometimes it is from within—technology gone awry, human greed run amok. Although there is some variety, most of the popular apocalyptic fictions cannot do without some element of hope. In contrast to the apocalypses of antiquity and the medieval period, when the eschaton was the moment for the inbreaking of direct divine rule, the aftermath of apocalyptic destruction in modern secular apocalypses is a time of tentative rebuilding, without any hope of external support. Though these apocalyptic imaginings tend to be resolutely nonreligious, they do ask ultimate questions about the nature of human being.

The sketch I have given of the flexibility of the phenomenon of the apocalyptic imagination is woefully inadequate, of course. Even as I have gestured to its variability, I have radically oversimplified it. And that is precisely why one needs volumes like the one Kelly J. Murphy and Justin Jeffcoat Schedtler have produced. Its three sections delineate three key movements in apocalyptic. Part I, Apocalypticism in the Ancient World, takes the reader back into the complexities of the origins of apocalyptic (chapters 2 and 3, by Christopher B. Hays) and into the origin of some of the most fundamental tropes that persist in the apocalyptic imagination up to the present day (chapter 4, by Jackie Wyse Rhodes). Although modern readers may tend to distinguish between religious and political modes of thought, the two were thoroughly enmeshed in antiquity, and chapter 5, by Robert

Williamson Jr. and Justin Jeffcoat Schedtler, explores the political dimensions of apocalyptic thought in anti-imperial resistance, a function that has continued to the present day. It is only because of the dominance of Christianity in the West, of course, and subsequently in much of the globe, that the apocalyptic imagination has become such a definitive presence. The last three chapters of Part I (by Greg Carey, Joshua Jipp, and Justin Jeffcoat Schedtler) explore how apocalyptic thought patterns pervade the thought world of early Christianity.

Part II, Apocalypticism throughout the Ages, traces the complex ways that the apocalyptic imagination funded a variety of different cultural and spiritual needs throughout the succeeding centuries. Although Christianity had a range of relations with the Roman imperial power throughout the first three centuries of its existence, the periods of persecution left a decided impact on its self-concept, and the confluence of apocalyptic ideas and narratives of martyrdom were an important way of thinking about this identity (chapter 9, by Karl Shuve). But as Christianity embraced apocalypticism, why did Judaism reject it? The history of the failed revolts of 66-70 CE and 132-135 CE turned Judaism toward ways of understanding its religious identity that were incompatible with apocalypticism (chapter 10, by Shayna Sheinfeld). Thus, ironically, the history of Jewish apocalypticism was preserved only because Christians found it vital to their own self-identity. And yet, when Rome embraced Christianity as the religion of the empire, apocalypticism, with its anti-imperial sub-text, had to be reinterpreted in ways that would make it compatible with the new relation to empire (chapter 13, by Brennan Breed).

As one might already expect from the ways in which the apocalyptic imagination morphed in order to address new cultural contexts in antiquity, the medieval period brought new transformations. The notion of the "millennium," anchored in the book of Revelation, created expectations of some transformative events either in 1000 CE (the anniversary of the incarnation) or 1033 (the anniversary of the crucifixion and resurrection). There was, not surprisingly, an upsurge in apocalyptic expectations. But no such transformation of the world occurred. Although scholars continue to debate the cause and effect, there was a striking transformation of piety in the decades that followed. More strongly effective forms of identification with the suffering of Jesus became the focus of piety, and some argue that the intensity of apocalyptic expectation was re-channeled into a kind of realized eschatology in the suffering and exaltation of Christ (chapter 11, by Travis Ables). It is important to remember, however, that apocalypticism, though born in Judaism and most prominent and culturally definitive in Christianity, also plays a significant role in Islam, as chapter 12, by Mohamed A. Mohamed, shows.

The presence of the apocalyptic imagination in contemporary culture might be best described in terms of an explosion. If one attempts to trace its effects, one is, by necessity, tracing fragmented patterns of impact. Even within Western secular culture, for example, the philosophical tradition and popular conceptions of progress indicate that the ghost of apocalyptic conceptualizations continues to have an impact, no matter how thoroughly the experts debate its extent (chapter 15, by Thomas Fabisiak). That explosion is well documented in the varied chapters in Part III. Although it is difficult to see any common core to the apocalyptic imagination that informs these contemporary expressions, perhaps one might focus on the relative interplay of focus on disaster and dissolution and on a possible future. Only in the cultic movements—whether they are formed out of traditional Christian elements, non-Christian ones, or some odd amalgamation—is there an expectation that bliss follows the trials of the eschatological woes (chapter 19 by Robert von Thaden Jr., and chapter 20, by Joe Laycock). But the apocalyptic imagination also serves in contemporary times to articulate the acute sense of the breakdown of assumed structures of civilization (chapter 14, by Michael Thate; chapter 16, by Matthew Rindge; chapter 17, by Ingrid Esther Lilly; and chapter 18, by James Perkinson). What is distinctly different about these apocalyptic imaginings is the lack of confidence in a plot in which the ills are only transitory woes on the way toward a glorious future. The most recent envisioning of apocalypse, the Zombie apocalypse (chapter 21, by Kelly J. Murphy), may seem just a bit of cultural camp. But the images with which it works—the living and the dead, the turning of the dead upon the living, the breakdown of civilization and its tentative reconstruction—these things bespeak profound disquiet and anxiety about the fundamental bases of our life together.

This volume brings together an extraordinary conversation about the apocalyptic imagination as it has informed western civilization for the past 2,500 years. It asks us to find those elements that persist and to ponder why they have been so resilient in our cultural imaginations. But it also asks us to identify the ways in which changing historical and cultural situations have called forth striking transformations of the apocalyptic imagination and to ask why those might be and how they have identified and addressed new anxieties and hopes. And finally, it asks us to look at our contemporary culture and to ask whether and how apocalyptically inspired forms of thought are framing our perceptions of our contemporary situations and whether or not we wish to endorse those ways of interpreting our contexts or to seek different frames of understanding.

Carol A. Newsom
Emory University

PART I

Apocalypticism in the Ancient World

1

Introduction—From Before the Bible to Beyond the Bible

Apocalypses throughout History

Justin Jeffcoat Schedtler and Kelly J. Murphy

KEY TERMS:
SEER
ZOMBIE APOCALYPSE
ESCHATOLOGICAL
REVELATION
CIPHER
CATHARSIS
CONTEXT
GENRE

Introduction

What is the first thing that comes to your mind when you hear the word "apocalypse?"

Armageddon.

Catastrophe.

Devastation.

The End.

The likelihood that such things immediately spring to your mind has a lot to do with the fact that you have lived most of your life in the last half of the twentieth century CE and/or the first couple of decades of the twenty-first century CE. In many facets of (especially American) culture, "apocalypse" and "apocalyptic" have become synonymous with doomsday scenarios and the harrowing drama they entail. Apocalyptic doomsday scenarios can take all sorts of shapes and appear in all sorts of popular media. Few of us were alive when Orson Welles famously read a fake news report of an alien invasion on live radio in 1938, which prompted listeners of the show—many of whom did not realize the report was fake—to react hysterically. This fake account of an apocalyptic event was based on H. G. Wells's 1898 novel, *The War of the Worlds*, a text that can be characterized as apocalyptic insofar as it depicted the invasion of earth by extraterrestrials (one of the first of its kind), which results in all kinds of catastrophes and a radical upheaval of the world as we know it.

Familiar apocalyptic scenarios in contemporary popular culture abound, and include an entire **genre** of Hollywood movies that depict "The End" (whether of the world itself or society). Some depict the world as it is ending, either from some kind of extraterrestrial threat or ecological disaster, as in *Deep Impact* or *2012*, or after the disaster has taken place, as in the most recognizable post-apocalyptic thrillers *Mad Max*, *Zombieland*, and *Interstellar* (to name only a few). On screens inside our living rooms, various apocalyptic shows keep us company in the night, such as *The Walking Dead*, which depicts life after a **zombie apocalypse**. So, too, are apocalyptic plots popular in literature, as in Richard Matheson's *I Am Legend*, Stephen King's *Cell*, Cormac McCarthy's *The Road*, Margaret Atwood's *MaddAddam* books, or Justin Cronan's *The Passage* (again, to name only a few).

Apocalyptic doomsday scenarios are not limited to the world of popular entertainment. In fact, apocalyptic scenarios—and, just as importantly, the apocalyptic mindset that produces them—are plainly evident in contemporary politics, religion, international affairs, and climate change debates. As recently as April 2015, former US Rep. Michele Bachmann claimed the rapture could happen within our lifetimes, blaming President Barack Obama's policies on Iran and the Marriage Equality Act. In a different vein, climate scientists predict the end of the environment, as we know it, if humans fail to make substantive changes in CO2 emissions; many religious practitioners continue to count the days until the (next) predicted end of the world and their own ascension to heaven; politicians look to events in the Middle East as signs of "The End Times." The list could go on and on—and does, from serious considerations to the use of "The End" in tongue-in-cheek disaster survival guides, such as the "Zombie Apocalypse Preparedness Guide" found on the Center for Disease Control's website. Even the Pentagon has a (humorous) "zombie plan" in place in the case of a zombie apocalypse. According to one report, "In an unclassified document titled 'CONOP 8888,' officials from U.S. Strategic Command used the specter of a planet-wide attack by the walking dead as a training template for how to plan for real-life, large-scale operations, emergencies and catastrophes."[1] A real-life worldwide zombie apocalypse is not necessarily expected, but the training scenario that imagines such a situation provides opportunities for educating students for how to act in the case of mass panic.[2]

While such end-of-the-world scenarios are clearly "apocalyptic" in terms of the most common contemporary use of the term—that is,

1. http://www.cnn.com/2014/05/16/politics/pentagon-zombie-apocalypse/.
2. http://i2.cdn.turner.com/cnn/2014/images/05/16/dod.zombie.apocalypse.plan.pdf.

meaning some sort of global catastrophe that somehow "ends" the world or radically changes society as we know it—the word "apocalypse" meant something quite different than this until very recently. If you happened to live, say, in the first several years of the first century CE—during which time the Roman Empire was just taking shape and Jesus walked the face of the earth—you would have had a very different understanding of the term. So, too, if you were living during Late Antiquity, the Middle Ages, the Renaissance, or the beginning of the Modern Period. So what did the word "apocalypse" mean in the first century, and how and why has its meaning changed over time?

The Importance of Genre

The word "apocalypse" derives from an ancient Greek word *apokalyptein*, which, quite literally, meant to "uncover, disclose, or reveal." One of the most common uses of this word in everyday Greek was to describe the process by which a husband lifted the veil covering the bride's face at a wedding ceremony. A common ritual—which, of course, still occurs in many cultures to this day—had the effect of *revealing* the bride to the husband. The process of unveiling the bride's face, which was initially either entirely or partially covered by the veil, allowed the bride's face to be seen clearly and in plain view of everyone present. The act of *uncovering* constitutes the essence of an *apocalypse*, and it provides a starting point for considering a body of ancient literature by the same name.

Though the building blocks for the group of ancient texts called *apocalypses* are evident in much earlier Babylonian, Persian, Egyptian, and Hebrew literature, the very first apocalypses *per se* appear to have been written by Jewish authors, beginning sometime in the third century BCE. You are likely familiar with some of these texts, most famous among them is the book of **Revelation** from the New Testament. However, the Hebrew Bible/Old Testament book of Daniel, which includes an apocalypse in chapters 7–12, is also an example of this genre of text. There are many other extant apocalypses (i.e., those which have been preserved for us to read today) with which you may be less familiar, but which were, no doubt, very popular among various Jewish groups in antiquity. 1 Enoch was among the most popular. It is a compilation of five originally distinct texts featuring Enoch, a figure from the book of Genesis (see Gen 5:18–24), as the central character. 2 Baruch, 4 Ezra, Apocalypse of Zephaniah, Apocalypse of Abraham, and the Testament of Abraham are additional examples of Jewish apocalypses that circulated widely in the third to the first century BCE. The list goes on. Despite the fact that what most Christians consider the "Bible" contains only two apocalypses, dozens of other apocalypses from that period still survive, indicating how popular the apocalypse was as a literary **genre**—a kind or form of literature—in antiquity.

This genre of literature continued to be popular amongst various Jewish groups into the first century CE and beyond, and importantly, among an emerging Jewish sect of "Christians." The last book in the Christian Bible, the book of Revelation (alternatively, the *Apocalypse of John*), may be the most recognizable, but a number of non-canonical apocalyptic texts were also produced by some of the earliest Christians and attributed to early Christian apostles, including, e.g., the *Apocalypse of Paul* and the *Apocalypse of Peter.*

Such texts depict all kinds of violence and destruction, to be sure. For example, 4 Ezra (sometimes called 2 Esdras) reveals in no uncertain terms the utter desolation that God will bring upon those who have forsaken God and God's commandments:

> Now concerning the signs: behold, the days are coming when those who dwell on earth shall be seized with great terror, and the way of truth shall be hidden, and the land shall be barren of faith.
>
> And unrighteousness shall be increased beyond what you yourself see, and beyond what you heard of formerly. And the land which you now see ruling shall be waste and untrodden, and men shall see it desolate.
>
> But if the Most High grants that you live, you shall see it thrown into confusion after the third period; and the sun shall suddenly shine forth at night, and the moon during the day. Blood shall drip from wood, and the stone shall utter its voice; the peoples shall be troubled, and the stars shall fall. (NRSV 4 Ezra 5: 1–5)

No doubt authors and audiences of ancient apocalypses would have recognized the kind of grand-scale destruction that presages the "end of the world" depicted in modern-day apocalyptic doomsday scenarios. In fact, they envisioned (quite literally) the "end of the world" and the annihilation that it entailed in all kinds of ways. But the impending and/or manifested End was only one constitutive element of the apocalypse proper. Just as important—and perhaps more so—were the *revelations of the present circumstances* that were giving rise to the doomsday scenarios. Just as the bride's veil, once removed, revealed her fully to her husband, so, too, apocalypses revealed a previously obscured reality to their audiences.

Let's look at one example in order to begin to understand this important phenomenon. In the book of Dan 7–12, the protagonist Daniel is said to receive a series of **visions** of various phenomena, including four great beasts coming out of the sea:

> In my vision at night I looked, and there before me were the four winds of heaven churning up the great sea. Four great beasts, each different from the others, came up out of the sea. The first was like a lion, and it had the wings of an eagle. I watched until its wings were torn off and it was lifted from the ground so that it stood on two feet like a human being, and the mind of a human was given to it. . . . (Dan 7:2–4)

The vision continues with descriptions of the second and third beasts, and finally, the fourth beast:

> After that, in my vision at night I looked, and there before me was a fourth beast—terrifying and frightening and very powerful. It had large iron teeth; it crushed and devoured its victims and trampled underfoot whatever was left. It was different from all the former beasts, and it had ten horns. (Dan 7:7)

At the conclusion of this vision, Daniel reveals his anxiety surrounding the contents of these visions, which he does not immediately understand. So, he asks an unknown figure—a heavenly intermediary, we are later told—to interpret the visions:

> He gave me this explanation: "The fourth beast is a fourth kingdom that will appear on earth. It will be different from all the other kingdoms and

will devour the whole earth, trampling it down and crushing it." (Dan 7:24)

The description of Daniel's first vision reveals several related elements of this apocalypse and the genre of apocalypses, generally speaking. First, we observe that Daniel is a somewhat unintentional—or at least unsolicited—recipient of a vision, the origins of which are not further specified, other than that they occur in a dream. Insofar as Daniel is the witness to the dream, he may be characterized as a **seer**. In an apocalypse, a seer is required to mediate the vision, though the circumstances surrounding the reception of the vision vary somewhat. At times, the seer is carried up to the heavens to witness the vision; at other times, the seer experiences visionary dreams while asleep. The authenticity of the vision experience is a matter of some debate, with some scholars arguing for the credibility of the visions (analogous to other "mystical experiences" in the ancient and modern world), and others suggesting that the vision sequence is simply a literary convention designed to impart a specific message to the intended audience of the apocalypse.

A second constitutive element of apocalypses is that their contents are very often presented in symbolic imagery and language. Given the inherently cryptic nature of symbols, the contents of these visions, taken at face value, are often ambiguous and/or unintelligible. Oftentimes, animals appear to represent human figures or otherworldly entities; at other times, people receive strange visions, such as the bowls of God's wrath (Rev 16). As such, the visions (or at least parts of the visions) are often interpreted for the seer—and thus, the audience of the seer's vision—by a divine mediator or a heavenly angel.

It is precisely the symbolic nature of the visions that make them appear esoteric to modern-day readers, which in turn attracts rampant speculation about who or what lies behind the symbols. The "number of the beast" (666), which appears in the book of Revelation, is one conspicuous example of this. Perhaps you've heard speculation as to the person, or entity, believed to lie behind "666." A quick Google search reveals that all sorts of people have been identified as the referent: Barack Obama, Saddam Hussein, and Bill Gates, to name just a very few. Others have concluded that the number actually refers to a particular entity: the Social Security administration, the Council on Foreign Relations, or Monster Energy Drink (no, we are not kidding!). The power of **symbology** can be quite stunning. For example, when Ronald and Nancy Reagan moved into their Bel-Air retirement home in 1989, they changed the address from 666 to 668 St. Cloud Road—a change based solely on readings of the book of Revelation that claim that "666" is the mark of the beast. (In reality, the earliest manuscripts of the book of Revelation attest that the number of the beast is 616, not 666.)

In fact, if you take a look further back in history, you will find that very, very many people have been identified with this number, as well as many other symbols in the book of Revelation (e.g., the Great Prostitute, the marks on the forehead, the battle of Gog and Magog, etc.). The number of possible contemporary referents to the symbols in the book of Revelation and in other apocalypses testifies to the popularity of understanding such symbols as **ciphers**, or *codes*, for contemporary events and figures. Indeed, the practice of interpreting symbols in these apocalypses as codes for contemporary events is nearly as old as the apocalypses themselves.

The Importance of Context

The irony is that specific figures and entities *do* lie behind the symbols. However, it is our contention (and the view of the vast majority of biblical and religious scholars today) that the symbolic contents of the vision reveal something, first and foremost, *about the present circumstances of the author and the author's community.* That is, the common denominator among ancient apocalypses is that they attempt to *reveal* some aspect (political, social, religious, etc.) of the order of things as they were in their own **context**—namely, in the time(s) and place(s) in which the apocalypse was written and/or edited to receive its final form.

Our previous example of the vision of the monstrous fourth Beast in Daniel 7 perfectly illustrates this phenomenon. Within the text itself, the heavenly angel interprets the Beast as "a fourth kingdom on earth that shall be different from all the other kingdoms; it shall devour the whole earth, and trample it down, and break it to pieces" (Dan 7:23). Though the historical referent to whom the Beast refers may remain a bit of a mystery to the twenty-first-century reader, who stands more than 2,000 years removed from the events being described in the text of Dan 7, the original audience would have surely recognized its identity (through the thinly veiled imagery) as the Seleucid Empire, which ruled over the land of Judea. (The evidence for this conclusion is conclusive and will be revealed in chapter 2.) Thus, in cloaked symbolic language, the vision *reveals* to Daniel the true identity of the Seleucid Empire and its rulers as monstrous entities who devour the earth and its inhabitants. Revealing that the Seleucid Empire and its rulers are indeed evil, and intent on decimating the peoples over whom it rules (including the author and audience who are stationed in Judea), is precisely the point of this apocalypse. In other words, the destruction that will ensue as a result of this evil Empire, as well as some of the mechanisms by which this will occur, is but one piece of a larger clarion call of the author(s) of the book of Daniel: "Beware! Your rulers are corrupt and they will eventually lead to your own destruction."

As sure as the author(s) of the book of Daniel may have been about the depravity of the Seleucid Empire and its rulers, this view constituted only one perspective among many about the true nature of the Seleucid Empire. In fact, there is evidence that some Jews living under Seleucid rule viewed the situation in much more favorable terms. So, this apocalypse, like all others, attempts to uncover a reality that may be *obscured or unrecognized by others*. The purpose of the apocalypse is, in other words, to alert the audience to a view of reality that they may not yet comprehend, or that may be in some dispute. At any rate, a common denominator among ancient apocalypses is that they view the present order of things as somehow dysfunctional and/or corrupt, and the purpose of the apocalypse is to make this known.

11

Reading an ancient apocalypse in its context—in other words, in terms that would be recognizable, first and foremost, to the author(s) and audience(s) of the original text—constitutes an interpretive approach that is quite different than the one most readers take today. As we saw above, and as we will see throughout this volume, the most popular method for reading ancient apocalypses instead consists of reading the symbols of ancient apocalypses as saying something specifically about the *present circumstances of the modern reader*. The reason why so many figures have been associated with the number "666," for example, is because people so often read these symbolic texts as ciphers for people and events in their own times and places. By contrast, when scholars ask, "To what does the number '666' refer?" or "Who are the Beasts in Daniel 7?" we begin by exploring the conceptual worlds of the original author(s) and audience(s), not those in the twenty-first century. Yet, outside of the scholarly world (and sometimes even within it), we often do not read the ancient texts in this way because *we are* too distant from the text's original contexts.

With these introductory comments in view, we can now consider a well-known definition of *apocalypse* as defined by a group of international scholars. Here, "apocalypse" is defined as

> a genre of revelatory literature with a narrative framework in which a revelation is mediated by an otherworldly being to a human recipient, disclosing a transcendent reality which is both temporal, insofar as it envisages **eschatological** salvation, and spatial, insofar as it involves another, supernatural world.[3]

This definition highlights an extremely important aspect of ancient apocalypses that has not yet been considered: the purpose of *revealing* something about the present circumstances of the Seer and his community—i.e., serious deficiencies with the present order of things—is both to be aware of their present and impending consequences, and perhaps more importantly, to convey a message of

---

3. John J. Collins, *The Apocalyptic Imagination: An Introduction to Jewish Apocalyptic Literature* (Minneapolis: Fortress Press, 1998), 5.

salvation for those living under them. The example above from Daniel is again illustrative:

> The fourth beast is a fourth kingdom that will appear on earth. It will be different from all the other kingdoms and will devour the whole earth, trampling it down and crushing it. The ten horns are ten kings who will come from this kingdom. After them another king will arise, different from the earlier ones; he will subdue three kings. He will speak against the Most High and oppress his holy people and try to change the set times and the laws. The holy people will be delivered into his hands for a time, times, and half a time.
>
> But the court will sit, and his power will be taken away and completely destroyed forever. Then the sovereignty, power, and greatness of all the kingdoms under heaven will be handed over to the holy people of the Most High. His kingdom will be an everlasting kingdom, and all rulers will worship and obey him. (Dan 7:23–27)

Central to Daniel's revelation is that while the "holy people" (read: the community of authors and audience of Daniel) may be suffering now under the policies of Antiochus IV, his rule will soon come to an end, at which point, power will be transferred to God and God's "holy people" will prevail. This is just one example of how apocalypses envisage both "eschatological salvation" (a temporal aspect) and a "supernatural realm" (a spatial aspect), and it is necessary to note that apocalypses envisage salvation in a myriad of ways. For example, sometimes the audience is tasked with certain behavior in order to bring about their salvation.

This seemingly soothing element of apocalypses has led many scholars to conclude that such literature was intended primarily to evoke **catharsis**. That is, through an imaginative uncovering of the current sociopolitical order, and the subsequent graphic display of their humiliating defeat, apocalypses provide comfort for their audience in the face of current hardships. But there may be a more obvious intended effect than this. Left unsaid in the technical definition of apocalypse (and absent from this particular example in Dan 7) is a scenario in which those who do *not* recognize the dangers of the present circumstances are under threat to be destroyed by them.

Put another way, failure to heed the warnings of the apocalypse, and failure to recognize the current deficiencies of the present social, economic, religious, and/or political order, often leads ultimately to absolute destruction.

Why the Apocalypse Matters

In the first season of AMC's *The Walking Dead*, one of the main characters, Andrea, is searching frantically through the RV of another character, Dale, looking for something to wrap a birthday gift in for her sister. She turns to Dale and says, "Wrapping paper, colored tissue, anything? How can you not have any?" Dale responds, "Well, if I'd been informed of the coming apocalypse I'd have stocked up" (*The Walking Dead*, Season 1, Episode 4).

In this case, the apocalypse is of a particular kind: the so-called zombie apocalypse. But the apocalypse is all around us today—on our televisions, in our theaters, crowding the bookshelves of libraries. At times, the apocalypse is fantastical and imaginary, as is the case in *The Walking Dead*. At other times, however, contemporary notions of the apocalypse have real-life, and often tragic, implications. For example, in 2011, a series of Family Radio Billboards dotted the American countryside, proclaiming, "He is Coming Again! May 21, 2011." Though Harold Camping, the leader behind the California-based church, had made (failed) predictions of the end of the world before, his announcements about the end of the world and Jesus's imminent return nevertheless resulted in a significant following. Followers donated their savings to Family Radio and sometimes left their families to travel across the United States and spread Camping's apocalyptic message. Of course, May 21, 2011, came and went, and the world did not end. Nevertheless, Camping's failed prediction profoundly impacted the lives of real people.

Fast forward to January 2015, where Utah police finished investigating the September 2014 deaths of the Strack family: Kristi and Benjamin Strack, a married couple, and the three Strack children, all found dead in their Springfield, Utah home. The police eventually concluded that the parents' deaths were suicides. It seems likely that the couple killed the youngest two children, but the death of their 14-year-old child remained "undetermined." According to police reports, the couple had been in contact with an imprisoned man named Dan Lafferty up until at least 2008; Lafferty self-identifies as the prophet Elijah. In Christian tradition, Elijah is often thought to be the herald of the Second Coming of Christ. Various news reports suggested that the couple committed suicide because they believed in a "pending apocalypse."

Yet, despite cultural fascination with The End—and the ways it shows up on our favorite television shows or in our most watched movies—what seems ordinary (oh, yes, another zombie show) becomes profoundly tragic in light of empty bank accounts, broken families, and suicides. Moreover, such tragic events remind us of the many ways that ancient texts continue to live on all around us, in both overt and implicit ways. This ongoing legacy of ancient apocalyptic texts is continually relevant, and not only to biblical and religious scholars. The litany of names is long: William Miller, Hal Lindsay, David Koresh, Harold Camping, Kristi Strack, Benjamin Strack. . . . All of these people are associated with (sometimes multiple) wrong predictions and assumptions about the end of the world. If, in their original contexts, books such as Daniel or Revelation functioned cathartically for their audiences, providing comfort in the face of then-current hardships, then how did these texts become linked with so many failed, and often tragic, predictions of the End of the World?

The questions we ask when we read literature are important, and it seems that readers such as William Miller and Harold Camping failed to ask the right kind of questions. Ancient apocalyptic texts are not handbooks to the end of the world, but they matter. At times, ancient texts determine house numbers (no 666 St. Cloud Road for Nancy and Ronald Reagan), while at other times they contain hidden messages, as in *The Walking Dead*. For example, in one episode, Rick walks into the church and a series of Bible verses are on the board that would normally contain the hymnal passages for the day's service (including

Rom 6:4; Ezek 37:7; Matt 27:52; Rev 9:6; Luke 24:5). Looking up the passages, readers discover each of them sound "zombie-esque": "Therefore we have been buried with him by baptism into death, so that, just as Christ was raised from the dead by the glory of the Father, so we too might walk in newness of life" (Rom 6:4); "So I prophesied as I had been commanded; and as I prophesied, suddenly there was a noise, a rattling, and the bones came together, bone to its bone" (Ezek 37:7); "The tombs also were opened, and many bodies of the saints who had fallen asleep were raised" (Matt 27:52); "And in those days people will seek death but will not find it; they will long to die, but death will flee from them" (Rev 9:6); "The women were terrified and bowed their faces to the ground, but the men said to them, 'Why do you look for the living among the dead? He is not here, but has risen'" (Luke 24:5). In their original contexts, of course, none of these texts had anything to do with zombies. Nevertheless, for the dedicated *The Walking Dead* fan who takes the time to look up the passages, it's hard not to think "zombie" when reading these passages out of context. Sometimes, ancient apocalyptic texts make for funny retirement stories about everyone's favorite Republican president. Other times, ancient apocalyptic texts are hidden, somewhat humorous, messages on our favorite television shows. And then, there are the times when apocalyptic texts are misread, and tragedy is the result.

In short, these ancient texts and their long history of interpretation *matter*. Both the book of Daniel and the book of Revelation reveal the earliest Jewish and Christian worlds. They help us to discover what people desired, feared, and yearned for *in their lifetimes*. As you will see in the following pages, many readers and interpreters have used the books of Daniel and/or Revelation in a number of ways throughout history—and continuing up to the present—without trying to predict the end of the world. These books are more than useless relics or failed predictions of the end of the Seleucid or Roman Empires.

Likewise, the many ways that the apocalypse plays out in our contemporary culture—from climate debates to art to film and beyond—also matter. Apocalyptic texts and their many afterlives reveal to us information about ourselves and about being human. Apocalyptic texts and their afterlives ask profound human questions that unite the past and the present, especially the following: What does it mean to be human? Why does history matter? Where are we headed?

In a recent work, Collins returned to the definition of apocalypse outlined above, writing, "Definitions are by nature synchronic and static. Genres, in contrast, evolve and are constantly changing" (Collins, 15). The following pages are interested precisely in the afterlives of the genre of apocalypse, and not only in its definition. What, if anything, connects ancient texts such as Ezekiel or the book of Revelation to current climatological crises and television shows such as *The Walking Dead*? How has the genre of apocalypse evolved over time? How does it continue to change? How has it stayed the same?

The volume you are about to read addresses this question while exploring what "apocalypse" has meant to different people in different places and at different times. Context, as you will see, continues to matter, as much as, if not more so than, official genre definitions. Part I consists of chapters on ancient apocalyptic texts and movements. Part II consists of chapters that explore the way that ancient apocalyptic trajectories continued through Late Antiquity, the Middle Ages, Reformation, and the Early Modern period. Part III consists of chapters that demonstrate the continuing prevalence and ongoing importance of apocalyptic thinking and the afterlives of ancient apocalyptic texts in the contemporary world.

2

———

The First Apocalypse (Daniel 7–12)

A Story Told Backwards

Christopher B. Hays

GETTING PREPPED:

1. What comes to mind when you think of the book of Daniel?
2. Read Daniel 2 and Daniel 7. What similarities and differences do you notice in these two texts? What seems strange or unfamiliar? Do you recognize anything from these texts?

KEY TERMS:
PROTO-APOCALYPTIC
COURT TALES
DIADOCHI
REDACTION
PSEUDEPIGRAPHY
EX EVENTU PROPHECY

ANTIOCHUS IV
LITTLE HORN

Introduction

From about 250 BCE to 250 CE, apocalypses flourished as a genre among early Jewish and Christian authors. However, despite the many other apocalypses written during this period, the only one that found its way into the canonical texts of contemporary Judaism and the canonical Old Testament of contemporary Christianity is in Daniel, chapters 7–12.

So where did apocalypses come from? The most common assumption among earlier generations of scholars who studied the origins of the genre was that Jewish apocalypses either: (1) directly depended on a similar genre from the ancient Near Eastern (ANE) world, or that they (2) developed in a relatively linear fashion out of (biblical) prophetic traditions, driven by shifts in the social realities and worldviews of early Judaism. Both of these earlier assumptions have proven problematic. Under closer scrutiny, no preexisting ANE genre or text provides a very close analogy for the early Jewish apocalypses. Furthermore, the differences between what have been called **proto-apocalyptic** prophetic texts (i.e., texts that demonstrate a nascent apocalyptic worldview) and actual apocalypses have similarly become more apparent. The apocalypse was a new invention of the Hellenistic period, but that is not to say that it was created *ex nihilo* (out of nothing). Rather, like all literature, the apocalypse can be imagined as a textile woven together out of strands of other texts already in existence. The maxim of the book of Ecclesiastes applies here: "there is nothing new under the sun" (1:9). So, again, where did apocalypses come from?

The story of the origins of apocalyptic is best told backwards, starting at the end of a long trajectory of ideas and historical events that culminated in the apocalypse now found in Dan 7–12. Accordingly, understanding the book of Daniel requires insight into four areas: (1) the book's literary contents (including its relationship to the "apocalypse" genre); (2) its composition (including its relationship to its historical contexts); (3) its main character (including its relationship to ANE myths and legends); and (4) the social context of its authors.

The book of Daniel divides into two halves. Chapters 1–6 are tales of Daniel and his Jewish compatriots at a foreign court—what scholars often call **court tales**. These are stories such as "Daniel in the Fiery Furnace" (Dan 3) or "Daniel in the Lion's Den" (6:16–24), familiar to many readers from their days in Sunday School or Hebrew School. In these stories, Daniel and his compatriots manage to stay faithful to YHWH, the God of Israel, despite living in the foreign Babylonian court and despite being enjoined by Babylonian kings to worship other gods. Something else entirely is found in Dan 7–12, which comprises a series of five strange visions that contain all of the necessary features to be labeled an "apocalypse."

Sidebar 2.1: Apocalypse

"a genre of revelatory literature with a narrative framework in which a revelation is mediated by an otherworldly being to a human recipient, disclosing a transcendent reality which is both temporal, insofar as it envisages eschatological salvation, and spatial, insofar as it involves another, supernatural world." (Collins, *Apocalyptic Imagination*, 5; cf. *Semeia* 14)

The contents of Dan 7–12 shed light on how these chapters came to be, what events they may have originally referred to, and why. The book of Daniel has consistently been used to predict the end of the world, from the ancient world until today, but no one has ever successfully used the book to predict accurately the time and date of the **eschaton.** That leaves us with a question, "What else might the book of Daniel be about?"

Daniel 7–12: The Hebrew Bible's Apocalypse

In the first vision (Dan 7:1-28), Daniel has a dream that begins with a vision of a stormy sea, out of which four beasts arise in succession. The text seems clear that Daniel remains in his bed, yet the things revealed to him are certainly from "another, supernatural world." The fourth beast, which is of greatest interest in the text, has ten horns, and then an eleventh horn grows. As the fourth beast is raging, suddenly thrones are set up, and one who is called "ancient of days" is seated, with thousands in attendance around him. By his command, the fourth beast is put to death and burned. Perplexed by the vision, Daniel seeks out one of the attendants (unlike in the previous chapters found in Dan 1-6, Daniel can no longer interpret dreams and visions—he needs an otherworldly mediator to interpret them for him). The attendant tells him that the beasts symbolize kingdoms, and the horns symbolize the kings of the fourth kingdom (compare the "Animal Apocalypse" in 1 Enoch 85-90). Just as the fourth kingdom is different and more terrorizing than the others, so too, the eleventh king is the worst, in that he will "speak words against the Most High, shall wear out the holy ones of the Most High, and shall attempt to change the sacred seasons and the law" (7:25). This king is generally understood to represent **Antiochus IV** (see below, under "History and the Formation of the book of Daniel"). But the attendant reassures Daniel that "kingship and dominion . . . will be given to the people of the holy ones of the Most High" (7:27).

Fig. 2.1. Daniel's vision of four beasts; engraving by Matthäus Merian, ca. 1630. Commons.wikimedia.org.

In the second vision (Dan 8:1–27), Daniel sees himself in the Persian city of Susa (see further below); the text does not specify where he is when he has the vision. By the river Ulai, he sees a powerful ram with two horns that none can resist, until a goat with single horn appears and tramples it. Afterward, the goat's horn breaks and is replaced by four horns, and then another **little horn**. The little horn taunts and abuses the host of heaven, taking away its offerings and its sanctuary. Daniel hears two "holy ones" talking, one asking the other how long this situation will last, and the other answering: "2,300 evenings and mornings; then the sanctuary shall be restored to its rightful state" (8:14). Another voice calls to the angel Gabriel to interpret the vision. Overawed by Gabriel, Daniel falls face-down, and then enters a deep sleep as Gabriel speaks; yet, Gabriel touches him and stands him up (perhaps in a dream within the vision). Gabriel explains to him that the horns of the ram are the kings of Media and Persia, and the goat is Greece, with the first king (i.e., Alexander the Great) as its horn. The four horns are his successors (i.e., the **Diadochi,** the generals who fought over Alexander the Great's kingdom after his death). Gabriel finally elaborates on the power and deceitfulness of the last king, the "little horn," but does not identify who it is. The last king will destroy the people of the holy ones and even "rise up against the Prince of princes" (8:25). But Gabriel reassures Daniel that "he will be broken, and not by human hands." He says that the vision is to be sealed up, because "it refers to many days from now" (8:26). Daniel is overwhelmed by the vision and stays in bed for days.

The third vision (Dan 9:21–27) is preceded by a lengthy prayer of confession (9:3–19), but is introduced by Daniel's statement, "I perceived in the books the number of years that, according to the word of the Lord to the prophet Jeremiah, must be fulfilled for the devastations of Jerusalem—seventy years." This is a reference to the 70 years Jeremiah prophesies for the exile (Jer 25:11–12; 29:10). Gabriel appears to Daniel and explains: "70 weeks are decreed for your people and your holy city" (9:24). He divides the 70 weeks into three periods: (1) seven weeks "from the time that the word went out to restore and rebuild Jerusalem until the time of an anointed prince"; (2) 62 weeks for Jerusalem to be "built again with streets and moat"; (3) after this, "an anointed one will be cut off" and "the troops of the prince who is to come shall destroy the city and the sanctuary. . . . He shall make a strong covenant with many for one week, and for half of the week he shall make sacrifice and offering cease." The precise meaning and timespan of the weeks has been extensively debated for years without consensus, but the destroying prince again seems to correlate with Antiochus IV.

The fourth vision (Dan 10:1–21) comes to Daniel after he has been mourning and fasting for three weeks. He is standing on the banks of the Tigris when "a man clothed in linen" appears to him, but whose clothing and physical features are described in terms of precious metals and gems, with eyes "like torches of fire" (10:6). As in the second vision (8:18), Daniel falls face-down in a deep sleep; the other people with him do not see the vision, but flee anyway. Then, one "in human form" (10:16, NRSV; or "in the likeness of the sons of men," RSV) lifts Daniel up. He explains that he has heard Daniel's words, but was detained, fighting against the "prince of the kingdom of Persia" until Michael came to relieve him. The message of this vision is relatively simple and can be summarized by the words in 10:19: "Do not fear, greatly beloved, you are safe. Be strong and courageous!" Then, he excuses himself again to go fight the prince of Persia, followed by the prince of Greece.

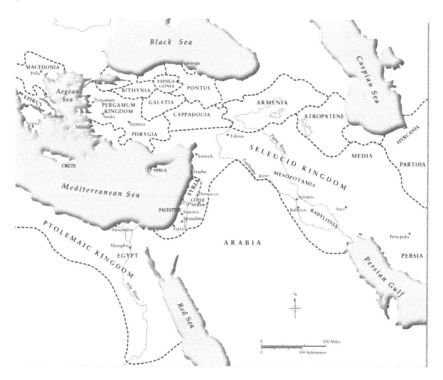

Map 2.1. The Hellenistic world after Alexander's conquests.

What follows in chapter 11 is an extraordinary survey of **Hellenistic** history (i.e., the history of the Mediterranean world in the aftermath of the conquests of Alexander the Great). It begins with a very cursory glance at the Persian kings who preceded the Greeks, but then goes into more detail about the rulers from the time of Alexander the Great to the battles between the Ptolemies and Seleucids (those rulers who succeeded Alexander) over Alexander's kingdom, and finally to the careers of Antiochus III and Antiochus IV (yet more figures who ruled in the wake of Alexander's conquests). Although none of these figures is named, the level of detail has made it easy to correlate the events with historical accounts. The narrative accurately portrays historical events up to the Antiochene persecution of 167 BCE (that is, the persecution of Jews under Antiochus IV), which would result in the Maccabean revolt described in the apocryphal books of Maccabees. The accuracy is such that many scholars conclude the author was working with a written source chronicling the events surveyed (rather than hazy memories of a remote past).

After verse 31, the discourse turns to the reactions of the people, and Antiochus IV's cultic and theological wrongdoings. The text offers a very vague prediction of Antiochus's demise (Dan 11:45: "he shall come to his end, with no one to help him"), but does not show awareness of the actual circumstances of Antiochus's death (which occurred in 164 BCE), nor of the Maccabean purification and rededication of the Jerusalem temple in 165 BCE. The discourse ends with the promise that "Michael, the great prince, the protector of your people, shall arise" (12:1; cf. 10:21). After a time of incomparable anguish, Daniel is told, those among his people who are "found written in the book" will be delivered. An eternal fate is envisioned, in which many (thus, presumably not all) "who sleep in the dust will awake, some to everlasting life, and some to shame and everlasting contempt" (12:2). But Daniel is told to "keep the words secret and the book sealed until the time of the end," until which "evil shall increase" (12:4).

Daniel 12:5–12 is sometimes treated as a separate vision, and as a **redactional insertion** (a text that was added later). The primary new piece of information given here is that "From the time that the regular burnt offering is taken away and the abomination that desolates is set up, there shall be one thousand two hundred ninety days," and it blesses "those who persevere and attain the thousand three hundred thirty-five days" (12:11–12).

The book ends with a message of hope, with the attendant telling Daniel, "But you, go your way, and rest; you shall rise for your reward at the end of the days" (12:13), placing Daniel with the other wise people whom the book predicts will be raised from the dead (see 12:2–3). Many scholars take this to be the first mention of the widespread resurrection of the dead in the Hebrew Bible. In any case, the idea that Daniel will be rewarded at the end of days is one of the reasons that these chapters can be classified as an apocalypse, fulfilling the "eschatological salvation" component of the definition.

The Book of Daniel: History

Some features of the book of Daniel, especially the formulas dating various stories and visions to specific years of the reigns of various kings, give the impression that the book is a recounting of events from the Neo-Babylonian Period and the early Persian Period—i.e., from the sixth century BCE. However, nearly all critical scholars agree that the visions of Dan 7–12 refer to and react to the persecutions of Jews carried out by the Greek emperor Antiochus IV Epiphanes (r. 175–164 BCE). Remarkably, the **Roman** philosopher Porphyry, in the third century CE, already recognized the connection between Dan 7–12 and Antiochus IV. Although Augustine, bishop of Hippo, condemned him for calling Daniel's visions **vaticinia ex eventu** (i.e., "after the fact" prophecies), Porphyry's position is now commonly accepted. Most scholars are content to grant that chapters 8–12 are largely unified compositions of the Antiochene period, but the situation is different with chapter 7. Some think it was also a mostly unified late composition, while others think parts of it were composed earlier, and then augmented.

Scholars reach these conclusions through a series of "clues" left in the text, which indicate that the book was composed later than the time period in which it is set literarily—and in the case of the visions, much later. One such clue is that the vision in Dan 8:1 puts Daniel in a place called Susa. Susa became a capital city of the Persian Empire under Darius I at the end of the sixth century BCE, but prior to this, it was not a place of any significance during the Neo-Babylonian Empire. In other words, it would have been a very strange and extremely improbable location for a wise man in an *actual* Neo-Babylonian court, but for those who lived under later Persian rulers, it is understandable to have *imagined* a wise man in Susa. A second clue is evident in a consideration of the kings named in the book. They are, in order, Nebuchadnezzar, Belshazzar, Darius ("the Mede"), and Cyrus ("the Persian"). Among various problems with this list and order, the most conspicuous is that it skips Nabonidus, who is known to have succeeded Nebuchadnezzar. This is an historical error of a sort that was very common among authors who were writing about the ANE from the vantage point of the Hellenistic world, such as Herodotus, Xenophon, or Berossus. Many details simply became fuzzy over time and were not included in later recollections/reconstructions of history. A third clue is found in the neat stylization of history into four kingdoms (Babylonian, Median, Persian, and Greek) in chapter 7. Such "periodization" of history was a common feature of Greco-Roman historiography, which further suggests that the Daniel traditions come from a later period (see the discussion on periodization of history in the next chapter). Furthermore, the way the historical reviews focus on the third and second centuries and culminate with the Maccabean period is enough to locate the composition in this period with confidence.

What marks chapter 7 as somehow different than chapters 8–12? One important sign that points to chapter 7 being the work of a later editor is the horns mentioned in 7:7–8, 11, 20–22, and 24–25, especially the **little horn** that "made war with the holy ones and was prevailing over them." This is almost universally taken to refer to Antiochus IV, who is said to have sold the high priesthood of the Jerusalem temple to the highest bidder (2 Macc 4:7–22), which created competition among priestly families. When the competition became violent in 170–69 BCE, Antiochus apparently took it as a rebellion against his own authority. He slaughtered the inhabitants of Jerusalem (1 Macc 1:29–36; 2 Macc 5:24–26) and decreed death to anyone who carried or adhered to the

Jewish book of the Law, or had their children circumcised (1 Macc 1:54–64; Ant 12.5.4–5 §§248–64). He also had pagan sacrifices carried out on the Temple's altar (1 Macc 1:54); this is referred to as "the abomination that desolates" in Dan 11:31 and 12:11 (see also 8:13; 9:17; 9:27). Antiochus's treatment of the Judean people eventually led to the Maccabean Revolt in the mid-160s. Thus, the appearance of the "little horn" is one clue that this passage in Dan 7 appears to have been written at a late date.

Sidebar 2.2: 2 Maccabees 5:11–14, on Antiochus IV

[11]When news of what had happened reached the king, he took it to mean that Judea was in revolt. So, raging inwardly, he left Egypt and took the city by storm. [12]He commanded his soldiers to cut down relentlessly everyone they met and to kill those who went into their houses. [13]Then there was massacre of young and old, destruction of boys, women, and children, and slaughter of young girls and infants. [14]Within the total of three days eighty thousand were destroyed, forty thousand in hand-to-hand fighting, and as many were sold into slavery as were killed.

There are also ideological differences that divide Dan 7 and 8. In Dan 7, the hope may be breathtakingly and unrealistically ambitious, but it is an ambition for *worldly* authority, a permanent restoration of Jewish self-rule over the land of Judea: "The kingship and dominion and the greatness of the kingdoms under the whole heaven shall be given to the people of the holy ones of the Most High; their kingdom shall be an everlasting kingdom, and all dominions shall serve and obey them" (7:27). By contrast, the hopes in Dan 8–12 are for the temple and its offerings (8:12–14) and for individual or sectarian **salvation** in the afterlife (12:2–3). In fact, the very meaning of salvation changes:

after a certain point, the visions do not even look for a judgment that would punish the wicked and effect salvation for the righteous in this world, but instead shift to "eschatological" salvation—i.e., at the end of time. This tension between salvation within and beyond history has continued to exist within Judaism and Christianity ever since.

The contrast between the worldviews of these visions, the connections between Daniel 2 and 7, and the fact that Daniel 2–7 is in Aramaic instead of in Hebrew are among the key factors that lead many scholars to conclude that Daniel 7 was originally composed *earlier* than chapters 8–12, and that the passages about the horns that are mentioned above were inserted by later editors. In this view, Daniel 7 would have been composed in the late fourth or early third century BCE (Newsom and Breed 2014, 215–20).

At all events, Dan 7–12 was composed much later than the period it narrates, and the events that it narrates are closely connected to the period in which it was composed. The predictions in the strange and highly symbolic visions that Daniel sees are mostly *vaticinia ex eventu* ("prophecies after the fact"), and they grow more specific as the passages get closer to the reign of Antiochus IV. The book of Daniel is primarily interested in the events of the second century BCE, and argues that God will intervene in history to restore what has been wronged by various evils—most notably, by the reign of Antiochus IV.

The Book of Daniel: The Character of Daniel

The name Daniel, which means, in Hebrew, "God is my judge," is not one that appears randomly chosen, since there were ancient and diverse traditions about sages named Daniel. Within the Bible, a certain Daniel is also mentioned as a prototypical wise man in Ezek 28:3, and as a person of exemplary righteousness, along with Noah and Job in Ezek 14:14, 20. But legends about Daniel even *predate* the Bible: in the Ugaritic Aqhat myth, from the Late Bronze Age, one of the major characters is a righteous king named Dani'ilu, cognate with Daniel. (It is hard to tell how wise Dani'ilu was supposed to be, since only parts of the text have survived.) The invention of stories about Daniel continued into the intertestamental period (the time between the writing of the Hebrew Bible/Old Testament and the New Testament) as well: a "Daniel" is also mentioned in the book of Enoch—another early apocalypse that did not make it into the biblical canons known to most Jews and Christians today, but which was certainly well known by early Jewish and Christian communities. In 1 Enoch 6:7, Daniel is named as one of the Watchers, i.e., the fallen angels who took human wives, an elaboration of the story in Gen 6:1–4 (see chapter 4 for more on Enoch). In another apocryphal book, the book of Jubilees (4:20), Daniel is mentioned as the uncle of Enoch, so that the two names associated with the earliest apocalypses are part of the same genealogy. While a man named Daniel is also mentioned in a genealogy of those who returned from Babylon to Jerusalem with Ezra after the exile (Ezra 8:2), nothing else is said about him in that context.

It is unlikely that the authors of each of the known texts about Daniel were intentionally referring to the others. Rather, it would seem that the various stories drew from a very longstanding tradition about this legendary wise man named Daniel; what survives are probably only fragments of a tapestry of "Daniel traditions" that were originally much larger and more complex. While it is impossible to prove a negative—that a historical Daniel at the Babylonian court *did not* exist—the general consensus is that the court tales and the visions coalesced around an essentially legendary figure named Daniel.

Since most scholars agree that the stories in Dan 7–12 are largely about a legendary figure and not the recordings of a historical man named Daniel, the book can be understood as an example of **pseudepigraphy**—much of the book is, after all, in the first person (e.g., 7:2: "I, Daniel, saw in my vision . . ."). Starting from the third century BCE, around the time Daniel was being composed, pseudepigraphy became a widespread practice. In Jewish circles, many new compositions were written in the names of major biblical figures such as Adam, Abraham, Moses, Elijah, Isaiah, and so on.

Pseudepigraphy was by no means a uniquely biblical or Jewish phenomenon; it had deep roots in the wider ANE. A number of major compositions from Egypt and Mesopotamia were cast as the words of famous deceased figures, especially former kings and wise men, e.g., the Egyptian "Prophecy of Neferti," "Teaching for King Merikare," and "Teaching of King Amenemhet I for His Son Senwosret," or famous scribes and wise men of old ("Maxims of Ptahhotep," "Lamentations of Khakheperre-sonbe"). In Mesopotamia, legends about famous, ancient kings such as Sargon the Great and Naram-Sin were written in the first person, pretending to be stela-inscriptions by the kings themselves. An even closer analogy to Daniel and Enoch is supplied by the Instructions of Shuruppak, who is identified as an antediluvian king. In the text, Shuruppak is portrayed as the father of the Sumerian flood hero, Ziusudra (analogous to the biblical Noah), and offers him his teachings.

Pseudepigraphical texts claim greater antiquity and authorship by placing them on the lips of revered individuals, and this was most likely the impetus for claiming Daniel as the author of the text that bears his name. That is, people would be more willing to accept the contents of the texts, including the visions in chapters 7–12, as authoritative if they were assigned to an author of Daniel's importance.

Daniel 7–12: Author(s)

If the book of Daniel was not simply written by a man named Daniel, then what can we say about its author(s)? We have already noted their historical horizons and their apparent knowledge of ancient literary traditions. This brings us to the topic of **apocalypticism**, which is a term for a social ideology, i.e., a way that a group collectively viewed their world (Hanson; Cook). Often, those who use the term assume that it arose uniquely in response to severe hardship. Although this was probably not true of all apocalypses, it is an understandable conclusion for the book of Daniel, since it is known to have been composed out of times of suffering and (perceived, if not actual) persecution. In short, the idea is that history has failed, events are out of control, and the tide has turned against the groups who composed the apocalypses; they are tormented, tortured, oppressed. The belief that the current sociopolitical order is capable of rectifying matters is abandoned, but the message of the apocalypses is that God is, nevertheless, in control. *Even if no one on earth and within human history can perceive it, God's justice will be done*—and those who are oppressed should hold onto hope.

Sidebar 2.3: Other Biblical Views of History

An "apocalyptic" view of history, thus, contrasts with the views of the authors of the biblical "Deuteronomistic History," i.e., the books of Deuteronomy through 2 Kings, which view divine justice as quite apparent and possible within normal sociopolitical structures. In those books, the prescriptions of Deuteronomy are applied to wide swath of history: those who do right are said to flourish in the land (Deut 4:40; 32:47, etc.), while those who do wrong are punished and expelled (e.g., Deut 4:26–27; 30:18, etc.). Somewhat remarkably, this theological-historical outlook survived even the destruction of Jerusalem in 587 BCE and the Babylonian Exile, which ended in 539 BCE with the rise of the Persian king Cyrus the Great, who allowed Jews to return to their land. Cyrus, despite being a foreign ruler, was seen as a messiah (Isa 44:28—45:13), and hopes were high.

Over the centuries, due to less benevolent rule by later foreign rulers and other factors, many strands of Judaism began to reconceptualize the shape of history in an apocalyptic manner (Mermelstein 2014). This is the case with most of Dan 8–12. It has abandoned any enthusiasm for foreign rulers, and its hopes are narrowed: it hopes for the free and correct execution of worship and the sacrificial cult in light of the edicts of Antiochus IV, especially concerning worship in the Temple, and it hopes for the individual afterlives of those who are faithful. The abandonment of the political sphere reflects pessimism among authors of the apocalypses. If this pessimism, and the associated withdrawal into sectarian groups, is a marker of apocalypticism, then one can find other late postexilic texts that show similar tendencies, notably Isaiah 56–66 and Zechariah 10–14; in such texts, pronouncements of doom outnumber promises and exhortations. As an example, one might take Isa 65:8–15, which threatens judgment, but only against *some* people. A group called "the servants" is to be saved. A representative passage reads: "My servants shall eat, but you shall be hungry; my servants shall drink, but you shall be thirsty; my servants shall rejoice, but you shall be put to shame" (65:13; cf. Dan 12:2). It would appear that the authors are part of a sect that regards itself as holier than others, and has given up on convincing the others to see things its way.

A similar distinction between groups seems to be operative in Daniel, and not only in terms of eschatological salvation. Daniel 11:32–35 distinguishes between "those who violate the covenant," having been seduced by Antiochus and/or the lures of Hellenistic culture, and "the people that knows its God (and) will stand firm," which presumably refers to those in the communit(ies) that produced and read the text that resisted Antiochus. The authors' favored people are repeatedly called "holy ones" (Dan 7:18–27; 8:24), and Daniel is told that the revelation he receives is "to help you understand what is to happen *to your people* at the end of days" (10:14). There is no national or even ethnic identity implied in this formulation; in the worldview of the author(s), some of those calling themselves Judeans or Jews are not *really* Daniel's people, or the holy ones of God. In short, the authors of Daniel provide a message presented in mythological and symbolic language: history is controlled by God, and not by imperial rulers such as Antiochus IV, despite what the present circumstances might suggest. The audience of the apocalypse should align themselves accordingly.

Conclusion

A long history of interpretation has posited that Daniel's prophecies refer to a future long after the lifetimes of the author(s) of chapters 7–12, but the text itself demands to be understood in its historical context and in light of the persecution of Judaism under the rule of

Antiochus IV. Set within its historical context, Dan 7–12 makes vivid and powerful claims: a human being receives a revelation from a divine messenger, the past and the present are explained in symbolic and coded detail, there is a focus on eschatological salvation as well as the dualistic nature of the world, and while things might look bleak at the present, there is hope for the future in the form of divine intervention in history. Daniel 7–12 is an apocalypse, but for contemporary readers it reveals more about life in the second century BCE than it does about any catastrophic end of the world in the distant future.

Although the genre of apocalypse was a product of the Hellenistic period, it was not, as noted at the beginning of this chapter, created *ex nihilo*. The following chapter will explore the ways that the apocalypse can be imagined as a textile woven together out of strands of other texts already in existence—both texts now found in the Hebrew Bible and others from the large ANE world.

Study Questions:

1. What are some of the sociopolitical forces that gave rise to the book of Daniel?
2. What can be said about the author of Daniel? How does the pseudepigraphic attribution of the text to this figure contribute to the meaning of the text?
3. What constitutes an "apocalyptic" view of history?

Bibliography and Further Reading:

Collins, John J. *The Apocalyptic Imagination: An Introduction to Jewish Apocalyptic Literature.* 2nd ed. Grand Rapids, MI: Wm. B. Eerdmans, 1998.

_____. *Daniel: A Commentary on the Book of Daniel.* Hermeneia. Minneapolis: Fortress Press, 1993.

Cook, Stephen L. *Prophecy & Apocalypticism: The Postexilic Social Setting.* Minneapolis: Fortress Press, 1995.

Goldingay, John. *Daniel.* Word Biblical Commentary 30. Dallas, TX: Word Books, 1989.

Hanson, Paul D. *The Dawn of Apocalyptic.* Philadelphia: Fortress Press, 1975.

Koch, Klaus. *The Rediscovery of Apocalyptic.* Studies in Biblical Theology 2/22. Naperville, IL: A. R. Allenson, 1972. (German original 1970: *Ratlos vor der Apokalyptik*).

Mermelstein, Ari. *Creation, Covenant, and the Beginnings of Judaism: Reconceiving Historical Time in the Second Temple Period.* Supplements to the Journal for the Study of Judaism 168. Leiden: Brill, 2014.

Newsom, Carol A. and Brennan W. Breed, *Daniel: A Commentary.* Old Testament Library. Louisville, KY: Westminster John Knox Press, 2014.

Plöger, Otto. *Theocracy and Eschatology.* Richmond, VA: John Knox Press, 1968. (German original 1962: *Theokratie und Eschatologie*).

Rowley, H. H. *The Relevance of Apocalyptic: A Study of Jewish and Christian Apocalypses from Daniel to the Revelation.* Third Edition. New York: Association Press, 1963.

3

"Proto-Apocalyptic" Constellations in the Bible and the Ancient Near East

Revelation, Interpretation, Combat, and Judgment

Christopher B. Hays

GETTING PREPPED:

1. How would you define "prophecy" or "prophetic texts"? How would you define "wisdom" literature?
2. What do you know about the Hebrew Bible/Old Testament's views on the afterlife? Make a list and cite any relevant texts.
3. According to most scholars, the Hebrew Bible/Old Testament (HB/OT) drew upon, and thereby reflects, a wide range of ideas from surrounding Ancient Near Eastern (ANE) cultures. In what ways might HB/OT authors have had access to such ideas? In what ways do you imagine the HB/OT made use of such ideas?
4. The genre of apocalypse developed out of its particular historical context, while also borrowing and (re)using motifs and ideas from

earlier literature (both biblical and extra-biblical). Based on the definition of apocalypse, what ideas, motifs, and/or themes might you expect to find in earlier genres of literature from which the genre of apocalypse drew?

KEY TERMS:
PROPHETIC BOOKS
WISDOM LITERATURE
REVELATION
INTERPRETATION
COMBAT
JUDGMENT
ESCHATOLOGY
PERIODIZATION OF HISTORY
THEOMACHY
ENTHRONEMENT
UNCREATION

Apocalyptic Precursors in the Hebrew Bible and the ANE

Scholars largely agree that the apocalyptic visions of Dan 7–12—from the four beasts in Dan 7 to the idea of the resurrection of the dead in Dan 12—are among the last additions to the Hebrew Bible. Accordingly, the quest for the origins of apocalyptic literature has often centered on precursors within the Bible itself. Some scholars claim that apocalypses grew out of prophecy, while others say that the apocalypses are a permutation of **wisdom literature**. In reality, certain facets of apocalypses can be found in *numerous* books and genres throughout the Bible, as well as extrabiblical texts. The current evidence indicates that the apocalypse was a new, hybrid genre invented under specific social and cultural conditions, and drawing from resources in surrounding ancient Near Eastern (ANE) and Greek cultures.

This chapter turns from exploring the specific contours of Dan 7–12 to tracing apocalyptic themes and motifs in this biblical apocalypse back into the earlier literature from which it has drawn. The material is organized around four conceptual "constellations": **revelation, interpretation, combat,** and **judgment.** The chapter closes by hypothesizing how and why a new synthesis of these conceptual constellations arose around the third century BCE—creating a genre of literature we now call "apocalypse."

Revelation: In the Bible and Beyond

Most of the revelations in Dan 7–12 take the form of visions and dreams. Dreams can be considered a subset of visions (i.e., visions seen while sleeping). Although the two are frequently treated as synonymous in Daniel (1:17; 2:28; 4:5; 7:1), in chapters 9 and 10–12, it seems that Daniel is not sleeping when his visions come to him, and it is not clear in chapter 8 whether or not he is sleeping. The idea that dreams reveal knowledge that is not normally available while awake is one of the most widespread religious ideas across cultures (not to mention, a foundational idea of certain psychiatric methods). Accordingly, some of the most significant events in the Bible are marked by dreams or visionary experiences, including, for example, the Abrahamic covenant (Gen 15:1); the various dreams of Jacob (Gen 31, 37, 46); Samuel's oracle against the house of Eli (1 Sam 3:9–15); Nathan's dynastic promise to David (2 Sam 7:16–17); and God's promise to Solomon (1 Kgs 3). Indeed, divination by dreams and visions was deemed such a normal practice that their absence was viewed as a curse in the case of the divinely disfavored Saul (1 Sam 28:6) and the fallen Jerusalem (Lam 2:9).

There is also a strong connection between visions/dreams and the prophetic tradition. God says in Num 12:6: "When there are prophets among you, I the LORD make myself known to them in visions; I speak to them in dreams." Furthermore, many of the prophetic books are described, in part or in whole, as visions, e.g., Isa 1:1; 21:2; 22:1, 5; Obad 1:1; Nah 1:1; Hab 2:2–3. On the other hand, dreamers and visionaries are sometimes condemned or mocked for purveying falsehoods, e.g., Deut 13; Jer 23:25–32; 29:8–9; Ezek 12–13; 21:29; 22:28; Zech 10:2; 13:4.

Two prophetic books, Ezekiel and Zechariah, are widely recognized as forerunners of the Danielic apocalypse. Both include elaborate dream reports, rich with theological and historical symbolism. Notable examples in the case of Ezekiel include his visions of the throne of YHWH (Ezek 1) and its departure from the Jerusalem Temple (Ezek 10); and his visions of the valley of dry bones (Ezek 37) and the restored Temple (Ezek 40–48). Each of these visions conveys a message about God's roles in *historical events*: the divine throne's departure reflects YHWH's abandonment of Jerusalem to destruction; the revivification of the dry bones looks to the restoration of the nation; and the vision of the temple anticipates its rebuilding.

What all these visions have in common, and what distinguishes them from Dan 8–12, is a *lack of* **eschatology** or concern with end times (from Greek *eschaton*, "end"). The end times can mean different things, of course, but for our purposes, eschatology refers to the end of human history because of divine intervention. Daniel refers to the end repeatedly (8:17, 19; 9:26; 11:35, 40; 12:4, 6, 7, 9). By contrast, Ezekiel's and Zechariah's visions relate specifically to events *within history*, not beyond it. Zechariah provides a striking comparison to Daniel in this respect. Zechariah 1–6 comprises eight visions, often mediated by angelic figures. The second is a vision of "four horns that scattered Judah" (1:21)—highly reminiscent of the horns in Dan 7–8—followed by four blacksmiths coming to strike them down. The latter parts of Zechariah, which contain oracles rather than visions, have struck some readers as eschatological. For example, Zech 13:8–9 looks to judgment on the Day of the Lord: "in the whole land . . . two-thirds shall be cut off and perish, and one-third shall be left alive; and I will put this third into the fire, refine them as one refines silver, and test them as gold is tested." (The dualism and the idea of a time of testing are characteristic of apocalypticism; compare Dan 12:10.) Furthermore, nature will also be changed to the point of being unrecognizable: "On that day there shall not be either cold or frost. And there shall be continuous day . . . not day and not night, for at evening time there shall be light" (Zech 14:6–7). However idealized and unlikely Zechariah's visions of the future are, they are visions of a future that is, in many ways, continuous with the present. The natural order is said to be upended, but this world is not passing away for Zechariah. These passages are still concerned with material wealth, nationalistic sentiments, temples, and annual festivals: "And the wealth of all the surrounding nations shall be collected—gold, silver, and garments in great abundance. . . . Then all who survive of the nations that have come against Jerusalem shall go up year after year to worship the King, YHWH of hosts, and to keep the festival of booths" (Zech 14:14, 16; cf. Isa 60; 66:20–23). Zechariah might contain most of the literary pieces that eventually coalesced in the apocalypses, but in the end, Zechariah does not make the leap *beyond or outside of history*, as Daniel and other apocalypses do.

If we move beyond the Bible to the ANE, the situation was not terribly different with respect to revelatory dreams and visions. The clearest picture of ANE dream interpretation comes from Mesopotamian sources. Scribes collected various types of omens into lengthy compilations, some of which concerned the meaning of dreams. But the entries in these lists are quite terse; they are not extended dreams or interpretations such as the ones we saw in Daniel. For example, one of the "dream books," entitled (in Akkadian) ^{d}*Zaqīqu* (after the god of dreams), reads as follows:

> If he (in his dream) goes to an orchard: (somebody) will pronounce his release.
>
> If he goes to a (vegetable) garden: his work will get worse, (or) he will be free of hardship.
>
> If he goes to set a wood-pile afire: he will see days of sadness. (Oppenheim, *The Interpretation of Dreams* (1956), 269)

As is clear from this example, the association between the dream-event and its interpretation is often not at all clear. Nevertheless, the dream-omen series indicate the regularity of dream interpretation as a religious practice in Mesopotamia.

There are also a number of extended reports of dream visions within narratives in Sumerian, Akkadian, and Middle Egyptian (Oppenheim 1956). Among the Egyptian examples is the Dream Stela of Thutmose

IV, in which the pharaoh recounts that he fell asleep in the shadow of the Great Sphinx when he was a boy. In a dream, the Sphinx spoke to him in the voice of his father, promising that he would be king if he would only dig the sphinx out of the sand that covered it. Similarly, the Famine Stela recounts a story about the Dynasty 3 pharaoh Djoser (r. 2667–2648 BCE), although the stela is thought to have been composed more than two millennia later, in the Ptolemaic period. In it, Djoser's Egypt is suffering from famine, but the god Khnum appears to him in a dream. Djoser worships the deity, who reassures him: "Gone will be the hunger years that begot borrowing from their granaries." He then wakes up, with his mind racing.

Fig. 3.1. Reproduction of the Dream Stela of Thutmose IV (original ca. 1500–1390 BCE, granite, located on the Giza Plateau); Rosicrucian Egyptian Museum, Cairo. Commons.wikimedia.org.

Dreams also figure in the less extensive literature preserved from Late Bronze Age Ugarit. In the Kirta myth, the eponymous king mourns his failure to produce an heir, and then, falls deeply asleep and dreams. In his dream, the god El, the "Father of Man, comes down" to comfort and advise him (KTU3 1.14 i–ii; author's translation here and following unless otherwise indicated). More surprisingly, near the end of the Baal Myth, El, the chief god, has a symbolic dream in which "the heavens rain oil and the wadis flow with honey" (1.6 iii.8–9, 12–13), symbolizing that Baal, a lesser god, has come back to life and the fruitfulness of the natural world is restored.

In Mesopotamia, dream visions are found in the royal inscriptions of well-known kings such as Gudea, Aššurbanipal, and Nabonidus, where they may convey to the kings words of advice or warning. They also figure in myths and legends about Dumuzi, Gilgamesh, and Enkidu. In the Gilgamesh Epic, the eponymous king has two vivid dreams about a heavenly body falling to earth that he, even with his great might, cannot move. Gilgamesh's mother interprets both dreams for him, concluding that he will meet someone as strong as himself, whom he will love—which turns out to be Enkidu (SBV I.243–300).

The interpretation of dreams was important, because failure to understand a dream was considered a curse—as in *Ludlul bel nemeqi*, a composition about suffering and deliverance that is often compared to Job. At one point, the sufferer laments:

> My omens were confused, equivocal every day,
> My oracle was not decided by diviner and dream interpreter.
> What I overheard in the street (portended) evil for me,
> (When) I lay down at night, my dream was terrifying. (SAACT 7 I.51–54)

Eventually, the sufferer has dream visions of a sequence of figures who are "clothed like a human but equal to a god" (III.32), who begin his process of healing and restoration. These heavenly helpers are reminiscent of Daniel's radiant mediator clothed in linen (10:5–6; 12:6).

A final example of a dream vision that is highly relevant to later apocalypses is the "Underworld Vision of an Assyrian Prince." The text, which comes from seventh-century BCE Assyria, describes multiple dreams of a crown prince called Kummay. The lengthiest dream that is preserved begins when Kummay "lay down to sleep and saw a night

43

vision" of the underworld and its many supernatural monsters with composite features. Lastly, he meets Nergal, the king of the underworld, who is "seated on a regal throne" and wearing a crown (r. 11). Nergal has to be dissuaded from killing the prince on the spot, and then warns him:

> Do not forget or neglect me! Then I will not pass a verdict of annihilation on you. (But) on the command of Šamaš, may distress, acts of violence and rebellion together blow you down so that, by their oppressive clamour, sleep may not come to you. (Livingstone, 74)

Nergal goes on to show Kummay the interred body of his royal father. The prince wakes up with his heart pounding, and he laments.

Certain similarities with Dan 7–12 will already be clear, such as the otherworldly vision of composite monsters, the encounter with an enthroned deity, and the protagonist's awed, fearful reaction. In addition to these, some have argued that the text indicates *ex eventu prophecy* (some of the troubles that Nergal threatens for Kummay, e.g., "distress, acts of violence and rebellion," could be understood as prophecy-after-the-fact, since Aššurbanipal did, in fact, experience just those things during his reign). It also employs various forms of dream interpretation and mediation. If these points were granted (the broken state of the text makes it difficult to be certain), then nearly all the key pieces of later apocalypses would be present already in this early text. But in reality, neither the *ex eventu* prophecy nor the divine mediation of knowledge are developed as fully as they are in Daniel—or in older ANE texts, as we shall see in the next section.

Interpretation: Mediation, Secrecy and Sealed Documents, and the Periodization of History

There was a long tradition of revelation through dreams in both the biblical texts and the larger ANE, but apocalypses add an element in their revelation that was previously more rare: mediation—that is, explanation of the dream or vision by another supernatural figure. (Recall that the presence of an otherworldly mediator is part of the definition of an apocalypse.) In some cases, there seems to have been no problem with the idea that human prophets could stand in the presence of God and receive visions and oracles directly, as if they were among the divine council. This was true of Moses, most famously (Exod 33:11), but also of Isaiah (Isa 6), and even Micaiah ben Imlah (1 Kgs 22). In other cases, a dream requires interpretation by a third party. In apocalypses, the dreams and visions seem to be too difficult for human interpretation; repeatedly, they require the mediation of a supernatural figure—an attendant to the heavenly throne room (Dan 7:16), or the angel Gabriel (Dan 8:16; 9:21). Moreover, Daniel's are not the first occurrences of this motif in the Bible; angelic interpreters figure prominently in the visions of Zech 1–6, and the first part of Ezekiel's vision of the restored Temple (Ezek 40–42) is mediated by an unnamed man, described in a manner similar to the figure in Dan 10:5, who tells him: "set your mind upon all that I shall show you" (Ezek 40:3–4).

The interpretation of dreams and visions was practiced in Mesopotamia as well. The data about who the interpreters themselves were is rather limited, but the role clearly existed. Since most of the ANE dream visions were attributed to kings, it is not surprising that mediation is uncommon in them. Kings were often seen as divine (as in Egypt), or at least as having a status akin to a high priest (as in Mesopotamia), so it would have been unbecoming to suggest that they needed a mediator to understand a vision. Nevertheless, the presence of mediators might be inferred. One is suggested, for example, by the story of Gilgamesh's dream being interpreted by his mother. In addition to dream interpreters, there were also seers who might experience a vision and interpret it for the king (SAA 9:xlvi–xlvii).

All of the aforementioned Mesopotamian interpreters were human figures, but the possibility of supernatural mediation was also possible. One of the most interesting examples of this consists of the dream dialogue between the famous Mesopotamian king Aššurbanipal and Nabû, the moon god. In the dream, Aššurbanipal prays, "Please, powerful Nabû, do not abandon me among those who wish me ill!"

Although Nabû himself speaks through the text, at this moment, another supernatural figure speaks for him: a dream god, or *zaqiqu*. This figure says, "Fear not, Aššurbanipal, I will give you long life," and so on (SAA III.13:22–24).

Besides otherworldly meditation, the difficulty of interpretation also manifested itself in the motif of the sealed book or scroll. This tradition developed over time. The earliest Hebrew prophets, such as Elijah and Elisha, were not associated with writing at all, but the prophecies of Isaiah are said to have been written down for later verification (Isa 8:1, 16; 30:8; cf. Deut 18:22). The textualization of prophecy continued to increase from there: Jeremiah had his own scribe, Baruch (Jer 36, etc.); Ezekiel receives revelation by a scroll (even God communicates in written form!), though he still must swallow it and speak it later (Ezek 2:9–3:4); and Zechariah also receives a scroll from the heavens (Zech 5).

This shift to writing correlates with a more general growth of literacy in the Levant from the ninth to sixth centuries BCE. Indeed, by the postexilic period, even kings were viewed by the biblical authors as quite bureaucratic; they were always having things looked up or written down (Est 2:23; 6:1; Ezra 6:2; Neh 7:5). Like many aspects of earthly kingship, this was reflected in the divine realm—now God, too, was said to keep heavenly ledgers to aid in the management of the universe (Dan 7:10; Mal 3:16). Human and divine kings also had expert mediators of knowledge around them to keep track of such details. In Dan 10:21, a mediating angelic figure interprets writing for Daniel, but in Dan 12:4, Daniel is instructed, "keep the words secret and the book sealed."

Secrecy of revelations and their interpretations was also a concern for ANE scribes. The concern for secrecy is especially evident in Mesopotamia, where scribes saw themselves as the inheritors of ancient knowledge from before the flood. The story of Enmeduranki's education concerning divination by Shamash and Adad in the Heavenly court was noted above; and another text promises: "Šamaš will give to the diviner the secret of Šamaš and Adad" (Zimmern, *BBR* 88, rev. 3). This secret knowledge was guarded jealously by the small set of "experts" who were trained in it. There is a very common annotation, appearing on the bottom of certain kinds of tablets, which reads: "An expert may show an(other) expert; a non-expert shall not see (it)" (Lenzi, *Secrecy and the Gods*).

In the case of Daniel (and perhaps, more generally) the call for secrecy introduces an intentional paradox: the book simultaneously reveals divine mysteries and claims to desire their secrecy. The effect is to invite readers into a community of "insiders." Thus, the motif of the secret, sealed writing is integral to apocalypses in various ways.

Another integral element of ancient apocalypses is the *ex eventu* prophecy, which claims to have foretold the future, but was in fact composed after the events in question. Consider the "Dynastic Prophecy": it appears to date from the late 330s BCE, the time of the conflict between Alexander and Darius III of Persia, and it summarizes the *past* reigns in the Neo-Assyrian, Neo-Babylonian, and Persian periods, but presents them as *future* predictions: for example, it says of Nabonidus, "A rebel prince will arise [. . .] The dynasty of Harran [he will establish. He will exercise kingship] for 17 years. He will oppress the land and festival of Esa[gil he will cancel.]" It then correctly describes the rise of Cyrus the Great: "A King of Elam will arise. . . He will remove him (i.e., Nabonidus) from the throne, etc." To that point, the text accurately reflects history. However, the Dynastic Prophecy appears to go on to wrongly foretell that Darius III would defeat Alexander the Great (Neujahr, *Predicting the Past* [2012], 58–71). This was, of course, an error—in its brief attempt at actual prediction, the Dynastic Prophecy failed.

The Dynastic Prophecy was only one of a number of *ex eventu* prophecies from ancient Mesopotamia, which spanned a wide swath of history and were used in numerous situations. The goal of *ex eventu* prophecy was typically to build authority leading up to an actual prediction. The audience is meant to think, "If the diviner was so accurate in predicting events up to this point, surely s/he is also correct about what's to come next!" Therefore, the more history, the better.

Ex eventu prophecy often went hand in hand with the **periodization of history,** or the attempt to define various blocks (i.e., periods) of history apart from other blocks of history. In Daniel, each of the first four visions periodizes history in a different way. History is organized by the various beasts and horns in chapters 7–8, and by the schema of "weeks" in chapter 9. The use of periodization is most elaborate in the detailed historical survey of chapter 11. The essential theological idea of historical periodization is that God is in control of history, even over imperial foreign empires that seem far beyond the power of the communities who read and embraced the apocalypses. The claim that God is more powerful than human empires has roots much deeper in Judean history. As early as the eighth century BCE, Isaiah asserted that Assyria was not acting entirely of its own accord, but that YHWH had taken it up as an instrument—as the rod of divine wrath (Isa 10:5). The claims of Daniel are even broader: they do not pertain only to a single instance of judgment, as Isaiah's initially did, but to the rise and fall of empires over centuries. The broader scope of Daniel's periodization comes out of the author's sense of the larger history of the nation and its region—a historical consciousness that may be due to the more extensive use of writing itself in the Levant (see above).

The ancient scribal traditions of ANE neighbors demonstrate that the periodization of history was well-established as early as the third millennium. The Sumerian King List attempted to record and systematize the reigns of ancient kings and their cities, going back to the dawn of creation. One prominent version of it names eight kings, their cities, and the lengths of their reigns, then summarizes: "In 5 cities 8 kings; they ruled for 241,200 years. Then the flood swept over" (WB i:1–39). It then resumes: "After the flood had swept over, and the kingship had descended from heaven, the kingship was in Kish. In Kish, Gushur became king; he ruled for 1,200 years . . . " and it continues in this way. Similar king lists come from Ugarit and Egypt.

The roots of the idea of the specific sequence of four great empires (as in Dan 2 and 7) have proven difficult to trace with greater precision. The idea of the "ages of man" is first attested in the Greek poet Hesiod (ca. 700 BCE), and is developed also in Ovid (43 BCE–17 CE), who reduced Hesiod's five ages to four: gold, silver, bronze, and iron. (*Metam.* I.89–150.) Hesiod (*Op.* 109–201) had included a "Heroic Age" between the ages of bronze and iron.)

Fig. 3.2. Lucas Cranach the Elder's Golden Age (ca. 1530), which is often thought to draw on Hesiod and/or Ovid's "ages of man." The "Golden Age" shows people living happily together, when peace and harmony prevailed. Each successive "age of man" grew increasingly worse, ending in the "Iron Age," where humanity was absolutely evil and abandoned by the gods. Hesiod thought he lived in the Iron Age. National Gallery, Oslo; Commons.wikimedia.org.

While the correspondence is not exact, the association in Dan 2 of the four empires with gold, bronze, iron, and mixed iron is certainly reminiscent of this older tradition. Except for the head of gold (2:38), the identity of the kingdoms here is never specified, and neither are the four beasts of Dan 7, but based on the rest of the book, they seem to correspond to Babylon, Media, Persia, and Greece. An almost identical order (Assyria, Media, Persia, and Greece/Macedonia) was mentioned by Herodotus (fifth century BCE) and Ctesias (fourth century BCE), both Greeks who were influenced by the rhetoric of the Persians (See *Hist.* I.95, 130; the inclusion of the Medes, who were otherwise not a concern for the Greeks or the Judeans, suggests a Persian [or at least, Eastern] perspective). By the time of the book of Daniel, this four-kingdom schema was also attested in numerous other Latin and Greek texts, where it often served as a prologue to Rome. Daniel's employment of the schema in the third and second centuries BCE was, thus, part of a widespread literary trend. Daniel's intense focus on the last empire, and specifically the Antiochenes, is one of the indications that the visions were (mostly) written in the first half of the second century BCE, and this means that the periodized historical surveys are not predictions as such, but rather *ex eventu* prophecies.

In sum, Daniel draws on ancient traditions in its emphasis on secrecy and references to sealed divine records. The difficulty of interpretation helps to explain the need for mediation of revelation by supernatural intermediaries. Among the secrets interpreted to Daniel by these intermediaries is the scope of history, periodized and described through *ex eventu* prophecies.

Combat

Often in ANE literature, gods and kings achieved victory through combat. One of the earliest connections drawn between biblical apocalypses and ANE texts was the idea that they reflect the "combat myth," which refers to a major deity's battle with, and victory over, the forces of chaos. The defeat and destruction of the supernatural beasts symbolizing empires in Dan 7 and 8 has been compared to the combat myth, and in the ANE, the two myths that have been most significant for comparison are *Enuma elish* (the most prominent of the Babylonian creation myths) and the Baal Myth from Ugarit. However, comparable myths of **theomachy** (divine combat) are present in numerous other cultures, and even in Mesopotamia and Ugarit, there are numerous other examples of the same motifs.

The myth of divine combat was so ancient and widespread that it is not clear where it originated, but it was already known in the Levant before Israel existed. For example, the Ugaritic Baal Myth portrays Baal fighting and defeating "Prince Sea" and "Judge River"—but Baal does not get to enjoy his victory for long. He is attacked and swallowed up by a demonic figure called, simply, "Death," and has to be saved. The beginning and end of the myth are lost to us, but it appears to reflect messages about both agricultural cycles and the politics of Ugarit's Late Bronze Age world.

The Babylonian myth *Enuma elish* is equally significant for comparisons with the Bible. In its most influential form, it was the story of the Babylonian god Marduk's birth, rise to power, and creation of the heavens and earth—with an emphasis on the city of Babylon and its temples. Marduk accomplishes his victory by killing Tiamat, the deified ocean, who has raised up an army of dangerous monsters and is threatening the other gods with destruction. The monsters are frightful and godlike; they are described as "giant serpents" with sharp teeth: "the Hydra, the Dragon, the Hairy Hero, the Great Demon, the Savage Dog, and the Scorpion-man . . . the Fish-man, and the Mighty Bull" (Lambert, 59). Tiamat's dispute with the other gods begins when her consort Apsu grows frustrated with the noise made by the younger gods; the situation escalates when Marduk's father, Ea, kills Apsu. Tiamat is enraged, and none of the gods are brave enough to stand against her until Marduk steps up. In response to his heroism, they endow him with their authority and glory. Marduk defeats Tiamat (who is portrayed as a kind of sea dragon) in a dramatic battle, then splits open her carcass, and with it creates the physical world. After this, he takes "the eleven creatures to which Tiamat had given birth," binds them, and breaks their weapons.

It is clear, on the basis of Ps 74:12–17, that some biblical authors were quite aware of the theme of creation-by-slaughter. One could multiply examples of God's battle with the sea: Ps 89:9–10; Isa 27:1; Job 26:12, among others. Job 9:13 recounts that "the helpers of Rahab [another biblical term for the watery chaos monster] bowed beneath" God, a text that likely shows awareness of Tiamat's helpers. Echoes of this combat myth are also evident in Daniel. For example, in Dan 7:11, we read: "the beast was put to death, and its body destroyed"; and in 8:25: "he will be broken, and not by human hands," which conjures specific events from *Enuma elish*. The fact that the beasts rise from the sea in Dan 7:3 is also important; the above examples indicate that "chaos" was often symbolized by oceans, seas, or rivers. It is likely that the authors of Daniel were quite aware of the combat myth, and deliberately chose to both evoke it and modify it.

Daniel also evokes combat myth themes in its threats of **uncreation**. For instance, when Dan 8:10 says that the little horn "threw down to the earth some of the host (of heaven) and some of the stars, and trampled on them," one could perceive it as a threat to the created order, where the primordial chaos that was previously overcome has returned. This is a theme apparent in other biblical and ANE texts. For example, in the story of Noah's flood, God undoes the separation he had made between the water and the dry land (Gen 1:6-7), so that "all the fountains of the great deep burst forth, and the windows of the heavens were opened" (Gen 7:11). Similarly, in texts that refer to impending divine judgment on the Day of the Lord, the ordering of darkness and light may be said to fail, so that he will "will make the sun go down at noon, and darken the earth in broad daylight" (Amos 8:9; cf. 5:8; Joel 3:15 [ET]; Jer 13:16, etc.). A very similar motif is used in the Mesopotamian Erra Epic, in which Marduk's departure allows not only the destruction of Babylon, but also the crumbling of the natural order: "When I left my dwelling, the regulation of heaven and earth disintegrated; the shaking of heaven meant: the positions of the heavenly bodies changed, nor did I restore them" (Foster, 887. I.133-34; see also *Enuma elish* IV.23-24).

A final major theme connecting Daniel's apocalypse with combat myths is that of the deity's **enthronement**. Not surprisingly, this motif is quite pervasive throughout the ancient world, even in material culture: The statues of deities that were used in many of the temples of Israel and Judah's neighbors were often supplied with thrones. YHWH, too, is seen seated on a throne by Micaiah (1 Kgs 22:19) and Isaiah (6:1).

YHWH is said to be "enthroned over the cherubim" in 1 Sam 4:4; 2 Kgs 19:15; Ps 9:7 (ET); Isa 37:16, and so on, and over the flood in Ps 29:10. Daniel 7:9's image of the throne ("his throne was fiery flames, and its wheels were burning fire") is quite similar to that of Ezekiel 1 and 10.

Enthronement of gods as a result of their conquering the forces of chaos is central to the aforementioned ANE myths as well. In a climactic moment of *Enuma elish*, the gods award Marduk a throne and celebrate him, saying, "Marduk is the king!" (IV.28) In the Baal Myth, the theme of Baal's throne is quite central; someone must sit on "the throne of his dominion" (1.3 IV.3) so that the world may be properly ordered. When Baal is swallowed up by Death, the question is discussed by the god; a lesser deity named Athtar tries to sit on it, but is embarrassingly inadequate to fill Baal's shoes: "His feet do not reach its footstool/ His head does not reach its top" (1.6 I.60–61). More specific to the use of thrones in biblical apocalyptic, in the Prophecy of Neferti, the restoration of justice by the expected king is symbolized by the enthronement of Ma'at, the goddess of justice and order: "Then Ma'at will return to her throne, and Chaos [Isfet] will be driven off" (ll. 71–72).

The scene of God's enthronement (upon multiple thrones!) in Dan 7:9–10 makes sense in this broader context. As in ANE and biblical antecedents, God rightfully sits upon the throne as a result of conquering all of the cosmic and earthly forces that might oppose God. Moreover, the precise placement of the thrones in Daniel 7 certainly also points to the restoration of divine order after the chaos caused by the "beasts." For the authors of the biblical apocalypses, the created world and all the history that it entails may have gone seriously awry, but they still stand ultimately under the authority of God.

Judgment

The image of thrones leads directly to a final constellation of ideas concerning judgment. Whereas the combat myth and the Day of the Lord are typically associated with divine victory and judgment in ways that are apparent within human history—be it in the natural world or in the political realm—this section focuses on eschatological judgment. Daniel 12 does not envision judgment on behalf of the righteous within history, but rather at "the time of the end" (12:4). This marks a fundamental break with reality as it has always been known, marked by "a time of anguish, such as has never occurred since nations first came into existence" (12:1). And the judgment is to be everlasting, whether it is "life" or "contempt" (12:2).

While postmortem judgment was scarcely attested in most ANE cultures, in Egypt it was a central aspect of the religion from an early period, and it provides some interesting comparisons for Dan 12. The judgment of the dead by a tribunal goes back to the Old Kingdom, and at least by the Middle Kingdom, where a distinct myth emerged in which the heart of the deceased was weighed to determine its righteousness by the measure of Ma'at (the Egyptian term for "justice," which referred to both an abstract concept and a goddess). Osiris oversaw the proceedings, while Thoth functioned as prosecutor.

The popular image of the Egyptian afterlife is of an idealized continuation of this life, but the Egyptians also wrote about the potential terrors of the afterlife. Those who failed the judgment could be portrayed as devoured by the monster Ammut, drowned, decapitated, bound, boiled in a cauldron, or burnt by snakes and other divine creatures spitting fire. (Of course, since decedents and their families paid for the production of the texts and images in question, punishment was always reserved for other people.) The flip side of the happy afterlife was a world that was "utterly deep, utterly dark, utterly endless" (Allen, *The Book of the Dead* (1974), Spell 175)—in short, not so different from the most baroque biblical and postbiblical images of hell.

Daniel similarly reflects an interest in the afterlife of individuals, and in particular, the idea that individuals are judged upon death. Daniel 12:3 specifically states that "those who make many righteous" will shine "like the stars, forever and ever." Interestingly, the idea that the blessed dead would be like stars was quite pervasive as well in Egyptian texts. It is attested repeatedly in the afterlife books, starting with the Old Kingdom Pyramid Texts, and continuing into the widely copied *Book of the Dead* in the New Kingdom and beyond. For example, *The Book of the Dead* Spell 136B reads: "The one who knows this spell sails in the bark of Re; he ascends on the light of the flame; he becomes a Star when he passes by you" (Allen 1974, 113). Spell 178 aspires for the decedent to "ascend to the Great God as a star that perishes not, possessor of eternity" (Allen 1974, 189). And perhaps most interesting for the present purpose, Spell 165 says that the deceased will "shine like the stars in the sky" (Allen 1974, 162).

Judgment of the dead is a logical final step in the divine restoration of order because although destruction and restoration might correct chaotic injustices going forward, those who lived in the times of the apocalyptists had still suffered unjustly. Only a judgment that addressed past wrongs and rewarded those who "stood firm" (Dan 11:32–35) would be worthy of God who, according to the most ancient confessions of faith, demanded faithfulness and carried out justice (Exod 20:5–6, etc.).

Conclusion

The diverse ideas and motifs that eventually coalesced in Dan 7–12 and other Jewish apocalypses were foreshadowed by the partial constellations of earlier texts. Daniel was a text deeply imbedded in its ANE environment. Among those that have proven especially suggestive for comparison are, from Egypt, the Prophecy of Neferti; from Mesopotamia, the Underworld Vision of an Assyrian Prince, the Dynastic Prophecy, and *Enuma elish*; and from Ugarit, the Baal Myth.

There is also much in Dan 7–12 that is continuous with earlier Judean theologies, as we can discern them in the Hebrew Bible. The framing genre of dreams and visions had extremely ancient roots, both in the Bible and beyond. The God of Israel, like the gods of surrounding nations, was believed to make his will known through such means. The book of Daniel also adapted from the prophets the idea that divine revelation requires mediation, a dissatisfaction with the social and cultic realities of the present, and a desire to foretell the future. From wisdom traditions came the idea that there are two options: the way of life and the way of death (Ps 1; Prov 12:28; 14:12). Moreover, there was the belief that history is under God's control, which was more apparent when it is viewed broadly. Although there is no single text that one can identify as "proto-apocalyptic," there are also biblical texts that show partial constellations of "apocalyptic" features: in particular, Ezekiel, Zechariah, Isaiah 56–66, and the Psalms have furnished significant points of comparison.

However, in Daniel, we see marked changes in the outlook and ideas of most earlier books of the Bible. The decline of prophecy meant that the human mediator (Daniel) needed additional, *supernatural* mediation to understand the revelations of God. God became a somewhat more distant sovereign figure, a master of imperial bureaucracy, separated from humankind by ranks of heavenly attendants. The difficulties of the community's life may have contributed to this sense of distance, as hardship made them feel God's absence. The peak of these troubles, the deadly persecutions of Jews during the Hellenistic period, surely contributed to the new emphasis on an afterlife judgment: if people could not trust in their outcomes within human life, and if God were just, then there must be an afterlife judgment to right the wrongs.

The authors of Daniel, however, were not concerned only with the fates of individuals, but with the *shape of history.* By the third century, those who lived in the Levant were conscious of the rise and fall of four enormous empires—Assyria, Babylonia, Persia, and Macedonia—within less than three centuries. They had also experienced, in various ways, the warring of Alexander the Great's successors. They were aware that principalities and powers came and went. The loss of their own political autonomy would have aided Judean authors in distancing themselves from these events. But eventually, the collision of a God said to be sovereign over history with the failure of history to live up to expectations led to the belief in a divinely ordained end to history. The authors summoned up the ancient combat myth, using the monsters of watery chaos to symbolize foreign empires subject to eventual defeat at the hands of God and God's allies.

In the final accounting, no particular text, or set of texts, was the "source" for Daniel's apocalyptic visions. The authors participated in a *koine* (or "common") culture, a diverse environment in which religious/theological/cultural ideas were shared, transposed, and reused in numerous contexts. Out of that shared heritage, the authors of early apocalypses wove cultural materials from their environments into a distinctive fabric, and an outlook that spoke to many people. Some of the key affirmations of apocalypses are:

- that God's ways are often mysterious, rather than clear

- that the righteous may be oppressed because of their faithfulness, instead of rewarded for it

- that the history in which people live is not all there is, or the only perspective

- that even God's creation may not be as secure as it appears, but may be threatened by disorder

- but that God is finally sovereign over all of human history, and judges impediments and oppressors in God's own time

Framed in this way, it is not hard to see why the apocalyptic has provided a matrix for much reflection—across contexts—ever since.

Study Questions:

1. Give one example from the Bible and one from an ANE text for each of the four conceptual constellations—revelation, interpretation, combat, and judgment—found in both apocalyptic literature and its precursors.
2. How are increased literacy rates in the ninth to sixth century BCE related to the motif of writing and the motif of secret, sealed documents found in the book of Daniel and other precursors to the genre of apocalypse?
3. In what ways does the book of Daniel draw on ANE ideas about chaos, creation, and uncreation, while also modifying those ideas?

Why do you think the author(s) of Daniel would both borrow and change these earlier ideas?

4. How does the book of Daniel both mirror and challenge earlier ideas about life after death?

Bibliography and Further Reading:

Allen, T. G. *The Book of the Dead: or, Going Forth by Day: Ideas of the Ancient Egyptians Concerning the Hereafter as Expressed in Their Own Terms*. SAOC 37. Chicago: Oriental Institute of the University of Chicago, 1974.

Annus, Amar and Alan Lenzi, Ludlul bēl nēmeqi: *The Standard Babylonian Poem of the Righteous Sufferer*. SAACT 7. Helsinki: Neo-Assyrian Text Corpus Project; Winona Lake, IN: Eisenbrauns, 2010.

Foster, Benjamin R. *Before the Muses: An Anthology of Akkadian Literature*. 3rd ed. Bethesda, MD: CDL Press, 2005.

George, Andrew. *The Epic of Gilgamesh*. Repr. ed. London: Penguin, 2003.

Goedicke, Hans. *The Protocol of Neferyt = The Prophecy of Neferti*. Johns Hopkins Near Eastern Studies. Baltimore: Johns Hopkins University Press, 1977.

Gunkel, Hermann. *Creation and Chaos in Primeval Times and End Times: A Religio-Historical Study of Genesis 1 and Revelation 12*. Grand Rapids, MI: Wm. B. Eerdmans, 2006. (German original 1895: *Schöpfung und Chaos in Urzeit und Endzeit. Eine religionsgeschichtliche Untersuchung über Gen. 1 und Ap. Joh. 12.*)

Lenzi, Alan. *Secrecy and the Gods: Secret Knowledge in Ancient Mesopotamia and Biblical Israel*. State Archives of Assyria Studies 19. Helsinki: Neo-Assyrian Text Corpus Project, 2008.

Livingstone, Alasdair. "The Underworld Vision of an Assyrian Prince" in *Court Poetry and Literary Miscellanea*. Edited by Alasdair Livingstone; SAA 3. Helsinki: Helsinki University Press, 1989.

Neujahr, Matthew. *Predicting the Past in the Ancient Near East: Mantic Historiography in Ancient Mesopotamia, Judah, and the Mediterranean World*. Brown Judaic Studies 354. Providence, RI: Brown Judaic Studies, 2012.

Nissinen, M. r Prophecies nor Apocalypses: The Akkadian
ts," in *Knowing the End from the Beginning: The*
c and their Relationship. Edited by L. L. Grabbe
T & T Clark, 2003), 135–48.

terpretation of Dreams in the Ancient Near East:
i Assyrian Dream-Book. Transactions of the
Society NS 46/3. Philadelphia: American
56.

ritic Narrative Poetry. SBLWAW 9. Atlanta:

hecies, SAA 9. Helsinki: Helsinki University

irst Tour of Hell: From Neo-Assyrian
vish Revelation." *Journal of Ancient Near*
51–69.

d Henry Beal, eds., *Creation and Chaos: A*
Gunkel's Chaoskampf Hypothesis. Winona

ire of Ancient Egypt: An Anthology of Stories,
Instructions, and Poetry. 3rd ed. New Haven, CT: Yale University Press,
2003.

Smith, Jonathan Z. "Wisdom and Apocalyptic" in *Map is Not Territory:*
Studies in the History of Religions. Studies in Judaism in Late Antiquity
23. Leiden: Brill, 1978.

4

Apocalyptic Literature beyond the Biblical Canons

Fallen Angels, Divine Journeys, and the Meaning of Life

Jackie Wyse-Rhodes

GETTING PREPPED:

1. What is a "canon?" What do you know about biblical canons, or other canons—for example, a literary canon (such as that of Shakespeare) or a musical canon (such as that of Beyoncé)? Who decides what to include in a canon and what to exclude? Are these decisions fixed, or do they change over time?

2. Have you ever heard of the biblical figure of Enoch? After thinking about this, read Genesis 5:18–24. Now, what do you know about Enoch?

3. Read Genesis 6:1–4. Are you surprised by these verses? What do you think they mean?

KEY TERMS:
1 ENOCH
CANONICAL
GENEALOGY
QUMRAN
TESTAMENT

Introduction

In previous chapters, you have learned that Jewish and Christian apocalyptic literature is deeply rooted in the Hebrew scriptures, especially the prophetic books and the wisdom traditions. You have also seen how apocalyptic literature is a product of its larger cultural milieu, a matrix that draws upon biblical materials, Babylonian wisdom traditions, Persian apocalypticism, and the "widespread Hellenistic conceptions" of otherworldly journeys and eschatological prophecy (Collins 1998, 34). You have already read extensively about the book of Daniel, the Hebrew Bible's only full-fledged apocalypse, as well as other apocalyptic passages in the Bible. Later, you will learn about the book of Revelation, the only apocalypse in the New Testament. Daniel and Revelation are considered "canonical" by some faith communities (Daniel by Jews and Christians; Revelation by Christians). A religious book is considered **canonical** when it belongs to the collection of scriptures that a certain faith community considers authoritative. A community's authoritative collection of scriptures is called a "canon," from the Greek word for "measuring stick," and when a book is added to that collection, it is said to have been "canonized."

Most other apocalypses in the Jewish and Christian traditions were never canonized (with the notable except of **1 Enoch,** which is included in the canon of the Ethiopian Orthodox Church). However, this does not mean that these books were never considered *authoritative.* On the contrary, many of these non-canonical apocalypses were read as authoritative scripture in ancient religious communities even if they were never canonized at a later point. For example, the New Testament book of Jude quotes 1 Enoch 1:9—a non-canonical text—with the same authority with which it quotes portions of the Hebrew scriptures (Jude 14–15). The process of canonization happened gradually and took many centuries, and by the time the Jewish and Christian canons had stabilized (during the second and fourth centuries CE, respectively), apocalypses had fallen out of favor with many religious communities. Indeed, Daniel and Revelation themselves were controversial choices for inclusion in their respective canons. However, as a whole, apocalyptic literature was popular in religious circles from the third century BCE to the early-second century CE for Jewish communities, and even longer for Christian communities.

What do we call this group of books—these formerly popular apocalypses that were never canonized? There are several options, some better than others. Because a portion of this literature was produced in the centuries after the latest books of the Hebrew scriptures were written down, but before the first books of the New Testament were composed, these apocalypses are sometimes considered "intertestamental literature." However, that term presupposes a Christian viewpoint, and for this reason, it is not used by the majority of scholars anymore. Another option is to call this literature "the non-canonical apocalypses," to distinguish them from the canonical apocalypses. But this is also an imperfect solution, since multiple canons exist, and some of this literature is included in one canon, but not another. Most often today, then, this literature is included among the Pseudepigrapha, a scholarly designation for early Jewish and Christian literature produced around the same time as much of the canonical biblical literature, but which was (usually) not canonized. However, the Pseudepigrapha includes other kinds of literature in addition to apocalypses, so it is not exactly the right term for the ground we are covering here either.

Unfortunately, all of the above designations are flawed, since they impose contemporary distinctions on ancient literature. In this chapter, I will simply refer to this literature as "early Jewish apocalyptic literature" or "early Christian apocalyptic literature," although sometimes, as we will see, it is not easy to tell the difference.

Enoch in the Bible

In the Hebrew Bible, we briefly meet Enoch in the context of an extensive **genealogy**: "When Enoch had lived sixty-five years, he became the father of Methuselah. Enoch walked with God after the birth of Methuselah three hundred years, and had other sons and daughters. Thus all the days of Enoch were three hundred sixty-five years. Enoch walked with God; then he was no more, because God took him" (Gen 5:21–24). The description of Enoch is remarkable when compared with the genealogies of the patriarchs who came before and after him. First, Enoch is the only one listed to have "walked with God," which indicates an especially pious life; other than Enoch, only Noah (Gen 6:9), Abraham and Isaac (Gen 17:1, 48:15), and Levi (Mal 2:6) are accorded this honor. Second, Enoch did not die, but rather was "taken" by God at the end of his life. Third, Enoch's lifespan is significantly lower than that of the other patriarchs; in fact, it totals 365 years (a long time by contemporary standards, but not when compared with the other patriarchs—for example, Noah is said to have lived 950 years), which corresponds perfectly with the number of days in a solar year. Finally, the fact that Enoch fathered the famously long-lived Methuselah is another indication of his special status.

This is all we know of Enoch from the Hebrew Bible. It is tantalizingly little, but still enough to indicate that Enoch was legendary among his peers. Enoch's extraordinary (and quite mysterious) status makes him a perfect biblical figure to serve as an apocalyptic visionary in the Jewish apocalypses 1 Enoch and 2 Enoch.

Fig. 4.1. Enoch, by William Blake (1807). British Museum; Commons.wikimedia.org.

Enoch and the Watchers

1 Enoch is a collection of five booklets written over a period of centuries, edited together, and eventually combined to form one of the earliest works of Jewish apocalyptic literature. All five booklets share a common narrator: Enoch himself. As we have seen, Genesis offers scant information about Enoch. The book of 1 Enoch takes up the questions raised by the biblical text in Gen 5:18–24—Who was Enoch? Why was he special? What does it mean that he "walked with God"?—and answers them definitively. In this way, 1 Enoch serves to interpret and expand upon this portion of Genesis.

The book of 1 Enoch also expands upon another brief and enigmatic biblical passage in Genesis, which follows:

> When people began to multiply on the face of the ground, and daughters were born to them, the sons of God saw that they were fair; and they took wives for themselves of all that they chose. Then the LORD said, "My spirit shall not abide in mortals forever, for they are flesh; their days shall be one hundred twenty years." The Nephilim were on the earth in those days – and also afterward – when the sons of God went in to the daughters of humans, who bore children to them. These were the heroes that were of old, warriors of renown. (Gen 6:1–4)

Once again, a confusing text confronts readers of Genesis. Who are the "sons of God" (which also can be translated as "divine beings")? How and why did they marry human women? Who are the *Nephilim*, and how do they relate to these divine beings? Were these marriages good or bad? Did the women have a choice in the matter? The book of Genesis leaves these questions unanswered, but the book of 1 Enoch does not.

The first booklet (chapters 1–36) of 1 Enoch is called The Book of the Watchers (BW). This booklet re-interprets the story of divine beings having sex with human women in Gen 6. In the BW, the divine beings are called "Watchers" and each is named individually. In fact, the reader is invited to listen in on their conversation as they decide to defy God by descending from the heavens to the earth:

> When the sons of men had multiplied, in those days, beautiful and comely daughters were born to them. And the watchers, the sons of heaven, saw them and desired them. And they said to one another, "Come, let us choose for ourselves wives from the daughters of men, and let us beget children for ourselves." And Shemihazah, their chief, said to them, "I fear that you will not want to do this deed, and I alone shall be guilty of a great sin." And they all answered him and said, "Let us all swear an oath, and let us all bind one another with a curse, that none of us turn back from this counsel until we fulfill it and do this deed." Then they all swore together and bound one another with a curse. (1 En 6:1–5)[1]

A number of differences between Gen 6:1–4 and 1 En 6:1–5 are immediately apparent. First, in 1 Enoch, the Watchers make the motivation for their actions abundantly clear: they want a family life, with wives and children. Second, the nature of their desire is evil. Shemihazah calls his plan a "great sin" and will not act unless his companions promise to support him. As the story unfolds in 1 En 6–16, the negative consequences of the Watchers' actions multiply. Their half-divine, half-human children are no longer "heroes of old," as in Genesis; rather they are monstrous, and grow increasingly so with each generation, until they devour much of life on earth and even turn

---

1. All quotations from 1 Enoch are taken from the following translation: George W. E. Nickelsburg and James C. VanderKam. *1 Enoch: The Hermeneia Translation* (Minneapolis: Fortress Press, 2012).

on one another. Additionally, readers of the BW soon realize that the Watchers descend from the heavens not only to procreate, but also to teach forbidden heavenly knowledge to their human companions. This illicit curriculum varies from subjects worthy of Hogwarts ("the cutting of roots" and "the loosing of spells"), to astrology and astronomy, to metalworking for the making of weapons, to the fashioning of jewelry from precious metals and the creation of cosmetics from stones and dyes.

Sidebar 4.1: The Watchers' Forbidden Curriculum

If you had been one of the Watchers' students, you would have been apprenticed in the following subjects:

- forging instruments of war
- making jewelry
- mixing cosmetics
- cutting roots
- casting spells
- sorcery and magic
- interpreting lightning flashes, shooting stars, and the movements of the earth, sun, and moon

(from 1 Enoch 8)

In 1 Enoch, the Watchers do not get away with such evil. The angels who still reside in the heavens observe the bloodshed, violence, and desolation on earth, all of which resulted from the illicit sex and destructive teachings of the fallen Watchers. They approach God with this information, and God sends them to Enoch. (Where has Enoch been all this time? We do not know, but we can assume that he has not been participating in the Watchers' schemes.) In turn, Enoch is sent to the Watchers to convey the following words of judgment: the world that the Watchers have corrupted will be washed away in a global flood, and the Watchers themselves will be imprisoned in the heavens forever. Understandably, the Watchers are "trembling and fear" (1 En 13:3), and they send Enoch back to God with a letter requesting forgiveness, which God denies. The Watchers' disobedience has sealed their fate, and there is nothing more to be done.

As modern readers, we are left with a number of questions. Why was it such a terrible offense for the Watchers to choose to leave their heavenly home? Why did it wreak such havoc when they shared their knowledge and technologies with humankind? In the book of 1 Enoch, the cosmos is held together by boundaries put in place by God, a cosmology that echoes the meticulously ordered creation in Gen 1:1–2:4b. In fact, the book opens with what scholars often call a "wisdom hymn" (1 En 2:1–5:4), which lauds the natural world as a model for human righteousness precisely because the stars, trees, waters, and seasons are orderly and obedient to God's commands. The Watchers, however, defied divine boundaries, descending to earth with their "stolen mysteries" (1 En 16:3) and sharing them freely with humankind. In the early Jewish imagination, one's children are one way (sometimes the *only* way) that a person can live beyond the grave. The Watchers, divine beings who were already immortal, greedily sought a "double dose" of immortality when they descended; not only would they never die, but they would also bear offspring to continue their family line. These actions transgressed the boundaries God set for the world at creation, and thus, the Watchers are portrayed as corruptors of the world.

When compared with the biblical book of Genesis, the BW can be interpreted to blame divine beings, in part for the introduction of evil into the world, rather than humankind and a serpent (see Gen 3:1–25 for an alternative story). In the BW, it is not Adam and Eve who sin first; rather it is the fallen angels. And even though humans cooperate with the Watchers' sinful project, it is unclear whether humankind would have chosen to sin on its own. In Gen 6–9, a global flood was deemed necessary by God because of human sin and corruption; in the BW, the fallen angels bear the brunt of the blame for the deluge God sends. What difference might it have made for the ancient reader to locate the origins of evil in the heavens rather than in human beings? Would they have viewed the world differently, and humankind's place in it? To be sure, the rest of 1 Enoch makes it abundantly clear that humankind will be held accountable at the final judgment for their own wrongdoing. Perhaps the BW serves as a kind of warning for human readers: as it was with the Watchers, do not let it be with you.

Enoch's Heavenly Journeys

The latter portion of the BW focuses on Enoch's tours of the heavenly realm. Though Enoch sometimes experiences visions in much the same way as Daniel (1 En 13:8–10), most of his activity as an apocalyptic seer (i.e., visionary) happens in a wakened state. Not only does Enoch see visions in his mind; he also experiences them bodily. The authors of 1 Enoch interpret Gen 5 rather literally. Since Enoch "walked with God," it made sense to them that he would have been physically transported to the heavenly realm in order to receive special divine knowledge to share with his descendants and the rest of humanity. The BW is explicit in its depiction of Enoch being borne up to the heavens, especially in 14:8:

> Look, clouds in the vision were summoning me,
> and mists were crying out to me;
> and shooting stars and lightning flashes were hastening me
> and speeding me along,
> and winds in my vision made me fly up and lifted me upward
> and brought me to heaven.

What does Enoch see when he arrives in the heavenly realm? In chapters 14–15, he visits God's throne-room in the heavenly temple. Here, God speaks with Enoch directly, uttering an oracle against the actions of the Watchers. The fact that no angelic mediator is required to facilitate the conversation between God and Enoch indicates Enoch's status as an especially worthy human being.

In chapters 17–19, as well as later in the book, angels usher Enoch through the heavenly realm on a kind of sight-seeing expedition, and many of the spectacles he encounters have to do with the natural world. Enoch sees "the mouth of all the rivers of the earth" (17:8); "the treasuries of all the winds" (18:1); the storehouses where the hail, winds, mists, clouds, sun, and moon are kept (41:4–5); and the angels who open the storehouse doors and release precipitation at the appropriate times (34:2, 41:4, 59:17–21). Enoch's heavenly journeys take him first to the foundation of the earth, then to the cornerstone of the earth, and finally, to the ends of the earth. Who could have guessed that a heavenly tour would have revealed so much about the world below? In 1 Enoch, earth and heaven are not opposed to one another, but are regarded as intricately connected, as part and parcel of the same reality. In this sector of the apocalyptic imagination, the lines between spiritual and the physical worlds blur, and material reality is held in high regard. In fact, in 1 Enoch 69, the creation of the world is depicted in terms of a covenant (or contract) between God and the created order. Unlike Gen 1, in which God is the lone actor in creation, in 1 Enoch 69, when God speaks, the stars answer and the natural world utters words of praise. The natural world is given agency in 1 Enoch and chooses to obey God's commands.

During his journeys, Enoch is shown not only the mysteries of the created order, but also the consequences of sin for both Watchers and humans. Twice, Enoch witnesses the prisons where the disobedient Watchers are bound (19:1 and 21:10), thus emphasizing the egregious nature of their transgressions. In 22:2, Enoch views a mountain with "four hollow places in it." An angel tells Enoch that these pits are holding places for human souls until the final judgment. Three of the four pits are dark and deep, but one is illuminated and contains a fountain. The first dark pit contains the souls of those who have sinned against their fellow humans (i.e., murderers), but did not receive a fitting punishment in their lifetimes. These will be "bound forever"

(22:11) at the final judgment. The second pit contains the souls of the ones who were wronged by their counterparts in the first pit. These weary souls are led by the spirit of Abel, murdered by his brother Cain in Gen 4:8, and they will presumably continue to cry out until the final judgment, when their demands for justice will be satisfied. The third pit contains the souls of sinners "who were godless, and they were companions with the lawless" (22:13), and these will be neither punished nor rewarded on the Day of Judgment. Finally, the illuminated pit contains the souls of the righteous, who will receive a favorable judgment when the time comes.

1 Enoch 22 offers its readers a glimpse into the heart of apocalyptic literature: a revelation of divine mysteries which are relevant to earthly realities. Here, we find one of the earliest known Jewish portrayals of an afterlife that includes different fates for particular kinds of human souls. With the possible exception of Dan 12:3, in which some of the wise are said to shine "like the stars forever and ever," the Hebrew Bible is close to unanimous in its portrayal of the afterlife as one undifferentiated destination for all souls, called Sheol, neither a place of judgment nor a place of reward. In the BW, written in the third century BCE, the concept of the afterlife is beginning to change. Otherworldly reward or punishment becomes an important feature of apocalyptic literature going forward, with later apocalypses frequently depicting scenes of eschatological judgment and speculating in detail about the ultimate fate of the dead.

The Rest of 1 Enoch

The BW features heavenly journeys and the revelation of divine knowledge to the chosen seer Enoch. The rest of 1 Enoch comprises four additional books, which share some concerns with the BW (such as the actions of the Watchers and the contents of the heavenly realm), but also explore different territory. The Book of the Parables (chapters 37–71) features a series of heavenly journeys, for example, and also includes narratives about Noah, casting the biblical flood in the light of eschatological judgment. The Book of the Luminaries (chapters 72–82) is likely the oldest Enochic composition, dating to the third century BCE. It contains treatises on astronomy which draw on ancient Babylonian "science" and presents a case for both a solar and a lunar calendar. Except for an eschatological passage in chapter 80, this book consists entirely of calendrical and geographical material based upon the predictable movements of the luminaries. It was likely attributed to Enoch because of his aforementioned affiliation with the solar year. In The Dream Visions (chapters 83–90), Enoch narrates two apocalyptic visions. The first conflates the biblical flood with the final judgment of humankind. In the second, called The Animal Apocalypse, Enoch envisions the history of the world as an allegory (see below). 1 Enoch ends with The Epistle of Enoch (chapters 91–105), an example of testamentary literature (see below). Enoch calls his sons to him and instructs them in righteous living before his death. His instructions include an Apocalypse of Weeks (91:11–17 and 93:1–10), in which Enoch narrates the history of the world from his own time until the final judgment and the subsequent renewal of creation. Similar to Dan 9:24–27, Enoch symbolically speaks of each epoch of time as a "week."

Sidebar 4.2: The Animal Apocalypse

The Animal Apocalypse (AA), found in 1 Enoch 85–90, is a famous example of an early Jewish historical apocalypse. Historical apocalypses interpret the past from a theological point of view, usually in light of God's judgment of the world. The AA proceeds allegorically. Humans are depicted as cattle. The Watchers are portrayed as stars that fall from the heavens, turn into bulls, and mate with the female cattle. Their offspring are elephants, camels, and asses—unexpected progeny from the unions of bulls and cows, but in harmony with the BW's portrayal of the half-divine, half-human offspring as monstrous and destructive. The allegory continues, tracing the biblical narrative from the time of

---

Noah to the history of the ancient Israelites (depicted as sheep) as their monarchy builds and is then destroyed by foreign empires (depicted as unclean varieties of beasts and birds). This historical recital leads up to events happening at the time the apocalypse was written, including the oppression led by the Greek king Antiochus IV Epiphanies and the reform movement of a young generation of Jews called the Maccabees, led by "the ram with the great horn" (Judas Maccabeus). According to the AA, the final epoch in human history will include the divine provision for a new Jerusalem, the return of all exiles, the resurrection of the dead, and the transformation of all peoples (Jew and Gentile) into the likeness of a Messiah figure portrayed as a "great white bull," like Adam and Noah before him.

The five books of 1 Enoch comprise a diverse collection of literature, from oracles to wisdom poems, from mythological retellings to eschatological visions, from an allegorical apocalypse to an astronomical treatise. These books were produced independently, but all came to be affiliated with Enoch, that rare example of a human being considered worthy to receive the secrets contained in the heavenly realm. In spite of the diversity of their genres, these five Enochic books share a common purpose: to inspire righteous living in early Jewish (and later, Christian) communities by reminding the faithful that the vagaries of their everyday lives are part of a much larger narrative, a cosmic story revealed to them by a trusted intermediary, which is meant to be passed down through the generations until the final events of human history have come to pass.

Qumran and the Dead Sea Scrolls

So far, we have explored the five booklets that comprise 1 Enoch, the earliest Jewish apocalypse. Less than 100 years ago, our knowledge of these Enochic writings was bolstered by the discovery of an extensive collection of ancient manuscripts preserved in caves. This library contained copies of familiar apocalypses like Daniel and 1 Enoch, along with many other texts, some of which were also apocalyptic. The manuscripts in this library are commonly called the Dead Sea Scrolls. They are one of the most important archaeological finds of the twentieth century, and they were discovered by accident.

In the late 1940s, a Bedouin shepherd boy stumbled upon ancient caves in Khirbet **QUMRAN**, located about ten miles south of Jericho on the northwest shore of the Dead Sea. Subsequent archaeological excavations uncovered eleven caves at Qumran, containing more than 1,000 scrolls—some relatively complete, some fragmentary—all dating from the mid-third century BCE to the mid-first century CE. Near the caves, the ruins of a Jewish settlement were found, complete with living quarters, a cemetery, copious pottery shards, and a number of large *miqva'ot*, or Jewish ritual immersion baths. Some scholars identify the Qumran community with the Essenes, an ascetic movement within early Judaism that emphasized both strict Torah obedience and ritual purity, though this is fiercely debated. Others have suggested that Qumran functioned as a kind of retreat center, with some members living there permanently, while others commuted back and forth from Jerusalem for shorter stays, possibly with their families.

Fig. 4.2. The caves near Qumran, where the Dead Sea Scrolls
were discovered. Photo by user Franco56;
Commons.wikimedia.org.

The scrolls from Qumran comprise a religious library or archive, collected and curated by the nearby community until its destruction by the Roman Empire in 67 CE. Among these Dead Sea Scrolls are the earliest surviving manuscripts of the Hebrew Bible, as well as other non-biblical texts, such as 1 Enoch, and the book of Jubilees, a retelling of Genesis and Exodus with apocalyptic overtones. The Qumran collection also includes a number of "sectarian texts," which are thought to have been written specifically by and for members of the community (though some of these scrolls may have originated elsewhere). The sectarian texts are unique to Qumran, and many of them have a marked apocalyptic bent. One such text, called The War Scroll, depicts an eschatological battle between the "sons of light" (the Qumranites themselves) and the "sons of darkness" (Gentile nations and their Jewish collaborators). The scroll uses military language and imagery, but its armies are commanded by priests rather than generals, and its weapons are inscribed with dedications to God. Proper sacrifices prepare the soldiers for battle, and about half of the scroll consists of songs of praise to God. Rather than offering a literal battle plan, the War Scroll depicts a future time when the righteous will prevail in a cosmic struggle.

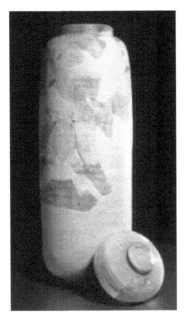

Fig. 4.3. Jars such as this one, found in a cave near Qumran, were used to store manuscript rolls of parchment, papyrus, and copper. First century BCE. Walters Art Museum, Baltimore. Commons.wikimedia.org.

Another sectarian text from Qumran, The Rule of the Congregation (11Q19), contains instructions for the initiation of new members into the community. It concludes by depicting an eschatological banquet attended by the faithful community members, the priest, and "the Messiah of Israel." The Temple Scroll (11QTemple) offers an idealized vision of the New Jerusalem in a glorious future, with a purified temple and a renewed sacrificial system. In The Treatise of the Two Spirits, a unit within the larger Community Rule (1QS), two spirits compete for the loyalty of the human heart: the spirit of truth and the spirit of injustice. In each human, one of the two spirits will eventually prevail, and to some extent, the end result is determined by God: "For God has sorted them into equal parts until the appointed end and the new creation" (1QS 4:25 [Garcia Martinez 1994, 8]). By living in a community set apart from the Jerusalem temple (which, in the Qumranites' view, had been corrupted), the residents of Qumran endeavored to live in such a way so that the spirit of truth would prevail. They were, in fact, quite confident that they were numbered among the "children of light" rather than the "children of darkness," looking forward to the day when their righteousness would be rewarded with eschatological vindication and a renewed, heavenly Jerusalem.

Sidebar 4.3: Pseudepigrapha: Two Meanings

As mentioned earlier, "Pseudepigrapha" is a scholarly designation for early Jewish and Christian literature produced around the same time as much of the Bible, but which was (usually) not canonized. The word "pseudepigrapha" can also refer to a particular genre of literature. A literary work is designated as "pseudepigraphic" if it is attributed to an ancient author who did not actually write it. (In fact, the word "pseudepigrapha" means "false writing" in Greek.) Using this latter definition, the book of 1 Enoch is pseudepigraphic because it is attributed to the ancient figure of Enoch, but was actually written by scribes in the Second Temple period. It so happens that 1 Enoch is also a part of the collection of literature called the Pseudepigrapha. However, other pseudepigraphic works are not part of the Pseudepigrapha, such as a number of the letters attributed to Paul in the New Testament. One easy way to tell whether a work is pseudepigraphic in genre or is simply a part of the Pseudepigrapha is to pay attention to whether the "p" in "pseudepigrapha" is capitalized.

Other Apocalypses: Jewish and/or Christian

In addition to Daniel, 1 Enoch, and the apocalyptic literature at Qumran, a number of other works of early Jewish apocalyptic literature played a significant role in early Jewish and Christian communities. We will briefly consider three of them—the Testament of the Twelve Patriarchs (TTP), the Testament of Moses (TM), and the Sibylline Oracles (SO)—before exploring a number of apocalypses with origins in early Christianity

As is apparent by their titles, the TTP and the TM are **testaments**, meaning that they offer parting words (or a "last will and testament") from one generation to the next. For example, the TTP is a pseudepigriphon (see above), which presents the last words of Jacob to each of his sons, whose descendants formed the twelve tribes of Israel. Eschatological themes pepper these testaments, with the Testament of Levi being especially apocalyptic in nature. Like Enoch, Levi is taken on a tour of the heavenly realm, and subsequently relates his visions to his children. It is unsurprising that Levi is chosen from among the twelve sons of Jacob for this honor, since his descendants were set apart as a tribe of priests. Likewise, TM presents Moses's parting words to Joshua. Moses's speech comprises a re-telling of biblical history from the conquest of Canaan to the establishment of the monarchy, to the downfall of kingdoms and the diaspora, to the return to the land, to the corruption of the Second Temple and its eventual destruction. The TM uses *ex eventu* prophecy ("prophesy after the fact," see Hays, chapter 2) to interpret its own time (the first century CE) as the beginning of the eschatological age, in which those who remain faithful to God's laws as revealed in the Torah will be rewarded.

The SO are a collection of fourteen apocalyptic oracles—or divine speeches mediated by human figures—that were influential for early Jewish and Christian communities. The SO do not feature biblical characters, but instead adapt the Greco-Roman figure of the sibyl: a female prophet who uttered divine speech. Sibyls were commonly consulted about matters related to politics or war. In the SO, these pagan prophetesses receive divine knowledge not from Greek or Roman deities, but from the God of Israel (and sometimes, from Christ). Book 3 is Jewish in origin and contains a variety of apocalyptic discourse, including *ex eventu prophecy*, reviews of history, and an eschatological vision of the future in which the destruction of humans and the natural world is followed by an age of blessing and restoration. In Book 3, the author's loyalties lie with the king of Egypt, who is called upon by God to oppose the Roman Empire and restore Israel. Book 5 of the SO, another Jewish composition, also decries Roman rule, but rather than looking to a contemporary political power for salvation, this oracle anticipates a heavenly savior. Book 4 (also Jewish) anchors hope for the future neither in political entitles nor in a heavenly figure, but rather in repentance, which will result in an improved existence after the resurrection of the dead. About half of the books in the SO were either edited by Christians (books 1, 2, and 8) or appear to be Christian in origin (books 6 and 7). The SO are, thus, a composite work, developed and edited over a long period of time—first by Jews and then by Christians. Though portions of the Jewish books date to the second century BCE, as a whole, the SO may have reached their final (Christian) form as late as the seventh century CE.

Sidebar 4.4: Who was a Sibyl?

In the fifth century BCE, Greek poet Heraclitus described a sibyl as follows: "The Sibyl, with frenzied mouth uttering things not to be laughed at, unadorned and unperfumed, yet reaches to a thousand years with her voice by aid of the god" (fragment 95). In Virgil's Aeneid (book VI), Aeneas visits the sibyl at Cumae (near modern-day Naples), and she accompanies him on his descent to the underworld.

Fig. 4.4. Michelangelo's depiction of the Cumean Sibyl in the Sistine Chapel, part of the Papal residence in Vatican City, painted in 1508–12. Commons.wikimedia.org.

Apocalyptic literature continued to be written by Jews through the end of the first century CE. Apocalypses written in the wake of the events of 70 CE, when the Romans responded to the first Jewish revolt by seizing Jerusalem and destroying the Second Temple, bristle with anti-Roman sentiments. These apocalypses include 4 Ezra, 2 Baruch, 3 Baruch, and the Apocalypse of Abraham, some of which are explored in detail in chapter 10. In many ways, these works show continuity with earlier apocalypses: not only are they all pseudepigraphic, but they also feature heavenly tours, scenes of eschatological judgment, and extensive conversations with angelic intermediaries. However, to a greater extent than their earlier counterparts, these later apocalypses emphasize questions of theodicy—in other words, questions which explore the judgments of God upon the world and whether or not they are justified. Accordingly, the visionaries and seers for whom these books are named repeatedly question the justice and righteousness of God. Baruch and Ezra are especially tenacious in seeking to understand why the Jewish resistance failed, and even more poignantly, why the Romans were successful in destroying the temple. These books carefully examine what it means to be a faithful Jew in the absence of a central location for the community to worship and offer sacrifices. In particular, 2 Baruch and 4 Ezra feature theological disputes between the apocalyptic seers and their angelic intermediaries—and once in a while, even arguments between the seers and their God. These apocalypses do not offer easy answers to the theological dilemmas their visionaries are facing, but the books do consistently suggest that there is yet some measure of hope, and that Jews who continue to obey the Torah can expect an eschatological restoration of their fortunes.

In 132–135 CE, the Jews revolted against the Romans for a second time. In turn, Rome quashed their resistance for good. In the wake of the second unsuccessful revolt, Jewish apocalypses began to wane in popularity, at least partially because the military actions of the Jewish people had not ushered in the cosmic heavenly victory that apocalyptic writers had foreseen. Many early Jews stopped anticipating that God would intervene in history as (soon as) they had expected, and therefore, apocalyptic literature lost some of its appeal. However, the decline of apocalyptic literature happened gradually, and a number of the SO were still produced in this period, along with another Enochic apocalypse called 2 Enoch. Christians continued to read Jewish apocalypses, and seem to have considered them authoritative, in part because this literature still spoke to the Christian expectation that Jesus would return within their lifetime to judge the world's inhabitants. Early Christians edited and added to some Jewish apocalypses (such as the SO), amending them theologically to include references to Christ. Christians also wrote a prologue and a second half for 4 Ezra. The longer Christian version of 4 Ezra, called 2 Esdras, is included in the Apocrypha, a set of books canonized by the Roman Catholic and Orthodox churches, but not by Protestant Christians.

Christians also penned apocalypses from scratch. Like the book of Revelation, the Shepherd of Hermas is a Christian historical apocalypse (see excursus on the Animal Apocalypse, above) in which an earth-bound human figure is shown heavenly visions and commissioned to share them with the wider Christian community. A former slave, Hermas is guided through his visions by a female figure who represents the church. Later in the book, he offers instructions to fellow Christians by sharing Similitudes, or "revelatory allegories" (Carey 2005, 198), concerning such quotidian matters as the temptation of material possessions as well as weighty topics such as the fate of the righteous and the wicked at the final judgment. Christians also wrote apocalypses featuring heavenly ascents. The Ascension of Isaiah (AI) builds on a prior Jewish legend called "The Martyrdom of Isaiah," which takes place in the time of the Israelite monarchy. According to this legend, Isaiah is sawn in half by King Manasseh because his prophecies are unfavorable toward the king and critical of Jerusalem. Christians re-interpreted this legend by casting Isaiah as a believer in Jesus, 700 years prior to his birth. In AI, the prophet Isaiah presents Manasseh with a review of history, which includes the coming of Jesus and God's eschatological judgment (3:13–4:22), and it is on account of this prophecy that Manasseh kills him. After his death, Isaiah ascends through the seven heavens (chapters 6–11) and describes what he sees on his journey.

Another Christian apocalypse which features a heavenly ascent (and hellish descent) is the Apocalypse of Peter. In this book, one of the Christian church's most important early leaders is cast in the role of visionary. The book takes place during events narrated in the New Testament book of Matthew: namely, the transfiguration of Jesus (Matt 17) and the apocalyptic teachings of Jesus on the Mount of Olives (Matt 24). As one of the disciples, Peter is granted special revelation into the meanings of Jesus's teachings by way of visions portrayed on the palm of Jesus's hand (rather like a miniature television screen). In these visions, Peter is taken on a tour of heaven as well as a tour of hell. In hell, Peter sees in graphic detail the *lex talionis* (measure-for-measure) punishments meted out to sinners. For example, those who blaspheme are hanged by their tongues, and adulterers from their hair, feet, or genitalia. These stomach-churning visions are meant to motivate listeners to repent of wrongdoing and to live righteously so that they might be gloriously rewarded in the afterlife.

The Apocalypse of Paul was written after the Apocalypse of Peter and is probably dependent upon it. Paul, another influential early Christian leader, implies in the New Testament book of 2 Corinthians that he himself had been taken up to the third heaven (12:1–5). Most manuscripts of the Apocalypse of Paul quote these verses, and then proceed to narrate what Paul saw on his otherworldly journey. Like Peter, Paul tours both heaven and hell. In the heavens, he witnesses the rewards of the blessed, and in hell, more gruesome measure-for-measure punishments. This apocalypse addresses theological questions about the afterlife, stating quite clearly that the soul leaves the body upon death, and is reunited with the body at the resurrection (a teaching still espoused by some Christians today). Also, more clearly than any biblical text, the apocalypses of Peter and Paul teach that heaven and hell are intended for divine reward and punishment and that all souls are destined for one or the other. Remarkably, Paul intercedes for the damned in the apocalypse that bears his name. In so doing, he succeeds in obtaining for them a small mercy: one day of rest, probably weekly. In Paul's apocalypse, even sinners suffering eternal torment are given respite on the Sabbath. This is unique among early Christian writings.

Conclusion

As we explored earlier, in 132 CE, under the leadership of the Jewish leader Simon Bar Kokhba, the Jews of Jerusalem revolted against the Romans for a final time. Hadrian defeated the followers of Bar Kokhba in 135 CE, and subsequently, scattered the Jews from Jerusalem and Judea, going so far as to re-name the region Syria Palaestina. In this new context, the eschatological hope offered by apocalyptic literature began to speak less powerfully than it had in previous generations. In the decades and centuries that followed, Jewish communities began meeting under the instruction of rabbis, seeking to remain faithful in the absence of a centralized place of worship by studying the Torah. Early Christian communities, especially those consisting predominantly of Gentiles, generally had not experienced the same kind of trauma as their Jewish siblings (though they too were disturbed by Rome's actions in Jerusalem). Because Christians were awaiting the imminent return of Jesus, apocalyptic literature remained compatible with their expectations for the culmination of history. However, as generations passed and Christ did not return, the relevance of the old apocalyptic visions gradually faded. In some ways, it is remarkable that apocalyptic books other than Daniel, Revelation, and 1 Enoch survived at all. Thankfully, even though religious canons came to exclude most apocalypses, some Jews and Christians kept reading them, making copies by hand to pass down the generations. In this way, the non-canonical apocalypses continued to influence the theology and spirituality of Jews and Christians throughout the centuries. Even today, if we venture into some religious services, we will hear eschatological claims that, in their fervor and sincerity, rival those of the ancient apocalypticists. Not only that, but when we go to the movies, we just might encounter a film featuring cosmic catastrophe and the end of the world. As humans, we remain obsessed with the security of our future and the ultimate fate of our planet. Though the ways in which we express our fears may differ from those of early Jewish and Christian writers, it is remarkable—and perhaps somewhat comforting—that we still share with our ancient forebears a number of fundamental questions about the meaning of life and our ultimate place within the cosmos.

Study Questions:

1. In the Book of the Watchers, divine beings are partly to blame for the introduction of evil into the world. As I asked earlier, what difference might it have made for an ancient reader to associate the origins of evil with the heavens and their occupants? Would they have viewed the world differently, and humankind's place in it?

2. Why is it significant that the idea of an afterlife developed gradually over time? What are the theological implications of the afterlife in 1 Enoch 22 compared with those of the afterlife portrayed in the Apocalypses of Peter and Paul?

3. Why do you think apocalyptic literature waned in popularity—in Jewish communities in the second century CE, and a few centuries later, in Christian communities? Did this genre of literature cease to answer the theological questions early Jewish and Christian communities were asking? If so, in what ways?

4. In this chapter, you were introduced to many examples of early apocalyptic literature. Did this chapter challenge any of your assumptions about apocalypses? Did this chapter change the way you think about modern apocalyptic genres, such as films and books which feature cosmic catastrophe and the end of the world?

Bibliography and Further Reading:

Carey, Greg. *Ultimate Things: An Introduction to Jewish and Christian Apocalyptic Literature.* St. Louis: Chalice Press, 2005.

Collins, John J. *The Apocalyptic Imagination: An Introduction to Jewish Apocalyptic Literature.* Grand Rapids: Wm. B. Eerdmans Publishing, 1998.

Garcia Martinez, Florentino. *The Dead Sea Scrolls Translated: The Qumran Texts in English.* Leiden: Brill, 1994.

Portier-Young, Anathea. *Apocalypse Against Empire: Theologies of Resistance in Early Judaism.* Grand Rapids: Wm. B. Eerdmans Publishing, 2011.

5

Apocalyptic Movements in Early Judaism

Dissonance and Resistance

Robert Williamson Jr. and Justin Jeffcoat Schedtler

GETTING PREPPED:

1. When you imagine the authors of the early Jewish apocalypses, how do you picture them? Were they rich or poor? Highly educated or poorly educated? Secluded from society or part of the mainstream?

2. What purposes do you think the early Jewish apocalypses serve? Do they threaten people? Or give people hope? Or encourage people to rise up against the ruling authorities? Why do you think people wrote apocalypses?

KEY TERMS:
SEER
EX EVENTU PROPHECY
DAY OF THE LORD/DAY OF JUDGMENT

WISDOM LITERATURE
ANTIOCHEAN CRISIS
COMPARATIVE SOCIOLOGY
DEPRIVATION MODEL
DISSONANCE MODEL
RELATIVE DEPRIVATION MODEL
QUMRAN
RESISTANCE LITERATURE
MANTIC WISDOM
VISIONARY PROPHECY

Introduction

Over the past few chapters, we have been examining the early Jewish apocalypses related to the figures of Enoch and Daniel, as well as their relation to other literatures of ancient Israel and the ancient Near East. In this chapter, we step back for a moment to consider Jewish apocalypticism as a social movement or, more likely, a series of loosely related social movements drawing on a common worldview that they deploy in diverse ways.

Who wrote the Jewish apocalypses? When you read the apocalypses related to Enoch and Daniel, what image of the authors do you have in your head? Are they rich or poor? Powerful or powerless? Are their lives in peril or just their lifestyles? These are important questions for our understanding of apocalypticism in early Judaism, but they are surprisingly difficult to answer. The reality is that we have very little evidence concerning the original authors and audiences of early Jewish apocalypses, apart from the texts they left behind. Other than the settlement at Qumran, where the Dead Sea Scrolls were found, we have little physical evidence of apocalyptic movements in ancient Judaism. And, as we discuss later, it is unclear whether the movement at Qumran is representative of Jewish apocalyptic groups as a whole.

The good news is that the early Jewish apocalypses themselves tell us quite a lot about the beliefs and values of the people who wrote them. Taken together, the early Jewish apocalypses reveal a common way of understanding the world—what biblical scholar John Collins refers to as an "apocalyptic imagination." By reconstructing that worldview from these texts, we can begin to understand the movements that comprised early Jewish apocalypticism.

Apocalypse as a Genre

As outlined in the introduction to this volume, the word "apocalypse" has been used in a number of different senses. Within our own Western culture, the word is most often invoked in descriptions of a catastrophic end of the world. However, as we have seen, the root meaning of the Greek *apokalypsis* is something closer to "unveiling" or "uncovering." Based on its usage in Rev 1:1 ("The revelation [*apokalypsis*] of Jesus Christ, which God gave to show his servants what must soon take place"; NRSV), the word "apocalypse" has come to describe a whole group of texts that are related to the book of Revelation in terms of theme, content, and worldview. As such, "apocalyptic literature" often refers to a *body of literature* in which the true nature of the human world is revealed through special insight from the divine realm.

A number of these texts were produced by Jewish groups, beginning in the middle of the third century BCE and extending through the end of the first century CE. The earliest of these apocalypses focus on a figure name Enoch (see Gen 5:18–24). They include the Astronomical Book, the Book of the Watchers, the Animal Apocalypse, the Apocalypse of Weeks, and the Similitudes of Enoch. Originally composed independently of one another, they are now collected together in a book called 1 Enoch (see chapter 4). A second set of early Jewish apocalypses now appears as a collection in the biblical book of Daniel (chapters 7; 8; 9; and 10–12). Other Jewish apocalypses include 2 Enoch, 2 Baruch, 4 Ezra, Apocalypse of Zephaniah, Apocalypse of Abraham, Testament of Abraham, and Testament of Levi 2–5. Indeed, insofar as the earliest Christians considered themselves Jews, it is reasonable to consider the earliest Christian apocalypses as constitutive of the Jewish apocalyptic literature composed during this period—including the last book of the Christian New Testament, Revelation. It is very likely that other apocalypses were composed by Jewish (and Jewish-Christian) groups during this time period, though they no longer exist in any form for the modern interpreter to consider.

Working from these apocalyptic texts, it is possible to identify a general worldview that characterizes early Jewish apocalyptic thought and distinguishes it from other ways of perceiving the world. Collins refers to this worldview as an "apocalyptic imagination," and describes it as follows:

> [T]he world is mysterious and revelation must be transmitted from a supernatural source, through the mediation of angels; there is a hidden world of angels and demons that is directly relevant to human destiny; and this is finally determined by a definitive eschatological judgment. In short, human life is bounded in the present by the supernatural world of angels and demons and in the future by the inevitability of a final judgment. (Collins, *Apocalyptic Imagination* [1998], 8)

From this description, we can identify several key features of the worldview among the early Jewish apocalyptic groups:

1. The world is mysterious and cannot be understood by human perception alone.
2. As such, humans require divine revelation in the form of dreams or visions, which are mediated by chosen ones, i.e., **seers**, and which are very often interpreted by heavenly beings.
3. The world is fundamentally characterized by a metaphysical dualism between the divine and human realms.
4. The world is also characterized by a moral dualism (righteous vs. wicked) that is paralleled in the divine realm by angels and demons (or by good and bad angels).
5. Human history is bounded by a final judgment of the righteous and the wicked.

These five elements of the ancient Jewish apocalyptic worldview(s) are embodied in various apocalypses in somewhat different ways. To begin, the precise form of mediation or revelation differs somewhat across the apocalyptic genre. A seer is oftentimes said to have attained visions by means of a dream. The apocalyptic section of the book of Daniel furnishes evidence of this trope:

> In the first year of King Belshazzar of Babylon, Daniel had a dream and visions of his head as he lay in bed. Then he wrote down the dream, "I, Daniel, in my vision by night saw. . . . " (Dan 7:1–2)

At the same time, in the very same sequence of texts, Daniel is said to receive visions by other means. In chapter 10, for instance, Daniel receives a vision on the bank of a river. Here, he is depicted as being fully awake, though apparently in an altered state as the result of three weeks of eating no "rich food, meat, or wine" (Dan 10:3).

In other cases altogether, a seer is said to be physically transported (most often, with the help of divine intermediaries) to a special location from which to observe—and subsequently, report—various phenomena. Consider, for example, the beginning of Enoch's otherworldly journeys in The Book of Watchers:

> And they took me and led me away to a certain place in which those who were there were like flaming fire; and whenever they wished, they appeared as human beings. And they led me away to a dark place and to a mountain whose summit reached to heaven. And I saw the place of the luminaries and the treasuries of the stars and of the thunders, and to the depths of the ether, where the bow of fire and the arrows and their quivers were and the sword of fire and all the lightnings. And they led me away to the living waters and to the fire of the west, which provides all the sunsets. . . and I departed for where no human walks. . . . (1 Enoch 17:1–4, 6; translation Nickelsburg and VanderKam, 1 Enoch [2012], 38–39)

From here on, Enoch's journey consists of being led from one fantastical place to another, and the text consists of his fanciful descriptions of all that he sees.

Just as the means by which the seer acquires the apocalyptic vision varies, so too the elements of metaphysical and moral dualism vary across apocalyptic literature. In this regard, apocalypses are typically thought to fall into two basic types: otherworldly journeys and "historical" apocalypses. Both otherworldly journeys and historical apocalypses manifest the basic ideas of the apocalyptic worldview, though they emphasize different aspects of it. For example, otherworldly journeys, such as they are found in the Astronomical Book and the Book of the Watchers, are concerned primarily with the spatial aspects of divine/human dualism, or in other words, with the places of the divine (the heavens/cosmos) and the places of humans (the Earth). As a result, they often focus on specific elements of these realms, e.g., topography, inhabitants, and/or the interaction between the divine and human realms.

Alternatively, the historical apocalypses, such as the Animal Apocalypse, Apocalypse of Weeks, and Dan 7–12, tend to focus on temporal aspects of that dualism, viewing human history in terms of cosmic struggles between the forces of good and evil, and anticipate these struggles culminating in a divine judgment, which will unfold either in their own times or in the immediate future. In other words, the historical apocalypses are concerned primarily with situating events within a sweeping narrative of past, present, and future histories.

Finally, ancient Jewish apocalypses present different portraits of the end time judgment. In Daniel 7, God (called "the Ancient One of Days") takes up a throne in the midst of the heavenly court. After opening the books, God destroys the fourth beast and deprives the first three beasts of their power, handing over the kingdom to "one like a son of man," presumably the archangel Michael, who will have "an everlasting dominion that will not pass away" (Dan 7:13–14). In this text, the eschatological judgment functions at a political level, focusing on the four kingdoms and their rulers. In the apocalypse spanning Daniel 10–12, the final judgment takes on a more individual character. In that text, the archangel Michael again arises to deliver the people, but this time, it is those individuals whose names are written in the heavenly book who are delivered (Dan 12:1). This vision of the final judgment includes the resurrection of the dead, both righteous and wicked:

Multitudes who sleep in the dust of the earth will awake: some to everlasting life, others to shame and everlasting contempt. Those who are wise will shine like the brightness of the heavens, and those who lead many to righteousness, like the stars for ever and ever. (Dan 12:3–4)

This text is the first clear reference to the resurrection and eschatological judgment of the dead in the Hebrew Bible.

The Origins of Jewish Apocalypticism

The earliest Jewish apocalypses, now preserved in the book called 1 Enoch (see chapter 4, this volume), first appear in the middle of the third century BCE. If we identify Jewish apocalyptic groups as those groups who held the worldview preserved in the Jewish apocalypses as described above, then it would be improper to speak of Jewish apocalyptic groups *per se* prior to the third century BCE. However, it is clear that Jewish apocalypticism did not appear out of thin air. Rather, it developed over time, influenced by traditions both native to ancient Israel and adapted from other cultures—notably, the Babylonians and Persians. Moreover, it can be considered as part and parcel of a more specific trajectory whose roots can be seen in particular biblical traditions—namely, the prophetic and wisdom traditions.

Israelite Traditions

Scholars have recognized that many of the elements of the Jewish apocalyptic worldview appear in nascent form in the prophetic literature of the Hebrew Bible, though not yet fully developed into the forms and patterns they would eventually take in the apocalyptic texts proper. For instance, the theme of the **Day of the Lord,** which appears as a popular topic in several Israelite prophetic texts dating to the eighth century BCE (e.g., Amos 5:18–20; Isa 13:6–13), has clear resonances with the concept of the **Day of Judgment** in the apocalypses. Each term refers to a time period during which God appears in order to render judgment upon, and ultimately, to destroy,

God's enemies, bringing about salvation and redemption to God's people.

The tradition of **visionary prophecy**, which appears in some of the earliest prophetic texts in the HB/OT (e.g., Amos 7), also resonates with later apocalyptic thought insofar as it provides a mechanism by which a person could receive divine revelation(s). That is, while in the prophetic tradition, God might reveal a vision to a prophet (and carry on a conversation with the prophet while doing so!), so, too, in the apocalyptic literature is the seer privy to divine visions and auditions. Thus, as these early biblical texts demonstrate, the dawn of specific elements of apocalyptic thought was clearly underway as early as the eighth century BCE.

Further examples of what might be deemed "proto-apocalyptic" thought can clearly be seen in the Exilic and early post-Exilic prophets, as well. For example, Ezekiel presents a cataclysmic battle in which God fights on behalf of Israel against the mythical forces of Gog and Magog (Ezek 38–39). Zechariah 1–8 presents a series of visions that require interpretation by an angel, a central aspect of later apocalyptic thought. Joel 2 envisions the pouring out of the spirit during "the last days," which shares clear affinities with the apocalyptic idea of the "end times" in which God's enemies are defeated and God's people are saved. Clearly, many of the elements of the Jewish apocalyptic worldview are present in these texts, but the worldview has not yet fully materialized.

While elements of Jewish apocalyptic thought clearly derive from biblical prophecy, it also has identifiable roots in traditional Israelite **Wisdom literature**. The clearest example of this appears in the book of Proverbs, which exhibits a "moral dualism" expressed in strong dichotomies between the wise and the foolish and between the righteous and the wicked. For example, a series of sayings in Proverbs 10 contrasts the fates of the righteous and the wicked:

What the wicked dread will come upon them,
but the desire of the righteous will be granted.
When the storm has swept by, the wicked are gone,

but the righteous stand firm forever. . . .
The fear of the Lord prolongs life,
but the years of the wicked will be cut short.
The hope of the righteous ends in gladness,
but the expectation of the wicked comes to nothing.
(Prov 10:24–25; 27–28)

Here, one can see analogues with apocalyptic tropes in which the "in" group (the "chosen"; the "righteous"; etc.) is distinguished from the "out" group (the "wicked"; the "unrighteous"; etc.) in the strongest possible terms. Moreover, in this Wisdom tradition, the wise and righteous are rewarded, while the foolish and wicked are punished—a notion that regularly appears in apocalyptic literature. Unlike later apocalyptic thought, however, Wisdom literature does not tend to connect these dualisms to the metaphysical realm. In other words, wisdom exists in the world (not outside of it) and is typically revealed to humans through natural (not supernatural) means, though figures such as Woman Wisdom and Woman Folly (see Proverbs 9) no doubt provide a mechanism for this later development.

Sidebar 5.1: The Babylonian Exile

At the very end of the seventh century BCE, the region of Judea found itself in the midst of a power struggle between the Neo-Babylonians (under the rule of Nebuchadnezzar) and the Egyptian Empire. The Judean King Jehoiakim equivocated in his allegiances to these powers, and as a result, Nebuchadnezzar besieged Jerusalem three times over a period of 20 years. Finally, in 586 BCE, the city of Jerusalem was destroyed, along with its central institution, Solomon's Temple, and many of its citizens were deported to Babylon. This marks the beginning of the so-called Babylonian Exile, which lasted until 538 BCE, when the Persian ruler Cyrus conquered the Neo-Babylonians and allowed the Judeans to return home. Cyrus's edict, which appears

---

multiple times in the OT/HB, not only allowed the Judeans to return home, but also to rebuild the Temple in Jerusalem. The rebuilding of this "second" Temple marks the beginning of the "post-exilic" period in Jewish history, as well as the inauguration of the "Second Temple period," which lasted until the eventual destruction of this temple at the hands of the Romans in 70 CE.

Fig. 5.1. The Ishtar Gate from ancient Babylon.

Pergamon Museum, Berlin;

Commons.wikimedia.org.

A number of additional elements evident in the Wisdom tradition are worthwhile inasmuch as they resemble elements in apocalyptic texts. Israelite Wisdom expresses an interest in cosmology—the beginnings and workings of the world—and its connection to morality, which is expressed particularly in Wisdom hymns such as Proverbs 8 and Job 28, as well as the somewhat later Ben Sira 42:15–43:33. That the early apocalyptic "authors" Enoch and Daniel are both depicted as sages further suggests a connection between Wisdom traditions and apocalypticism.

Foreign Influences

While Jewish apocalyptic thought has clear roots in the native traditions of ancient Israel, it also shows influences from the Babylonian and Persian cultures contacted during the exilic and post-exilic periods. In particular, Babylonian **"mantic" wisdom** (the interpretation of mysterious signs and dreams) likely contributed to the visionary emphasis of Jewish apocalyptic literature. Notably, both Daniel and Enoch are connected to the guild of Babylonian mantic sages, with Daniel being depicted as a member of the guild in Daniel 1–6 and Enoch being modeled on the Babylonian sage Enmeduranki, founder of the Babylonian *baru* guild of diviners. A second probable Babylonian influence comes from the Babylonian prophecies, which employ a phenomenon known as *ex eventu* **prophecy** (or "prophecy after the fact"). Such prophecy "predicts" the events of an earlier time by casting history as prediction, and then offering genuine predictions of events occurring in their own time. We find this phenomenon in a number of Jewish apocalypses, particularly those related to the Antiochean crisis. The Animal Apocalypse "predicts" the entire history of Israel from Adam to the Maccabean revolt, while Daniel 8 describes the rise of Alexander the Great, and then, of Antiochus. The most detailed *ex eventu* prophecy among the early Jewish texts appears in Daniel 11, which traces history accurately from the time of the last Persian kings until the rise of Antiochus (Dan 11:1–39). However, the final predictions of the demise of Antiochus in Dan 11:40–45 are not historically accurate, suggesting that the author wrote them as (ultimately incorrect) predictions in the midst of the Antiochean crisis.

Jewish apocalypticism also demonstrates influences from Persian thought, particularly in terms of cosmic dualism between good and evil and/or light and darkness. The extent of Persian influence on Jewish apocalypticism is disputed because the Persian traditions themselves are notoriously difficult to date. As a result, we cannot be sure whether particular Persian traditions: (1) influenced Jewish apocalyptic thought; (2) developed in parallel with Jewish thought; or (3) appeared in response to Jewish notions of apocalypticism. Nonetheless, the Persian belief in a cosmic struggle between light and darkness in the form of angels and demons is attested by Theopompus as early as 300 BCE, and the Persian belief in resurrection is assuredly ancient.

From such data, a plausible reconstruction of the origins of Jewish apocalypticism is possible. It is most likely that Jewish apocalyptic thought emerged among Jews living in the region of Mesopotamia during and after the period of the Babylonian Exile. It probably developed among highly literate Jews, those who were deeply immersed in the study of ancient texts, and familiar both with ancient Israelite (biblical) traditions as well as the religious thought of both the Babylonians and Persians. In particular, Jewish scribes, those who collected and transmitted texts in an age well before modern printing presses, were in a position to incorporate biblical and non-biblical elements into a relatively coherent "apocalyptic worldview." Accordingly, Jonathan Z. Smith has argued that both Wisdom and apocalypses are "essentially scribal phenomena" (Smith 1993, 74). That the central figures of many apocalypses (Enoch, Daniel, Ezra, and Baruch) have scribal backgrounds lends credence to this claim.

Sidebar 5.2: The Antiochean Crisis

In the late-fourth century BCE, Alexander the Great conquered much of the Ancient Mediterranean world, including the relatively tiny geographic area of Judea and its capital, Jerusalem. After the death of Alexander, his kingdom was divided among his generals, the so-called

---

Diadochoi. As the region of Judea lay in between two major centers of this power structure, the Ptolemaic kingdom in Egypt and the Seleucid kingdom to the East, it came under the power of each at various points. Judean responses to foreign rule varied, but a particularly violent protest occurred during the rule of Antiochus IV, the Seleucid ruler of Judea during 174–163 BCE. According to 1 and 2 Maccabees, a group of Jews led by Judas Maccabeus reacted against various measures enacted by Antiochus, ultimately establishing an independent Jewish state. Various apocalyptic texts seem to bear witness to these events.

Fig. 5.2. A coin from the Seleucid dynasty of Antiochus IV (175–164 BCE). Front: Antiochus IV crowned. Back: Zeus holding scepter with inscription: King Antiochus, Image of God, Bearer of Victory. Photo: CNG Coins; Commons.wikimedia.org.

While apocalyptic thought seems to have taken shape in Mesopotamia, many apocalypses were clearly composed in the region of Jerusalem and Judea, as they concern the events leading up to the Maccabean revolt in the second century BCE. For example, you read in chapter 2 that Antiochus IV most likely lies behind the description of the "little horn" in Dan 8:9–14. We must assume either that the Jewish apocalyptic groups that developed in the eastern Diaspora returned to Judea or that the traditions they developed gained popularity beyond their original authors, among those who remained in Judea.

Who Wrote Apocalypses Anyway?

The conclusion that the authors of the early Jewish apocalypses were most likely highly educated scribes flies in the face of a common misperception that apocalyptic thought emerges primarily among the poor and oppressed, or those who suffer persecution for their religious convictions. This **deprivation model** of apocalypticism, which proposes that the extreme rhetoric of apocalyptic texts (i.e., the violent destruction of the current sociopolitical order) was the product of a group that was disenfranchised and/or isolated in society, was common among scholars until quite recently.

However, more recent studies have shown that, while it certainly *possible* for apocalyptic views to be held by people living in situations of deprivation, apocalyptic thought is not *limited* to such situations. An important study by Stephen L. Cook used the method of **comparative sociology,** which analyzes data across disparate cultures, to demonstrate that apocalyptic views have been (and continue to be) held by groups in a wide range of social locations—both oppressed and oppressors, colonized and colonizers, poor and wealthy. Cook argued that there is nothing in particular about apocalyptic thought that is specific to those living in situations of desperation or deprivation.

In light of this conclusion, others have proposed a more moderate position, which might be called the **relative deprivation model**. According to this view, a person may hold apocalyptic beliefs (and write apocalyptic texts) if they *perceive* themselves to be deprived (financially, politically, socially, etc.), regardless of their absolute level of financial, political, or status in society. However, this model encounters difficulty in defining what constitutes "relative" deprivation (i.e., relative to what?), so that the category tends to become so broad as to be meaningless.

In light of these concerns, a more adequate description of the social location of apocalyptic thought may be considered by means of a **dissonance model,** in which apocalyptic thought is understood to emerge in situations where there is a perceived lack of fit between the reality of lived existence and the way that people feel the world "ought to be." While this sense of dissonance could potentially involve active persecution, economic deprivation, or political powerlessness, it could also emerge in less dire situations in which people of means and considerable power nonetheless feel unable to conform the world to their own sense of how it should be. Such might have been the experience, for example, of some of the post-Exilic returnees to Judea who are believed to be responsible for composing some of the earliest apocalyptic literature. As a more contemporary analogue to this ancient scenario, one might consider the resonance of the *Left Behind* series of apocalyptic novels, particularly among relatively wealthy, white, American Evangelicals in the early 2000s (see chapter 19, this volume), as well as other popular expressions of apocalypticism in contemporary popular culture.

What this means for the study of early Jewish apocalypticism is that we ought not limit our view of Jewish apocalyptic groups only to those experiencing powerlessness, deprivation, or persecution. Although it is certainly possible that some apocalyptic texts originated in such circumstances, Jewish apocalypticism also seems to have existed among wealthy, powerful, and educated members of society. That the authors of the early Jewish apocalypses associate themselves with the scribal figures Enoch and Daniel suggests that they were themselves scribes, and thus, members of an educated elite with some measure of access to wealthy and powerful people.

The Functions of Apocalyptic Thought in Early Judaism

Given all of this, what can we say about the *function* of apocalyptic thought in early Judaism? It has been common to think of apocalypses as "crisis literature" that emerges in periods of acute persecution. In fact, this view does accord well with some of the Jewish apocalypses, particularly those Enochic and Danielic texts related to the Antiochean crisis, as well as the book of Revelation. Those apocalypses address particular crises by giving their readers confidence that the persecution would soon end and that God would re-establish justice. Yet, other apocalypses are not so easily described as crisis literature. In particular, early Enochic texts such as the Astronomical Book and the Book of the Watchers do not seem to reflect any particular crisis. Nor does the apocalyptic community at Qumran (see more in the next section) seem to have existed in response to any immediate crisis so much as to a long-term sense of alienation from the Temple establishment in Jerusalem.

For this reason, the dissonance model, which we discussed earlier, may provide a better framework for understanding the function of apocalyptic literature. Both the "crisis" and "non-crisis" apocalyptic texts express a sense of dissonance between the world as it is and the world as it "should be"—the "crisis" texts simply experience the dissonance more urgently. In all cases, the apocalypses insist that God will intervene to resolve the dissonance, rewarding those who are righteous and punishing those who are wicked. In this way, apocalyptic texts can encourage their readers toward particular actions grounded in a transcendent reality and confirmed by an eschatological judgment. Much apocalyptic literature thus functions first to critique the status quo and then to encourage its readers to reject that status quo in anticipation of God's ultimate intervention in the form of eschatological judgment.

In this sense, it has become increasingly common to refer to the early Jewish apocalypses as **resistance literature.** In some cases, this resistance may refer to active resistance to an immediate crisis, as in texts such as the Animal Apocalypse and Daniel 7–12, which were produced during the reign of Antiochus. In other cases, the resistance may be more subtle. Anathea Portier-Young has shown how even the early Enochic apocalypses such as the Astronomical Book and the Book of the Watchers function as resistance by subverting the foundational myths of Hellenistic culture. For instance, the story of the fallen watcher Asael, as told in the Book of the Watchers, inverts the Greek myth of Prometheus, who brought fire and culture to humankind. By contrast, Asael corrupts humanity by teaching them warfare, sorcery, and astronomy, thus calling into question the cultural legacy of the Greeks. Similarly, the Book of the Watchers portrays the Greeks themselves as destructive "giants," born of fallen angels and human women and wreaking havoc on the earth. This story reverses the Greek mythology of the Gigantomachy, as told in Hesiod's Theogony, in which the Greek Olympian gods are the ones who destroy marauding giants to establish peace on the earth. While these stories in the Book of the Watchers do not seem to respond to a particular crisis, they do function as a general resistance to Greek rule over the Jewish people.

However, while the category of resistance is useful for understanding one of the significant functions of Jewish apocalyptic thought, not all Jewish apocalypses are accurately classified as resistance literature. For instance, a number of apocalypses, such as 4 Ezra, 2 Baruch, 3 Baruch, and the Apocalypse of Abraham, were composed in the wake of the destruction of the Second Temple by the Romans in 70 CE. These writings are more accurately described as reflections on that tragedy rather than as resistance literature.

The difficulty of identifying the single function of apocalyptic literature may, in fact, be a testimony to the adaptability of the apocalyptic worldview. It provides a way of framing *any* dissonance between the world-as-it-is and the world-as-it-should-be, whether that dissonance is an urgent crisis, a general disaffection with the predominant culture, or a national tragedy. Any of these dissonances can be addressed through an apocalyptic worldview, which casts the dissonance in terms of metaphysical and moral dualisms and promises an end to the dissonance in the form of an eschatological judgment. This "apocalyptic technique," to borrow from Collins, more than any particular social function, provides the common ground of early Jewish apocalyptic movements (Collins 1998, 41).

Early Jewish Apocalyptic Groups

We now turn to the question of what we can know about specific

Jewish apocalyptic groups in the Second Temple period. Unfortunately, there is little physical evidence of Jewish apocalyptic groups beyond the remains of the **Qumran** community, discussed below. As a result, we are left to reconstruct Jewish apocalypticism primarily from the texts of the apocalypses themselves. The earliest Jewish apocalypses suggest at least two apocalyptic communities existing side-by-side, one placing its primary emphasis on the Enoch traditions and the other on the Daniel traditions. While it is theoretically possible that these groups could be one and the same, their competing responses to the Antiochean crisis (see above) suggest otherwise. Most likely, we should not think in terms of *the* Jewish apocalyptic movement, but rather of multiple apocalyptic Jewish groups existing alongside one another, sharing a general "apocalyptic imagination," but with varied interests and emphases.

The Enochic Traditions

The earliest Enochic literature, consisting of the Astronomical Book, the Book of the Watchers, the Animal Apocalypse, and the Apocalypse of Weeks, are clearly related to one another, suggesting an Enochic apocalyptic movement (or perhaps, closely-related movements) with a consistent worldview, rather than simply a few disconnected texts related to Enoch. As noted earlier, this movement likely had its origins in the eastern Diaspora, given the similarities between Enoch and the Babylonian mantic sage Enmeduranki. However, the texts collected in 1 Enoch reflect a time after the group (or its traditions) had returned to Judea.

The earliest of the Enochic works, The Astronomical Book and The Book of the Watchers, focus centrally on Enoch's heavenly journeys. Unlike the historical apocalypses, these early Enochic books show little interest in history itself or in the specifics of divine intervention in human affairs. Nonetheless, they do express a feeling of dissonance with the cultural milieu. Both texts give an explanation of why the world has drifted from the way it should be. The Astronomical Book describes "the days of the sinners" (1 En 80:2) when "many heads of the stars will stray from the command and change their ways and actions" (1 En 80:6). The Book of the Watchers, which shares this worldview, attributes the waywardness of the world to the actions of fallen angels, led by Shemihazah. Both texts likewise expect an eschatological intervention in which God will judge those who have gone astray and set the world aright. In contrast to the historical apocalypses produced during the Antiochean crisis, these early apocalypses seem to reflect a time of relative peace, or at least, a lack of urgency about the state of things.

The later Enochic traditions, known as the Apocalypse of Weeks and the Animal Apocalypse, reflect a more urgent view of the world. They respond to the events of Antiochean persecution and the Maccabean revolt, around 167 BCE. The Animal Apocalypse presents an *ex eventu* prophecy of the history of the Jewish people, from Adam down to the Antiochean persecution. It closes with a judgment of the wicked, both divine and human, and the establishment of a new society (1 En 90:20–27). Interestingly, both the Animal Apocalypse and the Apocalypse of Weeks seem to refer to the members of the Enochic group itself. The Apocalypse of Weeks refers to "witnesses of righteousness from the everlasting plant of righteousness" (1 En 93:10). The Animal Apocalypse describes a group of sheep who are given a sword to go out and slaughter all of the other animals. Thus, the Enoch group appears to have supported the Maccabean revolt by encouraging its readers to take up arms against the Greeks. It is possible that this Enoch group is to be identified with the Hasidim (or Hasideans) in 1 and 2 Maccabees (1 Macc 2:42; 7:12–13 and 2 Macc 14:6), who likewise fought in support of Judas during the Maccabean revolt. However, the connection remains speculative.

The Daniel Traditions

Like the Enoch traditions, the Daniel traditions also seem to have their roots in the Eastern Diaspora. The Court Tales of Daniel 1–6 situate the figure of Daniel in the court of the Babylonian and Median kings, and the emphasis on Daniel as a dream interpreter has deep connections to Babylonian **mantic wisdom,** in which humans gain access to divine knowledge in particular through dream interpretation and visionary experiences. While the Court Tales are not themselves apocalyptic, the connections between the Four Kingdoms motif of Daniel 2 and the four beasts of Daniel 7, as well as the choice of Daniel as a visionary, suggest that the apocalyptic texts are rooted in a community for which the Court Tales were foundational stories.

If this is the case, then the Daniel traditions, like the Enoch traditions, have origins in the eastern Diaspora, but ultimately took root in the region of Judea and Jerusalem during the Hellenistic period. The apocalypses of Daniel 7–12 emerge from the same historical milieu as the Animal Apocalypse and the Apocalypse of Weeks, suggesting that apocalyptic thought was particularly relevant during the period of Antiochean persecution, though not exclusively then.

Like the Apocalypse of Weeks and the Animal Apocalypse, the Daniel apocalypses present Jewish history in the form of *ex eventu* prophecy, attributed to the Babylonian-era figure Daniel, but written at the time of the Antiochean crisis. Daniel 7 describes four beasts emerging from the sea, representing four successive empires. It presents Antiochus Epiphanes IV as a little horn with "a mouth speaking arrogantly" (Dan 7:7). At the conclusion of the apocalypse, the fourth beast is judged and destroyed by God, the Ancient One seated on the throne. Daniel 8 presents a similar review of history, this time presenting Greece as a goat, again with Antiochus as a horn that "acted arrogantly," specifying that "it took the regular burnt offering away from him and overthrew the place of his sanctuary" (Dan 8:11). The long apocalypse of Daniel 10–12 presents a detailed *ex eventu* prophecy, again culminating in the reign of Antiochus.

However, it is significant that the apocalypses of Daniel encourage a different response to the Antiochean persecution than do the Animal Apocalypse and Apocalypse of Weeks. While the Enoch texts encourage their followers to take up arms against the Greeks, Dan 11:33 describes "some among the wise" who "shall fall by sword and flame, and suffer captivity and plunder," a reference to martyrs. Nowhere in Daniel are the people encouraged to take up the sword. Rather, Daniel encourages its readers to wait for the archangel Michael to intervene on their behalf, commending nonviolent resistance and even martyrdom in the meantime.

This difference between the Enoch and Daniel traditions suggests that they should not simply be identified as belonging to the same apocalyptic movement. Rather, it appears that two apocalyptic groups, both with roots in the eastern Diaspora, existed side-by-side during the time of the Antiochean persecution, and yet manifested and encouraged different responses to it. This observation gives further credence to the claim that we should not think of *the* Jewish apocalyptic movement, but rather of multiple Jewish apocalyptic movements existing at the same time and not always toward the same ends.

The Qumran Community

The third and most tangible example of an early apocalyptic Jewish group is the sectarian community living at Qumran, at the northern tip of the Dead Sea, from perhaps the middle of the second century BCE until its destruction by the Romans in 70 CE. This "Qumran Community," as it has come to be known, collected a significant number of religious texts, both biblical and extra-biblical, which are commonly called the Dead Sea Scrolls. The collection included numerous copies of both the Enoch apocalypses and the book of Daniel, suggesting that both traditions were important to the community. As a result, the Qumran Community cannot properly be described as either Enochic or Danielic but rather as a distinct movement that saw itself as related to both traditions.

Curiously, the Qumran Community did not themselves produce any apocalypses *per se*, though a number of the texts composed by the community clearly express an apocalyptic worldview more generally. One of their foundational documents, known as the Community Rule (1QS), includes a passage that divides humanity into the Sons of Light and the Sons of Darkness, each of which has a corresponding angelic or demonic force. It envisions a cataclysmic battle at the end of days in which the Sons of Light will defeat the Sons of Darkness. Similarly, the community's War Scroll (1QM) contains detailed plans for the final battle between the community and the demonic forces arrayed against it. Another collection of texts known as the *pesharim* ("interpretations") views the prophetic books of the Bible as containing concealed mysteries about the community's own time, which must be unraveled by a visionary interpreter. Other texts known as the *Hodayot* ("thanksgiving songs") view the members of the Qumran Community as already having a lot among the angels, where they will live like stars after death.

In this way, the Qumran Community gives us one example of what an apocalyptic Jewish group might have looked like toward the end of the Second Temple period. They were founded by a charismatic leader, known as the Teacher of Righteous, and withdrew into the wilderness, apparently out of protest against the ruling parties of Jerusalem and their administration of the Temple. The community had an extensive initiation process that required members to give up their personal possessions into the common treasury. They appear to have been mostly celibate males, though this point remains in dispute.

However, we should not view the Qumran Community as the picture of what all apocalyptic Jewish groups were like. The community had a particular interest in purity rules and a strictly hierarchical organizational structure that are not evident in the apocalypses of Enoch and Daniel, making it unlikely that the movements that produced those texts held the same views. More importantly, the foundational documents of the Qumran Community itself makes it clear that not all Jewish apocalyptic groups consisted of celibate men separated from society. A text known as the Damascus Document (CD) acknowledges that even the Qumran Community was part of a broader movement that included married Jews who lived dispersed among the cities and towns of Judea, rather than separated in an enclave such as Qumran. Thus, even members of the same apocalyptic movement could lead lives that were quite different from one another.

Conclusion

If our examination of early Jewish apocalypticism has taught us anything, it is that we should be careful in the assumptions we make about the groups that wrote and read these apocalypses. While in the popular imagination, apocalyptic groups are often thought of as radical groups existing on the margins of society, our study has suggested that such is not always the case. Even in the case of the Qumran community, which did withdraw into the wilderness near the Dead Sea, it is clear that the movement extended beyond Qumran into the cities and towns of Judea among people who probably were indistinguishable from their non-apocalyptic neighbors. Thus, we should think of Jewish apocalyptic movements not only at the periphery of society but also at the center, among those with some degree of access to both wealth and power.

It is clear that the authors of the Enochic and Danielic apocalypses were highly educated scribes familiar with the traditions of the Jewish scriptures as well as Greek and ancient Near Eastern mythologies. They had a keen enough grasp of history to write *ex eventu* prophecies with a high degree of accuracy. They wrote in opposition to the influence of the Greeks on Jewish culture generally, and in the time of Antiochus, specifically against what they understood as a desecration of the Temple in Jerusalem. They were anti-Greek scribes in a period when those in power were welcoming of Greek culture, and they encouraged resistance to Greek influence among their followers—whether violent, in the case of Enoch, or nonviolent, in the case of Daniel.

However, we should recall that the historical apocalypses produced in response to the Antiochean crisis do not represent the totality of early Jewish apocalypticism. Not all of the apocalypses respond to particular crises, and the otherworldly journeys, in particular, generally refrain from the direct political commentary we find in the historical apocalypses. In these non-crisis texts, the categories of dissonance and resistance remain useful, but less directly so. Often, dissonance takes the form of a general wariness of the influence of those in power, whether politically or culturally, and resistance may be as subtle as asserting the superiority of Jewish traditions over those of the dominant culture.

All of this should caution readers of apocalyptic literature against making quick assumptions about the social locations and motivations of the people who wrote apocalypses. They can be written by people from all parts of society—those in the center and those at the periphery, those with access to power and those with very little power, those who are actively persecuted and those who have a general sense of wariness about the state of the world. As readers, then, the best approach is to search the individual texts themselves for information about the identities of the authors and the concerns that motivate them to write. By rejecting the assumption that all apocalyptic groups are basically the same, we can appreciate the richness and variation of these texts and of the people who wrote them.

Study Questions:

1. What difference does it make to your reading of an apocalypse whether it was written by someone powerful or powerless, rich or poor?
2. Can you think of examples from our own time of apocalyptic groups from different social locations within society?
3. If you were going to write an apocalypse today, what kind of dissonances would motivate your writing? In what ways do you perceive the world as not being what it "should be?"

Bibliography and Further Reading:

Collins, John J. *The Apocalyptic Imagination*. 2nd ed.; Grand Rapids/ Livonia, MI: Wm. B. Eerdmans/Dove, 1998.

____, ed. *Apocalypse: The Morphology of a Genre*. Semeia 14; Missoula, MT: Scholars Press, 1979.

Cook, Stephen L. *Prophecy & Apocalypticism: The Postexilic Social Setting*. Minneapolis: Fortress, 1995.

Nickelsburg, George W. E., and James C. VanderKam. *1 Enoch.* Hermeneia; Minneapolis: Fortress Press, 2012.

Portier-Young, Anathea E. *Apocalypse against Empire: Theologies of Resistance in Early Judaism.* Grand Rapids: Wm. B. Eerdmans, 2011.

Smith, Jonathan Z. "Wisdom and Apocalyptic," in *Map is Not Territory: Studies in the History of Religions.* 2nd ed. Chicago: University of Chicago Press, 67–87.

6
———

Apocalyptic Currents in Early Christianity

One-Trick Ponies?

Greg Carey

GETTING PREPPED:

1. What assumptions do you bring to apocalyptic literature? What do you assume it talks about? How do you imagine that people use it?
2. Do you think apocalyptic ideas are closer to the core or to the margins of early Christian literature?
3. Many people associate apocalyptic literature with striking or bizarre symbols. How do you think early Christians found meaning in those symbols?

KEY TERMS:
APOCALYPTIC DISCOURSE
APOSTASY
ENTHYMEME

RAPTURE

REDACTION

Introduction

One way to imagine the Christian New Testament would be to say that it begins with the stories of Jesus (the four Gospels) and concludes with Revelation. In that final book, we encounter cosmic conflict between the forces of God and those of the devil, a return of Jesus to set things right, a final judgment of the living and the dead, and a new Jerusalem in which people live without pain or fear. On account of its graphic portrayals of the end times, grotesque cosmic creatures, vivid cosmic battles, and seemingly unintelligible symbology, we tend to isolate Revelation from the rest of the New Testament (and of early Christianity in general). In doing so, we allow Revelation to define apocalyptic thinking for many people.

An alternative way to describe the New Testament—and much of early Christian discourse—would place **apocalyptic discourse** much closer to the center of the story. Our best evidence suggests that the New Testament came together in stages, as early Christians created and circulated copies of the literature they read aloud in their gatherings. The first pre-canonical collections available to us include the four Gospels and the book of Acts, along with at least ten letters attributed to the apostle Paul. Later material seems to have accumulated around that core, with varying groups of documents being copied and read more often in some areas than in others. The book of Revelation, for example, was far more popular in the Roman West than in the East. Yet that core—the four Gospels, followed by ten Pauline letters—clearly constitutes the most widely circulated material from earliest Christianity.

Apocalyptic discourse heavily shapes most of the earliest, core Christian literature, not just Revelation. This chapter will briefly track the influence of apocalyptic literature upon the canonical Gospels and the Pauline literature—topics other chapters in this volume explore more fully. It then turns to explore several diverse ways in which apocalyptic literature "worked": that is, the different ways in which several early Christians used apocalyptic topics to influence behavior and shape belief. Our examples of early Christian apocalyptic literature are hardly one-trick ponies. In this literary corpus, apocalyptic discourse proved a remarkably adaptable resource for early Christian imagination.

Apocalyptic Discourse in Christian Contexts

I often rely on a single thought experiment to underscore the foundational contribution of apocalyptic discourse to early Christianity. Let's imagine a very smart person who reads the Bible all the way through, from beginning to end. Sometimes, she needs help to understand certain items, but she comes to the Bible as a relatively blank slate. All of this is new to her. Yet this imaginary reader remembers everything she encounters. Beginning with Genesis, she reads the entire Old Testament (or Hebrew Scriptures), and when she finishes Malachi (the last book in the Protestant Old Testament) and begins to read Matthew, she learns she's entering the New Testament.

The thought experiment hinges on what happens when our reader enters the New Testament. That is, what happens when she moves from Malachi to Matthew? I would say she encounters some surprises—ideas that are either totally new or much more developed than what she's seen in the Old Testament so far. For example, Matt 1:1 introduces Jesus as the "messiah" or "Christ." Both *messiah* (from Hebrew and Aramaic) and *Christ* (from Greek) indicate one who is anointed for a special purpose, and our reader has already met biblical characters in the Old Testament who have been "anointed" for one purpose or another. But as she works through the New Testament, our reader realizes that only one person is identified in that way now. Why now is only Jesus recognized as the messiah? She also meets angels and demons. In the Hebrew Scriptures, she has encountered angels on occasion, especially "the angel of the LORD," but she hasn't really met evil spirits. In fact, in the Hebrew Scriptures, "evil spirits" always come from God (Judg 9:23; 1 Sam 16:14-23; 18:10; 19:9). In Matthew, she will soon meet the devil, or Satan. The Hebrew Scriptures mention a Satan, but he is not the mighty supernatural adversary that so concerns early Christian writers. Matthew is quite fond of describing a final judgment, and the concept of resurrection from the dead pervades his gospel and much of the rest of the New Testament. In the Hebrew Scriptures, however, our reader has met these ideas only in the book of Daniel. Some people might see references to resurrection in other Hebrew Bible passages (e.g., Isa 26:19; Job 19:25–26; Ezek 37:1–14), but none of those cases are explicit. Instead, we often find the expectation that the realm of the dead is bitter, lifeless—and permanent (e.g., Ps 88:3–12). This is why the Sadducees in the New Testament do not believe in a resurrection (see Mark 12:18–27 par.).

Our imaginary reader has encountered four important new, apocalyptic ideas—a single messiah, a personal Satan and the demons, a final judgment, and resurrection—when she entered the New Testament. These apocalyptic ideas are hardly peripheral; instead they lie close to the core of early Christian proclamation. There's no separating early Christianity from apocalyptic thinking, and one can scarcely imagine early Christian discourse without them. In fact, the centrality of this **apocalyptic discourse** to the early Christian message led German scholar Ernst Käsemann to declare apocalyptic "the mother of all Christian theology." Yet, none of these ideas had attained a developed form within the scriptures of Israel. So then, where did they come from?

These key concepts all emerged or crystallized within Jewish apocalyptic literature of the second and first centuries BCE. The apocalyptic literature of ancient Judaism, almost all of it non-canonical (i.e., not included in the final form of the Old Testament as we now know it), provided a foundation for the ministry of Jesus and the emergence of the church.

Many—but certainly not all—early Christians bought into the apocalyptic storyline. The non-canonical Gospel of Thomas, for example, explicitly rejects apocalyptic speculation. There Jesus warns the disciples against those who say God's kingdom is in the sky: if it were so, wouldn't the birds get there ahead of us (Gos. Thom. 3)? And when the disciples ask Jesus about the end, Jesus rejects the question entirely: the key to understanding lies in one's origins rather than in one's end (Gos. Thom. 18). Some early Christian documents, while not completely rejecting apocalyptic thought, nevertheless show considerably less interest in certain aspects of apocalyptic discourse. For instance, while the epistle of James considers the role of Satan and the final judgment, it never mentions Jesus's resurrection. On the whole, however, apocalyptic topics constitute a basic feature of early Christian discourse.

Deploying Apocalyptic Discourse

When many people today hear the word "apocalyptic," their imaginations turn in one of three directions. First, there's the association of apocalypticism with destruction. Apocalyptic topics bring us in touch with the common human desire to envision The End. This kind of "apocalyptic" imagination can invoke alien invasions, super-diseases, nuclear threats, and dramatic manifestations of cosmic change. As such, the genre of apocalyptic and post-apocalyptic films seems never to exhaust itself. Alternatively, the word "apocalyptic" reminds many of a particular kind of preaching, usually evangelistic. In this model, concepts like the end or a final judgment are deployed to motivate people to avoid the punishments of hell and embrace God's love. (We set aside for the moment the question of why someone would embrace as loving a God who condemns billions of people to hell.) Third, there's the motif of comfort. For example, when someone dies, other people often say things such as, "She's in a better place now," or "I'm sure he's looking down at us from heaven." People often turn to the idea of heaven—itself an apocalyptic motif—for solace in the face of great loss.

So common are these three associations—a violent end, the threat of judgment, and heavenly solace—that they make the stuff of humor. A film such as *This Is the End* uses a last-days scenario as a setting for all sorts of juvenile misbehavior. Homer Simpson sells his soul for a donut, only to have donuts shoved down his throat as torture in hell. Cartoon characters accidentally blow themselves to bits, awakening to find themselves playing harps on fluffy clouds.

Early Christians demonstrated remarkable ingenuity and flexibility in their adaptation of apocalyptic discourse. (So did ancient Jews.) The examples I provide below could easily be multiplied. Nevertheless, these examples show that early Christians not only relied heavily upon apocalyptic concepts, they also used them in diverse contexts and for diverse ends.

Theological Responses to Emerging Problems

Contemporary readers often struggle to imagine just how fluid was the environment of early Christianity—its texts, practices, and even its beliefs. For decades, even centuries, the churches held no set standard of teaching and no canonical collection of authoritative books. Instead, they relied upon traditions associated with Jesus, the Jewish scriptures as translated into Greek, their own religious experience, and creative argumentation to resolve their challenges. We see this process at work in 1 Thess 4:13–18, the passage typically associated with what some Christians call the "Rapture." According to rapture theology, Jesus will return just before the end of history to gather believers to meet him in the air—leaving the rest of humanity to face a horrific period called the great tribulation before history ends (think of the basic plotline of any of the *Left Behind* movies). The New Testament passage certainly includes the image of Jesus coming to gather believers, but it says nothing about other people being left behind to suffer or about the end of history. In any event, Paul is writing to address a different question entirely, apparently one he had not anticipated.

First Thessalonians likely represents our oldest extant Christian document. Paul relates that when he first preached in Thessalonica, he proclaimed Jesus's death, resurrection, and return (1 Thess 1:9–10). Even as he writes, Paul himself believes that Jesus's return will occur during his own lifetime: "We who are alive, who are left, will be caught up in the clouds together with them [i.e., those who have died]" (4:17,

NRSV). Paul's tone, however, suggests that he—or perhaps the believers in Thessalonica—has been taken by surprise. During the period between Paul's preaching and the composition of this letter, some believers have died. And that's created a problem in Thessalonica: "If we die before Jesus returns, have we missed out?"

Paul's reply indicates that he's been forced to get creative. Let's break down part of Paul's argument. Paul begins by acknowledging the problem. Some have died, and the Thessalonians are distressed.

> But we do not want you to be uninformed, brothers and sisters, about those who have died, so that you may not grieve as others do who have no hope. (1 Thess 4:13)

Paul then addresses the problem in two stages. First, he develops a creative argument of his own.

> For since we believe that Jesus died and rose again, even so, through Jesus, God will bring with him those who have died. (1 Thess 4:14)

This tiny argument requires some unpacking. It's an example of an **enthymeme**, an argument that leaves one of its basic premises unstated. It's left to us to discern what that missing piece might be. Let's take a look.

STATED PREMISE: We believe that Jesus died and rose again.

CONCLUSION: God will bring with Jesus those who have died.

What is Paul's unstated premise that links Jesus's resurrection to the resurrection of believers who have died? We must fill in this gap, but we have good reasons to feel confident in our guessing. Paul makes an extended argument about the resurrection in 1 Cor 15, where he expresses a view that was common to everyone who believed in a future resurrection: the resurrection is a corporate event that marks the end of history. Thus, Jesus's resurrection marks just the "first fruits" of a larger process that will include all the righteous (1 Cor 15:23). To restate Paul's argument, *Since we believe that Jesus rose* (stated), and *since Jesus's resurrection must be the beginning of a total resurrection* (unstated in this particular passage, but a valid premise, based on other known passages), then *God will raise deceased believers along with Jesus* (stated).

This first (of two) arguments relies on apocalyptic logic to draw a new conclusion. Apparently, Paul had not taught the Thessalonians what would happen to believers who died before Jesus's return. If he had, he could simply have reminded them so. Instead, he builds a new argument to meet this unexpected situation. Paul reinforces that first argument with a second, and it works very differently.

> For this we declare to you by the word of the Lord, that we who are alive, who are left until the coming of the Lord, will by no means precede those who have died. (1 Thess 4:15)

Instead of building an argument, Paul appeals to "the word of the Lord"; that is, he bases his case upon the authority of Jesus. This likely means one of two things: either Paul is appealing to a mystical revelation from Jesus that has happened since Jesus's career (Paul does that, as we shall see), or he is claiming that he has heard that Jesus taught such a thing. This is when Paul spells out the image of Jesus riding on clouds to gather his believers—a set of images we find in Mark 13:26–27 (see Matt 24:30–31; Luke 21:27). It seems likely Paul's second argument has its roots in traditional sayings ascribed to Jesus. In 1 Thess 4:13–18, then, Paul deploys apocalyptic discourse to provide a theological response to an emergent question. In doing so, he also speaks words of both comfort and encouragement to the Thessalonians. Paul begins and ends his argument with the question of comfort. He doesn't want the Thessalonians to "grieve as others do who have no hope" (4:13), and he encourages the Thessalonians to comfort one another with his words (4:18). Then, Paul moves on. He knows the Thessalonians have been well instructed concerning the return of Jesus (1 Thess 5:1–3). Now, he turns this apocalyptic knowledge into a pep talk. If Jesus is coming soon, and at a time no one knows, believers had best remain alert (1 Thess 5:11).

Claiming Authority

Paul also resorts to apocalyptic language when he's asserting—or defending—his own authority. We see this process at work in Paul's two most impassioned letters, 2 Corinthians and Galatians. In each letter, he names opposing teachers: he calls them "super-apostles" in 2 Corinthians, and "those who are troubling you" (my translation) in Galatians (1:7). In both letters, and only in these letters, does Paul talk about "a different gospel" (Gal 1:6–9; 2 Cor 11:4). In Galatians, he curses his opponents and denies the possibility that another gospel could exist! In these most polemic of his letters, and again only in these letters, Paul alludes to his own mystical experiences, or *apokalypseis.* In Galatians, he offers an extended argument that his gospel message comes directly through an apocalypse and not through the teaching of others (1:11–16). (By "apocalypse," Paul means not a literary apocalypse, but an apocalyptic visionary experience.) Even his consultation with other apostles occurs because Paul has received a revelation, i.e., an apocalypse (Gal 2:2). As for 2 Corinthians, Paul argues that he exceeds the "super-apostles" "in visions and revelations of the Lord" (12:1–10). He describes a particular experience in which he journeyed to the "third heaven" and heard words he may not repeat (12:4). In the two letters in which Paul most directly confronts competing teachers, including their "other gospels," Paul directly appeals to his own revelatory experiences—that is, his own personal apocalypses.

And it's not just Paul. In the book of Revelation, the author John claims his own revelation directly from Jesus Christ (1:1–2). He even goes so far as to bless those who keep the vision and curse those who do not (1:3; 22:18–19). Moreover, the Synoptic Gospels (Matthew, Mark, and Luke) narrate apocalyptic mystical experiences at the outset of Jesus's story. Upon his baptism, Jesus sees the heavens open, with the Holy Spirit descending upon him and a heavenly voice declaring Jesus as Son of God (Mark 1:9–11; par. Matt 3:13–17; Luke 3:21–22). Jesus then overcomes a period of temptation by the devil (Mark 1:12–13; par. Matt

4:1–11; Luke 4:1–13). In Luke, Jesus's disciples return from a preaching mission and inform him that demons are submitting to them in Jesus's name, a clear indication of Jesus's supernatural authority. Jesus replies: "I watched Satan fall from heaven like a flash of lightning," then affirms the authority he has bestowed upon his disciples (10:17–20).

Correcting Belief and Behavior

At first glance, Paul's first letter to the Corinthians looks like an organizational mess. After four chapters about divisions in the church, Paul seemingly tackles one topic after another with no obvious organizing principle. However, Paul begins the letter by affirming the Corinthians' spiritual gifts and knowledge as they await Jesus's return (1:4–8), and the letter concludes with a lengthy argument concerning the resurrection of the dead (15:1–58). Many interpreters believe that these two issues—spiritual gifts and eschatology—fuel the conflicts reflected throughout the letter. Paul provides an extensive argument concerning the Corinthians' overestimation of their own wisdom (1:18–2:16). Later, he demotes knowledge as less valuable than love (8:1–13).

An extensive section of 1 Corinthians, the longest argument devoted to a single conflicted issue, involves how church members express their spiritual gifts during their gatherings (12:1–14:40). Essentially, Paul affirms the Corinthians' gifts, but not the competitive and exclusive ways in which they express them. Right in the middle of the argument occurs one of the Bible's most famous passages: Paul's encomium to love (13:1–13). Many readers recognize this passage from wedding ceremonies without recognizing that Paul composed it to address church conflict. Again, Paul elevates love above all other spiritual gifts: these gifts include speaking in tongues (heavenly languages) and prophecy, the very issues at stake in chapters 12–14. As the passage climaxes, Paul deploys apocalyptic discourse: love never fails, but prophecies, knowledge, and tongues will all pass away. Moreover, at the return of Jesus, believers will learn that their wisdom and spiritual gifts are merely partial, awaiting fulfilment beyond the boundaries of history (13:8–12). The Corinthians rely too heavily upon their own spiritual attainments, which will mean little in the light of Jesus's return.

Political Critique

The great literary apocalypses of ancient Judaism and early Christianity often feature sharp criticism of the ruling powers of their day. Daniel, which stands alongside parts of 1 Enoch as our oldest surviving apocalypse, offers guidance and inspiration to Jews who desire to remain faithful during a particular political crisis, the Maccabean Crisis (176–164 BCE). Daniel 7 describes a series of four great beasts coming up from the sea: one like a lion but with eagles' wings, a second like a bear, a third like a winged leopard, and an especially dreadful fourth beast with ten horns. Daniel later learns that these four beasts correspond to a series of empires that has oppressed Israel and Judah. We know them as the Babylonian, Median, Persian, and Hellenistic (or Greek) empires. Daniel then depicts the arrival of "one like a son of man" who comes with the clouds to exert rule over all the nations.

This book features an entire chapter devoted to the New Testament book of Revelation, so we will treat it only briefly here. Revelation adapts Daniel's political critique in its attack against Rome. Chapter 13 introduces the Beast, who receives worship from the general population, controls commerce, and wages war against the saints. The Beast represents Rome, which extorted enormous wealth by means of its military might: "Who is like the beast, and who can fight against it?" (Rev 13:4). Revelation rolls the features of Daniel's four beasts into one horrific adversary. With ten horns and seven heads, it resembles a leopard, with feet like a bear's and a mouth like a lion's. In contrast to the Beast, Revelation presents two major images for Jesus: "one like the Son of Man" (Rev 1:13; see Dan 7:13) and a Lamb that stands, although it has been slain. Addressed to seven churches in the Roman province of Asia (part of western Turkey today), where worship of the Roman emperors was especially prominent, Revelation portrays the Lamb's conquest of the Beast, much as Daniel's Son of Man defeats the fourth beast. Where the Beast now rules the earth, the Lamb shall; and where the Beast now receives worship, the Lamb is worthy of eternal worship (Rev 5:9–14).

Interpreting Times of Crisis

Apocalyptic literature tends to flourish when groups or individuals experience intense dissatisfaction with the world. Judaism's great literary apocalypses emerged in response to two primary crises: the Maccabean Revolt, in which Daniel and much of 1 Enoch were composed, and just after the sack of Jerusalem by Roman forces (70 CE), when 2 Baruch, 3 Baruch, 4 Ezra, and the Apocalypse of Abraham appeared. If the ancient apocalypses have a primary function, it may well involve interpreting challenging times in order to shape how individuals and communities respond to those crises.

We see similar patterns within early Christian apocalyptic discourse. We have seen how the book of Revelation promotes both criticism of and resistance to Roman imperial politics. More general, however, are the "little apocalypses" Jesus delivers in Mark 13, Matthew 24, and Luke 21. Though these speeches differ in some of their specifics, they all prepare disciples to maintain discipline when faced with wars and other conflicts.

All of these little apocalypses refer to a calamity in Jerusalem, probably the city's destruction by the Romans, but they lack the sharp political critique we find in Revelation.

If Revelation voices immediate political dissatisfaction, and possibly, a response to persecution, and the synoptic "little apocalypses" offer a more generalized response, we also observe a far more generalized trend among early Christians. Some early Christian texts warn of a general end-time **apostasy**, when believers find themselves plagued by false teaching. For example, Second Thessalonians warns believers of an apostasy that must precede the end. In that period, a "lawless one" will occupy the temple and declare himself divine (2:1–12). First and Second Timothy alike indicate the spread of false teaching in the last days (1 Tim 4:1–5; 2 Tim 3:1–9; 4:3–4). First and Second John also announce the presence of "antichrists" in the last days, who promote false doctrine (1 John 2:18; 2 John 7).

Promoting Discipline by Managing Expectations

This final category of examples is also the most slippery, as it involves **redaction**, the ways in which Matthew and Luke adopt and adapt Mark's message. Almost all scholars agree that Mark's story provides the foundation for those of Matthew and Luke, and that, in fact, Matthew and Luke include much of Mark's original material in their own Gospels. Yet, Matthew and Luke each contain much material that is not found in Mark. The origin of this unique material is a question for another day, but when Matthew and Luke do deviate from Mark's account, they are usually trying to make a very specific point. These redactional changes are hardly random; instead both Matthew and Luke do their editing in thematic and significant ways that are worthy of our attention. Matthew and Luke do so with respect to Mark's apocalyptic content, and we have space only to sample how they do so.

We saw above that Mark 13, Mark's "little apocalypse," deals with the coming of the Son of Man. Most interpreters understand Mark to be discussing the fall of Jerusalem in 70 CE, as if Jesus had "predicted" those events. If so, Mark is alerting its readers that Jerusalem's fall marks the beginning of the end—an *imminent* end. No one knows the time of the end exactly, but disciples should remain vigilant (13:32–37). Mark 13 prepares its audience for faithful discipleship in trying times, with the expectation that Jesus will return very soon.

Written after Mark, Matthew and Luke necessarily interpret time a little differently. Matthew tends to emphasize what lies beyond the end, a final judgment, rather than the imminence of the end itself. For example, to Mark's account, Matthew adds several images concerning a final judgment, and Matthew is especially fond of describing judgment in terms of "weeping and gnashing of teeth," a phrase that occurs only once in Mark and Luke. With respect to judgment imagery, Matthew features images of sorting the good from the bad (13:41–43; 47–50), along with parables in which some are included, but others excluded (22:11–14; 25:1–13, 14–30) or Jesus denies knowing would-be followers (7:23). The most prominent example of Matthew's sorting and judging imagery is the parable in which the Son of Man separates the sheep from the goats (25:31–46). Matthew applies the weeping and gnashing of teeth image to those in the outer darkness (8:12; 22:13; 25:30), to those cast into "the furnace of fire" (13:42, 50), and to one who is cut in pieces (24:51). With the exception of Matt 7:23, all of these examples occur in Matthew—but not Mark or Luke.

- Where Matthew admonishes its audience to prepare for a final judgment, Luke tends to diminish interest in Jesus's immediate coming while emphasizing what it means to follow Jesus in the here and now. We can see this especially by comparing Jesus's apocalyptic speech in Luke 21 with the one in Mark 13. Where Mark's Jesus warns that "Many will come in my name and say, 'I am he!'" (13:5), Luke adds, "and, 'The time is near!'" (21:8). Luke opposes not only false messiahs, but those who claim to know the end.

- In Mark 13:7, Jesus declares, "the end is still to come." Luke redacts this to, "the end will not follow immediately" (21:9).

- Mark 13:8 interprets wars, earthquakes, and famines as signs of the end: "This is but the beginning of birth pangs." Luke 21:10–11 mentions the portents, but eliminates the reference to birth pangs.

- Luke and Mark alike regard the siege of Jerusalem as a time of great suffering. In Mark, God intervenes to "cut short" this period (13:20); Luke omits any reference to divine intervention here and introduces an indefinite period: "Jerusalem will be trampled on by the Gentiles, until the times of the Gentiles are fulfilled" (21:24).

- Like Mark, Luke refers to the Son of Man's arrival "with power and great glory" (21:27). Luke adds that only when the Son of Man returns—not when catastrophes ravage the earth—Jesus's followers will know that their redemption has drawn near (21:28).

- Luke adds material at the end of the little apocalypse (21:34–36).

Disciples must remain alert, for "that day" will arrive suddenly. They must not allow excessive pleasures to weigh them down, nor should even "the worries of this life" hinder them.

Luke affirms the belief that Jesus might return at any moment, but Luke's emphasis lies with following Jesus in the here and now.

Conclusion

Apocalyptic concepts provided a constitutive element for the emergence of Christian discourse. Moreover, apocalyptic topics played varied roles in the arguments early Christians used to shape community attitudes and behaviors. We should neither assume that the New Testament texts agree with one another on every particular, nor that they relate to apocalyptic discourse in identical ways. In this chapter, we have seen how apocalyptic argumentation could inform *constructive theology*, as Christians offered innovative responses to unexpected questions. We might imagine the use of apocalyptic topics as a kind of *rhetoric*, a form of argumentation in which people use basic building blocks to construct more or less complex arguments. Some forms of apocalyptic argumentation work through the *poetry* of images, as we see in imagery such as weeping and gnashing of teeth or Revelation's network of lamb, beast, and whore. Apocalyptic discourse offered a flexible set of conceptual and persuasive resources for early Christian authors and preachers. In turn, early Christians applied apocalyptic discourse to diverse persuasive ends.

Study Questions:

1. If you had to explain the importance of apocalyptic discourse for early Christianity to a casual friend, what would you say?
2. How do you understand the relationship between apocalyptic literature and claims to authority?
3. Can you identify three ways in which early Christians used

apocalyptic discourse to influence one another's behavior or beliefs?

Bibliography and Further Reading:

Bauckham, Richard, and Trevor Hart. *Hope Against Hope: Christian Eschatology at the Turn of the Millennium*. Grand Rapids: Wm. B. Eerdmans, 1998.

Carey, Greg. *Ultimate Things: An Introduction to Jewish and Christian Apocalyptic Literature*. St. Louis: Chalice Press, 2005.

Collins, John J. *The Apocalyptic Imagination: An Introduction to Jewish Apocalyptic Literature*. Biblical Resource Series. Grand Rapids: Wm. B. Eerdmans, 1998.

____, ed. *The Oxford Handbook of Apocalyptic Literature*. New York: Oxford University Press, 2014.

O'Leary, Stephen D. *Arguing the Apocalypse: A Theory of Millennial Rhetoric*. New York: Oxford University Press, 1994.

7

Paul—The Apocalyptic Apostle

Joshua W. Jipp

GETTING PREPPED:

1. What do you know about Paul and his teaching?
2. Paul (then known as "Saul") was once a great persecutor of Christianity. How did Saul eventually come to believe that Jesus was the Christ?
3. If you've been a part of a Christian community or organization that has read Paul, can you think of any of his apocalyptic statements? How have these been interpreted or used in that community?

KEY TERMS:
GOD'S CURSE
RESURRECTION
THE PRESENT AGE/COMING AGE

PARTICIPATION
JUSTIFICATION BY FAITH
EPISTEMOLOGY
BINARIES
PAROUSIA

Introduction

By almost anyone's account, Paul—or Saul, as he was first known—was an intensely passionate and charismatic personality. While much of his pre-Christian life remains inaccessible due to lack of information, both Paul's own letters as well as the Acts of the Apostles indicate that the pre-Christian Saul was a violent persecutor of those Jews who worshipped Jesus of Nazareth (1 Cor 15:9; Acts 8:1–3; 9:1–6, 21). Paul himself states that it was public knowledge that he "persecuted God's church to an extreme degree and tried to destroy it" (Gal 1:13). Saul's desire to destroy the church was rooted in his being "incredibly zealous for the ancestral traditions" (Gal 1:14), which contradicted the testimonies of early Christians who gave their allegiance to a Jew who—so it seemed to Saul—was under **God's curse**. God's Law had declared that "anyone hung on a tree is under God's curse" (Deut 21:23). In other words, Jesus of Nazareth was publicly crucified on a wooden cross, thereby he "hung on a tree," and was thus understood by Saul to have been "cursed by God." In fact, the allusive use of language such as *hung on a tree/wood* suggests that much of the offense of Jesus's crucifixion for Paul lies in the thought that he was cursed by God, and thereby, could not be Israel's messiah (Gal 3:10, 13; cf. Acts 5:30; 13:29; 1 Pet 2:24). Violent and total opposition, then, best describes the relationship between the pre-Christian Saul and the proclamation of Jesus of Nazareth as Messiah.

What happens next is as well-known as it is inexplicable. Saul the Pharisee meets the resurrected Jesus on a road, and from that point on, does a complete about-face, becoming an apostle of Christ and changing his name to Paul. From this point, Paul lived the rest of his days entirely devoted to establishing Christian communities all over the Mediterranean world. While many have tried to guess at the psychological motivations or the personality type that would help explain this momentous event within the history of Christianity, there are no real convincing rational explanations for Saul's transformation. Some of the earliest Christians were baffled to hear of Saul's conversion: "Isn't this the one who in Jerusalem was destroying those who called on this name [i.e., Jesus] and then came here in order to take them to the chief priests as prisoners?" (Acts 9:21)

Paul does not provide us with a rational explanation for his transformation. There is no sense that *anything* within Paul's prior experiences or thought-world prepared him for his encounter with the resurrected Jesus Christ (Gal 1:13-14). In other words, Paul's transformation was the result of something completely extraordinary, and he characterizes this extraordinary encounter as an *apocalypse*:

> I did not receive [the gospel] nor was I taught it from humans, but rather by means of *an apocalypse [apokalypsis] of Jesus Christ.* (Gal 1:12)

> God . . . was pleased *to reveal [apokalyptein] his son* in me so I could preach him among the nations. (Gal 1:15-16)

But what exactly does Paul mean here when he says that he received an *apocalypse*? J. Louis Martyn characterizes this event as one in which "God opened [Paul's] eyes to the presence of the risen Lord Jesus Christ in the church" (Martyn, *Theological Issues* [1997], 99). In other words, Paul has a *revelation*, given to him by God and through the vision of Jesus, which results in a re-evaluation of his own Jewish heritage and traditions. And so begins Paul's journey of rethinking the relationship between what he thought he knew (tradition) and what God had revealed to him (apocalypse).

For Paul, this act of rethinking the relationship between his former traditions and his apocalypse of Jesus Christ is no philosophical matter, for Paul's very commission, to which he has devoted his life, is founded on his encounter with Jesus Christ. In what follows, we will examine four broad aspects of Paul's worldview that have been shaped by Jesus Christ's apocalypse to Paul.

The Present Evil Age and the Age to Come

Paul believes that the end-time ("eschatological") event whereby God acts to defeat God's enemies and reclaim the cosmos has *already happened* through the life, death, and **resurrection** of Jesus Christ. When Paul says, "when the fullness of time had come, God sent his Son" (Gal 4:4a), he draws attention to the fact that the Son comes to the cosmos from *outside* of it. Further, the advent of Jesus Christ into the world gives Paul insight into God's climactic plan for the cosmos and all of human history. Again, Martyn states it clearly: "In short, the Son's sending is an invasion of cosmic scope, reflecting the certainty that redemption has come from outside, changing the very world in which human beings live, so that it can no longer be identified simply as 'the present evil age' (1:4)" (Martyn 1997, 408). Thus, one of the defining features of apocalyptic thought, that God intervenes decisively in human history, is present in Paul's thought: God has redeemed the world by sending Jesus Christ into the world.

So, how does the coming of Jesus Christ into the world effect redemption in Paul's theology? It cannot be stated too strongly that, for Paul, the death of Jesus Christ on the cross and God's raising him from the dead is the singular event that ushers in God's future age for his people, i.e., a new creation and a new world. This event almost certainly provides the impetus for Paul's re-evaluation of the crucified Jesus of Nazareth as cursed by God to his belief that Jesus is God's Messiah. Thus, it is God's act of resurrecting the crucified one from the dead that proves to Paul that God has vindicated Jesus, and, even more importantly, shows that the risen Jesus is still alive in a more powerful way (e.g., Rom 4:24–25; cf. 1 Tim 3:16). That is, God's resurrection of the Messiah from the dead is the event whereby God enthrones Jesus as the powerful cosmic LORD who rules over the cosmos (Rom 1:1–4).

Paul believes that the resurrection from the dead—an event that was generally seen as occurring at the end of the age (e.g., Dan 12:1–3; Mt 12:32) —has *already happened* to God's messianic son. That is, God's future has invaded the present time, meaning that Paul does not think there is a simple chronologically linear movement from the **present age** to the future **coming age.** Rather, these two ages, or as Paul refers to them elsewhere, "this present evil age" (Gal 1:4) and "new creation" (Gal 6:15; 2 Cor 5:17), overlap and conflict with one another. In a sense, the *future* in which Jesus rules the cosmos has already happened, and yet, co-exists with the *present* world. Thus, a second important aspect of apocalyptic theology, the notion of God's future invasion of the world to redeem it from the present worldly forces of evil, has already occurred.

Paul thinks of his churches as living within the tension or the overlap between these ages; they are, in other words, those "upon whom *the end of the ages has come*" (1 Cor 10:11b). Paul conceptualizes this conflict between these two ages, or, perhaps better, two worlds with a variety of metaphors to show their irreconcilable opposition toward one another.

The Present Evil Age	The Age to Come
Flesh	Spirit
Adam	Christ
This cosmos	New creation
Death	Life/Resurrection
Sin	Grace/Righteousness
Unrighteousness	Righteousness
The dominion of darkness	The kingdom of God's Son
Slaves	Sons and Daughters
Condemnation	Love of God
Elemental principles of the cosmos	Christ

The list is not comprehensive, but it functions to demonstrate Paul's belief that God has invaded the present age through Christ and the Spirit, thereby resulting in an implacable conflict between two worlds. Paul sees reality, then, in apocalyptic terms, as divided between two worlds and their attendant and competing powers.

The Deliverance of Humanity
from the Evil Age and Its Powers

Given the conflict between the old world powers of death, sin, and flesh that dominate and enslave humanity and God's new creation that has broken into the world, Paul conceptualizes salvation as *liberation from the powers of the present evil age and transferal into the new world marked by Christ and the Spirit.* Paul, or a follower of his, emphasizes the liberative nature of salvation when he speaks of God as the one "who rescued us from the dominion of darkness and transferred us into the kingdom of his beloved Son" (Col 1:13). Throughout Gal 3:19–4:11, Paul speaks of those who are outside of Christ as "under the power of sin" (3:22), "confined" and "imprisoned" (3:23), under the tutelage of a guardian (3:24–25; 4:2), as slaves (4:1), "enslaved to the elemental forces of the world" (4:3, cf. 4:8–9), and "under the law" (4:5). This is why cleansing or forgiveness from sins, necessary as it is, is not enough to procure salvation in Paul's apocalyptic thinking. Rather, just as Paul was grasped by the apocalypse of Jesus Christ (Gal 1:12–17), so Paul conceptualizes Christ's death as *snatching* the Galatians out of this present evil age (Greek *exelētai*, Gal 1:4b). Christ invades the cosmos that is under the sway of evil powers in order to rescue humanity from its bondage to the powers of the old world order (Gal 3:13, 24–25; 4:1–7). As Paul says in Gal 5:1, "Christ has freed us for the purpose of freedom" (cf. Gal 5:13). Instead of being under the authority of a guardian, those who are rescued become "God's sons and daughters through Jesus Christ" (3:26). They are "purchased" by God, and thereby, adopted into God's family such that they even receive the "Spirit of [God's] Son" (Gal 4:7).

This language is apocalyptic insofar as Paul conceptualizes the invasive coming of Christ as resulting in *the death of the old world and the creation of a new cosmos.* And Paul is clear that the cross of Christ destroys the old world order: "But may it never be true that I would boast except in the cross of our Lord Jesus Christ, through which the cosmos has been crucified and I myself to the cosmos" (Gal 6:14). Those who die with Christ experience the painful death of the old cosmos, but this also results in their **participation** in "new creation"—a new space or world where the fundamental structures of the universe are re-imagined. In other words, while one world has died, a radically new one has come into existence.

The same conceptualization of salvation as liberation from the old world order and transfer into the new age/creation is evident throughout many of Paul's letters, but is perhaps nowhere as clearly set forth as in Rom 5–8. In Rom 5:12–21 Paul speaks of Adam and Christ as representative figures who each have their own kingdom that exerts its dominion over its people. Adam, standing for the old world order, is identified with death, sin, transgression, and unrighteousness. But Christ's single act of giving his life on the cross and God's ensuing resurrection of Christ overpower the dominion of Adam and result in humanity receiving God's gift or grace, eternal life, and righteousness. This contrast between Adam and Christ appears to be somewhat fundamental to Paul's thinking as elsewhere, he describes all of humanity as **participating** in one of these figures—"in Adam all die, so in Christ all will be given life" (1 Cor 15:22). Again, Paul here conceptualizes salvation as liberation and rescue from Adam's dominion of death, for it is only by participating in Christ's death, burial, and resurrection that one is "liberated from sin" (Rom 6:7). Note that by participating in Christ's death and resurrection, the individual shares in the crucifixion, that is to say, the violent destruction of the old humanity dominated by sin and death: "our old humanity has been co-crucified, so that the body of sin might be destroyed" (Rom 6:6). At the same time, this destruction entails liberation from the old world, and those who do so are described by Paul as experiencing the realities of grace (6:14), freedom from sin (6:18), the Spirit of God (8:2, 9–11, 13–16), renewed cognitive capacities that please God (8:5–8), resurrection (8:10–11), life (8:13), inheriting with Christ (8:17), the redemption of their bodies (8:23), the eradication of condemnation (8:1, 33–34), and the powerful love of God (8:35–39).

A New Epistemology

Given that the death and resurrection of Christ is the singular revelatory action of God, Paul articulates an apocalyptic-new-creation *way of knowing and thinking*, i.e., **epistemology**, that seeks to transform how one views all of reality. One of Paul's agendas is to transform the cognitive faculties of his churches by teaching them how to think, believe, perceive, and behave in a way that is congruent with the new world order brought into existence by Christ's death and resurrection. The apocalyptic contrast between two ways of knowing is perhaps best exemplified in Paul's words in 2 Cor 5:16–17: "From now on, therefore, we regard no one from a human point of view; even though we once knew Christ from a human point of view, we know him no longer in that way. So if anyone is in Christ, there is new creation. Everything old has passed away; see, all has become new." There is, in other words, a way of knowing that is human and belongs to the dead old world order, and there is a new way of knowing that corresponds to God's act of new creation through the death and resurrection of Christ.

But what exactly does this new epistemology look like? In short, as the definitive revelation of God, *Christ* is the new pattern or prototype for humanity. Paul's use (or creation) of a baptismal formula indicates his belief that God's apocalyptic act in Christ has created a new humanity that looks and acts fundamentally differently from the old: "there is neither Jew nor Greek, neither slave nor free, neither male or female; for you are all one in Messiah Jesus" (Gal 3:28; cf. 1 Cor 12:13; Col 3:11). While one's social status (slave or free), gender (male or female), and ethnic identity (Jew or non-Jew) are not eradicated, Paul does use this trope of the new humanity as legitimating his churches as sites of inclusion and ecclesial participation for slaves, women, and non-Jews. And while one may debate whether Paul was faithful to all of the implications of his apocalyptic theology (e.g., 1 Cor 7:21–23), one can easily find plenty of evidence within his letters that Paul not only included, but also *empowered* slaves, women, and non-Jews within his churches.

In 1 Cor 1:18–2:16, Paul constructs a new way of thinking that is based on the apocalyptic realities of the cross and the spirit of God. There is a fundamental contrast in this passage between the wisdom and knowledge of "this present age" (1:20; 2:6) and the wisdom of God/Christ (1:24–25; 2:7). Such **binaries** are typical of apocalyptic language. So, the wisdom of this age values the wise, the powerful, and the nobly born, whereas the wisdom of Christ means God has chosen the foolish, the weak, the lowly and despised (1:26–28). This latter wisdom and perception is something that "God has revealed to us by means of the Spirit" (2:10a), but this wisdom is inaccessible and remains hidden to those who are wise and powerful, according to this age (2:6–8). This new apocalyptic epistemology that is based on the cross means that divine wisdom is revealed in the lowly and humiliating act of the cross of Jesus—something that appears as foolish, shameful, and weak to those who belong to the old world order (1:25–28). But given that the cross is the event whereby God has initiated the death of the old world order, it functions for Paul as the wisdom of God. Paul seeks, then, to inculcate "the mind of Christ" (2:16) into the Corinthian church so that they will not boast in human achievement (1:30–31) or evaluate Paul's preaching according to popular orators (2:1–5), and will reject boasting over their favorite leaders (3:1–5).

Perhaps most remarkable, however, are those statements where Paul devalues the Law of Moses due to God's revelation in Christ. Paul's apocalyptic belief that "this world in its current form is passing away" (1 Cor 7:31) provides, in part, the ground for his rejection of the Law of Moses dividing the world into Jew and non-Jew: "Circumcision is nothing and uncircumcision is nothing, but [what matters is] keeping God's commandments" (7:19). Paul says something remarkably similar where the distinction between circumcision and uncircumcision is relativized due to "faith working through love" (5:6) and "new creation" (6:15). Though not as neatly encapsulated into a single statement or verse, Paul's contrast between the Torah and the work of Christ and the Spirit in Rom 7–8 calls the believer to a new way of thinking and acting based on God's apocalyptic event.

Torah (Old World) – Rom 7:7–25	Christ/Spirit (New World) – Rom 8:1–39
Condemnation	Justification
Death	Life
Flesh	Spirit
Bondage	Freedom
Body of death	Resurrection body
Sin	Righteousness

Paul's devaluation (not rejection, note 7:7, 14) of the Torah stems from his belief that God's apocalyptic action has taken place *not by means of the Law of Moses, but rather through the world-altering, life-giving event of Christ's death and resurrection and the outpouring of the Spirit.* Paul's incredible claims about the relativizing of the Torah are retrospective, then, in that Paul is looking backwards upon this old world order as the sphere in which God has not acted. Further, the epistemological consequences of these world orders are significant. Those who live within the realm of the Torah are divided between their desires to please God and their ability to actually make good on these desires by acting in a way that pleases God (Rom 7:14–25). Paul states simply: "the mind of the flesh is death . . . because the fleshly mind is hostile toward God, for it does not subject itself to God's law, since it is not even able to do so" (Rom 8:6a, 7). The cognitive faculties, however, of the person who belongs to God's new world order are exactly the opposite: "the mind of the Spirit is life and peace" (Rom 8:6b). Thus, in Paul's apocalyptic worldview, God through Christ has not only redeemed humanity from the old world, but has also given humans the ability to experience God's new creation in the present.

The Future Victorious Return of Christ

Despite Paul's insistence that God's apocalyptic action has taken place in Christ, he still looks forward to a catastrophic, public, visible return of Christ from heaven in order to bring history to its conclusion. One day, the overlap of these two world orders will be broken, Paul believes, as Christ will return from heaven in order to destroy the old world completely and to bring forth a new and perfectly restored new creation. Paul uses the language of apocalypse (1 Cor 1:7; 2 Thess 1:7) and **parousia** (1 Cor 15:23; 1 Thess 2:19; 3:13; 4:15; 5:23)—namely, the glorious and triumphant return of the enthroned Christ—to describe Christ's return to establish his kingdom on earth. This belief, while incredible to many, is articulated in almost all of Paul's letters (though only minimally in Galatians). This public (re)-appearance of Christ will result in the resurrection unto life for God's people (1 Cor 15:20-23, 35-50), the full coming of God's salvation and rescue of his people (Rom 13:11-14), the full reunification of Christ with his people (1 Thess 4:13-18), the restoration of creation from its corruption (Rom 8:18-25), the end of death and suffering (Rom 8:18-19; 1 Cor 15:23), and the supreme and unopposed reign of God (1 Cor 15:24-28). Whereas in the Hebrew Bible, this day of reckoning was frequently spoken of as "the day of the Lord," Paul speaks of "the day of the Lord Jesus Christ" (Rom 2:16; 1 Cor 1:8; Phil 1:10; 1 Thess 5:2; 2 Thess 2:2). Paul believes that Jesus's return will initiate this final day and result in judgment and wrath for the wicked, but salvation and resurrection for the righteous. Paul is clear that people will be judged *according to* (not on the basis of) their actions in this life. In other words, the quality of their life will provide the proof of their salvation (Rom 2:6; 1 Cor 3:11-15; 2 Cor 5:10).

Apocalyptic and Christian Theology

Paul's theologizing in his epistles is held together by his apocalyptic interpretation of God, human action, sin, salvation, and the eschatological denouement. Paul's apocalyptic theologizing has significant consequences for Christian theology for these matters.

God: Paul's knowledge of God is based squarely on his apocalyptic encounter with Christ. Christ has a priority over everything else—even the Torah—in mediating divine revelation. All that Paul knows about God, then, results from the revelation (apocalypse) of Jesus Christ to him.

Human Action: Given the priority of Christ over all other forms of knowledge, Paul grounds human perception and action upon God's activity in Christ. God has created a new world order and a new humanity based upon Christ and the Spirit. To know how to think and act rightly is contingent upon this new world order. This new world order does not privilege male over female, Jew over non-Jew, or free over slave. Christ, who dismantles such societal structures, is alone the prototype for this new human existence.

Sin and Salvation: Sin is such a domineering tyrant that enslaves and imprisons its subjects to the death-dealing old world order that humanity cannot overcome it or contribute to humanity's salvation. On the contrary, only God's actions through Christ can liberate humanity from the powers of sin, as attested by Paul's frequent use of metaphors that stress God's liberative action in Christ: Humanity is rescued from this present evil age; is purchased out of slavery for God; is rescued from the dominion of darkness; is justified and reclaimed to live under God's sovereign lordship.

Eschatology: Currently, the "old world" and "new world" exist in tension. However, this overlap of the ages, Paul believes, will not hold sway forever. Christ will return for both judgment and salvation. While the former will experience wrath, the latter will be raised from the dead in order to reign with God in a restored creation. This public and catastrophic event will result in God's full and complete reclamation of the world and God's total supremacy and sovereignty.

Study Questions:

1. Is Paul's thinking in binaries (that is, in either/or terms) more likely to be liberative or oppressive?
2. What is the relationship between Paul's ancestral traditions and his apocalypse of Jesus Christ?
3. If Paul were alive today, what contemporary categories might he use to describe God's liberation of humanity?

Bibliography and Further Reading:

de Boer, Martinus C. "Paul, Theologian of God's Apocalypse." *Interpretation* 56 (2002): 21-33

Brown, Alexandra R. *The Cross and Human Transformation: Paul's Apocalyptic World in 1 Corinthians.* Minneapolis: Fortress, 1995.

Davis, Joshua B. and Douglas Harink. Editors. *Apocalyptic and the Future of Theology: With and Beyond J. Louis Martyn.* Eugene, OR: Cascade, 2012.

Harink, Douglas. *Paul among the Postliberals: Pauline Theology Beyond Christendom and Modernity.* Grand Rapids: Brazos Press, 2003.

Martyn, J. Louis. *Theological Issues in the Letters of Paul.* Nashville: Abingdon, 1997.

8

The Beast or the Lamb in the Apocalypse to John

Will the Real Emperor Please Stand Up?

Justin Jeffcoat Schedtler

GETTING PREPPED:

1. What do you know about the book of Revelation? Can you recall any specific figures, images, or events in the text?
2. Can you think of ways in which historical or contemporary figures have been associated with figures (for example, the "number of the Beast—666") in the book of Revelation?
3. In what ways does the book of Revelation continue to play a role in contemporary religious, political, and/or cultural discourses?

KEY TERMS:
BRANCH OF DAVID
CIPHER
VICE-REGENT

IMPERIAL CULT

IDEOLOGY

GEMATRIA

Revelation in Contemporary Culture

In chapter 20, you will read about the Branch Davidian sect as a "New Religious Movement" (NRM), and the protracted standoff between members of that group and Federal authorities, which led ultimately to the fiery destruction of their religious compound and their own violent deaths. Here we use this story as a backdrop for considering the fascinating way in which the leader of the group, David Koresh, understood the book of Revelation to contain information about the end of the world and his own role in it. His story serves as an example of a very common tendency in popular interpretations of Revelation: to understand the text and its many symbols as a blueprint for current events in the interpreter's own time and place. It is also a somber reminder that such interpretations can lead to horrific consequences. Thus, we consider such interpretations and the logic behind them, as well as alternative readings of Revelation.

The Backdrop: David Koresh, the "Branch Davidians," and Biblical Apocalypses

The name and **ideology** of the Branch Davidian sect derived from a very specific notion in biblical prophecy that one day, there would arise a descendant of David (i.e., a righteous **Branch of David**), ancient Israel's first king, in order to re-establish the royal dynasty on earth (e.g., Jer 33:15). The Davidians understood themselves to be the manifestation of this "branch" and believed that they were ordained by God to re-establish the Davidic kingdom in Jerusalem.

In the mid-1980s, after a power struggle among rival factions which included, among other things, a "resurrection contest" between challengers for control of the group, leadership was eventually assumed by Vernon Howell, who had joined the group several years earlier as a worship leader and musician. At about the same time, Howell reported that he began to receive prophetic visions in which God revealed to him that he was the anointed one (i.e., the "messiah") chosen to bring about God's kingdom on earth. Howell claimed to receive one particular vision in which he was revealed to be the modern-day manifestation of the ancient Persian ruler Cyrus (Persian: *koresh*), who himself had been anointed by God (i.e., as a "messiah") to deliver the Israelites from Babylonian captivity (Isa 45:1). As a result of this, Howell assumed the name David Koresh to reflect his new self-understanding, and Koresh and his followers assumed ownership of a large compound on the outskirts of Waco.

At the center of Koresh's theology was the notion that *biblical apocalypses provided specific information about himself and his own community*. Koresh believed that the book of Revelation, in particular, provided symbolic information that God would soon judge the world, and that he and his community would play a critical role in this event. He understood this in quite specific terms. He began by identifying himself as the "Lion of the Tribe of Judah and the Branch of David" in Rev 5:5. (While the language here is indeed symbolic, it is not at all ambiguous; it clearly refers to the crucified Jesus, i.e., "the Lamb who was slain" [Rev 5:12]). Having discovered that the figure in the text refers to himself, Koresh goes on to project himself into the narrative throughout Revelation: *he* is the one who is "able to open the scroll and its seven seals" (Rev 5:5); *he* is the one who rides the "white horse," holding a bow and "bent on conquest" (Rev 6:2); and so on. Perhaps most importantly for understanding the eventual siege and demise of the Branch Davidian compound, he identifies himself as the one who is called "Faithful and True," who is called to wage war against his enemies:

> I saw heaven standing open and there before me was a white horse, whose rider is called Faithful and True. With justice he judges and wages war. His eyes are like blazing fire, and on his head are many crowns. He has a name written on him that no one knows but he himself. He is dressed in a robe dipped in blood, and his name is the Word of God. The armies of heaven were following him, riding on white horses and dressed in fine linen,

white and clean. Coming out of his mouth is a sharp sword with which to strike down the nations. "He will rule them with an iron scepter." He treads the winepress of the fury of the wrath of God Almighty. (Rev 19:11–21)

The fact that Koresh understood himself to be the central character in the narrative provides some context for understanding his decision to stockpile heavy weaponry in the Branch Davidian compound (the event that would eventually raise the suspicion of the Federal Bureau of Alcohol, Tobacco, and Firearms) and to raise up an "army of God" in order to prepare for the End.

How is it that someone could come to such a conclusion? Was David Koresh a mentally unstable individual who lured followers into a dangerous religious cult? This seems likely. Indeed, the end-time interpretations of David Koresh and his adult followers in the Branch Davidian compound may be considered radical insofar as they were willing to die—and did, in fact, die—in order to defend their apocalyptic outlook. The very fact that they ultimately came under such a severe threat most likely instilled confidence in their belief that the End was near. However, while the consequences of their interpretation were indeed severe, you may be surprised to learn that the interpretive methods they employed are not so far removed from the most common methods of interpretation of the vast majority of folks who have read Revelation throughout history and to this very day.

Interpreting Revelation: Reading Me, Myself, and I into the Text

David Koresh understood the symbolic language in the book of Revelation as a **cipher**, i.e., a code in need of decryption. In the end, he concluded that the symbols, in fact, referred to his own circumstances: the heroic protagonists in the text referred to himself and his community, the grotesque creatures referred to his enemies, and so on. In this way, he was able to read the book of Revelation (alongside other biblical apocalypses) as a kind of symbolic roadmap for deciphering his own life's mission, projecting his own circumstances onto the story of clash of the forces of good and evil as they are presented in the text. To be sure, David Koresh and his Branch Davidian community took their interpretation of the book of Revelation to the furthest extremes, but their methods of interpretation are representative of a very common approach to the text.

We encounter many such examples in this volume. For example, in chapter 18, we will see that Protestant Reformers depicted the Pope as the very unholy "Beast" from Rev 13, and the Holy Roman Emperor as a figure worshipping this Beast. Martin Luther went so far as to explicitly identify the Pope as the Antichrist in one of his writings:

> We here are of the conviction that the papacy is the seat of the true and real Antichrist. . . . Personally I declare that I owe the Pope no other obedience than that to Antichrist. (Froom, 256)

For their part, the Catholic faithful returned the favor by depicting Luther and his Reformers in league with the devil. This kind of identifying and "mapping" one's enemies from the text of Revelation continued in all sorts of ways: William Blake portrayed various elements of the British Empire as the "Whore of Babylon" as a critique of British Imperial authority during the French Revolution; Nazi resistor Max Beckmann portrayed the Four Horsemen of the Apocalypse (Rev 6:1-7) as elements of the Nazi regime; Hal Lindsey identified the Cold War as the precursor to the battle of Armageddon. And so on.

A quick Google search reveals how frequently and easily people do this. Try it! As such, Koresh's attempt to equate himself with Revelation's messianic Lamb, and his enemies with the horrific enemies of the Lamb, while egregious in certain respects, is nevertheless representative of a popular strategy for interpreting Revelation's symbols. And while it may seem reasonable, in some instances, to identify the evil characters in the text with known monsters in contemporary society (e.g., to associate the Nazi regime with the Four Horsemen of the Apocalypse), such interpretations most often end up being simple projections of peoples' own peculiar haunts and fears. What is to stop people from associating Revelation's symbols with whomever they want? (Hint: people rarely identify *themselves* with the evil characters!)

The ease with which someone can locate their own personal enemies in the text, and the very fact that Revelation has functioned so often in this way to such disparate results, might itself serve as a caution against using it in this way. There is another reason to challenge this kind of reading. When people read a biblical text as a map for their own personal circumstances, they diminish or altogether discard those meanings the text may have had for the people who composed it as well as for those who first read it. In other words, such a reading presumes the text has meaning only or primarily for those interpreting it in the present-day, thereby subsuming all other historical contexts and meanings under a quite literal and *self-centered* interpretation. So, what alternative interpretation is available if Revelation is not best understood as a cipher for one's own present circumstances?

A Long Time Ago, in a Galaxy Far, Far Away . . .

In order to understand the many dimensions of Revelation, we need first to put ourselves in the shoes of someone who may have read the text when it was first composed almost 2,000 years ago. The first audiences of the book of Revelation were likely congregations of small churches living in the western coast of modern-day Turkey, in an area called Asia Minor, sometime in the late-first century CE.

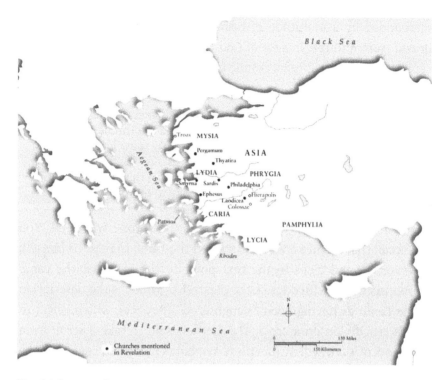

Map 8.1: Roman Asia.

So much can be determined from the fact that Revelation is explicitly addressed to "the seven churches that are in Asia" (Rev 1:4), and in fact, contains individual letters (full of all kinds of admonitions and warnings) addressed to each of these churches (Rev 2–3). While the precise demographics of the individual congregations are less certain, the location of the first audience of Revelation in Asia Minor is critical to its interpretation, insofar as this area constituted a political entity within the Roman Empire, the geographic center of which was Rome, and the conceptual center of which was the Emperor.

This political milieu provides an important first clue to interpret the text. After an introduction of the author, who claims to be exiled to the island of Patmos, where he receives a "revelation of Jesus Christ," which he is commanded to write down (Rev 1), and the contents of the seven letters to the churches in Asia Minor (Rev 2–3), the vision proper begins with a description of the Lord God sitting on a throne, surrounded by a multitude of heavenly angels and other creatures. Drawn from multiple images of God in the Old Testament, this vision depicts God as the supreme cosmic ruler:

> ...there in heaven stood a throne, with one seated on the throne! And the one seated there looks like jasper and carnelian, and around the throne is a rainbow that looks like an emerald. Around the throne are twenty-four thrones, and seated on the thrones are twenty-four elders, dressed in white robes, with golden crowns on their heads. Coming from the throne are flashes of lightning, and rumblings and peals of thunder, and in front of the throne burn seven flaming torches.... (Rev 4:3–5)

The vision then depicts a Lamb sharing the throne with God. You will recall that David Koresh understood the Lamb to refer to himself; however, several clues in the text point to the fact that the Lamb represents the crucified Jesus, the clearest of which is the description of the Lamb as having been "slaughtered" (Rev 5:6), which refers to Jesus's crucifixion on a cross. The Lamb is said to take a scroll from the hand of God, which functions symbolically to indicate that the Lamb—i.e., the crucified Jesus—shares the authority of God.

Ultimately, the contents of this vision function to establish God as a sovereign, cosmic, and eternal ruler, and the crucified Jesus as God's **vice-regent**. In so doing, the vision implicitly contrasts the rule of the heavenly Lord God and Lamb as it is depicted in Revelation with that of the earthly ruler, the Roman Emperor, as it was known in the Roman Empire in the first century CE. Though an explicit distinction is never made here or anywhere in Revelation, such a contrast was achieved through the visual imagery and the language used to describe God. That is, the vision of God and the Lamb sitting upon a cosmic throne, surrounded by a heavenly retinue that is constantly praising them, would have evoked a comparison with the image of the earthly Emperor who received similar honors. The implication is that God and the Lamb are the ultimate, eternal, and rightful rulers of the Universe, over and against the earthly ruler, who pales by comparison. What was implied through visual metaphors is proclaimed by the various songs of the heavenly chorus, for example:

Holy, holy, holy, the Lord God the Almighty, who was and is and is to come. (Rev 4:8)

To the one seated on the throne and to the Lamb, be blessing and honor and glory and might forever and ever! (Rev 5:13)

Left unstated in these hymns, but something that would have no doubt been recognized by the audience to this vision, is the implicit claim that the Roman Emperor was *not* holy and was entirely *unworthy* to receive these honors. This dynamic, whereby the legitimacy of the rule of the Roman Emperor is challenged by the claim of the rightful rule of God and the Lamb, begins here and provides an interpretive lens to view the entire book of Revelation. That is, the rest of the story of Revelation tells the story of the eventual victory of God over what is perceived to be the present evil age *of the author and audience of the text.* This provides the clue to reading Revelation's symbolic imagery.

In short, the subsequent visions depict—in symbolic, yet graphic detail—the coming battles between the forces of God and the Lamb and their adversaries, who are imagined here to be the entire Roman Imperial apparatus and anyone who participates in this Imperial system, as well as the spiritual forces that are believed to undergird this system. All of the symbolic characters line up according to their place along the battlefront. On the side of God and the Lamb are, for example, the "Four Horsemen" (Rev 6), 144,000 with the seal of the living God on their forehead (Rev 7), the Two Witnesses (Rev 11), the Woman Clothed with the Sun (Rev 12), and the armies of heaven (Rev 19). Opposed to these are the Dragon who makes war on the Woman Clothed with the Sun (Rev 12), two Beasts who derive their power from the Dragon (Rev 13), the Great Whore of Babylon (Rev 17), and Satan and the armies of Satan (Rev 20).

Accordingly, the battles between these characters are depicted in symbolic terms. For example, by opening each of "seven seals," the Lamb unleashes the Four Horsemen and various meteorological phenomena, which wreak havoc upon the earth (Rev 6); likewise, when heavenly angels sound the seven heavenly trumpets (Rev 8-9), or dispense the contents of seven "bowls of the wrath of God" (Rev 15-16), the destruction on earth intensifies. The end result of this war is nothing other than the complete annihilation of the adversaries of God and the Lamb, and the establishment of the rule of God and the Lamb upon the earth (Rev 21–22).

As we have seen, interpreters of this text tend to project their *own* stories and circumstances onto this text, thereby associating the symbolic figures with their own friends and foes, and correlating the symbolic events with specific circumstances in their own lives. What happens instead if we consider the symbolic imagery in the context of the stories and circumstances of the original author(s) and audience(s) of the text—that is, in terms of the experiences of the author(s) and audience(s) living in a Roman Imperial context?

Test-Case: The Two Beasts—Who or What Are They?

The First Beast

The clearest evidence that the object of attack throughout the book of Revelation is the Roman Imperial system appears in Rev 13, wherein we encounter two beasts, one "from the sea" (Rev 12:18–3:10) and another "from the earth" (Rev 13:11–18). Like most of the symbolic figures that are negatively characterized in the text, these beasts are marked by their grotesque appearance: the first beast is said to have ten horns and seven heads, with crowns on each horn, and blasphemous names written on each head (13:1); likewise, the second beast is said to have "two horns like a lamb" and speaks like a dragon (13:11). So, too, are the beasts said to perform destructive acts. Consider the actions of the first beast:

> The beast was given a mouth uttering haughty and blasphemous words, and it was allowed to exercise authority for forty-two months. It opened its mouth to utter blasphemies against God, blaspheming his name and his dwelling, that is, those who dwell in heaven. Also it was allowed to make war on the saints and to conquer them. (Rev 13:5–6)

The actions of the second beast coordinate with those of the first:

[The second beast] exercises all of the authority of the first beast on its behalf, and it makes the earth and its inhabitants worship the first beast. ... It performs great signs, even making fire come down from heaven to earth in the sight of all; and by the signs that it is allowed to perform on behalf of the beast, it deceives the inhabitants of the earth, telling them to make an image for the beast.... (Rev 13:12–14)

Without a precise social, historical, political, and religious context as a starting point to consider these symbolic images, it is easy to see why people project their own stories and circumstances onto them. Without any knowledge of the ways in which the original author(s) and audience(s) of Revelation may have understood these symbols, it becomes easy for people to associate them with figures in their own time and place. All one has to do is identify someone who is "uttering haughty words" or "blaspheming God" (in their view) and that person can become the beast; likewise, anyone perceived to be "deceiving the inhabitants of the earth" can be associated with the second beast. And so on.

If instead these symbols are viewed in light of the symbolic world in which the original author(s) and audience(s) lived, that is, life in Asia Minor under Roman Imperial rule at the end of the first century CE, the potential meanings of these symbols become somewhat more bounded, and thus come into much clearer focus. To begin, there are very good reasons for associating the first beast with the Roman state itself, or some aspect thereof. It was quite common in ancient Judaism to portray oppressive foreign nations as "beasts," "monsters," and "sea-monsters" (Aune, *Revelation*, 2:732–733). In Dan 7:1–8, for example, four beasts represented four successive oppressive Empires (see chapters 1 and 2, above). Indeed, associating national enemies (and their leaders) with beasts has a long history in the Hebrew Bible, and for this reason alone, it makes sense to identify the Roman Imperial state, the very one under which the author(s) and audience(s) of Revelation were living, as a likely candidate for the first beast in Revelation 13.

But, in fact, there are more specific clues that point to this conclusion, including the very first descriptor of the first beast, which is said to have "ten horns and seven heads and ten crowns upon the horns" (13:1). Both horns and crowns symbolized power in the ancient world, and accordingly, these features often appeared symbolically in the Hebrew Bible to indicate powerful entities. For example, the fourth beast in the vision in Dan 7 is said to have "ten horns" (Dan 7:7), which are later in the same text explicitly identified as "ten kings" (Dan 7:24). Similarly, the book of Revelation depicts another entity, the "Whore of Babylon," sitting upon a scarlet beast that has seven heads and ten horns (Rev 17:3). The heads of the beast are later identified as "seven mountains" and "seven kings" (Rev 17:9), symbols that most scholars believe refer to the "seven hills" of Rome as well as seven Roman leaders. The ten horns are said to refer to "ten kings who have not yet received a kingdom," which most take to refer either to future Roman Emperors or to contemporaneous Roman client kings (Aune, *Revelation*, 3:944–952). It seems, then, that the description of a horned and crowned beast in Revelation 13 constitutes a grotesque caricature of the Roman Imperial state and its apparatus. No doubt a first-century Jewish audience would have recognized such an image, having become well-acquainted with such symbolic caricatures in their sacred scriptures.

Read in this light, the remaining symbolic imagery relating to the first beast can be fully appreciated. For example, the fact that Rome ruled most of the known world makes sense of the claim that the beast was "given authority over every tribe and people and language and nation" (Rev 13:7). In this vein, the well-known military superiority of the Romans seems to lie behind the statement of those who claim, "Who is like the beast, and who can fight against it?" (Rev 13:4) Moreover, the claim that the beast was "allowed to make war on the saints and conquer them" (Rev 13:7) can be understood to refer to Roman persecution of Jesus-followers, a theme which is prominent throughout the book of Revelation (e.g., Rev 2:8–11; 2:12–17; 6:9–11; 7:9–17; 11:1–13; 12:1–6; 17:1–18; 18:24).

Sidebar 8.1

The description of one of the heads of the beast as seemingly having received a "death blow" that "had been healed" (Rev 13:3) may refer to Emperor Nero (37 CE–68 CE). Popular legends circulated in the wake of Nero's death in 68 CE that he would somehow return to power. Some versions of the *Nero Redivivus* ("Nero Reborn") legend claim that he never died, but instead fled to Parthia, and that after some time, he would return to Rome. Importantly, such legends were popular during the time of the composition of Revelation, i.e., the end of the first century CE. Moreover, during this same time, several frauds are known to have pretended to be "Nero Redivivus." This lends weight to the notion that Rev 13:3 refers specifically to Emperor Nero.

Fig. 8.1. A marble bust of Nero; Antiques Museum in the Royal Palace, Stockholm. Photo: Wolfgang Sauber; Commons. wikimedia.org.

The Second Beast

Having identified the Roman Empire lying behind the depiction of the first beast in chapter 13, it remains to consider the identity (or identities) of the second beast in the second half of the chapter. The fact that it is said to exercise "the full authority of the first beast on its behalf" and "compels . . . inhabitants of the earth . . . to worship the first beast" (Rev 13:12) has led many to conclude that the second beast represents a particular aspect of Roman rule, including, perhaps, the Roman Emperor himself, Roman provincial governors, or the priests of the imperial cult (Aune, *Revelation*, 2:756). The **imperial cult**, or some element of the cult, appears most likely in light of the actions of the second beast relating to a particular cult statue that he commanded to have built "in honor of the first beast" and through which he performs impressive miracles (Rev 13:14–15).

The key to decrypting the symbolism in the passage rests on identifying what lies behind the reference to the cult statue, which is most likely a statue of the Emperor that would have occupied a prominent place in the Imperial cult. Though the term "cult" has pejorative connotations today, in Asia Minor (where Revelation was composed and first circulated) and throughout the Roman Empire in the first century CE, the imperial cult was a prominent and widely accepted element of the Imperial apparatus. The grounds of the Imperial cult were often quite impressive, displaying visually the grandeur of the Emperor and his family (including statues of the imperial family), as well as his great virtues, many accomplishments, and the generous benefactions he has granted to his subjects. Here, Roman citizens would congregate on certain days to offer sacrifices in honor of the Emperor and his family, to eat and drink with their neighbors, and to participate in accompanying civic festivities, which functioned (among other ways) to coalesce their identity as members of the Roman civic sphere.

If the "cult statue" represents the statue of the Emperor in the imperial cult, the Beast is some entity that supports the cult, e.g., the priests who maintain it. So much makes sense of the fact that the second Beast is said to "exercise the authority of the first Beast," that is, the Roman imperial apparatus, as well as the fact that the second Beast ordered the construction of the cult image and causes those who dwell upon the earth "to worship it" (Rev 13:12–14). Such an interpretation also makes sense of several additional details given about the actions of the Beast. For example, the claim that the Beast is able to "give life to the cult image . . . in order that [it] might speak" (Rev 13:15) likely refers to the well-known ancient phenomena of the animation of cult statues. Like many venerated statues and shrines today, such statues were believed to turn, sweat, weep, and even speak, and the cultic priests were often thought to be capable of producing such responses (see Aune, *Revelation*, 2:762–64).

Moreover, the text states that the second Beast determines whether people will live or die (Rev 13:15) on the basis of whether or not they worshipped the cult image. It seems that many early Jews and Christians conscientiously objected to the practice of honoring the Emperor (as well as the Roman gods) in this way. So much is suggested in a letter written in the year 112 CE to the Emperor Trajan by Pliny, a Roman governor in the area of Bithynia-Pontus (the northern coast of modern-day Turkey), who claimed that no "genuine Christian" could be induced to make offerings of wine and incense to the statue of the Emperor (Pliny, *Ep.* 10.96.5). In a similar vein, Tertullian, a prominent Christian theologian who was active nearly a century after Revelation was written, claimed that one of the main charges against Christians was their unwillingness to sacrifice on behalf of the Roman emperors (Tertullian, *Apol.* 10.1). By refusing to participate in imperial cultic sacrifices, many Christians were likely ostracized, and may have been persecuted outright. While it is unclear to what extent Christians were actually persecuted for failing to offer such sacrifices, it was a known trope among early Christians (see, e.g., Apocalypse of Peter 2). This is one way to make sense of the claim in Rev 13:15 that one's life hangs in the balance on the basis of one's response to the cult statue (of the Emperor).

The very last verse in chapter 13 includes what is perhaps the best known symbol in the book of Revelation, and maybe even the entire Bible: the "number of the beast," which is "666" (Rev 13:18). The text clearly indicates that this number refers to a person, and for this reason, commentators throughout history have attempted to identify a particular referent (to see such attempts, just Google it!). Some scholars have attempted to identify the personage behind "666" by means of a well-known ancient numerological code called **gematria,** in which letters and words were associated with particular numbers (e.g., the first letter of the Greek letter *alpha* equals 1, while *omega*, the last letter, equals 800). When the name of the Emperor "Nero Caesar" is transliterated from Greek (the language in which the text of Revelation was composed) into Hebrew, *QSR NRWN*, the total number equals 666.

Identifying the Emperor Nero in such negative terms makes sense in light of the violent persecution of Christians during his reign. The most flagrant event occurred in the aftermath of a destructive fire that burned in Rome for almost a week, which Nero falsely blamed on the Christians. The Roman historian Tacitus writes:

> Therefore, to stop the rumor [that he had set Rome on fire], he [Emperor Nero] falsely charged with guilt, and punished with the most fearful tortures, the persons commonly called Christians. . . . Accordingly first those were arrested who confessed they were Christians; next on their information, a vast multitude were convicted, not so much on the charge of burning the city, as of "hating the human race." In their very deaths they were made the subjects of sport: for they were covered with the hides of wild beasts, and worried to death by dogs, or nailed to crosses, or set fire to, and when the day waned, burned to serve for the evening lights. (Tacitus, *Ann.* 15.44; Translation in Bettenson, *Documents*, 1–2)

Inscribing Ideology: Revelation as Counter-Imperial Text

Thus, we see here that the symbolic figures and imagery in this chapter *can* be understood as a coded message, a cipher in need of interpretation. It is simply a matter of possessing the right key in order to decrypt the message. Again, I argue that this key is the knowledge that Roman imperial authority constitutes the proper object of attack throughout Revelation. By depicting the Roman Empire and various elements of its apparatus as "Beasts," the vision paints a picture of the Empire in very unflattering terms, and its overarching claim is clear: the Empire is an evil entity that blasphemes God, destroys God's followers, and deceives its own inhabitants. In this way, the vision represents a particular perspective—a particularly negative one—on the nature of Roman Imperial authority. Clearly, not all those living under Roman rule would have understood it in such negative terms, and indeed, we have evidence that many Jews and Christians did not consider it so negatively. But this is precisely the perspective conveyed in the visions in the book of Revelation, and it appears that the purpose of propagating the vision was to sway an audience toward this position.

How exactly did the text achieve its goal of convincing its audience that the Roman Empire was, in no uncertain terms, a monstrously evil entity? In short, the visions in Revelation create a symbolic space in which an audience can consider negative representations of the Empire, especially in contrast with other representations in which the Empire was presented in a wholly positive light. In other words, the visions invite an audience to enter the symbolic world opened up—or created—by them for the purpose of garnering support for its negative view of Roman Imperial authority. The visions seek to "'channel' the audience's understandings, emotions, and identifications in such a way that it is persuaded and moved to the desired action," which, in my proposed reading, would have constituted a realization that the Empire itself is fully corrupt (Schüssler Fiorenza 1998, 188). In this way, then, the visions inculcate their own anti-imperial **ideology** into its audience(s).

Once one recognizes anti-Roman ideology as a critical interpretive frame for the book of Revelation, it becomes much more difficult simply to project one's own circumstances onto the text. For example, once one identifies the Beasts in chapter 13, and the infamous number 666 with which they are associated, as negative characterizations of elements of the ancient Roman imperial apparatus as they existed in the time of the original author and audience of Revelation, it becomes more challenging simply to identify them as Barack Obama, Adolf Hitler, or anyone else outside of the imperial Roman context from which they were generated. In this way, then, careful consideration of the original sociopolitical contexts of the text helpfully limit the ways the text and its many symbols can be interpreted in modern contexts. Such considerations can be thought of as useful antidotes against the perverse ways in which the book of Revelation is read in many contemporary contexts today, and the horrific consequences that can result from such readings, such as those that occurred in Waco, Texas, at the Branch Davidian compound.

Study Questions:

1. In what ways have many interpreters of Revelation understood its symbolic imagery? What alternative interpretive method is suggested in this chapter?
2. What are some of the inherent problems in understanding Revelation's symbols to refer primarily to the circumstances of the modern reader of the text?
3. Given the interpretive approach suggested in this chapter, in what ways do you imagine Revelation could be appropriated in a modern context?

Bibliography and Further Reading:

Aune, David E. *Revelation.* 3 vols. Word Biblical Commentary. Nashville: Thomas Nelson, 1997–1998.

Bettenson, Henry, ed. *Documents of the Christian Church.* 2d ed. New York: Oxford University Press, 1963.

Collins, Adela Yarbro. *Crisis and Catharsis: The Power of the Apocalypse.* Philadelphia: Westminster Press, 1984.

Friesen, Steve. *Imperial Cults and the Apocalypse of John: Reading Revelation in the Ruins.* Oxford: Oxford University Press, 2001.

Froom, Le Roy Edwin. *The Prophetic Faith of Our Fathers: The Historical*

Development of Prophetic Interpretation. Vol 2. Washington, DC: Review and Herald, 1948.

Keller, Catherine. *Apocalypse Now and Then: A Feminist Guide to the End of the World*. Boston: Beacon Press, 1996.

Schüssler-Fiorenza, Elisabeth. *The Book of Revelation: Justice and Judgment*. Minneapolis: Augsburg Fortress, 1998.

PART II

Apocalypticism throughout the Ages

9

The Transformation of the Apocalyptic
Heritage in Late Antique Christianity

Karl Shuve

GETTING PREPPED:

1. What are some of the reasons why the apocalyptic genre had become so popular in Second Temple Judaism and Early Christianity?
2. How do you imagine that apocalyptic ideology could continue to thrive when Christianity was no longer at odds with the state?

KEY TERMS:
ETIOLOGY
LATE ANTIQUITY
RESCRIPT

MARTYROLOGY
CHILIASTIC

Introduction

As we read in earlier chapters, the first apocalypses were written by Jews living in a culture that had been recently transformed by the conquests of Alexander the Great. The earliest examples of the genre, the Astronomical Book and the Book of the Watchers, reflect a new interest in nature, cosmology, and the afterlife, which they convey through stories of the antediluvian patriarch Enoch's miraculous travels to heaven and the ends of the earth. Written in the voice (and consequently, with the authority) of Enoch himself, they relate his visions of the movements of celestial bodies, the places of post-mortem punishment, and even the throne room of God. Soon thereafter, this new kind of visionary literature was used to make sense of the whole sweep of history, first during a time of persecution by the Seleucid king Antiochus IV when people were suffering for their adherence to Torah, and then again, following the destruction of the Second Temple in 70 CE. These "historical" apocalypses looked forward to the future redemption of the righteous, often precipitated by the advent of the Messiah, and the punishment of their wicked persecutors. But of the many apocalypses that were written by Jews in Hebrew and Aramaic during the Second Temple period, it is striking that the book of Daniel alone—the only apocalypse to be included in the Jewish scriptures—can still be read in full in its original languages of composition. The others, like the Book of the Watchers, the Book of Dreams, 3 Baruch, and 4 Ezra, survive only in translations that were produced by later Christians readers, who spoke a dizzying array of languages, many of which will be unfamiliar to people in the contemporary Western world: Greek and Latin, as well as Armenian, Coptic, Ge'ez (Ethiopic), Georgian, and Slavonic.

Although the Jews of the Second Temple Period wrote the first apocalypses, it was the Christians of **Late Antiquity** who transmitted those texts to the modern world and ensured that apocalyptic thought would remain popular down to the present day. For reasons that you will learn about in a later chapter, rabbinic Jews became deeply suspicious of apocalyptic literature and did not encourage its transmission. By contrast, early Christians were ardent proponents of the genre. Not only did they preserve earlier Jewish apocalypses and write a large number of their own, they also allowed apocalyptic ideology to give a distinct coloring to the way that they portrayed the world around them: persecution, martyrdom, the afterlife, and even, ethics. The Christian affinity for viewing the world apocalyptically should not, however, be surprising. The earliest followers of Christ came from Jewish communities and continued to see themselves as Jews. Texts such as the Book of the Watchers were part of their literary and theological heritage and shaped how they understood the nature of the world and the way God worked within it. In this chapter, we will explore the many ways that apocalyptic literature shaped Christian self-definition in Late Antiquity, in that crucial period when Christianity emerged as a separate religion from Judaism—that is, during a time known in contemporary scholarship as the "Parting(s) of the Ways." (See chapter 10, this volume).

Translation, Transmission, Transformation: Late Antique Christians and the Second Temple Apocalypses

Before we consider how early Christians were responsible for preserving apocalypses written by Second Temple Jewish authors, we need to establish an important point: in the decades—and even centuries—following the birth of the Jesus movement, there was no rigidly defined canon of scripture. That is, most Christian readers in the second century CE did not make distinctions between apocalypses such as Daniel and the Book of the Watchers, and both were considered to be authoritative writings, since they were believed to be revelations from venerable figures of the distant past. Therefore, the Christian impetus to read, copy, and translate the apocalypses is in no way a strange phenomenon, and Christians treated them in very much the same way as they did the books of Genesis, Isaiah, or the Wisdom of Solomon.

The Book of the Watchers is perhaps our clearest example of this, and in fact, it complicates any clear distinctions we might be tempted to make between "canonical" and "non-canonical" apocalypses. You will already have learned about the plot of this text: how the Watcher angels, understood to be the "sons of God" from Gen 6:1-4, came to earth, corrupted humans with their teaching of illicit knowledge, and begot a race of giants through intercourse with human women; how Enoch, the "scribe of righteousness," was sent to intercede for them; and, finally, how Enoch toured the ends of the earth. The **etiology** of evil presented in this text—that human suffering and misery was precipitated by the descent of the Watchers—as well as its claims about post-mortem punishment were profoundly influential in early Christian theology.

Most strikingly, the Book of the Watchers makes an appearance in the epistle of Jude, which came to be included in the New Testament. Jude is writing to warn about the need to maintain "the faith that was once for all entrusted to the saints," which is now being corrupted (Jude 3; NRSV trans.). He reminds his readers of the condemnation that awaits those who go astray, and he uses as an example the angels who left their dwelling place and whom God consequently "has kept in eternal chains in deepest darkness for the judgment of the Great day" (Jude 6). Later in the epistle, Jude actually quotes a passage from the Book of the Watchers (1 En 1:9) to reinforce his belief in the truth of the coming judgment of the ungodly. This Enochic apocalypse deeply informed Jude's understanding of eschatological judgment and punishment. Moreover, Jude introduces his quotation in the same way as he does other biblical prophecies, suggesting its authoritative status.

Additionally, the influence of the Enochic apocalypse is clear in a number of later Christian texts from the second and third centuries. Most prominent among them is the *Second Apology* of Justin Martyr, a Christian philosopher who wrote in the middle of the second century to the Roman Emperor Antoninus Pius, in order to protest the persecution of Christians. In a short, but dense passage, Justin blames "every evil" on the Watcher angels, who in addition to teaching magic to humans begot a race of "demons (*daimones*)" that constantly torment and oppress them (2 Apol. 5; ET Barnard, 1997). Indeed, Justin insists that their offspring were mistakenly worshipped by human beings as gods—in classical Greek, the word *daimōn* referred to an intermediary god—and he thereby indicts the whole of Greek and Roman religious practice as a gigantic fraud perpetrated by the Watchers. Unlike Jude, Justin does not quote from the Book of the Watchers itself, nor does he mention it by name, but he is intimately familiar with its message, which he takes to be both true and authoritative. Alongside Justin, we could place several other early Christian authors who were clearly familiar with the Enochic corpus and re-appropriated key themes from Enoch's apocalypse(s) throughout their own texts. Irenaeus, in his *Against the Heresies*, uses the post-mortem punishment of the Watchers to warn the ungodly about their own fate (Haer. 1.10.1), very much as Jude did; Tertullian includes in his *On the Apparel of Women*, a lengthy rumination on how the Watchers corrupted women by teaching them about make-up and jewelry (Cult. fem. 1.2; cf. 1 En 7–8); and the anonymous second-century author of the *Pseudo-Clementine Homilies*, a narrative written in the name of Clement of Rome, blames the flood on the giants who were begotten from the union of the Watchers and human women (Hom. 8.12–17).

Popular though this Enochic apocalypse was in the early years of the Christian movement, by the late fourth century, its authenticity had been seriously questioned and most Christian communities ceased to read from or copy it. Although Jude, which, by this time, had been included in the New Testament, treated it as an authoritative writing, very few would accord it canonical status. But there is one significant exception: Christians in Ethiopia remained convinced that it was a genuine revelation of Enoch. As such, the text was accepted into the scriptural canon in the Ethiopian Orthodox Church, as part of a larger collection with the Similitudes of Enoch, the Astronomical Book, the

Book of Dreams, and the Epistle of Enoch. These five apocalypses, which together are known as 1 Enoch, survive in full only in their translation into Ge'ez, the language of the Ethiopic church, and are included in Ethiopic bibles as scripture. Thus, by an interesting accident of history—one that should forcefully remind us of the close relationship between Judaism and Christianity in antiquity—scholars are able to assess the significance of Enoch and his revelations in Second Temple Judaism because of the reading habits and apocalyptic predilections of late antique Christians.

Touring Heaven and Hell

Christians not only translated and transmitted earlier Jewish apocalypses; they also composed many of their own, often in the names of authoritative figures from the early Jesus movement. The Revelation to John, the last book in the Christian Bible, is by far the most famous. Because of Revelation's immense popularity in the history of Western culture, it can be tempting to imagine that Christians were interested primarily, if not exclusively, in the eschatological element—i.e., the "end of times"—of the apocalyptic genre. But the majority of extant apocalypses from the period are concerned with the revelation of hidden knowledge, whether of the origins of the universe or the nature of the afterlife. It was, as we shall see later in this chapter, in the stories of martyrs that the influence of the historical apocalypses can most clearly be discerned. In the present section, we will consider the many tours of heaven and hell imagined by late antique Christian authors.

Until quite recently, many scholars believed that late antique texts that narrated tours of hell were indebted to ancient Greek accounts of descents into Hades. The most famous of these is Book 11 of the *Odyssey*, which, in the classical world, was referred to by the Greek word *nekuia*—a term that originally denoted rites for calling up the dead. But Martha Himmelfarb has instead demonstrated that these works are most closely related to Second Temple Jewish ascent apocalypses, particularly the Book of the Watchers, in which Enoch saw the places where the fallen angels were punished as part of his tour of the cosmos (Himmelfarb, 2010). As we saw in the previous section, the Book of the Watchers was a popular and authoritative text in many early Christian communities. Central to Himmelfarb's argument is the observation that these are tours in which an angel serves as a guide, and which are punctuated by the visionary's questions and the angel's answers, which frequently begin with a demonstrative pronoun (e.g., "This is the place . . ."). These features are shared with the Book of the Watchers (esp. 1 En 17–19), but not with classical Greek sources. Also indicative of a debt to Jewish apocalypses is the fact that many tours of hell in Christian literature are coupled with tours of heaven, mirroring Enoch's own purported journey.

The earliest Christian vision of hell, which can be dated to the middle of the second century (just after the composition of the final book of the Bible), is the Apocalypse of Peter. It survives in two versions: a shorter Greek one and a longer Ethiopic one. The Ethiopic text, which is thought to reflect the earliest version of the story, begins on the Mount of Olives, with the disciples asking Jesus to tell them about the end times (cf. Matt 24). After Peter asks a question about the fate of sinners, Jesus launches into a lengthy description of the kinds of punishment that they will face following the final judgment, many of which are meant to fit the crime: blasphemers are hanged up by their tongues; adulteress women are hanged up by their hair and male adulterers by their genitals; liars have their lips cut off, and so forth.

The Ethiopic text is not, however, a tour properly speaking, since Jesus only describes the places of post-mortem punishment. But its vision of hell was, at some point in the following centuries, transformed into a tour, as that subgenre of apocalyptic literature grew in popularity. The Greek fragment—which dates to the eighth or ninth century CE, but may well reflect an earlier form of the text—begins not on the Mount of Olives, but at the scene of the Transfiguration, where Jesus is met by Moses and Elijah on a mountain and his status as a prophet ordained by God is further revealed. The vision of Moses and Elijah (who are not named) prompts Peter to ask Jesus about the fate of the righteous dead and he is then taken to "a very great region outside

171

of this world" (Apoc. Pet. 15; ET James, 1924). Peter first visits paradise, whose inhabitants have become like the angels (Apoc. Pet. 18–19)—a claim that we also find in some Enochic apocalypses (cf. 1 En 104–106; 2 En 22.9). But most of his tour is spent in hell, where he witnesses many of the punishments that were described by Jesus in the Ethiopic text.

Far more famous and influential than the Apocalypse of Peter is the Apocalypse of Paul. Also written in Greek, it was composed more than two hundred years after the Apocalypse of Peter, and it survives in a complete Latin translation as well as in Coptic, Greek, Old Russian, and Syriac translations. According to the text's prologue, it was "discovered" in 388 CE in the floor of a house that had once belonged to Paul, by a man who received an angelic visitation telling him of its existence (Apoc. Paul 1). Of course, this prologue was a clever way to explain why no one had ever heard of this text before, despite Paul having allegedly written it over three centuries earlier. We need not, moreover, take the date of 388 as the exact year of composition, for its specificity helped to create an aura of plausibility.

The tour is introduced by Paul's claim in 2 Cor 12:2 that he had been "caught up to the third heaven," a reference that again lends legitimacy to the work. He is first taken by his guide up to the firmament, where he sees many angels stationed—some who are appointed to watch over and tally the sins of the wicked, and others who are appointed to care for the righteous and escort them to judgment at their death. Paul is even granted a terrifying vision of souls being judged by God. Following this, Paul is taken to the "third heaven," which is the place where the righteous—that is, those who have "kept goodness and pureness of their bodies"—are rewarded (Apoc. Paul 19; ET James, 1924). Significantly, the first person whom Paul meets in the third heaven is none other than Enoch himself, "the scribe of righteousness," who weeps over the wickedness of humanity (Apoc. Paul 20). Once again, we see the deep influence of the Enochic literature on late antique Christian apocalypses. It turns out that Enoch and Elijah are the only two men in the third heaven, for they alone (at least, according to canonical biblical accounts) did not die. Alongside them, the righteous dead are said to reside in the "city of Christ" on Lake Acherusia, which Paul also visits, where they await the millennial reign of Christ and the final judgment. After these joyful, edifying sights, Paul is then taken to hell, and his somber reaction is captured in the words, "I sighed" (Apoc. Paul 31). This is a far more elaborate hell than we find in the Apocalypse of Peter, with a large number of very different sins meriting their own places of punishment. The taxonomy of sin is so specific that committing fornication directly after receiving the eucharist is treated differently from committing fornication on another day. Moreover, the kinds of sins that are emphasized are quite different. The Apocalypse of Paul presupposes a culture that has been heavily Christianized—as the Roman Empire was in the late fourth century—and focuses on people such as unworthy deacons, priests, bishops, and monastics (Apoc. Paul 34–36, 40) as well as insufficiently holy Christians, who were not zealous enough (31), did not place their trust in the Lord (32), or mocked the Word of God (37).

What was a relatively minor element in the Book of the Watchers, i.e., a vivid descent into hell, was transformed by Christians in Late Antiquity into its own subgenre of apocalyptic literature, including later works such as the Ethiopic Apocalypse of Mary and the Ethiopic Apocalypse of Baruch. Indeed, these works are ultimately ancestors of Dante's *Divine Comedy*, whose significant debt to apocalyptic literature often goes unremarked. Tours of heaven and hell found particularly receptive audiences in a culture that was far more worried about sin and corruption *within* the church than it was about persecution from those without—not, of course, that internal concerns were ever totally absent, as the Revelation to John shows. As we saw especially with the Apocalypse of Paul, these texts were used to construct an account of the ideal Christian and to enforce it through fear of very specific punishments. Whereas historical apocalypses such as Revelation shaped Christian visions of history and the end of time, these tour apocalypses shaped Christian visions of the self in the present time.

Subversive Revelations: "Gnostic" Apocalypses

There is one specific group of late antique Christians for whom the apocalyptic genre was particularly important: the Sethians. Often referred to as "Gnostics"—along with groups such as the Valentinians and Marcionites that are, in fact, very different from them—the Sethians adhered to a complex cosmology, according to which the material world is an imperfect copy of a higher, intelligible realm that was created by an ignorant or malevolent deity. They are called "Sethians" because they idealize the figure of Seth, introduced in the Bible as the third son of Adam, from whom they believe the elect are descended. Salvation comes through the knowledge that the human soul is not a part of this material, visible world, but is estranged from its true homeland in the intelligible realm.

Sidebar 9.1

One of the greatest repositories of early Christian texts was discovered in 1945 in Nag Hammadi, Egypt. Included in the find were 12 codices, or ancient books, of Christian documents in Coptic.

Fig. 9.1 The final page of the Apocryphon of John, a second-century CE Sethian Gnostic text, from a fourth-century codex. Coptic Museum, Cairo; Commons.wikimedia.org.

Until the middle of the last century, most of what we knew of this group came from reports of hostile writers who identified their beliefs as "heresies." But in 1945, a large number of their texts, along with those belonging to other marginalized groups, were discovered in Coptic translation at Nag Hammadi in Upper Egypt. One of the most striking things about this discovery is that the majority of the Sethian treatises—the Apocryphon of John, Apocalypse of Adam, Allogenes, Zostrianos—are apocalypses. These works often claimed to be the revelations given to authoritative figures such as Adam and the disciple John about the true nature of the cosmos and humanity's place within it. Perhaps one reason why the theme of the secret revelation was so important for the Sethians was that they were turning the biblical view of creation on its head: the creator God is not the only god, but an intermediate deity who is blind to his own lack of authority. Not only is the world that this god created *not* "very good," it is deeply flawed and shot through with evil. Human history is, in essence, one long story of deception and fraud, and thus a direct revelation of the truth to a worthy individual becomes absolutely essential.

The most influential and widely read Sethian apocalypse is the Apocryphon (Secret Book) of John, which survives in four different copies from Nag Hammadi. The work opens after the ascension of Jesus, with John being chastised by a Pharisee for having followed a false teacher who died on a cross. As John despairs his ignorance of Jesus's teachings and his inability to defend them, the heavens open, the earth shakes, and a shape-shifting figure appears before him "in multiple forms." He is instructed by this figure—which identifies itself as Father, Mother, and Child—to lift up his head and accept his teachings so that he can transmit them to his "fellow spirits." This opening narrative serves as a frame for Jesus's lengthy teachings about the deficiency of the material world and the need for righteous souls to escape it. Unlike most other apocalypses, John neither travels nor has visions; Jesus instead describes everything to him.

But the Sethians did compose ascent apocalypses, such as the lengthy and esoteric Zostrianos. The visions described in the text are not attributed to an earlier authoritative figure, but rather to an otherwise unknown visionary named Zostrianos. During a time of great despair, the "angel of the knowledge of eternal light" appears to Zostrianos, and leads him to the "great eternals" above and a vision of that which is truly real. He leaves his body behind on earth and ascends through a number of "aeons" or emanations of the divine. Each time he ascends to a new heaven, he is baptized—sometimes multiple times—which leads to a transformation of his soul. After his fourth baptism at the fourth aeon, he becomes "a perfect angel"—a claim that is highly reminiscent of Enoch's angelic transformation in 2 Enoch. He is then instructed by the great ruler "Authrounios" about how the material world came to be, before descending back to the earth to take up his body and instruct the elect in what he saw. It is very likely that the secret knowledge contained in this apocalypse was meant to accompany a distinct set of ritual practices, demonstrating again the way in which this genre played an important role in the process of self-definition in antiquity.

Dying for God: Martyrdom and Apocalyptic Ideology

The Revelation to John seems not to have had many imitators in the first few centuries after its composition. Whereas the Apocalypse of Peter opened the floodgates to a large number of tour apocalypses and the Sethians frequently couched their speculations about the origins of the universe in secret revelations, few historical apocalypses were written. Those that were composed, like the Apocalypse of Adam, are more concerned about articulating an account of world history in defense of their re-reading of the biblical narrative than anticipating the final judgment. But this may be because after a period of hesitation concerning its authority in the second century, Revelation so permeated the Christian imagination that no new versions were needed. Indeed, the way that early Christian communities understood their place in the Roman Empire—particularly in the face of persecution—was thoroughly shaped by the apocalyptic eschatology of Revelation and earlier Jewish historical apocalypses such as Daniel.

The persecution of Christians in the pre-Constantinian Roman Empire is so deeply engrained in our cultural imagination—even among those who know little else about the history of Christianity—that it can be easy to overemphasize. It was not until the Emperor Decius issued an edict in 249 CE requiring all citizens in the Empire to sacrifice to the gods that there was anything resembling an Empire-wide persecution—and even in this case, the goal was not the suppression of Christianity. They did not have to live or worship underground. But this does not mean that it was always safe to be a Christian. Because religion was so closely tied to civic life, Christians could easily be accused of misanthropy, and when something went wrong—a natural disaster, famine, an economic downturn—it was easy to blame them for upsetting the gods. A **rescript** written by the Roman Emperor Trajan around the year 110 in response to a local disturbance in the province of Bithynia and Pontus on the Black Sea makes clear that Christians can be arrested and even executed simply for professing to be Christian. He tempers this, however, by telling his governor, Pliny the Younger, not to go hunting them down.

Sidebar 9.2

A letter from the Emperor Trajan to the governor of Bithynia-Pontus, regarding the proper punishment of Christians:

> You have followed the right course of procedure, my dear Pliny, in your examination of the cases of persons charged with being Christians, for it is impossible to lay down a general rule to a fixed formula. These people must not be hunted out; if they are brought before you and the charge against them is proved, they must be punished, but in the case of anyone who denies that he is a Christian, and makes it clear that he is not by offering prayers to our gods, he is to be pardoned as a result of his repentance however suspect his past conduct may be. But pamphlets circulated anonymously must play no part in any accusation. They create the worst sort of precedent and are quite out of keeping with the spirit of our age. (*Ep.* 10.96; trans. Radice, 1969)

However dangerous it actually was to be a Christian in the late ancient Mediterranean, it is clear from the writings of Christians themselves that being a "persecuted" minority was central to their self-definition. We see this in the proliferation of stories about martyrs—known as **martyrologies**—beginning in the late second century. These texts, produced in communities across the Roman Empire, fall somewhere between fact and fiction: in many (but not all) cases, they feature actual historical figures who were put to death by Roman authorities, but they are artfully re-imagined to highlight the sanctity of the martyrs, who are often represented as imitators of Christ, and to include miraculous details. An outsider might be inclined to argue that any group which so believes itself to be the subject of persecution cannot possibly enjoy the favor of God or the gods; indeed, Justin Martyr tells us he was asked to respond to this exact objection (2 Apol. 4). These martyrologies provide an answer to this question by pulling back the curtain of history to reveal a larger divine purpose.

The answer that they reveal is largely in keeping with what we find in apocalypses such as Daniel, written during the tumult of the Seleucid persecution, and in Revelation, composed in the wake of the Second Temple's destruction, as well as in many sayings attributed to Jesus about suffering in the present life: despite any seemingly unfavorable present circumstances, God is ultimately in control of all earthly powers, and history is inexorably moving to a time beyond time when the Messiah will come to reward the righteous and to punish the wicked. Death is not the final word, and redemption is coming.

The *Martyrdom of Polycarp*, a deeply influential martyrology written about the death of the aged Smyrnian bishop Polycarp c. 155 CE, is exemplary in this regard. This text is remarkable for its clear allusions to the Gospels in its depiction of Polycarp's arrest and execution—even in such a minute detail as naming the police magistrate Herod—and for the reverence it shows to Polycarp's burned, "purified" body. And it is informed clearly by apocalyptic ideology. Polycarp says very little in the course of the narrative, but when he is pressed by the governor to recant his beliefs in order to spare his life, he replies, "The fire that you threaten me with burns merely for a time and is soon extinguished. It is clear you are ignorant of the fire of everlasting punishment and of the judgment that is to come, which awaits the impious" (Mart. Pol. 11.2; ET Musurillo, 1972). Polycarp's execution signifies not the weakness of God, but the disorder of an evil world that will soon be put right by God at the final judgment. Indeed, God's power and control is demonstrated by the fact that the bishop's body cannot be burned by fire, which serves only to purify it, "as gold or silver in the smelting-furnace" (Mart. Pol. 15.2). His body witnesses the coming resurrection.

Of course, in terms of genre, martyrologies are often quite different from apocalypses. The *Martyrdom of Polycarp*, for example, neither includes any guided tour of the cosmos nor offers any coded vision of human history. But there is one significant exception, the Passion of Perpetua, which blurs the lines between the two genres and reveals the striking debt to apocalyptic thinking in martyr literature. Edited at the turn of the third century in North Africa, it is a composite work that includes several different texts, including selections from the diary of the eponymous Perpetua, a literate noblewoman who faced death after her conversion to Christianity. In her diary, Perpetua records a series of visions she received from God while in prison, the first being of particular interest to us. In this vision, she saw a ladder, covered in spikes and hooks, "reaching right up to heaven" (*Pass. Perp.* 4; ET Musurillo, 1972). To climb up this ladder, Perpetua needs to step on the head of a dragon, evoking language from Gen 3:15. After an arduous climb to the top, she enters a lush garden in which an old man, surrounded by thousands of people dressed in white, was milking a sheep. In an image heavy with eucharistic overtones, he offers her a drink of this milk, which she takes from her own cupped hands. Upon awaking, Perpetua realizes that this vision reveals to her that she must die for Christ.

The diary itself is not an apocalypse. She has no angelic guide or interpreter, and it is more a sequence of dreams that reveal her fate as a martyr and the power to intercede on behalf of others that she acquires as a result of her faithfulness. But, like the heroes of many of the apocalypses, Perpetua makes an ascent to heaven—even putting herself in danger to do so—where she has a vision of God. This is not the indescribable God sitting on a fiery throne, but the Good Shepherd of the Gospels. She does not see angels, but she does see the righteous—presumably other martyrs—who are clothed in white, much like martyrs under the altar in Revelation, who were "given a white robe and told to rest a little longer" (6:11). From Daniel and the Book of Dreams through Revelation and 4 Ezra to the late antique martyrologies, we see a stable and consistent way of responding to the violence, threatened or realized, of hostile authorities: God temporarily permits suffering and injustice in the course of a much larger, cosmic plan meant to restore justice and ensure the permanent peace of the righteous.

Apocalypticism after the Peace of the Church

In closing, we will want to consider what happened to apocalypticism, particularly its eschatological dimension, after Christianity became Rome's favored religion. In 312 CE, the emperor Constantine made a public proclamation of his allegiance to the Christian God, and all emperors subsequent to him—with the exception of Julian, the so-called Apostate (360–363 CE)—were professing Christians. Constantine began promoting Christianity—spending large sums on church buildings, offering patronage to Christians—and by the late fourth century, it was the Roman Empire's official religion. This remarkable change was so enthusiastically embraced by Christians that the great scholar and bishop Eusebius of Caesarea, in his *Oration in Praise of Constantine*, could refer to the Emperor as possessing the "likeness of heavenly sovereignty authority" (3.5). What would happen to apocalyptic views of history, which generally presupposed that the righteous were in a position of relative powerlessness and in need of heavenly redemption?

What we see in the late fourth and early fifth centuries is a new approach to the interpretation of Revelation. During the second and third centuries, **chiliastic** interpretations of this apocalypse flourished. Christians believed that human history would span seven thousand years—for, as Psalm 90 says, "with the Lord, one day is as a thousand years" (90:4)—and that they were in the sixth age, on the verge of the millennial reign of Christ spoken of in Rev 20:4–5. Drawing on John of Patmos' clear identification of Babylon as Rome (Rev 17) and the beast as the emperor (Rev 13), they found firm evidence that they were living in the final days. But with the peace of the church, agnosticism about being able to precisely predict the end of the world took hold, and new modes of interpretation were devised to avoid identifying Babylon with Rome. Rather than read Revelation as a kind of road map of human history that clearly identified the timeline of the final judgment, some Christians read the text as an interior account of the soul's journey to God.

The most famous example is Saint Augustine's ruminations on the final judgment in the twentieth book of his monumental *City of God*. Augustine began writing this work shortly after the sack of Rome in 410—a traumatic event that shook the confidence of many in God's providential guidance of the newly Christianized Roman Empire. For Augustine, it was a mistake to invest any earthly polity—even Rome—with a sense of divine mission and it was utter folly to believe that one could predict the end of the world from political events and natural disasters. He begins the twentieth book by making it absolutely clear that, at some future time, Christ will come from heaven to judge the living and the dead once and for all. The vision of all history culminating in a great time of judgment is, for him, non-negotiable. But Augustine believes that his fellow Christians have missed a point of fundamental importance: there are *two* resurrections. The first is a spiritual resurrection, which occurs when Christians are baptized and raised from their state of being "dead in sin" (*Civ.* 20.6); the second is a bodily resurrection that will occur at the final judgment. This has led to what in his mind is a gross misinterpretation of Revelation 20, which was the cornerstone of the chiliastic view. For Augustine, this passage speaks about the *first* resurrection—that is, the turning of the Christian from idolatry to new life in Christ—and thus it is about the spiritual life and not a historical reign of one thousand years. Augustine also asserts as a corollary of this reading that the devil has been bound since the incarnation of Christ, which is what allowed the church to spread through the earth, and that the reign of Christ is happening through the life of the church. Moreover, he interprets the battles in Revelation as an interior struggle against vice, rather than as a cosmic battle that will usher in the end of the world (*Civ.* 20.9).

Augustine's interpretation of Revelation allowed for the text to be read and appreciated in contexts where the church was not in stark opposition to the ruling power, and it was wildly popular throughout the Middle Ages. But it was always easy enough to see the end of the world on the horizon, and thus apocalyptic eschatology never faded into the background. This is nowhere more evident than during the most significant political transformation the Mediterranean had seen since the time of Alexander the Great—the Arab conquests. Between the middle of the seventh and the middle of the eighth centuries, the Sasanian Persian empire utterly collapsed, and much of the Eastern Roman Empire—including Spain, North Africa, Egypt, Palestine, and Syria—fell to the Islamic invaders. Faced with this dramatic loss of territory—which included the ancient and important Christian cities of Antioch, Alexandria, Carthage, and especially Jerusalem—Christians needed a way to make sense of history. Thus they turned again to writing historical apocalypses.

The first and most famous apocalypse produced in the wake of the spread of Islam is a text written in the name of the third-century bishop Methodius of Olympus. It was composed in Syriac in the Byzantine Empire, and was quickly translated into Greek and Latin. The text lacks many formal features of the apocalyptic genre, such as a narrative framework or angelic guide, and it is called a discourse (*logos*) rather than apocalypse (*apokalypsis*) in the superscription of the Greek text. But its chiliastic chronology—dividing the world into seven millennia—and use of symbolic language to map the arrival of the eschaton merit its classification as an historical apocalypse, though one with strong ties to the prophetic literature of the Jewish Scriptures.

The Apocalypse of Pseudo-Methodius, as scholars now call it, begins with the expulsion of Adam and Eve from the Garden of Eden and proceeds to narrate the whole of human history, showing particular interest in the biblical chronology of the ANE and the conquests of Alexander. The author of the text believes himself to be living at the dawn of the seventh, and final, millennium. The sixth millennium in his scheme witnessed the rise of Rome and its subsequent Christianization, and this kingdom of the Christians is, he believes, the supreme and unconquerable power in the world. This last age of the world will witness a great struggle between Rome and the "seed of Ishmael"—that is, the Muslims (*Pseudo-Methodius* 11.1; ET Garstad, 2012). The Ishmaelites will be initially successful on account of the sinfulness of Rome; the Arab invaders have been given license to conquer by God "because of the sin of lawlessness" (*Pseudo-Methodius* 11.5). The increasing power given to the seed of Ishmael will be a time of testing for Christians, during which "the elect will be revealed" (*Pseudo-Methodius* 13.5). But after this time, God will aid the Romans in conquering the Arabs, ushering in a period of peace, which will be temporarily be disrupted by the Antichrist—the "son of perdition"—whose false righteousness is exposed by Enoch and Elijah, before the Son of Man "will arrive on the clouds of heaven" (*Pseudo-Methodius* 14.13). This is a particularly interesting text because its explanation is quite different from what is usually found in historical apocalypses. For apocalyptic writers, suffering was usually endured *in spite of* rather than *because of* the conduct of God's people, but for Pseudo-Methodius, God allowed Islam to rise because of the sins of Christians.

Conclusion

In the modern world, when we speak about the "apocalyptic," we generally refer to discourses about the end of the world. And it is in large part because of late antique Christian apocalyptic eschatology that this is so. But as you have learned by reading about the origins and development of this literature, apocalyptic texts were as concerned with disclosing the secrets of the cosmos and history as it was with divining the precise time of the end of the world. As popular as historical apocalypses were in Late Antiquity, it is arguable that Christians in this period were as, if not more, interested in the revelation of cosmological secrets and the nature of the afterlife than they were with speculations about the end of history and the final judgment.

Study Questions:

1. In what different ways did late antique Christians ensure the survival of Second Temple Apocalypses?
2. What are some reasons that apocalypticism was such an important part of late antique Christianity?
3. How did Christianity's changing relationship to the Roman state affect its apocalyptic worldview?
4. In what ways is the late antique Christian legacy evident today?

Bibliography and Further Reading:

Boustan, Ra'anan S. and Annette Y. Reed. *Heavenly Realms and Earthly Realities in Late Antique Religions*. Cambridge: Cambridge University Press, 2004.

Burns, Dylan. *Apocalypse of the Alien God: Platonism and the Exile of Sethian Gnosticism*. Philadelphia: University of Pennsylvania Press, 2014.

Himmelfarb, Martha. *The Apocalypse: A Brief History*. Oxford: Wiley Blackwell, 2010.

James, M. R. *The Apocryphal New Testament*. Oxford: Clarendon, 1924.

Justin Martyr. *The First and Second Apologies*. Translated by Leslie Barnard. New York: Paulist Press, 1997.

Musurillo, Herbert. *The Acts of the Christian Martryrs*. Oxford: Clarendon Press, 1972.

Pliny the Younger. *Letters, Volume II*. Translated by Betty Radice. Harvard: Harvard University Press, 1969.

Reed, Annette Yoshiko. *Fallen Angels and the History of Judaism and Christianity: The Reception of Enochic Literature*. Cambridge: Cambridge University Press, 2009.

10

The Decline of Second Temple Jewish Apocalypticism and the Rise of Rabbinic Judaism

Shayna Sheinfeld

GETTING PREPPED:

1. How might the destruction of the Second Temple in 70 CE be reflected in apocalypses written after the event?
2. What attributes do you think the Messiah has? Where do your ideas of the Messiah come from? Are your ideas of the Messiah similar or different from that of your classmates?
3. Does your idea of the Messiah coincide with the descriptions of the Messiah in the apocalypses you have read so far?

KEY TERMS:

JOSEPHUS

ESCHATON

ZION

PSEUDEPIGRAPHON

DAVIDIC DYNASTY

PROOFTEXT

RABBI

GENTILES

THE PARTING OF THE WAYS

The Destruction of the Second Temple

Beginning in 66 CE, Jews in Judaea revolted against Roman rule. The reasons for the revolt were myriad, stemming, in part, from poor leadership by both Romans and Jews, cultural tensions between Jews and non-Jews in the area, and a widening gap between the aristocracy and lower classes. First-century Jewish historian **Josephus** is our main source of details on the revolt, including the devastating destruction of the Second Temple in Jerusalem in 70 CE.

While all Jews did not venerate the Second Temple, it constituted the center of Jewish worship in antiquity. Judaism, like all religions in Greco-Roman antiquity, was organized around sacrifices to its God. Unlike other cults in antiquity, however, there was a strong tendency to view the Jerusalem temple as the sole locus of Jewish worship. Therefore, the destruction of the Second Temple was particularly devastating to Jews throughout the Roman Empire, and likely meant, for many Jews, the end of the worship of their God.

Sidebar 10.1: Flavius Josephus (c. 37–100 CE), born Joseph ben (son of) Matthias, was a first-century Jewish historian born to a priestly father and a mother who came from royal lineage. Josephus participated in the first Jewish revolt against the Romans, leading forces in the Galilee before he surrendered to the Romans in 67 CE. Josephus first served as a slave and interpreter to the leader of the Roman forces, Vespasian, who became emperor of Rome in 69 CE and founded the Flavian dynasty. Josephus then served Titus, the son of Vespasian who took over leading the military after his father. This service meant that Josephus was present when Jerusalem—including the Second Jewish Temple—was destroyed by the Romans in 70 CE. Following the war, Josephus was freed and granted Roman citizenship by the emperor Vespasian. Josephus returned to Rome with Titus and worked under the patronage of the Flavian family, writing first a history of the Jewish revolt against the Romans, called the *Jewish War,* and then a history of the world from a Jewish perspective, called *Jewish Antiquities.* These works serve as the primary—and often only—source for the historical reconstruction of the Second Temple period, especially the Jewish revolt against Rome.

In the *Jewish War,* Josephus describes the complete destruction of Jerusalem by the Romans:

> It [Jerusalem] was so thoroughly laid even with the ground by those that dug it up to the foundation, that there was left nothing to make those that came there believe it had ever been inhabited. This was the end which Jerusalem came to by the madness of those that were for innovations; a city otherwise of great magnificence, and of mighty fame among all humankind. (Josephus, *Jewish War* 7.3–4)

Josephus describes the destruction of Jerusalem as being so complete that a visitor could not tell that there had ever been such a magnificent city present. Josephus also describes the triumphant parade the Romans organized in Rome when the military returned, including a description of the booty that they took from the Jewish temple. In 82

CE, an arch commemorating Titus's victory over Judaea was erected in the Roman forum. A close-up of one of the reliefs on the arch shows the treasures from the temple, including a six-branched menorah. The Arch of Titus can still be seen in Rome today.

Fig. 10.1. Relief from the Arch of Titus showing Roman soldiers carrying the menorah from the Jerusalem Temple. Commons.wikimedia.org.

There was precedent, however, for dealing with the destruction of the temple of the Jewish God. In 587/6 BCE, the Babylonians sacked the first Jewish temple, and the Israelite elite were exiled to Babylon. This marks what is called the Babylonian exile (587/6–538 BCE). During the Babylonian exile, some of the Jewish elite grappled to understand their identity as a people without a temple, and part of their response was to compile a corpus of texts that spoke to the national and religious origins and history of the Israelite people. This compilation, with some variation, would eventually come to be known as the Hebrew Bible. Scholars think that it was during the Babylonian exile that many of the texts that are found in the current Jewish canon (i.e., the Hebrew Bible, which is analogous in some ways to what Christians call the Old Testament) were compiled. Thus, upon the return of many Jews to Judaea in 538 BCE, there existed a sense of Jewish identity that was not reliant upon a standing temple. It was not long, however, before another Jewish temple was constructed in Jerusalem, known as the "second temple."

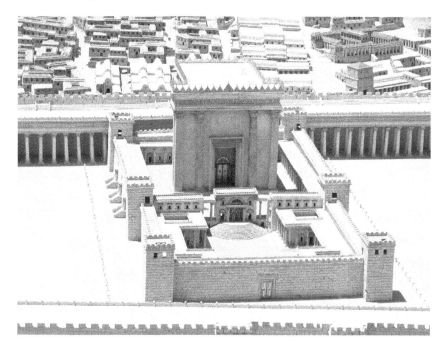

Fig. 10.2. Model of the Second Temple after Herod the Great's renovations. Israel Museum, Jerusalem. Photo by user Ariely; Commons.wikimedia.org.

With the destruction of the Second Temple in 70 CE, Jews once again turned to their national history, and especially to the parallel event from 587/6 BCE, to interpret their current realities. This response is nowhere clearer than in the apocalypses 4 Ezra and 2 Baruch, each written around 100 CE. Both texts draw on biblical characters—Ezra from the books of Ezra-Nehemiah and Baruch from the book of Jeremiah—who, according to the literary traditions of the Hebrew

Bible, experienced the destruction of the first temple or the repercussions of that life-altering event in ancient Israel's historical memory. In this way, while the apocalypses address the aftermath of the destruction of the Second Temple, the situation is conflated literarily with the destruction of the first temple. Accordingly, the texts could offer comfort in the current crisis: while they confirm that the destruction of the Second Temple is horrible, they offer solace by reminding readers that the temple has been destroyed before and that the Jewish people survived and even thrived despite it. Not only this, but both 4 Ezra and 2 Baruch go so far as to imagine a positive consequence as a result of the destruction of the Second Temple: the **eschaton**, or end time, must be imminent. In this way, the texts suppose that—despite the current predicament which seems bleak—it will not be long before the enemies of Israel (in this case, the Romans) would receive their punishment, just as they imagined the Babylonians (who destroyed the first temple) to have been punished by God through the hand of Cyrus the Great, the ruler of the Persian Empire who succeeded the Babylonians in their control over the land of ancient Israel.

4 Ezra

4 Ezra (known as 2 Esdras 3–14 in the Apocrypha) is a complex apocalypse that addresses why God has placed the Jewish people under the rule of the Babylonians after the destruction of the temple. The narrative is split into seven episodes that follow the protagonist Ezra through his questioning of the current crisis. Within these seven episodes, Ezra goes from questioning God's actions (episodes 1–3), to seeing a vision of a woman who then turns into the eschatological **Zion**, an alternate name for the temple mount and also a name used synonymously for Jerusalem (episode 4), to dream visions of the end-times (episodes 5–6). Finally, in the last episode (episode 7), Ezra re-receives the Torah and other divine books, which he is able to share with the larger community, and through them, to teach the people how

to reach salvation. The divisions of 4 Ezra can be seen more easily in the chart below:

Episode Number	Chapter(s)	Type of Episode
1	3:1–5:20	Dialogue
2	5:21–6:34	Dialogue
3	6:35–9:25	Dialogue
4	9:26–10:59	Dialogue/Eschatological Vision
5	11:1–12:51	Eschatological Vision
6	13:1–13:58	Eschatological Vision
7	14:1–14:48	Climax (Dialogue with God and Community, Revelation)

4 Ezra is a **pseudepigraphon**, that is, a text that claims to have been written by an earlier figure of biblical history. In this case, the narrator claims that he is Ezra, a character from what became the biblical books of Ezra-Nehemiah, which would place the narrative of 4 Ezra nearly 600 years earlier than the time that scholars know 4 Ezra was actually written. This may seem odd to modern readers, but writing under other, more authoritative names was quite common in antiquity, and nearly all Jewish apocalypses are works of pseudepigraphy. The selection of Ezra as the moniker of the author for this particular apocalypse is important: according to the narrative of Ezra-Nehemiah found in the canonical Hebrew Bible, Ezra lived after the destruction of the *first* temple, and led a group of aristocratic and priestly Jews home from Babylon to Judaea. So, too, was he responsible for the rebuilding of the temple (Ezra 7) and for the enforcing of Jewish law that had since been neglected (Neh 8). Thus, it appears that the author of 4 Ezra wanted to associate himself (while we do not know for certain the gender of the author, it is most likely that he was male) with the attributes of the biblical Ezra, and to build on them with his portrayal of Ezra in this narrative: as a survivor, a leader, a builder, and a Torah-abiding Jew. 4 Ezra does, indeed, emphasize the need to remember and observe the law. The narrative also encourages the belief in the

imminent eschaton, when all that is wrong with the world will be corrected.

2 Baruch

Like 4 Ezra, 2 Baruch is a pseudepigraphon written around 100 CE. Also like 4 Ezra, the text of 2 Baruch follows the story of a character associated with the time of the destruction of the first temple; i.e., Baruch. In the biblical book of Jeremiah, Baruch appears as the scribe and companion of the prophet Jeremiah. Baruch is essentially Jeremiah's sidekick: assisting the prophet with scribal tasks, running errands, and delivering news when Jeremiah is in hiding. However, in 2 Baruch, Baruch takes on the primary role of leader, prophet, and teacher, while Jeremiah is only referred to in passing as the one who is sent to Babylon to prophesy to the Jews in exile. In other words, in this text, Baruch has become the main prophetic figure.

The beginning of 2 Baruch sets the stage for how the reader should interpret the destruction of the Second Temple. At the beginning of the narrative, the temple is still standing. God informs Baruch of God's intention to destroy the temple, and then tells him about the new, eschatological Jerusalem that was pre-existent from the time of the Garden of Eden (2 Bar 4:1-7). This vision of the eschatological Jerusalem is meant to offer comfort to Baruch; while the worldly temple and city will be destroyed, they are not the *real* temple or Jerusalem. Baruch then observes angels depositing ritual objects from the temple deep into the earth, where they will be kept safe until the time of the coming of the eschatological temple (2 Bar 6:1-9). Finally, Baruch witnesses the angels destroying the walls and foundations of the temple, in order that no other people could ever claim to be better than Israel (2 Bar 7:1-8:2). Thus, even with the devastation of the worldly temple and Jerusalem's destruction, the reader should take comfort, knowing that such destruction was planned by God, that the sacred ritual objects of the temple have been saved, and finally, that no nation could actually compete against Israel's God—only through God's will could Jerusalem be conquered.

2 Baruch offers similar messages of comfort throughout its narrative, focusing heavily on the dialogues and revelations between Baruch and God, as well as Baruch's interaction with his community. In several places, Baruch's visions are apocalyptic in nature, with a special emphasis on the coming of the Messiah, who will be responsible for the judgment and destruction of the wicked. In fact, 2 Baruch's Messiah acts specifically to punish the enemies of Israel. According to 2 Baruch, their destruction is the task of the messiah alone, and therefore *not the job of the Jews.* That is, 2 Baruch promotes pacifism by claiming that the Messiah will judge the wicked in the eschaton, and therefore, the people should not take up arms against their enemies. While 4 Ezra and some other apocalypses also highlight the Messiah's job as judge, 2 Baruch is unique in encouraging the people to remain non-militaristic.

The last ten chapters of 2 Baruch consist of a letter that Baruch writes to the lost tribes of Israel. These chapters, known as the Epistle of 2 Baruch, serve as a kind of summary of the rest of the apocalypse, avoiding apocalyptic language to instead emphasize the lessons that the author of 2 Baruch taught throughout the rest of the book. At some point in the book's reception history these chapters were detached from the rest of the apocalypse and were distributed separately. The Epistle of 2 Baruch must have been popular, since numerous copies have been discovered in multiple languages, while the rest of 2 Baruch was only rediscovered in 1855. It could be that the last ten chapters were more popular because they avoided the apocalyptic imagery found in the rest of the narrative, but it could also be that the pacifism encouraged by 2 Baruch was not well-received. That such pacifism might have met with resistance is evident in the popularity and initial success of the violent Bar Kokhba revolt, which took place in Judaea about 30 years after the writing of 2 Baruch.

Bar Kokhba Revolt

Between 132 and 135 CE, Jews remaining in Judaea once again revolted against the Romans. Led by a purportedly charismatic Jewish leader named Simon bar Kosiba, the revolt constituted the last Jewish armed resistance against Rome. Bar Kosiba attempted to restore Jewish self-rule in a line similar to the rule held by the Hasmoneans, also known as the Maccabees, in the second and first centuries BCE. While it was likely one of his goals, it is doubtful that bar Kosiba ever regained control of Jerusalem from the Romans. What is known is that his campaign concluded with the total expulsion of Jews from Jerusalem and the surrounding countryside, which severely diminished the likelihood that the temple would be rebuilt in a timely manner, if ever again. The failure of the Bar Kokhba revolt also likely squelched the hope in the imminence of the eschaton as it was depicted in 4 Ezra and 2 Baruch.

Bar Kosiba's nickname (Bar Kokhba) suggests that at least some of his followers saw him as a Messiah figure. This nickname represents a play on words for a messianic figure based on a passage from the biblical book of Numbers: "I see him, but not now; I behold him, but not near—a star ("kokhba") shall come out of Jacob, and a scepter shall rise out of Israel; it shall crush the borderlands of Moab, and the territory of all the Shethites" (Num 24:17). This verse, understood in the stream of messianism that arose in the second temple period, and especially in relation to the **Davidic dynasty**, the royal lineage of King David that was promised by God to always exist (see 2 Sam 7:16), was read to refer to the future savior of the Jews, the Messiah. Bar Kokhba, "son of a star," thus becomes the star that emerges from Jacob in Num 24:17, and hence, the long-awaited messiah figure.

Sidebar 10.2: The Jewish Messiah

The word *messiah* derives from the Hebrew word *moshiach* and means anointed one; "Christ" or *christos* in Greek also means anointed one. The title *messiah* was initially used in biblical texts to refer to a person in a divinely ordained position of authority, usually a king. In the Second

---

Temple period, especially in apocalyptic literature, the messiah could refer to an eschatological figure who serves as the agent of God's will. This figure could be portrayed with any of the following traits:

- Mortal

- Angelic

- Royal

- Priestly

- Prophetic

- Militaristic

Not all Jews universally accepted the idea that there might be a Jewish messiah (and the same can be said of Jewish texts, including apocalypses). That being said, when a messiah was hoped for, the type of messiah was diverse and could fulfill any number of the positions listed. In addition, a messiah described in a particular text may be responsible for a national restoration, a cosmic upheaval, judgment of the wicked, or any mixture of these. Even individual texts that portray a messiah may draw upon more than one attribute. For instance, a messiah as found in the person of Jesus, according to the early Jesus-followers, might be described as a suffering servant, as interpreted through Isaiah, or as a kingly messiah, as described through the Gospel of Matthew's genealogy (1:1–17). Likewise, the Dead Sea Scrolls community expected *two* messiahs—one royal from the Davidic dynasty, the other a priestly messiah. In the world of early Judaism, there was no prescribed understanding of a messiah, except as an eschatological agent of God. This is why some Jews came to believe in Jesus as the messiah, while others found the figure of the messiah in

> the person of Bar Kosiba, and others are still awaiting the arrival of a
> messiah even to this day.

Combined with the military nature of the revolt, it is possible that those who participated in the revolt hoped bar Kosiba would bring about the eschaton, when the enemies of Israel would be punished and the temple would be rebuilt. Accordingly, several later sources support the idea that bar Kosiba was a military messiah figure. The well-known Rabbi Akiva is said to have heralded bar Kosiba as the Messiah (y Ta'anit 4:8; see sidebar 10.3 on Rabbinic Literature), citing the reference from the Torah found in Num 24:17 as a **prooftext**, or evidence from a biblical source to prove an argument. According to the narrative, another Rabbi, Yohanan bar Torta, responds to Rabbi Akiva that "grass will grow between your jaws and still the son of David will not yet come!" That is, Rabbi Akiva will be dead and buried long before the Messiah—the "son of David"—will have arrived. Yet another rabbinic source (midrash *Lamentations Rabbah* 2.5) suggests that bar Kosiba's name should not be read as "star" (*kokhba*), but as "liar" (*kozav*). This play on similar sounding words contributes to the suspicions with which bar Kosiba was viewed in rabbinic literature, especially in response to the eventual failure of the revolt. These competing rabbinic positions on bar Kosiba as the Messiah, and the nature of messianism more generally, also illustrate the diversity of positions that various Jewish groups could take with respect to such issues.

Early Christian literature also remembers bar Kosiba in a negative light. No contemporaneous Christian sources refer to bar Kosiba or the Bar Kokhba revolt, and it is not until the church father Eusebius (260/265–339/340 CE) mentions him in his *Ecclesiastical History* 4.6 (Eusebius.

Ecclesiastical History Vol. 1) that there is evidence that Christians were at all aware of the revolt. Eusebius lists the name of the leader of this revolt as "Bar Chochebas," a bandit who relied on the meaning of his name ("star") to argue for a heavenly origin to his leadership. Eusebius also claims that followers of Jesus took no part in the Bar Kokhba revolt: if bar Kosiba was seen as a messianic figure, it is understandable why Eusebius would not want to portray Jesus-followers as participating in the revolt, since support of bar Kosiba could be viewed as questioning Jesus's own unique, messianic status.

While scholars have only material evidence from the time of the actual revolt, in the form of coins and letters (see picture below), such material evidence, combined with the later Jewish and Christian literature, suggests that bar Kosiba was indeed seen by some as the messiah—a figure common in many Jewish apocalypses. It is not clear that bar Kosiba was attempting to bring about the eschaton, but it is known that he was trying to re-establish the self-rule of the Jews in Judaea, with the intention to bring about the rebuilding of Jerusalem and the third temple, all of which were to occur in the eschatological age in apocalypses such as 4 Ezra and 2 Baruch.

Fig. 10.3. Coins minted during the Bar Kokhba revolt. Note the temple imagery (left), and the lulav and etrog (right) which are Jewish ritual objects associated with the holiday of Sukkot, also called Tabernacles. Commons.wikimedia.org.

Judaism in the Rabbinic Period

4 Ezra, 2 Baruch, and the Bar Kokhba revolt were three distinct Jewish responses to the destruction of the Second Temple. Following the failure of the Bar Kokhba revolt and the subsequent banning of all Jews from Jerusalem, Jews remained in a precarious social position. The failed revolts meant that Jews as a whole were already on the wrong side of the Roman authorities, and contributing to these tensions were suspicions around a rapidly growing Jewish sect known as Christians. Thus, it should come as no surprise that the Jewish group that rose to dominance after the Bar Kokhba revolt appears to have downplayed apocalyptic and messianic expectations in exchange for a focus on self-preservation under Roman rule. This response to the situation caused by the destruction of the Second Temple can be found through the literature created by the rabbis. The Hebrew word *rabbi* means "my teacher," although in the rabbinic period it also refers to any member of Jewish society who produced literature between the second and sixth centuries CE. The rabbis were groups of Jews in the Roman province of Palestine and in Babylon who were learned in specific interpretations of Jewish scripture. These groups attempted to enforce their understanding of what it meant to be a Jew onto other non-rabbinic Jews after the destruction of the Second Temple. The rabbis eventually succeeded, and rabbinic Judaism succeeded in becoming the primary form of Judaism even up to the present day.

The rabbis attempted to establish their authority at least as early as 200 CE, and eventually succeeded in leading many Jewish communities to an understanding of Jewish practice and scripture as they knew it. The early rabbis, led by the patriarchate headed by Rabbi Judah the Prince, began compiling their oral traditions. Since the two apocalypses discussed above—4 Ezra and 2 Baruch—were written after the destruction of the Second Temple and in response to that destruction, and since the early Christian apocalypse called the Book of Revelation (the last book in the canonical New Testament; see chapters six and eight in this volume) was written around the same time as these apocalypses, one might expect that the earliest rabbinic literature would also contain apocalypses. Interestingly, however, rabbinic literature does not include any developed sense of apocalypticism, nor was there a concern for the imminence of the end time in their literature.

Instead, the Mishnah, the earliest of the rabbinic texts, is predominantly a law code focused on the (by this time, defunct) temple and its cult, as well as on specific legal cases and their resolution. The Mishnah, then, like the post-destruction apocalypses and the Bar Kokhba revolt, is a response to the destruction of the Second Temple; however, the Mishnah does not address the eschaton with any sense of urgency. Instead, some scholars suggest that the Mishnah's lack of apocalypticism or emphasis on the eschaton are a result of either the rabbis' confidence in the impending restoration of the temple, or because the rabbis were attempting to correctly remember *how* to serve God through temple worship, and did so through their study. Neither of these options, however, addresses the lack of apocalypticism in the Mishnah.

Sidebar 10.3: Rabbinic Literature

While this section focuses only on the Mishnah, this is only one of numerous types of literature written and compiled by the rabbis.

Mishnah: The collection of Jewish legal traditions compiled by the patriarch Rabbi Judah the Prince, circa 200 CE. When Mishnah is presented in the lowercase (mishnah), it refers to a specific paragraph of code from the Mishnah.

Tosefta: Compiled around 250 CE, this legal code contained the traditions not included in the Mishnah, and is arranged in a similar manner.

Gemara: Commentary on the Mishnah by later rabbis. Codified in the Talmud (see Talmud, below).

Talmud: The collective enterprise of the Mishnah combined with the Gemara. There are two talmudim (plural of talmud), based on their geographic origins. The Jerusalem Talmud (y) was codified in the fourth century CE in the Galilee, while the Babylonian Talmud (b) was codified around the late fifth and early sixth centuries CE in Babylonia. While there are overlapping traditions in the talmudim, there are also many differences.

Midrash: A type of biblical interpretation that was popular in rabbinic times as well as earlier. The term can also refer to a collection of interpretations compiled by the rabbis.

The Social World of the Mishnah

As discussed above, the Mishnah—and subsequent rabbinic literature—was compiled only after the failure of two revolts against Rome. Jews had not only lost the temple, they were now forbidden from entering Jerusalem, which was rebuilt as a Roman city named Aelia Capitolina. Archaeological evidence is unclear, but the Roman Historian Cassius Dio (155–235 CE) claimed that a temple to the Roman god Jupiter was to be built over the remains of the Jewish temple on the temple mount. The devastation caused by the revolts to the Jewish temple cult and to Judaism throughout the Roman Empire was extreme, and it was in this environment that rabbinic Judaism began. The minimal apocalypticism found in the Mishnah and subsequent rabbinic literature is likely a result of such a hostile historical context, and an environment in which many Jews were now trying to keep the attention of the Romans away from them. That is, after two failed revolts, the rabbis did not want to make matters worse by focusing on the things most often emphasized in the apocalypses: an idealized future where the enemies of the Jews would be punished and the temple would be rebuilt. The apocalypses look to the near future where the Romans would soon be punished, and Bar Kokhba's militarized attempt to throw off the Roman yoke and establish self-rule led to a violent end for many Jews. Thus, the Mishnah remembers the temple cult as an idealized past, a way to maintain knowledge of proper observance. Accordingly, any material that *could* be construed as encouraging active revolt against the Romans is nonexistent. The rabbis, as seen through their literature, primarily turned away from discussions of the interactions of Jews with non-Jews, and instead focused on how Jews should observe the laws in the Torah, and through that, how they should worship God.

The rabbis' inclination to avoid drawing attention to themselves may have resulted not only from the failed results of the revolts, but due to the spread of another Jewish group known by that time as the Christians. While Christianity would soon become a religion that was made up predominantly of **gentiles** (that is, non-Jews), it began as a sect well within Judaism. As such, it took time before the Roman authorities considered the early Christians as a group distinct from the Jews. As Christianity grew, its leaders attempted to distinguish themselves from Jews who did not believe in the messianic status of Jesus. Likewise, the rabbis attempted to distinguish themselves from the "heretical" Jews who believed Jesus was the christ (from the Greek *christos*, meaning "messiah"). The discussion of when and how Jewish and Christian groups distinguished themselves from one another during this period is called the **parting of the ways** in scholarly literature. There is significant disagreement among scholars as to whether this separation happened early (perhaps around the destruction of the Second Temple in 70 CE) or as late as the early medieval period (sixth through seventh centuries CE). It is most likely that the Jews and Christians separated from one another at different points in different geographic locations and under a variety of circumstances.

During the rabbinic period, the genre apocalypse continued to be popular within early Christian circles, and therefore the rabbis may have shunned this genre in particular in order to further distinguish themselves from the Christians. Thus, the rabbis likely avoided composing and transmitting apocalypses for two reasons: out of a desire to keep away from the attention of the Roman authorities and because of its association with the early Christians.

Mishnah Sotah 9:12-15

Nevertheless, one text from the Mishnah does reflect directly on the end times, and it is worth a brief examination in order to highlight just how different it is from the apocalypses discussed above and found within early Christianity. Tractate Sotah in the Mishnah deals primarily with the laws concerning the woman who is accused of adultery (see Num 5:11-31). At the end of Sotah chapter 9, the text shifts to a discussion of biblical rites that are no longer practiced, including the test given to potential adulterers. Sotah 9:12-13 shifts again to the decline of the Israelite nation. First, the text examines what was lost when the former prophets died (the text is ambiguous about who qualifies as the former prophets in this case), including the "Urim and Thummim" and prophecy as a whole, then it moves to a discussion of what was lost when the first temple was destroyed, including the "savor of the fruits," the "fatness of the corn," and "faithful men," so much so that "there has been no day without its curse." The loss of the "Urim and Thummim" refers to ritual objects associated with the breastplate of the High Priest that, as far as can be determined, assisted with judgment (see Exod 28:30). The loss of these ritual objects, combined with the loss of the former prophets, suggest that everything associated with the priests and prophets were lost at this point. Thus, at that point, God was no longer thought to speak to Israel through prophecy or omens. Likewise, with the destruction of the first temple, the rabbis would suggest that all the "fatness" associated with foods which were previously offered at the temple was now gone. In short, this means that direct access to God through the prophets and the richness of the food of the land were cut off from Israel.

The Mishnah then moves seamlessly from the destruction of the first temple to the destruction of the second (Sotah 9:14), not unlike the conflation of the two events in 4 Ezra and 2 Baruch. Here, during the "war of Vespasian" and the "war of Titus," (i.e., the first revolt against the Romans in 66–72 CE), regular festal activities associated with weddings were abolished due to the military conflict. Next, the "Last War" (i.e., the Bar Kokhba revolt) is mentioned together with a disagreement on whether a bride could move about in a litter (a celebratory way to transport the bride). Sotah 9:15 then proffers a list of thirteen early sages—wise teachers—and the mishnah lists what was taken from Israel upon their deaths. In most of the cases, there is an obvious connection between the rabbi and his attribute: for instance, "When Rabbi Ishmael ben Piabi died the splendor of the priesthood ceased," since Rabbi Ishmael was known to be a high priest of the Jerusalem temple. In the other examples, the sage is associated with a more generic but highly valued attribute, such as "When Rabban Johanan ben Zakkai died the splendour of wisdom ceased." Each of the sages and their attributes suggests a continued decline in the world: what good once existed, like the priesthood or the presence of wisdom, no longer exists.

What is especially noteworthy in these sections of Mishnah Sotah is that the rabbis consistently look back and mourn the changes that took place *in the past*. While the apocalypses may do this as well, they also look forward, anticipating the time of the eschaton when the wicked will be punished and the righteous will be rewarded. The apocalypses offer a sense of hope and comfort, whereas up to this point, this mishnah offers only a reflection on what has been lost. Mishnah Sotah 9:15 finally turns toward a description of the eschatological future. But here, too, rather than offer hope of what will come, the time *leading up* to the messianic age is described. As we find in other texts that describe this age, the mishnah here depicts the earthly situation as getting worse: "With the footprints of the messiah presumption shall increase and dearth reach its height, the vine shall yield its fruit but the wine shall be costly; and the empire shall fall into heresy, and there shall be none to utter reproof. The council chamber shall be given to fornication [. . .]." Here, too, the future is bleak: before the messiah arrives, things will only get worse. The shining hope and comfort that follows in many of the apocalyptic works is largely absent.

However, the mishnah does end on a more positive note:

> Rabbi Phineas ben Jair says: Heedfulness leads to cleanliness, and cleanliness leads to purity, and purity leads to abstinence, and abstinence leads to holiness, and holiness leads to humility, and humility leads to the shunning of sin, and the shunning of sin leads to saintliness, and saintliness leads to [the gift of] the Holy Spirit, and the Holy Spirit leads to the resurrection of the dead. And the resurrection of the dead shall come through Elijah of blessed memory. Amen. (*Sotah* 9:15)

The final section of this mishnah turns away from the eschaton, from which the rabbis did not seem to draw hope. Instead, the passage offers a description of the virtues *any* person can accomplish in the present time, and which will lead, eventually, to the resurrection of the dead (i.e., the eschaton). For the rabbis, virtuous behavior, rather than a messianic figure or cosmic upheaval, leads to a reward of the Holy Spirit and the resurrection of the dead. Such a focus on the actions and day-to-day practices of the individual is remarkably different from apocalyptic texts in which cosmically-oriented events are described.

Mishnah Sotah 9:12–15 is not a typical example of the kind of materials found in the Mishnah (yet another reminder that the rabbis largely eschewed apocalyptic thinking during the period of the Mishnah's composition), but it is an example of how the early rabbis dealt with questions of the eschaton: indirectly, uncomfortably, and predominantly in a negative manner. While the earlier Jewish apocalypses share similar descriptions of the birth pangs of the eschatological era, they ultimately end with the rewards for the righteous remnant and the punishment of the wicked. The rabbinic material seems to assiduously avoid encouraging a strong hope in the eschaton, and instead largely focuses on the here and now (or, rather the there and then).

The Development of Jewish Mysticism

While apocalypticism as a worldview seems to have fallen out of favor in rabbinic literature, a new genre arose within Judaism that had some similarities to apocalypses: Jewish mystical literature. Mysticism differs from apocalypticism on multiple levels. First, unlike the apocalypses that reflect an experience of divine revelation interpreted though a heavenly mediator, mystical experiences reflect private, unmediated encounters with the divine. Many examples of apocalypses and of mystical texts include ascents to heaven and visions of the heavenly chariot (*merkavah*) or throne (*hekhalot*) of the divine. However, the similarities found within the content should not equate a continuous literary trajectory: mystical texts, while drawing from many of the same biblical traditions that the apocalypses drew from, function at a different level. Jewish mystical texts seem to represent written directions for how a worthy individual may reach the divine. The texts suggest that most people will not be worthy to reach this experience; they likewise seem to contain a warning as to the danger associated with attempting to reach the divine. That is, while both apocalypses and mystical texts pass along revelation, mystical texts seem to contain an aspect of praxis in order for an individual to reach the divine, while apocalypses are meant to function as a way to pass along specific information. It is not clear whether there is more to the relationship between apocalypticism and mysticism beyond an overlap in narrative context. What is clear, however, is that the rise of rabbinic Judaism brought with it a decline of the Jewish apocalyptic outlook and an increase in text study, including the study and composition of mystical texts.

Sidebar 10.4

Babylonian Talmud *Hagigah* 14b is a story about what happened when four rabbinic scholars entered paradise. In its original context in the Tosefta, this passage is meant to serve as a warning against transmitting mystical teachings of the divine chariot to unqualified disciples. According to the famous medieval Jewish commentator Rashi, ben Azzai died from gazing at the divine presence, ben Zoma lost his sanity, Acher's "cutting down the plantings" refers to him becoming a heretic after the experience. Only Rabbi Akiva (the same rabbi who thought Bar Kosiba was the messiah!) was able to gaze at the divine chariot and leave unharmed, and tradition has it that he became the greatest rabbinic sage of his day:

> The Rabbis taught: Four entered the Pardes (paradise). They were ben Azzai, ben Zoma, Acher and Rabbi Akiva. Rabbi Akiva said to them, "When you come to the place of pure marble stones, do not say, 'Water! Water!' for it is said, 'He who speaks untruths shall not stand before My eyes' (Psalms 101:7)." Ben Azzai gazed and died. Regarding him the verse states, 'Precious in the eyes of G-d is the death of His pious ones' (Psalms 116:15). Ben Zoma gazed and was harmed. Regarding him the verse states, 'Did you find honey? Eat as only much as you need, lest you be overfilled and vomit it' (Proverbs 25:16). Acher cut down the plantings. Rabbi Akiva entered in peace and left in peace.

Study Questions:

1. What are the reasons that the destruction of the Second Temple was conflated with the destruction of the first temple in the post-destruction apocalypses?

2. How does messianism play a role in the apocalypses? In the Bar Kokhba revolt? In Mishnah Sotah 9?

3. Compare and contrast what you know about the Jewish apocalypses with what you now know about Jewish mysticism. What relationship, if any, do you see between the two?

Bibliography and Further Reading:

Collins, John J. *The Scepter and the Star: Messianism in Light of the Dead Sea Scrolls*. 2nd ed. Grand Rapids, MI: Eerdmans, 2010.

Eusebius. *Ecclesiastical History*. Vol. 1. Translated by Kirsopp Lake. LCL 153. Cambridge, MA: Harvard University Press, 1926.

Henze, Matthias. *Jewish Apocalypticism in Late First Century Israel: Reading 'Second Baruch' in Context*. Tübingen: Mohr Siebeck, 2011.

Himmelfarb, Martha. *Ascent to Heaven in Jewish and Christian Apocalypses*. Oxford: Oxford University Press, 1993.

Josephus, *Jewish War*. Translated by W. Whiston. Grand Rapids: Kregel Publications, 1999.

Reinhartz, Adele. "A Fork in the Road or a Multi-Lane Highway?: New Perspectives on the 'Parting of the Ways Between Judaism and Christianity" in *The Changing Face of Judaism, Christianity, and other Greco-Roman Religions in Antiquity*, eds. Ian H. Henderson and Gerbern S. Oegema. Gütersloh: Gütersloher Verlagshaus, 2006, 280–95.

Schäfer, Peter. *The Bar Kokhba War Reconsidered: New Perspectives on the Second Jewish Revolt Against Rome*. Tübingen: Mohr, 2003.

"The Soncino Talmud on CD-ROM." *Judaic Classics Library* (Davka Corporation Version 2.2. 2001. Print ed.: *The Babylonian Talmud*. Edited by Isadore Epstein, 30 vols. [London: Soncino Press, 1990]).

Warren, Meredith. "'My Heart Poured Forth Understanding': *4 Ezra's* Fiery Cup as Hierophagic Consumption." In *Studies in Religion/Sciences Religieuses* (2015): 320–33.

11

The End of the World . . . Again?

Apocalypticism in Medieval Christianity

Travis Ables

GETTING PREPPED

1. Can you think of times when you've heard about predictions of the end of the world? What kind of effect do you think that might have on those who believe such predictions? Have you ever thought that "the end" was near?
2. What does the word *mysticism* make you think of? What kind of connection to apocalypses do you think it might have?
3. What do worries about the apocalypse say about the way we view ourselves and the world? Are there political dimensions (issues of power and class) tied up with apocalyptic concerns?

KEY TERMS:

MILLENNIALISM

MILLENNIUM OF THE INCARNATION

MILLENNIUM OF THE PASSION
AFFECTIVE DEVOTION

Introduction

"It's the end of the world."

"Again?"

These two lines of dialogue, from a fourth-season episode of *Buffy the Vampire Slayer*, called "Doomed," demonstrate two things about apocalypticism: how powerfully it can be used to generate dramatic tension, and how easily overextended apocalyptic themes can be. The end of the world is the ultimate threat, constitutes the very highest dramatic stakes; but it also immediately raises the question of what happens *after* the end of the world fails to come to pass.

By this point in its run, *Buffy* had evoked the end of the world so many times that it had started to wink at its audience about it, but it also was continuing a theme begun in the first season that used the apocalypse as a backdrop to sketch major character transitions. Much of the episode deals with the fallout of the previous installment, a famous episode entitled "Hush," in which a supernatural silence had fallen upon Sunnydale, a silence that allowed a band of demons to surgically extract the still-beating hearts of their victims without fear of discovery. Buffy stopped them, of course; but "Hush" was all about how the suspension of the normal order of things was, at the same time, both a threat (in the hush, no one can hear you scream!) and a kind of revelation. In the loss of speech, Buffy and her friends (including a boyfriend whom she was hiding her Slayerhood from) had to find new ways to communicate, and it turned out that being forced to communicate through gesture and physical touch opened up spaces for characters to express things to one another they had been unable to vocalize. Secrets were spilled, hidden desires were revealed, and relationships were permanently altered.

It is something of a truism that apocalyptic texts—or TV episodes, especially genres such as sci-fi and fantasy—reveal the anxieties of the age that produces them, be it the crushing oppression of imperial Rome in the book of Revelation, the post-Hiroshima nuclear trauma of the original *Godzilla* films, or the banal horror of everyday life in high school (dramatized as a monster movie). This is obvious in the Middle Ages, too—for example, in the explosion of apocalyptic curiosity surrounding the dawn of the year 1000, as well as the fervor surrounding the Crusades and the Black Death in the eleventh and fifteenth centuries. But what these events reveal, and what the sketch from *Buffy the Vampire Slayer* above suggests, is that what happens in the wake of apocalyptic expectations—and their failure—is at least as interesting as the predictions of the end themselves.

The end of the world, again: failed apocalyptic expectations abound in the Middle Ages, but instead of focusing on this, we will investigate how apocalyptic disappointment reshaped practices of devotion, understandings of the self and community, and conceptions of agency and authority. Apocalyptic themes and texts produce certain kinds of people. So far, the end has not yet come, but Christians keep coming up with new and creative ways of responding. This chapter will document a few.

In popular parlance, *apocalyptic* calls to mind the scenes from, say, a Roland Emmerich film (*Independence Day, The Day after Tomorrow, 2012*): epic catastrophe, mass death and disaster, destruction that is both seemingly uncontainable and universal. At least in blockbuster versions, apocalypses also most often entail the survival of the worthy few (invariably, the rugged hero and *his* family). In biblical and intertestamental texts, it has a much different sense, as an "uncovering," and by extension, "revelation," of a larger reality that is accessible only to those who are able to see it, usually by a supernatural gift. But the focus of the apocalypses on eschatological (end-of-time) matters as part and parcel of this "revelation"—both in medieval times and in other epochs—means that the word often lends itself to the sense more familiar to us: a concern with the imminent end of the age, the goal toward which history is moving, and the fate of the chosen community within the tribulations of that history. So, in medieval studies (as well as in modern discourse), *apocalyptic* typically refers to the imminence of the end of the age and the accompanying expectation; moreover, this expectation is often *millenial* or *chiliastic* in character—that is, anticipating the reign of God on earth (sometimes, a literal thousand years, sometimes not), after a period of ruin and apostasy, in which the vindicated faithful live in harmony and peace.

In line with these ideas, this chapter will cover three areas of medieval apocalypticism. The first section explores the importance of the millennium (1000 CE) in medieval Christian chronicles of history. Here, I will also look at the impact of these anxieties on medieval devotion, reform, and social phenomena. Second, I will discuss the re-emergence of apocalyptic themes in the thirteenth century, considering especially the Franciscans and the polarizing figure of Joachim of Fiore. Finally, I will briefly discuss apocalyptic belief and rhetoric in a select subgroup of medieval spirituality—female spiritual writers. The common thread throughout all of this is how apocalyptic expectations constantly morphed into new and surprising forms of spirituality once a predicted "end of the world" scenario failed to manifest. The end of the world . . . again? That's the story of apocalypticism in the Middle Ages.

Between Two Millennia: The Years 1000 and 1033

> After the many prodigies which had broken upon the world before, after, and around the millennium of the Lord Jesus Christ, there were plenty of able men of penetrating intellect who foretold others, just as great, at the approach of the millenniun of the Lord's Passion, and such wonders were soon manifest. (Rodulfus Glaber, quoted in Fulton, *From Judgment to Passion* [2002], 162)

In the first half of the eleventh century, the historian Rodulfus Glaber wrote a history of the world centered on the apocalyptic significance of the millennium. Apart from a spectacular increase in church building (which would eventually help lead to the creation of the modern parish system), some of the "many prodigies" of which Rodulfus wrote included healings of the sick, abundance of crops, and the spread of peace across Europe, but these had been preceded by more pernicious signs: demonic miracles, heresy, famine, and widespread crime. Other writers related even more spectacular phenomena accompanying the millennium. Ademar of Chabannes (d. 1034) describes the vision of a monk who saw a great weeping crucifix in the stars, in the midst of typical apocalyptic natural events (floods, droughts, disease, eclipses; Fulton 2002, 64–65). In the same period, popular interest in the reclamation of Jerusalem from Muslim rule began to simmer, leading to pilgrimages, and soon enough, to the Crusades. The first sporadic and localized persecutions of Jews in Europe also date to this period. The thread that ties all these events together is a widespread apocalyptic fervor, although there was debate about which date was more important, the **Millennium of the Incarnation** (1000) or the **Millennium of the Passion** (1033).

This debate was relatively new; early Christianity had followed a different chronology of history. In the beginning of the fifth century, Augustine's *City of God* had marked a transition in early Christian eschatology. Augustine opposed a literal intepretation of the thousand-year reign of Christ in Rev 20, arguing instead that scripture prophesied the invisible, spiritual era of the church (so-called *amillennialism*; see *City of God* 20.7; Landes, "The Fear of an Apocolyptic Year 1000" [2000], 110–18). Early Christian theologians, such as Irenaeus and Hippolytus, believed in an earthly millennium that would complete the six historical ages of the world (in correspondence with the six days of creation); Augustine spiritualized this idea, but did not reject the idea of a seventh sabbatical age as such. Despite his influence, however, the temptation toward calculable typologies of history and the end was too strong, and millennial thinking persisted. Indeed, there was significant belief around his time, no doubt owing largely to the collapse of the Roman Empire, that the Antichrist was alive and well, and that the end of the age was nigh. So, for instance, Sulpicius Severus, a near-contemporary of Augustine, wrote the *Chronicles* of the world in part to calculate the date of the apocalypse (he guessed c. 500 CE), and in his *Life of Martin*, he stated that Martin of Tours had faced great demonic opposition as the activity of Satan increased before the "end of the age" (Severus 2015, 228–29; 50). Likewise, the bishop Maximus of Turin preached about the impending millennium in vivid pictures of judgment and comfort, placing the fears of his Italian hearers in a cosmic context as the Roman social structure crumbled around them (Daley 1991, 124–67).

The year 500 passed without the end, but beginning with the eighth-century historian Bede, the year 1000—one millennium after Christ—became the new focus of expectation for the final age of history (Landes 2000, 116; Emmerson and McGinn 1992, 38–50). Two centuries later, Adso of Montier-en-Der wrote a treatise that collected the scattered biblical Antichrist traditions into a new apocalyptic schema, and portrayed the Holy Roman Empire as the only force that held back the "mystery of lawlessness" (2 Thess 2:7). But by the the mid-tenth century, Rome seemed to be crumbling yet again: no emperor was on the throne, and once more, invaders threatened. Given this social unrest, and these new speculations, populist preachers began to promote the idea of Christ's return at the millennium. It was widely believed that this last stage of history before the millennium would see the appearance of the Antichrist, and would be portended by the apparent triumph of "heretics," "pagans," and "infidels." Indeed, the first heretics burnt in the Middle Ages, at Orleans in 1022, date to this period (Moore, *The Formation of a Persecuting Society* [2007]).

But, of course, Christ failed to come (either at the year 1000 or 1033!). Rather than eliminating apocalyptic expectation once and for all, the disappointment surrounding the failed millennium instead marked a major transformation in devotion and piety. We can trace the beginnings of the great traditions of affective spirituality to this period—movements of deeply emotional penitence over personal sin and imaginative attachment to the Savior, which would develop into the movements of mysticism, popular devotion, and reform in the later Middle Ages. Increasingly, piety centered on the figure of the suffering, crucified Christ, a tectonic shift that would permanently reshape Western spirituality. As Richard Landes writes, "Since the very crucifixion of Jesus represents the first apocalyptic disappointment of Christianity . . . the intensification of his agony may well reflect the intensity of disappointment at the passage of 1000" (Landes 2000, 114).

The roots of this spiritual transformation lie in the apocalyptic expectation leading up to the millennium—an example of **millennialism**. As the quote from Glaber indicates above, one of the most conspicuous results of the expectation of the millennial apocalypse was the perception that "prodigies," or natural phenomena, were abounding. Yet another result is evident at the popular level. There were mass pilgrimages to Jerusalem in 1026 and 1033, motivated, in part, by the desire to supplant Muslim occupation, but also by the desire to stand where Christ had stood, to "suffer with Christ, to abide with Him, and to be buried that [one] might be granted through Christ to rise again in glory with Him" (Hugh of Flavigny, quoted in Fulton 2002, 66). Likewise, Rodulfus speaks of a pilgrim who, upon reaching the Mount of Olives, "threw himself to the ground, his arms extended in the form of a cross, and with many tears exulted in the Lord: . . . 'I believe that, just as I have followed thee in the body to come to this place, so my soul, unharmed and rejoicing, will follow after thee into heaven'" (quoted in Fulton 2002, 68).

The theme of these quotes is of close identification with Christ—geographic in nature, but emotional and affective in character. They foreshadow a distinct change in the eleventh century in prayer, visual depiction and devotion, and the eucharistic liturgy: an increased emphasis upon the historical Christ, who is no longer simply a triumphant heavenly monarch (as with the famous Pantocrator at Ravenna—see Fig. 11.1), but is now depicted as the suffering, crucified Savior, familiar from the ubiquitous crucifixes of the Middle Ages. The famous Gero Crucifix, for example, is one of the earliest examples of the newly developing piety in medieval material culture: it is a realistic, unflinching portrayal of the dying Christ (Fig. 11.2), a Christ who had died in history in the presence of human beings.

Fig. 11.1. Mosaic of Christ and the angels, sixth century; Basilica di Sant' Apollinare Nuovo, Ravenna, Italy. Photo: user Mattis; Commons.wikimedia.org.

Fig. 11.2. The "Gero Crucifix," late tenth century, Cologne Cathedral, Germany. Photo: Elke Wetzig; Commons.wikimedia.org.

That is not to say, of course, that such a change happened overnight, nor that the failure of the apocalypse was the only cause. Nevertheless, by the end of the eleventh century, texts such as Anselm's *Prayers and Meditations* would witness this unprecedent change: Christ was not just a heavenly monarch or the transcendent Word of contemplation, but a thoroughly historical and fully human figure, whose suffering and passion were vividly real, intimately close, and a focus for devotion. Rachel Fulton documents the process behind this change: first, there was the intense fear of Christ's judgment in preparation for the end of the age, which changed to contrition for his failure to appear (perhaps he had not returned because the church was not yet ready? See Fulton 2002, 60–141). This took the form of a desire to share in Christ's sufferings, the better to express penitence and the better to prepare for the apocalypse (again!), which most Christians still believed was just around the corner. I will examine this spirituality more in the next section.

The Aftermath of the (Non)-Apocalypse: Affective Devotion

We saw above how Rodulfus quoted a pilgrim who fell to the ground on the Mount of Olives, expressing a desire to be present with Christ. Following the failure of the millennium, the shift toward this mode of spirituality is conspicuous: the historical gap between Christ and the believer has contracted as the end draws near, even if the judge yet awaits to be appeased. Anselm's *Prayers and Meditations*, written in the 1070s for aristrocratic lay readers, exhibits this longing and desire for the reality of Christ's historical flesh. The prayers are essentially a recasting of monastic *lectio divina*, the meditative spiritual reading of scripture as compiled in the readings and confessions of the Daily Office, for the benefit of laity; they therefore seek to excite the same patterns of devotion for such readers who cannot benefit from the intensely regimented life of the Benedictine monk. They are written with a heightened rhetorical style designed to excite contrition and mourning over sin in the readers (*compunction*, as it was known in monastic circles), but Anselm does not admonish the reader to identify herself with Christ; he expresses a deep longing to be present *with* Christ and experience his passion firsthand, to express devotion by proximity:

Alas for me, that I was not able to see
the Lord of Angels humbled to converse with men,
when God, the one insulted,
willed to die that the sinner might live. . . .
Why, O my soul, were you not there?
(Anselm 1973, 95)

Thus, the passion of the pilgrim who longs to be present with Christ has been relocated to the cell of the monk and the parlor of the reader of Anselm's treatise.

The traditional division between monk and laity would be further blurred with the mendicant movement of the early thirteenth century: Dominicans and Franciscans left the cloister and went out into the world, living on alms, enacting the mission of the apostolic life, and expressing their devotion as literally as possible in imitation of Christ. Anselm's emotionally realist spirituality was ideal for this new form of faith, which often attracted lay followers, and the Franciscans, in particular, adopted his tempestuous emotional rhetoric to express their adoration of Christ's passion. In this, they followed the practice of Francis of Assisi, whose awareness of his identity with Christ was so strong that the very wounds of Christ appeared in his flesh before he died (the famous "stigmata"). Thus, instead of being content with being imaginatively present at the crucifixion, like Anselm, they focused on direct identification with Christ. Bonaventure, the great mystical writer and minister general of the order in the 1270s, would begin one of his treatises (like Anselm's, written for lay readers) with this admonition: "With Christ I am nailed to the cross. . . . The true worshiper of God and disciple of Christ, who desires to conform perfectly to the Savior of all men crucified for him, should above all, strive with an earnest endeavor of soul to cary about continuously, both in his soul and his flesh, the cross of Christ" (Bonaventure, *The Soul's Journey into God* [1978], 119).

For lay readers, Francis's life made Christ's person and significance concrete and accessible. His re-enactment of the evangelical narrative of Christ bore an apocalyptic significance: he came to be viewed in eschatological terms by followers such as Bonaventure, who, in his biography of Francis, portrayed him as the apocalyptic angel who opens the sixth scroll in Rev 7. By his life of exemplary poverty and perfection, he announced the imminent end (Bonaventure 1978, 179). In fact, Francis so replicates the journey of the humbled, poor, crucified Christ into glory that, in the Lower Church of Assisi, Giotto de Bondone portrayed him in terms that recall the traditional "pantrocrator" (i.e., ruler of all things) motif: as the triumphant Christ rules and judges the world, so now, Francis is crowned in glory.

Fig. 11.3. Saint Francis in Glory, fresco by Giotto di Bondone (1330); Lower Church, Assisi. Web Art Gallery; Commons.wikimedia.org.

Thus, Francis would later be known as an *alter christus*, "another Christ," by some of his followers, who became known as the Spirituals due to their intense and literal devotion to his example of poverty. As the Franciscan order became more and more institutionalized, they became increasingly radicalized, and by the late thirteenth and fourteenth centuries, they viewed the struggle between themselves and the "conventuals" (mainstream Franciscans) as the final apocalyptic tribulation. They believed that the battle was between the apostate church, led by the Antichrist pope, and the faithful remnant, the true Spirituals, who would lead the faithful into an age of peace

221

(McGinn 1979, 156–57). Canonical scripture and the church would be rendered obsolete in the new millennial sabbath that was dawning.

The Spirituals took their cue from the prophecies of Joachim of Fiore, one of the great apocalypticists of the Middle Ages. Unlike the traditional seven ages that early Christians used to calculate the end of the world, for Joachim, there were three: one of the Father, from Adam to Christ; an age of the Son, from King Josiah of monarchical Israel to the present; and an age of the Spirit, beginning with Benedict of Nursia and lasting until the end.

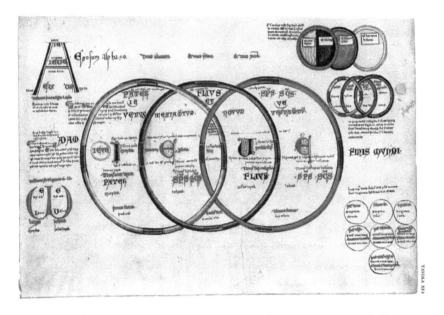

Fig. 11.4. The three trinitarian circles of history, according to Joachim of Fiore (from the thirteenth-century Il Libro delle Figure); Bodleian Library MS CCC 255A f. 7v; Commons.wikimedia.org.

But Joachim's intentions were actually more subtle than simply mapping out a schematic of world history: he was focused on the mystical interpretation of scripture through a trinitarian lens. The Trinity provided an interpretive key for the "concordance" of the testaments, as well as an overall pattern for history. Moreover, Joachim did not write about three distinct *ages*, but rather three overlapping, qualitative states (Joachim's term was *status*): one could move into the third "age" by one's religious dedication and mystical insight. Joachim's apocalypse was a contemplative one of apocalyptic insight, not cataclysmic event—about becoming a certain kind of person.

The end of the world—again? As it happened, an apocalyptic third age did not irrupt into history; instead a new spirituality began with Francis—one focused on identity and cosuffering with Christ, which closed the gap of history between the believer and Christ, and made contemporaneity with him a reality of **affective devotion**, evangelical poverty, and re-enactment of his mission. And, as we have seen with Joachim, apocalyptic spirituality blended with a sense of the mystical, the hidden interpretation of scripture revealed to the contemplative devout. This leads us to our final section, the apocalyptic theology of three female writers.

The Apocalypse in Women's Spiritual Writing

With Joachim, we can see the overlap between two terms: *apocalyptic* and *mystical*, both of which come to modern readers with a great deal of semantic baggage. *Mystical* calls to mind the mysterious, the esoteric, the ecstatic *experience* of something supernatural. But in their original sense, both *mystical* and *apocalyptic* had a much simpler sense: the unveiling of the hidden. The *mystical* in the Middle Ages was, above all, simply the spiritual or allegorical sense of the scriptures, discerned through contemplation, prayer, and solitude. Mystics did speak of ecstatic union with God, but such experiences were rare and fleeting and occurred in the discipline of the monastic, cloistered, or devoted life. Hildegard of Bingen, the twelfth-century abbess, offers a perfect example.

Hildegard is most famous for her *Scivias* (an abbreviation of *Scito vias [Domini]*, "Know the ways [of the Lord]"), a kind of visionary systematic theology. After a revelation in 1150 led her to found the convent of Bingen, she received a subsequent vision that led to the writing of the text; her description of the vision illustrates the importance of understanding mysticism as a species of apocalyptic, and both as a mode of understanding the truth of scripture:

> When I was forty-two years and seven months old, Heaven was opened and a fiery light of exceeding brilliance came and permeated my whole brain, and inflamed my whole heart and my whole breast, not like a burning but like a warming flame, as the sun warms everything its rays touch. And immediately I knew the meaning of the exposition of the Scriptures . . . though I did not have the interpretation of the words of their text. (Hildegard, *Scivias* [1990], 59)

The *Scivias* consists of three cycles of visions covering the traditional orders of the creation of the world, the redemption offered in Christ, and the sanctification achieved in the age and administration of the church. There are twenty-six visions total in the *Scivias*, each beginning with a description of what Hildegard saw, accompanied by an illustration commissioned by her, and followed by an explanation and elaboration of the vision for the reader. They, thus, cover the whole of salvation history—from creation to the end of the age—as a single revelatory work. The fact that for Hildegard, each vision was an "exposition of Scripture," a revelation of the meaning of the Bible, has quite a lot to do with her context, in which the experience of scripture was primarily from the liturgy of the Mass and from the Daily Office, the same template Anselm worked from in the *Prayers and Meditations*. As Anselm sought to channel monastic *lectio divina* for lay readers, so in a different sense, Hildegard's visions reveal the meaning of scripture for cloistered lay women outside of the normal channels of clerical mediation.

That in itself has a fair claim to being apocalyptic, if we understand the term in its biblical sense of "revelation." But, of course, Hildegard also narrates a vision of the end. Vision 11 of book 3 narrates a time of great trial and deception culminating in the witness of Enoch and Elijah, who preserve the Catholic faithful before the end of the age. That Hildegard understood herself to be living in such a time seems clear: drawing on the traditional seven ages of the world, she states that the world is in the last, seventh age, with her own prophetic call indicating the laxity of the church and the peril of the times: "But now the Catholic faith wavers among the nations and the Gospel limps among the people. . . . For this reason, I [i.e., God] now speak through a person who is not eloquent in the Scriptures or taught by an earthly teacher" (Hildegard 1990, 499). Hildegard's vision reflects many of the anxieties of the age, anxieties that ultimately have to do with maintaining Christendom and the reform of the church. But we shouldn't miss how her claim to apocalyptic revelation is a source of authority and agency—something she foregrounds by noting the scandal of her gender.

Concern with the state of the church, and the desire to draw on apocalyptic themes to promote reform, also characterize the work of the late-twelfth-century writer Herrad of Hohenbourg, abbess of the convent of Mount Sainte-Odile. Herrad led the compilation of the *Hortus deliciarum* (Garden of delights), a sprawling pastiche of patristic writings, music, pictures, and narration that recounted the history of the world from creation to consummation, on analogy with Augustine's *City of God*, Sulpicius Severus's *Chronicles*, and Rodulfus Glaber's *History*. Herrad's text is interesting because its vision backs away from the apocalypse as a time of judgment, focusing instead on the end as a way of admonishing her canonesses to work as laborers in the vineyard and to share in Christ's eschatological sufferings (remember the weeping crucifix in the stars—Christ suffers for an unfaithful church). Drawing on the parable of the vineyard in Matt 21, the *Hortus* portrays the faithful as besieged by the Antichrist, but protected by the few diligent priests and teachers who suffer with Christ:

> Christ alone treads the winepress, for by the suffering of the Cross he brought redemption to all believers. For when the saints present their grapes, this signifies that as they sweat with holy and dutiful labors in this vineyard—the Church—and as they imitate and venerate the Lord's suffering, they untiringly bear the weight of the day's heat all the way until the time of judgment. (Quoted in Campbell, "Lest He Should Come Unforeseen" [2015], 102)

Herrad portrays secular (nonmonastic) clergy as being deceived by the Antichrist's preaching. The true church, on the contrary, suffers like laborers in the vineyard; the iconography of the *Hortus*'s illustrations consciously recalls martyrdom narratives that unite the faithful with Christ: "The *imitatio Christi* that is at the spiritual center of martyrdom is also at the iconographic center of the witness of the faithful against the Antichrist" (Campbell 2015, 106). Whereas her contemporaries were preoccupied with the politics of extending and preserving Christendom through the conversion of the Jews and Muslims, and on tensions between the church and the Holy Roman emperors, Herrad's focus is on reform and pedagogy. Still, it illustrates the paradoxical anxiety of Christian empire, which has been characterized by apocalyptic anxiety at its moments of greatest hegemony, and always seems to find its pretensions to universality under threat by the heretical or infidel other in its midst (Moore 2007; Cohn 1970).

A very different kind of apocalyptic spirituality is seen in the next century in the beguine mystic Mechthild of Magdeburg. Mechthild's *The Flowing Light of the Godhead*, written in the mid-thirteenth century, is a compendium of visions, poetry, hymns, moral texts, admonitions, allegories, and so on. She writes of an apocalyptic scenario in which the mendicant Dominican order, with which she was associated, is persecuted by the Antichrist (Mechthild, *The Flowing Light of the Godhead* [1998], 170–75), echoing the Franciscans' perception of themselves as being persecuted for their exemplary spirituality. But she also offers another version of apocalypticism throughout *Flowing Light*, in which the veil of the earthly is peeled back and the mystical (the hidden) is apocalyptically revealed. She regularly portrays vision of heaven, hell, purgatory, and the populations of these spiritual realms. One particularly fascinating vision carries her before a heavenly altar to reveal the operations of the saints behind the scenes of the liturgy of the church. Before the altar stand John the Baptist, the apostles John and Peter, and Mary. John the Baptist carries the lamb to the altar, is dressed in clerical vestments with John and Peter, and with Mary apparently at this side, presides over the Mass. At Mary's behest, the lamb offers itself to Mechthild. The offering at the altar oscillates between being a lamb and a host, a common trope in medieval Eucharistic imagery, but what is startling is the conclusion of the vision, in which Mechthild receives the body and is united to Christ: "I no longer saw the host, but only a bleeding lamb hanging from a red cross. . . . St. John took the white lamb with its red wounds and placed it between her teeth in her mouth. Then the pure lamb lay down onto its own image in her stable and began to suckle from her heart with its sweet mouth" (Mechthild 1998, 75).

The vision is surprising because Mechthild reverses the relationship of nurture from the Lord's Supper: instead of being nourished by the "body of God," as she feeds on the lamb, she is united to Christ (it "lay down onto its own image"), but in turn, Christ feeds from her heart. The Eucharistic or communion imagery is significant: Mechthild wrote at a time in which the communion cup was withheld from laity (a major issue of complaint in the Reformation). Medieval theologians responded with a theology of "concomitance" (which stipulates that the body and blood of Christ is present in the wafer alone, eliminating the need for the cup of wine to achieve the effect of the sacrament), but Mechthild represents a different response, one in which the spiritual benefit of the Mass was given directly by Christ, bypassing the recalcitrant priest altogether. Other women, such as Lutgard of Aywières, had even more unambiguous visions, in which Christ or the cup would fly across the nave and directly to the thirsting communicant (Bynum 1987, 118).

The imagery is of intimate spiritual union, but this union was not simply for her own enjoyment: Mechthild elsewhere describes a vision of her own soul as clothed in the garments of the apocalyptic woman of Rev 12 who defeats the dragon of the enemies of God (Mechthild 1998, 63). Like Herrad, Mechthild wrote with concern over inadequate leadership in the church and desire to share directly in the life and sufferings of Christ. And similarly to Hildegard, Mechthild adopts apocalyptic themes as a source of prophetic authority, for her text ultimately portrays her not simply as concerned with her own union, but suffering with Christ on behalf of his church, the better to bring salvation history to an end.

Conclusion

The end of the world . . . again? When we discussed the *Buffy* episode "Doomed" above, the end of the world didn't seem nearly as big a deal as dealing with the emotional and relational fallout of "Hush." The trick with the apocalypse is navigating the transformations in character that it causes; the end of the world always manages to be delayed, but the aftershocks of failed expectations of the end are not so easily evaded. The apocalypse in the Middle Ages is something like that. We have reviewed the apocalypse as a backdrop for education and pedagogy (Herrad), revolutionary changes in spirituality (Anselm, Francis, Bonaventure), navigating political and ecclesiastical reform (Hildegard, Mechthild), and for unlocking the hidden meaning of the scriptures (Joachim, Hildegard, Mechthild). A common thread throughout has been how the apocalypse opens up a direct pathway to participation in Christ: for medieval people, this meant partaking in his sufferings, but it also meant participating in his mission and cooperating with him for the continuing redemption of the world. The idea that the world would end with the transition into a seventh, sabbatical millennium runs throughout the era, but as tends to happen, the end fails to come and prophets move their calendars forward a few centuries. But as this process runs in the background, something different and potentially more interesting occurs: people look into the oncoming storm and emerge transformed.

Study Questions:

1. How did the belief in the imminent apocalypse transform into a form of spirituality? How is that tied to changes in Christology (belief in Christ)?
2. This chapter emphasizes spirituality in the Middle Ages that focuses on the historic sufferings and death of Christ. How is

this different from contemporary views of Christ? What do you think accounts for those differences? How do you account for the dramatically different portrayals of Christ in figures 1 and 2?

3. How do the terms *apocalyptic* and *mystical* overlap? Are they used differently in this chapter than in contemporary life?

4. One implication of this chapter is that in history, belief in the apocalypse is less important than the *effects* of that belief. Explain that distinction; are there other areas of religion (Christian or otherwise) in which it is helpful to distinguish between belief and its effects?

Bibliography and Further Reading:

Anselm. *The Prayers and Meditations of St. Anselm.* Translated by Benedicta Ward. New York: Penguin, 1973.

Baumgarner, Frederic J. *Longing for the End: A History of Millennialism in Western Civilization.* New York: St. Martin's Press, 1999.

Bonaventure. *The Soul's Journey into God, the Tree of Life, the Life of St. Francis.* Edited by Ewert Cousins. Mahwah, NJ: Paulist Press, 1978.

Bynum, Caroline Walker. *Holy Feast and Holy Fast: The Religious Significance of Food to Medieval Women.* Berkeley: University of California Press, 1987.

Campbell, Nathaniel. "'Lest He Should Come Unforeseen': The Antichrist Cycle in the *Hortus Deliciarum.*" *Gesta* 54, no. 1 (2015): 85–118.

Cohn, Norman Cohn. *The Pursuit of the Millennium.* Rev. ed. New York: Oxford University Press, 1970.

Daley, Brian E. *The Hope of the Early Church: A Handbook of Patristic Eschatology.* New York: Cambridge University Press, 1991.

Emmerson, Richard K. and Bernard McGinn. *The Apocalypse in the Middle Ages.* Ithaca, NY: Cornell University Press, 1992.

Fulton, Rachel. *From Judgment to Passion: Devotion to Christ and the Virgin Mary, 800–1200.* New York: Columbia University Press, 2002.

Hildegard of Bingen. *Scivias.* Translated by Columba Hart and Jane Bishop. New York: Paulist Press, 1990.

Landes, Richard. "The Fear of an Apocalyptic Year 1000: Augustinian Historiography, Medieval and Modern." *Speculum* 75, no. 1 (Jan. 2000): 97–145.

____, Andrew Gow, and David C. Van Meter, eds. *The Apocalyptic Year 1000: Religious Expectation and Social Change, 950-1050.* New York: Oxford University Press, 2003.

McGinn, Bernard, ed. *Apocalyptic Spirituality.* New York: Paulist Press, 1979.

Mechthild of Magdeburg. *The Flowing Light of the Godhead.* Translated by Frank Tobin. New York: Paulist Press, 1998.

Moore, R. I. *The Formation of a Persecuting Society: Authority and Deviance in Western Europe 950-1250.* 2nd ed. Malden, MA: Blackwell, 2007.

Noxon, Marti, David Fury, and Jane Espenson. "Doomed." *Buffy the Vampire Slayer*, season 4, episode 11. Directed by James A. Contner. Aired Jan. 19, 2000. Beverly Hills, CA: Twentieth Century Fox, 2005. DVD.

12

Apocalypse in Islam

Mohamed Mosaad Abdelaziz Mohamed

GETTING PREPPED:

1. How similar or different is apocalypse in Islam to apocalypse in Judaism and Christianity?
2. Is Jesus Christ the Messiah in Islam, whose coming will mark apocalypse?
3. Why is the apocalyptic narrative central in many radical Islamic movements today?
4. What are the major and minor signs that indicate an imminent apocalypse in Islam?

KEY TERMS:
ḤADĪTH
MINOR SIGNS
MAJOR SIGNS

Introduction

There might be no area in Islam that has as many contradictions as apocalypses. The Qur'ān focuses on the Day of Judgment, not any events leading to it, while the corpus of Ḥadīth elaborates on these apocalyptic events. The exceptional recent popularity of the topic among both scholars and laity contradicts its relative theological insignificance in traditional Islamic scholarship. In fact, being a popular theological topic itself is contradictory to Islam's traditional emphasis on rituals and the law, not beliefs and theology. Historically, narratives of apocalypse have regularly been used by all conflicting Muslim groups and factions. Each of these groups and factions knew how to prove that the text was on its own side. Currently, the topic is excessively used by political Islamists, radical terrorists, and Muslim pacifists.

Sidebar 12.1

Ḥadīth is the speech of the Prophet, as preserved in a number of collections. Though it is a foundational text of Islam, it comes next to the Qur'ān in significance. The latter is considered the direct speech of God.

The Emergence of Apocalyptic Narratives in Islam

The reader of either the Qur'ān or Ḥadīth will not miss an urging and warning tone of the imminent end of the world in these texts. Sūrat al-Qamar, the fifty-fourth chapter of the Qur'ān, starts with this verse: "The Hour draws near; the moon is split" (Noble Qur'ān, 54:1; trans. Haleem, 2010, 350). The Hour is one of several names of the Day of Judgment, and the verse warns readers of its imminent coming. The corpus of Ḥadīth includes numerous reports that emphasize the imminent end of the world as well. For instance, in several instances, the texts report that Prophet Muḥammad joined his forefinger with the middle finger and said, "I and the Last Hour have been sent like this!" (Muslim al-Nīsābūrī, 2006, 2:1350) In numerous other reports, the Prophet warned Muslims against the antichrist, who in Arabic is called al-Dajjāl. In one of these reports, he said, "I warn you of him and there is no Prophet who has not warned his people against the Dajjāl. Even Noah warned (against him) but I am going to tell you a thing, which no Prophet told his people. You must know that he is one-eyed and Allāh, the Exalted and Glorious, is not one-eyed" (ibid., 2:1338). Here, the Prophet is both expecting the coming of the antichrist, and providing Muslims signs to identify him.

In fact, there are several reports that show the Prophet actively investigating Ibn Ṣayyād, a Jewish boy who lived in Medina, whom the Prophet suspected to be the future antichrist. In one of these reports, the Prophet asks Ibn Ṣayyād if he bears testimony to the fact that Muḥammad is the Messenger of God. Playfully, Ibn Ṣayyād replies with a question, "Do you bear testimony to the fact that I am the messenger of God?" Muḥammad then asks him, "What do you see?" Ibn Ṣayyād answers, "I see the throne over water!" Approvingly, the Prophet says, "You see the throne of Satan upon the sea!" "What else do you see?" the Prophet asks. Ibn Ṣayyād answers, "I see two truthful ones and a liar or two liars and a truthful one." Here, Muḥammad objects and says to his companions, "Leave him! He has been confounded" (Muslim al-Nīsābūrī, 2006, 2:1336). The investigation indicates how soon the Prophet expected the end of the world to come.

Signs and Stages of Apocalypse

From the textual sources of the Qur'ān and Ḥadīth, Muslim scholars have established a long list of apocalyptic signs that will precede the end of the world. Scholars have further classified these signs into **"Minor Signs"** and **"Major Signs."**

The Minor Signs of Apocalypse

There are different collections of what has been classified as Minor Signs, the numbers of which vary from a few dozens to several hundreds. Scholars have divided these Minor Signs into two groups. The first group includes the signs of events that have already happened. For example, since Muḥammad indicated that his mission was quite close to the end of the world, both his mission and his death were considered two of these Minor Signs. Through interpreting Ḥadīth texts, or even fabricating some of this text, all early intra-Muslim wars were added to this list of Minor Signs, and so were the major conquests of Egypt and Persia.

The rest of the long list reflects a negative perspective of how history unfolds. Ignorance overcomes knowledge; obedience to one's parents disappears; the unqualified assume offices; bad people are the community leaders; adultery and usury proliferate; God's law is forgotten, and so on. In short, the list paints a picture of continuous deterioration of faith and community. These "minor" signs have provided an easy framework of interpretation: a less-than-ideal reality is a sign of imminent apocalypse. Since order, where Muslims follow diligently the Islamic rules and laws, has not come true, a complete disorder, an end of the world, is to be expected.

The second group of signs that has not been realized includes a few good expectations, numerous bad expectations, and a number of extraordinary events. Of the good expectations, one finds signs such as the overgrowth of money and its spread among people, the earth spilling out its treasures, the emergence of a mountain of gold out of the Euphrates, the prosperity of Jerusalem, and the turning of the Arabian desert into valleys and rivers. Bad signs are more numerous: the Qur'ān will be forgotten; Muḥammad's tribe of Qurayš will go extinct; other tribes will revert to paganism; and the Kaʿbah, the most holy house in Islam, will be destroyed. Disorders in nature will become common. There will be frequent huge cracks in the earth, asteroids, congenital abnormalities, heavy rain that does not produce crops, and even the vanishing of mountains. Extraordinary phenomena will top these signs: trees, stones, beasts, inanimate objects, and even sandal straps and whip ends will speak up!

Muslims believe that these Minor Signs will be followed by wars and tribulations. There are numerous reports here. Though not all of these reports are quite authentic, in terms of their attribution to Muḥammad, most of them have the typical structure of "The Day of Judgment would not come until such and such happens." For instance, we find this report where the Prophet says, "The Last Hour would not come until the Muslims fight the Turks—a people whose faces would be like hammered shields wearing clothes of hair and walking (with shoes) of hair" (Muslim al-Nīsābūrī, 2006, 2:1331). In other reports, Muslims will fight the Persians. Al-Bukhārī narrates a report of Ḥadīth that says, "The Last Hour would not come until you fight with Khūz and Karmān from among the ʿAjam" (al-Bukhārī, 1993, 3:1315). Though ʿAjam literally means "non-Arabs," it is traditionally used to refer to the Persians. In addition, most scholars located Khūz in Iran, and Karmān in Western Afghanistan (al-ʿAsqalānī, 1959, 6:607). Even though the Prophet prophesied that tribulations and wars will come from the east (al-Bukhārī, 1993, 6:2598), there are many reports of Ḥadīth that refer to future wars with the Romans. In al-Mustadrak, we find a report that Muslims and al-Rūm, the Romans, will together win a war against a common enemy. However, a religious dispute following this victory will result in a war between the two allies. Overwhelmingly victorious, al-Rūm will proceed to invade the Muslims' land under eighty banners (Muḥammad al-Nīsābūrī, 1993, 4:467).

The most frequently narrated war in today's literature, however, is the predicted war against the Jews. The report in Ṣaḥīḥ Muslim says, "The last hour would not come unless the Muslims will fight against the Jews and the Muslims would kill them until the Jews would hide themselves behind a stone or a tree and a stone or a tree would say: Muslim, or the servant of Allah, there is a Jew behind me; come and kill him; but the tree Gharqad would not say, for it is the tree of the Jews" (Muslim al-Nīsābūrī, 2006, 2:1335).

The Africans are not spared from these wars as well. In Ṣaḥīḥ al-Bukhārī, there is a report where the Prophet says, "The Kaʿbah [believed to be God's house in Mecca] would be destroyed by an Abyssinian having two small shanks" (al-Bukhārī, 1993, 2:579). All these wars are followed by even greater tribulations and wars, many of which are, in fact, among Muslims. (The details of these wars are beyond the scope of this chapter, but interested readers should look to the chapters that address apocalypse in Ṣaḥīḥ al-Bukhārī [al-Bukhārī] and Ṣaḥīḥ Muslim [Muslim al-Nisābūrī]—the two most authentic collections of Ḥadīth.) However, what is of ultimate interest here is the emergence of a heroic character, a pious Muslim leader, who will eventually unite all the believers. This leader will be called al-Mahdī, or the Guided One.

Al-Mahdī, according to several reports, will have the same name of the Prophet: Muḥammad Ibn ʿAbd-Allāh (al-Tirmidhī, 1996, 4:84, 85). His lineage would go back to al-Ḥasan Ibn ʿAlī, the grandson of Muḥammad and the son of Muḥammad's daughter, Fāṭimah, and her husband, the Prophet's cousin, ʿAli Ibn Abī Ṭālib (al-Suyūṭī, 2006, 52). Several reports of Ḥadīth indicate that his rise is preceded by severe intra-Muslim wars, and a time of frequent earthquakes (Ibn Ḥanbal, 2011, 5:2668). He will have supporters and enemies, but his crowning, as the King of Arabs, will happen against his personal will. In *Musnad Aḥmad*, we find a report, in which the Prophet said:

> Disagreement will take place at the death of a Caliph. A man from Medina will come forth fleeing to Mecca. Some of the people of Mecca will come to him, bring him out against his will and swear allegiance to him between the Corner of the Kaʿbah and the Maqām. An expeditionary force will then be sent against him from al-Šām (Syria) but will be swallowed up in the desert between Mecca and Medina, and when the people see that, Abdāl al-Šām (the Saints of Syria) and ʿAṣāʾib (groups of people, each made of 30-40 persons) of Iraq will come to him and swear allegiance to him. (Ibn Ḥanbal, 2011, 12:6446)

Overcoming his Muslim enemies, and uniting his forces, al-Mahdī will prevail over his enemies among non-Muslims. However, peace and prosperity, instead of wars and tribulations, will seem to predominate during his reign. There are several reports that indicate that he will fill the earth with justice and fairness, following the injustice and tyranny that will precede him (Muḥammad al-Nīsābūrī, 2006, 4:600). In another report in *al-Mustadrak*, the Prophet says:

> Al-Mahdī will be born during the last days of my *Ummah* (the community of Muslims). Allāh will provide him with heavy rain; the earth will grow its produce; he will distribute money in abundance among the people; cattle will be in plenty; and the *Ummah* will be held in great esteem. He will live (as a ruler) for seven or eight years. (Ibid., 4:601)

Those prosperous seven or eight years, however, will start with two of the Major Signs of apocalypse: the emergence of al-Dajjāl, or the antichrist, and the return of Jesus.

The Major Signs of Apocalypse

A list of ten Major Signs appears in several authentic reports, and included in these ten Major Signs are always the emergence of al-Dajjāl and the descent of Jesus—or his return from Heaven to earth. For instance, in *Ṣaḥīḥ Muslim*, we find a report of Ḥadīth, where a Companion of the Prophet says:

> Allah's Messenger came to us all of a sudden as we were busy in a discussion. He said, "What do you discuss about?" They (the Companions) said, "We are discussing about the Last Hour." Thereupon he said, "It (the Day of Judgment) will not come until you see ten signs." He made a mention of the Smoke, al-Dajjāl, the Beast, the rising of the sun from the west, the descent of Jesus son of Mary, the Ya'jūj and Ma'jūj (Gog and Magog), and land-slides in three places, one in the east, one in the west and one in the Arabian Peninsula, at the end of which fire would burn forth from Yemen, and would drive people to their *maḥšar* (place of their assembly in the Day of Judgment). (Muslim al-Nīsābūrī, 2006, 2:1327)

Numerous reports of Ḥadīth address al-Dajjāl, and warn Muslims about him. He will claim to be God, but in Ḥadīth texts, Muslims were given a detailed description of him so that they can recognize him and not be deceived by his extraordinary tricks. In reports of Ḥadīth, he was described as short, thick, and with frizzy hair. He does not walk straight because of a deformity in his leg. The most recognizable physical feature, however, is that he will be one-eyed. His left eye is blind, neither protruding nor sunken, and looks like a floating grape (Ibn Ḥanbal, 2011, 10:5641, 5642). Three conspicuous signs will help believers to recognize him: the blind eye, that he rides only on donkeys, and the three letters written in between his eyes, K F R, which is shorthand for "blasphemy."

Al-Dajjāl's actions seem miraculous. It will rain on his order. He will kill a man and restore him back to life. He comes with heaven and hell, a river, water, and a mountain of bread. Yet, Muslims must be aware of his tricks: his heaven is hell, and his hell is heaven. Everything he says is trickery. He stays for forty days: one day of which is as long as a year; one day is as long as a month; one day is as long as a week; and the rest of his days are regular days. He will go everywhere, except to four mosques: the Mosque in Mecca, the Mosque in Medina, the Mosque in Jerusalem, and the Mosque in Mount Sinai (Ibn Ḥanbal, 2011, 10:5641–3). Muslims are advised to steer clear from him in order to avoid his deception (Muḥammad al-Nīsābūrī, 2006, 4:576).

The second Major Sign of apocalypse is the Descent of Jesus, for the vast majority of Muslims believe that Jesus was neither crucified nor killed on the cross. They believe that God made the betraying disciple, Yeahuda, to look like him, and that the Romans killed Yehuda, thinking he was Jesus, while God actually raised Jesus to Heaven. Jesus, according to the majority of Muslims, is alive in Heaven, but will descend to earth at the End of Time. The Qur'ān says, "They did not kill him, nor did they crucify him, though it was made to appear like that to them; those that disagreed about him are full of doubt, with no knowledge to follow, only supposition: they certainly did not kill him—No! God raised him up to Himself. God is almighty and wise" (Noble Qur'ān, 4:157; trans. Haleem, 2010, 65). In *Ṣaḥīḥ al-Bukhārī*, there is a report of Ḥadīth that the Prophet said, "By Him in Whose Hands my soul is, Son of Mary will shortly descend amongst you people as a just ruler. He will break the Cross, kill the pig, and abolish the Jizyah [a tax taken from the non-Muslims, who are in the protection of the Muslim government]. Then, there will be abundance of money that nobody will accept more of it" (al-Bukhārī, 1993, 2:774). Several reports of Ḥadīth describe Jesus as neither tall nor short, white, wearing two yellowish garments, with his head appearing to drip with water, even if it is not wet (Ibn Ḥanbal, 2011, 4:1942). In a report narrated in *Ṣaḥīḥ Muslim*, Jesus will also perform pilgrimage to Mecca with Muslims (Muslim al-Nīsābūrī, 2006, 1:572).

The main role of Jesus after his descent is associated with al-Dajjāl, insofar as Jesus is the one who will kill al-Dajjāl with his spear and protect the believers from al-Dajjāl's deception and evil. The context of this confrontation is especially intriguing. In a chapter titled "The Conquest of Constantinople, the Emergence of al-Dajjāl, and the Descent of ʿĪsā Ibn Maryam (Jesus son of Mary)," *Muslim* narrates this report of Ḥadīth:

> The Last Hour would not come until the Romans would land at al-Aʿmāq or in Dābiq [a place in Syria, close to Damascus]. An army of the best people on earth at that time will come from Medina to confront them. When they will arrange themselves in ranks, the Romans would say: Do not stand between us, and those, who took prisoners from amongst us. Let us fight with them; and the Muslims would say: Nay, by Allah, we would never get aside from you and from our brethren that you may fight them. They will then fight and one third of the army would run away, whom Allah will never forgive. Another third of the army would be killed, and those are the best martyrs in Allah's eye. One third of the army, who would never have doubt in their faith, would win, and conquer Constantinople. And as they would be busy in distributing the spoils of war, after hanging their swords by the olive trees, the Satan would cry: al-Dajjāl has taken your place among your families. They would then come out, but it would be of no avail. And when they would come to Syria, al-Dajjāl would come out while they would be still preparing themselves for battle drawing up the ranks. Certainly, the time of prayer shall come and then Jesus son of Mary would descend, and would lead them in prayer. When the enemy of Allah would see him, he would disappear just as the salt dissolves itself in water. If Jesus were to leave him alone, he would have dissolved completely, but Allah would kill him by his hand and Jesus would show them al-Dajjāl's blood on his spear. (Muslim al-Nīsābūrī, 2006, 2:1342)

There are several reports of Ḥadīth that give a similar account.

However, once we step outside the two most authentic sources of Ḥadīth—namely, Ṣaḥīḥ al-Bukhārī and Ṣaḥīḥ Muslim—we find a prominent presence of al-Mahdī in these final events, who overshadows Jesus. It is al-Mahdī who leads the prayer in Jerusalem, where Jesus descends and prays behind al-Mahdī. Those reports approve the killing of al-Dajjāl by Jesus, but Jesus here is presented as a supporter of al-Mahdī, who plays the central role in these final events. For instance, there is a report of Ḥadīth, where the Prophet says, "Jesus son of Mary will descend [to earth,] so their [Muslims'] leader, al-Mahdī, says, 'Come to lead our prayer!' Then, Jesus will say, 'No, their [Muslims'] leader must be one of them! That is how Allāh is honoring this Ummah [Muslims' community]'" (al-Jawziyyah, 2008, 147). Though the name of the military leader of the final and brutal war at Dābiq, the one who will defeat the Romans and proceed to conquer Constantinople, is never explicitly mentioned in Ḥadīth reports, many scholars have concluded that he is al-Mahdī himself (for instance, see Ḥassān, 2007, 461–68).

The next Major Sign of apocalypse is the emergence of Ya'jūj and Ma'jūj, known in biblical literature as the characters Gog and Magog, which are mentioned in both the Qur'ān and Ḥadīth (see the book of Ezekiel in the Hebrew Bible for the biblical accounts of Gog and Magog). In Chapter 18 of the Qur'ān, they are associated with Dhū-al-Qarnayn, or the Two-Horns One, a great and pious warrior. The Qur'ān says, "They said, 'Dhū-al-Qarnayn, Gog and Magog are running this land. Will you build a barrier between them and us if we pay you a tribute?' He answered, 'The power my Lord has given me is better than any tribute, but if you lend me your strength, I will put up a fortification between you and them'" (Noble Qur'ān, 18:94, 95; trans. Haleem, 2010, 189). Following the Jewish tradition, many Muslim scholars have identified this emperor with Alexander the Great, and the dam with the iron gates that keep Gog and Magog in. The breaking down of the dam, and the emergence of those numerous corrupters, is considered one of the Major Signs of apocalypse (Noble Qur'ān 21:96). In al-Bukhārī, there is a report of Ḥadīth that indicates a gradual breaking of this dam, which has already begun. Here, the Prophet says, "Woe to the Arabs from the great evil that has approached them. Today, a hole has been opened in the dam of Gog and Magog like this." The narrator of the report said, "The Prophet made a circle with his index finger and thumb" (al-Bukhārī, 1993, 6:2609). This report indicates that a small hole, the size of the circle made by the two fingers, was made at the time the Prophet made this warning.

In *Muslim*, there is a report that refers to Jesus as the leader of the Muslim community at that time and who, after killing al-Dajjāl, is warned against the emergence of Ya'jūj and Ma'jūj, and is advised to avoid any confrontations with them. The report is quite long, but there is one especially relevant part, in which the Prophet says:

> Allāh would reveal to Jesus these words: I have brought forth from amongst My servants such people against whom none would be able to fight; you take these people safely to al-Ṭūr (the Mountain of Sinai.) Then, Allāh would send Gog and Magog and they would swarm down from every slope. The first of them would pass the lake of Tiberias and drink out of it. When the last of them would pass, he would say: There was once water there. (Muslim al-Nīsābūrī, 2006, 2:1341–43)

In this report, Jesus and the Muslims pray to Allāh to save them, so Allāh destroys Ya'jūj and Ma'jūj and creates peace and prosperity for the believers.

Two of these Major Signs emerge almost simultaneously: al-Dābbah, or the Beast, and the rise of the sun from the west. In *Ṣaḥīḥ Muslim*, we find a report where the Prophet says, "The first Sign would be the rise of the sun from the west, and the emergence of the Beast before the people in the forenoon. Which of the two happens first, the second one would follow immediately" (Muslim al-Nīsābūrī, 2006, 2:1345). In fact, the Qur'ān too mentions the Beast. In chapter 27, the Qur'ān says, "When the verdict is given against them, We shall bring a creature out of the earth, which will speak to them: people had no faith in our revelations" (Noble Qur'ān, 27:82; trans. Haleem, 2010, 243). These two Signs: the rise of the sun from the west and the emergence of a speaking beast, will be an announcement of the imminent end of the world. At this moment, there will be no space for humans to return to God. The time of voluntary human action would have passed (al-Bukhārī, 1993, 6:2605, 6).

Yet, two final Signs would follow: the Smoke and the Fire. The Smoke is mentioned in the Qur'ān in chapter 44, which, in fact, is called al-Dukhān, or the Smoke! Here, the Qur'ān says, "[Prophet], watch out for the Day when the sky brings forth clouds of smoke for all to see" (Noble Qur'ān, 44:10; trans. Haleem, 2010, 321). The Day is seemingly the Day of Judgment. The Smoke, therefore, is an announcement of a transition from signs of the apocalypse into the first stage of the Hereafter: the Day of Judgment. The Smoke is followed by the Fire, which pushes humans to the place where they will be accounted for their actions. In al-Bukhārī, we find two reports of Ḥadīth. In the first report, the Prophet says, "As for the first portent of the Hour, it will be a fire that will collect the people from the East to West" (al-Bukhārī, 1993, 4:1628). In the second report, the Fire that collects the people comes out from al-Ḥijāz, the western part of Arabia. Here, the Prophet says, "The Hour will not be established till a fire will come out of the land of al-Ḥijāz, and it will throw light on the necks of the camels at Buṣrā (a city in South Iraq)" (al-Bukhārī, 1993, 6:2605). A report in Musnad Aḥmad nevertheless locates the Fire further south in Yemen. In this report of Ḥadīth, the Prophet states that "A fire will come out of Ḥaḍramawt that pushes people away." The Companions asked the Prophet what they should do then. He answered, "Go to Syria!" (Ibn Ḥanbal, 2011, 3:1042)

Apocalypse Past and Present

Ever since the death of the Prophet, nostalgia and romanticization of the past have caused many Muslims to expect an imminent end of the world. Virtually any signs of what some Muslims may see as imperfection can be framed as signs of apocalypse. Reviewing the numerous books on apocalypse, which are available on the market today, one would find a long list of those "signs," such as the spread of adultery, ignoring prayers, drinking wine, the taking of offices by the less qualified, the flourishing and widespread singing, dancing and playing music, the monopoly of a few merchants over the market, frequent lying, expensive dowries, leaders becoming ribald, ostentatious houses, disobedience of one's parents, frequent false testimonies, etc. This imperfect present reality is often contrasted with a romanticized past, where those vices are imagined to have been quite rare. So, as we have seen elsewhere in this volume, dissatisfaction with present circumstances is one major impetus of apocalyptic discourse today in Islam, just as it is in Christianity and other religious movements.

What first promoted the development of a discourse and doctrine of apocalypse, however, was the ferocious war among Muslims in early Islamic history. It is in this context that we find the emergence and establishment of the doctrine of al-Mahdī, which has become the central part of all Islamic apocalyptic movements. The early intra-Islamic wars divided the Muslim community into two denominations: the Sunni and the Shiite. Unlike the Sunnis, Shiite Muslims believe that both religious and political leadership must be combined under the authority of an infallible Imām, who comes from the House of the Prophet. They believe ʿAlī (599–661 CE), the Prophet's cousin and son-in-law, should have been the first Caliph, after the Prophet's death. After ʿAlī, al-Ḥasan (625–670 CE), ʿAlī's son and the Prophet's grandson, should have been the next Imām, then al-Ḥusayn (626–680 CE), his younger brother.

Two important phenomena characterized the early history of Shiite Muslims. First, the Shiite community was fragmented into many groups; most of them ended up as small, or even extinct, sects. It happened because of the lack of authority to assign the next Imām. For instance, al-Kīsāniyyah wanted Muḥammad Ibn al-Ḥanafiyyah (641–700 CE), a half-brother of al-Ḥusayn, to be the Imām. A majority of Shiites at that time wanted ʿAlī Zayn al-ʿĀbidīn (658–713 CE), al-Ḥusayn's son, to be the next Imām after the death of his father. In other words, dispute over proper authority is one of the main reasons why the chain of Imāms has indeed branched out into many groups.

Second, except for the Ismāʿīliyyah groups of Shiite Muslims, who still maintain continuous chains of Imāms, several other Shiite groups have had their chains interrupted by the death of each group's last Imām. Accordingly, some of these groups developed a doctrine of *Ghaybah*, or Occultation. According to this doctrine, the last Imām on the chain did not really die; he is just "hidden." In Twelver Shiite, which claims the majority of Shiite Muslims today, the death of the Eleventh Imām, Ḥasan al-ʿAskarī (846–874 CE) was followed by a claim that he had a four-year-old son, Muḥammad, who went into occultation—that is, into hiding. In Twelver Shiite Islam, Muḥammad, the son of Ḥasan al-ʿAskarī, is believed to be both the Twelfth Imām *and* al-Mahdī, who will come with Jesus at the end of time to establish peace and justice in the world.

The situation among Sunni Muslims is less clear. The complete absence of any mention of al-Mahdī in the two most authentic sources of Ḥadīth among Sunni Muslims, *al-Bukhārī* and *Muslim*, is striking. These two sources do include chapters that address apocalypses. Yet, in these chapters, we find only the descent of Jesus, and his leadership of the Muslim community. In fact, a few prominent Sunni scholars, past and present, denied the existence of al-Mahdī, and referred his existence outside *al-Bukhārī* and *Muslim* to Shiite infiltration of Sunni thought. Nevertheless, a majority of prominent medieval and modern Sunni scholars have authenticated the reports of al-Mahdī that exist in other sources of Ḥadīth, such as *Musnad Aḥmad*, *Musnad Abī Dawūd*, and *al-Mustadrak*. Unlike the Twelver Shiite, however, al-Mahdī in Sunni Islam is not identified by any person who went into occultation. He is simply identified as a future, pious Muslim leader, who will emerge toward the end of time.

For a variety of reasons, several Muslims have been identified with al-Mahdī. This is true both in the earliest periods of Islam and in the present day. For example, Muḥammad Ibn al-Ḥanafiyyah (642–706 CE) was identified by his Shiite followers as the Imām. After his death, a group of those followers identified him with al-Mahdī and claimed that he is still alive, living at Raḍwā Mountain, guarded by a lion and a tiger, next to a spring of water and a spring of honey (al-Ašʿarī 1980, 19). It seems that pious Caliph ʿUmar Ibn ʿAbd-al-ʿAzīz (682–720 CE) too was thought of by some Muslims as al-Mahdī (al-Dhahabī, 2004, 2:2910). Most of those claiming to be al-Mahdī were aspiring politicians, or ardent rebels. For instance, Abū ʿAbd-Allāh Ibn Tūmart (1080–1128 CE), the Moroccan founder of a religious and political movement, called al-Muwaḥidīn, claimed that he was al-Mahdī—a claim that helped him attract masses of people, eventually take the Almoravid Dynasty out of power, and establish Almohad Caliphate in its place by his successor, ʿAbd-al-Muʾmin al-Kūmī (d. 1163 CE). In their sermons, his followers used to describe him as "the Infallible Imām, the Known Mahdī, whom You (God) promised in Your revelation, embraced in Your bright light, the Rising Just, who filled the earth with justice and fairness, after it was filled with oppression and injustice" (Ibn Taymiyah, 1986, 4:98, 99). Another example is Muḥammad al-Mahdī (1843–1885 CE). A Sudanese Sufi, Muḥammad al-Mahdī founded a political religious movement, al-Mahdiyyah, and led a militant war against both the British occupation in Sudan and its Egyptian agents. To attract the masses, he identified with al-Mahdī, and claimed that God and His angels supported him and that it would be apostasy to doubt his status (Šalabī, 2001, 132–34).

On November 20, 1979, Juhaymān al-ʿUtaybī (1936–1980 CE), the leader of a Saudi radical group, al-Jamāʿah al-Salafiyyah al-Muḥtasibah, attacked the Meccan Mosque with two hundred followers and occupied it. Al-ʿUtaybī was convinced that the world had become so corrupt that it must be the end of time. Inside the Mosque, he announced that one of his aides, by the name of Muḥammad Ibn ʿAbd-Allāh al-Qaḥṭānī—a name that conforms with the name of the Prophet, as well as the name of al-Mahdī—is the awaited al-Mahdī himself. He asked his supporters to give their allegiance to al-Mahdī at al-Kaʿbah, something that will also conform with one of the major signs of al-Mahdī: that he will receive allegiance from Muslims at al-Kaʿbah. The armed confrontation with the authorities resulted eventually in the killing of the purported al-Mahdī and the arrest of al-ʿUtaybī and his supporters. This incident should not be interpreted as an isolated event conducted by some eccentrics, but as an event in continuity with other existing movements and trends in modern Saudi Islamic movements.

The twenty-first century is witnessing an unprecedented increase in the popularity of apocalyptic literature, and the daily use of such literature in interpreting contemporary reality. Just during the last year, four persons have claimed to be al-Mahdī: one in Morocco, one in Egypt, one in Saudi Arabia, and another in Iraq. In fact, a Yemeni self-claimed Mahdī, named Nāṣir Muḥammad al-Yamānī, can be checked online, since he has several websites, a blog, a YouTube channel and a Facebook page (see e.g., http://www.mahdi-alumma.com). On these cyber avenues, he answers questions, writes long letters to his followers, refutes criticism, interprets the Qur'ān and Ḥadīth, prophesies about the future, and even sends letters to the King of Saudi Arabia to advise him on how to handle the current war between Saudi Arabia and Yemen (see http://albayan-alhak.blogspot.com/2015/04/blog-post_12.html). There are numerous websites and cyber forums that focus almost exclusively on apocalypses. For instance, a visitor to the Cairo Book Fair will find literally hundreds of shelves devoted to books that address apocalypses. Audiovisual material on apocalypses is not in shortage either. This material, whether informative or interactive, provides readers and users with frames of interpretation to their everyday reality. On a forum such as al-Fitan (http://www.alfetn.org), which literally means "the tribulations," one cannot only consult with other members about the relationship between some news he or she heard over television and a piece of Ḥadīth that was narrated fourteen centuries ago, but this member can also share with other members his or her visions, asking for interpretation. Here, one can find an interesting interaction among an archaic text, a contemporary reality, and a metaphysical experience (http://www.alfetn.org/f26-montada). On this particular site, you may find a question from someone who saw volcanoes erupting in Mecca, or another one who saw the ousted Egyptian President Muḥammad Mursī in a vision and had a brief conversation with him.

What promotes this discursive movement among the historical

text(s), the present reality and the imagined future are geographical and racial descriptions in addition to the features of a few mythical characters. When the text is recalled, it brings forth places, such as Afghanistan, Yemen, Iraq and Syria, and the names of specific cities that continue to be important to Muslims today, such as Mecca, Medina, Constantinople, Damascus and Dābiq. The fact that Khurāsān, today's Iran, Iraq, Syria and Yemen are the very countries that witness global and civil wars make the boundaries between the historical text and the present reality easier to remove. When *some* Muslims read in the Ḥadīth about the Army that carries the Black Flags coming from Khurāsān, as the Army that will support al-Mahdī, they easily identify this Army with al-Qāʿidah Group, which has black flags. They may identify it also with ISIS, for it, too, has raised black flags. In fact, ISIS's monthly magazine is called Dābiq, for they are waiting there (in the small town of Dābiq) to fight the "Big Fight" with the Romans (Wood, 2015). In this context, the Romans named in the Ḥadīth come to be identified with contemporary Europeans. Once some Muslims read in the Ḥadīth about the fight with the Jews in Jerusalem, they immediately identify it with today's Israeli–Palestinian conflict. Ṣaddām Ḥusayn was frequently identified with the mythical character of al-Sufyānī, a brutal Muslim leader, who will eventually be stopped by al-Mahdī. In fact, until today, and in spite of his execution, Ḥusayn is still believed by several visitors of apocalyptic websites to be alive, for al-Sufyānī will be killed only on the hands of al-Mahdī (see e.g., "Ṣaddām Ḥusayn is Alive," *Al-Fitan*, http://www.alfetn.org/t16131-topic).

Apocalypse: Present and Future

The question we have to pose at the end of this chapter is important, but simple. What consequences does a prophecy—any prophecy, and not just apocalyptic prophecies—have on a believer's life and action? In *al-Muwāfaqāt*, al-Šāṭibī wrote:

> As an example, Averroes was asked a question about a ruler who had two credible witnesses testifying before him in some matter. Then, the

ruler had a vision, in which he saw the Prophet saying to him, "Do not rule according to this testimony! It is false!" Such a vision cannot be considered in a commandment or a prohibition. Nor does it provide a practical promise or threat. This vision, and all sorts of these things, violates a basic principle of the principles of the law. (al-Šāṭibī, 2003, 2:457)

Since, according to authentic reports of Ḥadīth, a vision of the Prophet *always* comes true (al-Bukhārī, 1993, 6:2567, 2568), al-Šāṭibī must be indeed excluding the notion of *Truth* from his ruling, and from the operation of the law. The truth that the law is interested in is a legal, not ontological, truth. The Islamic tradition classifies reality into *ghayb* and *šahādah*; the first refers to unseen reality, such as the angels and Heaven; the second to the seen reality, such as trees and fruits. The rulings of the law must be based on *šahādah*, not *ghayb*; on physical proofs, not visions.

In fact, the Prophet himself had a vision before the battle of ʿUḥud. In this vision, the Prophet saw cows being slaughtered, a crack in his sword, and his hand getting in a protective shield. His interpretation of his vision was that a group of his Companions will be killed, one of his relatives will be killed, and he should rather stay in Medina to fight his enemy in the city, and not go to fight them in the open desert (al-Qasṭalānī, 2004, 1:392, 393). Nonetheless, he listened to the majority of opinions of his Companions, who wanted to rush to the war outside the city and not wait the arrival of the enemy. Not only did he act against his own vision, but the dire consequences, according to his biographers, matched the vision: seventy-two of the Companions were killed; his uncle was killed. Obviously, he should have sought protection in Medina. Nonetheless, he never blamed anyone for the results. Actions and decisions, again, must be rooted in the laws of the physical world.

It is important here to recall one more report of Ḥadīth. In this curious report, the Prophet says, "If the Last Hour comes while you have a palm-cutting in your hands and it is possible to plant it before the Hour comes, you should plant it" (al-Albānī, 1997, 181). If the report about the Prophet's vision is important in producing legal rules, this report is important in locating the *taklīf*—responsibility or duty. Responsibility, according to this report, must not be rooted in the future, or any foreknowledge of it; it has to be rooted in the *present moment*. Obviously, there is no future for the palm-cutting to grow, but the responsibility of the believer is tied to the present moment. She or he has to plant it!

Similarly, there is a report in the Ḥadīth, considered highly authentic (*ṣaḥīḥ*) by Islamic scholars, that Muslims and Jews will fight at the end of the world. Here, Muslims can *believe* all they want that this war will eventually happen. However, today, their actions cannot be affected by their belief in this prophecy. Practically and legally, the prophecy has no consequences at all. Decisions of war and peace must be taken based on the objective rules of the physical world—that is *šahādah*, not *ghayb*. That is not to deny that individual Muslims may have feelings of hatred toward the Jews or that they root these feelings in the text of the prophecy. However, *feelings*, unlike in Christianity, are not centralized in the legal tradition of Islam. The Qur'ān does not instruct Muslims to love their enemies. It instructs them to be just with their enemies, even if they hate them (Noble Qur'ān, 5: 8). In addition, the fact that anti-Jewish feelings among individual Muslims have emerged only recently after the creation of the State of Israel makes one wonder if those sad feelings really originated from a fourteen centuries-old piece of text, or if an apocalyptic report of Ḥadīth was suddenly invited to contextualize a political crisis? Similarly, is it the mentioning of the small town of Dābiq in a report of Ḥadīth that created ISIS and made the terrorist organization to wait for a global war to start off in this town, or is it simply the fact that ISIS had occupied Northern Syria, including the small town of Dābiq, that gave this old report of Ḥadīth a new significance?

Here comes the necessary question: why then did the Prophet pass on this knowledge? The short answer is twofold. First, like Truth and *ghayb*, this knowledge is a matter of faith, not a matter of action. Second, the consequence of this knowledge is for the believer to get prepared for the Last Hour, by nurturing faith and acquiring piety, not by joining black-flag armies, or waiting for the "Romans" in Dābiq.

Study Questions:

1. What are the "minor signs" of apocalypse in Islam, and what functions did they play in the Muslims' interpretation of reality?
2. What are the Major Signs of apocalypse in Islam?
3. Compare the figure of the Messiah in Islam to that in Judaism and Christianity.
4. Discuss the role of apocalyptic narratives in today's terrorist organizations discourse.
5. Compare the figure of al-Mahdī, and his role in both Sunni and Shiite Islam.
6. What effect does Islam's focus on the law have on Muslims' dealing with apocalyptic prophecies?

Bibliography and Further Reading:

Albānī, Muḥammad Nāṣir al-Dīn al-. *Ṣaḥīḥ al-Adab al-Mufrad li-al-Imām al-Bukhārī*. Al-Jubayl, Saudi Arabia: Maktabat al-Dalīl, 1997.

Amanat, Abbas. *Apocalyptic Islam and Iranian Shi'ism*. London: I. B. Tauris, 2009.

Anonymous. "Saddām Ḥusayn is Alive." *Al-Fitan*. http:// www.alfetn. org/t16131-topic. Post on public forum; accessed Sept. 22, 2015.

Ašʿarī, ʿAlī Ibn Ismāʿīl al-. *Maqālāt al-Islāmiyīn wa Ikhtilāf al-Muṣallīn*. Wiesbaden: Franz Steiner, 1980.

ʿAsqalānī, Aḥmad Ibn ʿAlī Ibn Ḥajar al-. *Fatḥ al-Bārī Šarḥ Ṣaḥīḥ al-Bukhārī*. 13 vols. Beirut: Dār al-Maʿrifah, 1959.

Bukhārī, Muḥammad Ibn Ismāʿīl al-. *Ṣaḥīḥ al-Bukhārī*. Damascus: Dār Ibn Kathīr, 1993.

Cook, David. *Contemporary Muslim Apocalyptic Literature*. Syracuse, NY: Syracuse University Press, 2008.

_____. *Studies in Muslim Apocalyptic*. Princeton, NJ: The Darwin Press, 2000.

Dhahabī, Šams al-Dīn al-. *Siyar Aʿlām al-Nubalā'*. 3 vols. Beirut: Bayt al-Afkār al-Dawliyyah, 2004.

Filiu, Jean-Pierre. *Apocalypse in Islam*. Oakland, CA: University of California Press, 2011.

Haleem, Abdel, M.A.S. *The Qur'an: A New Translation*. New York: Oxford University Press, 2010.

Ḥassān, Muḥammad. *Aḥdāth al-Nihāyah wa Nihāyat al-ʿĀlam*. al-Manṣūrah: Maktabat Fayyāḍ, 2007.

Ibn Ḥanbal, Aḥmad. *Musnad Aḥmad ibn Ḥanbal*. 14 vols. Dār al-Minhāj, 2011.

Ibn Taymiyah, Aḥmad. *Minhāj al-Sunnah al-Nabawiyyah*. 9 vols. Riyadh: Jāmiʿat al-Imām Muḥammad Ibn Suʿūd, 1986.

Jawziyyah, Ibn Qayyim al-. *Al-Manār al-Manīf fī al-Ṣaḥīḥ wa al-Ḍaʿīf*. Mecca: Dār ʿĀlam al-Fawā'id, 2008.

Lawson, Todd. *Gnostic Apocalypse and Islam: Qur'an, Exegesis, Messianism, and the Literary Origins of the Babi Religion*. New York: Routledge, 2011.

McCants, William. *The ISIS Apocalypse: The History, Strategy, and Doomsday Vision of the Islamic State*. New York: St. Martin's Press, 2015.

Nīsābūrī, Muḥammad Ibn ʿAbd-Allāh al-Ḥākim al-. *Al-Mustadrak ʿAla al-Ṣaḥīḥayn*. 5 vols. Beirut: Dār al-Kutub al-ʿIlmiyyah, 2002.

Nīsābūrī, Muslim Ibn al-Ḥajjāj al-Qušayrī al-. *Ṣaḥīḥ Muslim*. 2 vols. Riyadh: Dār Ṭībah, 2006.

Qasṭalānī, Aḥmad al-. *Al-Mawāhib al-Ladunniyyah bi-al-Minaḥ al-Muḥamadiyyah*. 4 vols. Beirut: al-Maktab al-Islāmī, 2004.

Šalabī, ʿAbd-al-Wadūd. *Al-Uṣūl al-Fikriyyah li-Ḥarakat al-Mahdī al-Sudānī wa Daʿwatih*. Cairo: Maktabat al-Adāb, 2001.

Šāṭibī, Ibrāhīm Ibn Mūsā al-. *Al-Muwāfaqāt fī Uṣūl al-Šarīʿah*. 6 vols. Riyadh: Dār Ibn al-Qayyim and Dār Ibn ʿAffān, 2003.

Suyūṭī, Jalāl al-Dīn al-. *Al-ʿUrf al-Wardī fī Akhbār al-Mahdī*. Beirut: Dār al-Kutub al-ʿIlmiyyah, 2006.

Tirmidhī, Muḥammad Ibn ʿIsā al-. *Al-Jāmiʿ al-Kabīr*. 6 vols. Beirut: Dār al-Gharb al-Islāmī, 1996.

Velji, Jamel. *An Apocalyptic History of the Early Fatimid Empire*. Edinburgh, UK: Edinburgh University Press, 2016.

Wood, Graeme. "What ISIS Really Wants." In *The Atlantic*. March 2015. Accessed via http://www.theatlantic.com/magazine/archive/2015/03/what-isis-really-wants/384980, Sept. 22, 2015.

Yamānī, Imām Nāṣir Muḥammad al-. "Urgent from Imām Nāṣir Muḥammad al-Yamānī to King Salmā˜Ibn Abd-al-ʿAzīz." Blog post; accessed Sept. 22, 2015 via http://albayan-alhak.blogspot.com/2015/04/blog-post_12.html.

Yücesoy, Hayrettin. *Messianic Beliefs and Imperial Politics in Medieval Islam: The ʿAbbasid Caliphate in the Early Ninth Century*. Columbia, SC: University of South Carolina Press, 2009.

13

What Kind of World Is Possible?

Biblical Apocalyptic Literature and Visual Art

Brennan Breed

GETTING PREPPED:

1. Are there any vivid images you recall from the books of Daniel and Revelation?
2. When you think of the end of the world, what images come to your mind?
3. Why do you think someone would paint a picture of the end of the world?
4. Can you think of any famous pictures about apocalyptic themes?

KEY TERMS:
IMAGINATION
ICONOGRAPHY
FORMALISM
CONTEXTUALISM

VISUAL EXEGESIS
TRINITY
ILLUMINATED MANUSCRIPT
ICONS
ANASTASIS
LAST JUDGMENT
MANDORLA

Imagination, Apocalypse, and Art

The word "apocalypse" means "unveiling." It is a visual metaphor, implying that reading these texts will remove ignorance, which covers your mind. Apocalyptic texts claim to give you special knowledge that is otherwise hidden from your mental sight. Apocalyptic literature, with its shocking imagery, paints verbal pictures to open the minds of readers to the structure of the cosmos, the true course of history, and the nature of the divine realm. With such vivid visions, it is no surprise that apocalyptic texts have been popular sources of inspiration for artists over the past two millennia.

The verbal images in apocalyptic texts stimulate the **imagination** in both senses of the word. As the philosopher Immanuel Kant explained, "imagination" means two different things: first, it describes the ability to see the world as it actually exists. We all have difficulty properly understanding ourselves and our world, but we can try to use our imaginations to think carefully, analyze, and critique what we think we know, and learn more. Second, the word "imagination" describes the capacity to think of something truly new. People with imagination can think of entirely new and different ways of living. Often, art provides an avenue for imaginative people to create solutions to the world's problems.

Apocalyptic texts do the same: they can re-frame the world, re-narrate history, and offer glimpses of alternative realities. They present interpretive puzzles, number games, and subtle allusions to historical events that force readers to use their own imaginations to make sense of it all with only the few hints given in the text. And the lack of temporal specificity to their imagined futures—it's not clear exactly *when* the end will come—allows all readers throughout history to imagine themselves as part of the solution.

Artists throughout history and across the globe have found deep reservoirs of imagination in apocalyptic texts. They have produced a staggering amount of visual art portraying scenes from biblical apocalypses. One can find biblical apocalypses depicted in an impressive array of media, including sculpture, architecture, paintings, woodcuts, drawings, frescoes, tapestries, stained glass, **illuminated manuscripts**, advertisements, political cartoons, comic books, and more.

When studying visual art in relation to texts such as the Bible, it is important to note that biblically themed images are not usually "illustrations" of texts. Artists do not produce images that represent only what one finds in the words. Likewise, the biblical texts do not serve as captions to the images, nor do they merely label the elements of the picture. The relationship between biblically themed visual art and biblical texts is much more complicated than this. Viewers should examine both the biblical text and the image and ask: what is the relationship between text and image? What happens at the intersection of this text and this image? How does the image depict, depart from, fill out, or ignore the text?

One can study biblical art in many different ways. For example, one might study the **iconography** of apocalyptic art. Iconography is the practice of identifying the subject matter depicted in an image (i.e., "this picture shows the woman clothed with the sun, referencing Revelation 12"), followed by an explanation of what the image means. Often, iconographical studies will search for earlier artistic sources of the image, such as a previous illumination of the Woman Clothed with the Sun that seems to have influenced a later artist. Alternatively, **formalism** is the study of an image based on its visual qualities alone, especially its color, shape, space, line, volume, and texture. One could also ask **contextualist** questions about the life of the artist, the patron who paid for the work of art, and the space in which the artwork was originally displayed.

This chapter, however, focuses on the variety of ways that Christian artists interpret biblical apocalyptic texts, especially Daniel 7–12 and the book of Revelation, in their visual art. Scholars usually call this sort of study **visual exegesis**. By looking at what scenes artists and patrons choose to depict, where the images are placed, and how they seem to read the source text, an art historian can discern how the artist and patron *exegete* (that is, interpret) the biblical text. Visual exegetical studies use the insights of formalism and **contextualism**, but also ask about the role of the biblical text in the production of the image. With attention to visual exegesis, we can learn something about how these texts mattered to people, and what they thought those texts were saying.

This chapter organizes the history of visual interpretation of the books of Revelation and Daniel 7–12 into two broad themes: (1) imperial power, and (2) societal and religious engagement. Within each theme, I note trends and counter-traditions along the way, each of which demonstrate that these images of the End are, ironically, open to endless interpretations.

Imperial Power

Both books of Daniel and Revelation offer literary responses to various problems facing communities living under the regimes of foreign empires. For Daniel 7–12, that foreign power is the Seleucid Empire, and for Revelation, it is Rome. Perhaps it is surprising, then, to learn that artists often depicted scenes from Daniel and Revelation in support of powerful empires.

Until the Roman Emperor Constantine began supporting the Christian religion in the early fourth century, Christian visual art was limited to engravings on personal items, tombstones, and frescoes on catacomb walls. After official recognition by the Roman Empire and with the help of wealthy patrons, Christians soon built churches and other monumental spaces that offered Christians opportunities to display massive artworks, such as mosaics, sculptures, and panel paintings.

In the huge apse mosaic of the Roman church of Santa Pudenziana (fig 13.1), built and decorated around the year 400 CE, Christ appears draped in the robes of the Roman Emperor. He is seated on a throne that recalls both the Emperor's seat and Jupiter's throne on Capitoline Hill. But it also evokes the thrones mentioned thought the book of Revelation, complete with a stream flowing from its base (Rev 22:1–3). Christ's throne rests in the midst of a cityscape that recalls both Rome and the architecture of the New Jerusalem in Rev 21–22. The gleaming mosaic tiles used in Santa Pudenziana, and in many early Christian churches thereafter, evoke the precious jewels from Rev 21–22. The artists used mosaics to make viewers feel as though they had walked into the New Jerusalem itself, symbolized by the space of the church. Above Christ float the four living creatures from Rev 4 (cf. Ezek 1), which many Christian artists represented as the four Evangelists. Overall, the message is clear: the New Jerusalem that the book of Revelation anticipates is emerging in the present through the Roman Empire's adoption of Christianity.

Fig. 13.1. The mosaic in the apse of the sixth-century basilica of Santa Pudenziana, Rome; photo: Sixtus, enhanced by T. Taylor. Commons.wikimedia.org.

Throughout the history of Christian art, especially in the Latin West and in the Eastern Orthodox churches, one commonly finds depictions of Christ enthroned in majesty. Christ sits in power as sovereign of the world, portrayed in the likeness of a Roman emperor, and, with the addition of a beard, the Roman high God Jupiter. In fourth-century Roman churches, these depictions present Jesus as the Roman Empire's patron deity.

Revelation's adaptation of imperial rhetoric invited the Empire to strike back: Eusebius, the first Christian Emperor Constantine's court theologian, argued that Rome was the eternal kingdom foretold in Daniel and Revelation. According to Eusebius, Constantine placed a cross above the entrance to his palace, flanked by images of himself and his sons. Below them was a serpent pierced by a weapon and cast down into the sea, recalling Michael's defeat of the dragon in Rev 12:7–9 (as well as Isa 27:1; Ps 91:13).

Likewise, one of Constantine's imperial coins (Fig. 13.2) depicts his Roman military standard, topped with the Christian *Chi-Ro* symbol, piercing a serpent. Eusebius points out that this serpent refers both to the devil and Constantine's political enemy, Licinius, whom Eusebius had earlier called "that dragon." At once, Rome's supporters were identified as the holy ones, and Rome's enemies were identified with figures of pure evil, such as the Serpent (Rev 12), the Beast (Rev 13), and the Whore of Babylon (Rev 17–18). Instead of radical change constituted by an overthrow of the Roman imperial apparatus, which is portended in the book of Revelation itself, symbols drawn from Revelation and re-appropriated in Roman Imperial contexts ironically functioned to reassure the Romans that the Christianization of the Roman Empire was itself God's decisive intervention in history.

Fig. 13.2. A coin of Constantine the Great, ca. 312 CE.
Commons.wikimedia.org.

It was not long after Rome had adopted Christianity as the official religion of the Empire that its power began to wane. (Many non-Christian Roman authors saw this as no small coincidence!) Even by the time Santa Pudenziana was under construction, the Roman Empire was tottering on the brink of collapse. In response to this, some Christian theologians developed an alternative tradition—one that shares similarities with the original intentions of Revelation—that the Antichrist would arrive only if the Roman Empire faltered (drawing from 2 Thess 2:7, and interpreting the Roman empire as the "restrainer"). Yet, even after the fall of the Western Roman empire, the Eastern or "Byzantine" Roman Empire centered in Constantinople continued to depict the imperial Christ with symbols drawn from Revelation to promote its self-identity as a chosen kingdom.

For the most part, the gleaming Byzantine mosaic domes depict Christ as ruler of the world, sitting on a royal throne, calmly blessing the Byzantine Empire. In the Byzantine imperial church of San Vitale in Ravenna, for example, images of Emperor Justinian and Empress Theodora flank the main altar (Figs. 13.3a, b). Above them, one sees a mosaic of a purple-robed Christ sitting on a globe-shaped throne, from which streams flow (Gen 2:10; Rev 22:1; Fig. 13.3c). Far above the image of Christ enthroned is a lamb adored by angels (Rev 4–5). Such imagery is not only imperial; it also projects a carefully orthodox Christian theology about the **Trinity**, and reflects themes of the Eucharist ritual, which appears on the altar just below it. Nevertheless, it is carefully crafted to reinforce the imperial propaganda of the Byzantine Empire.

Fig. 13.3a, the Emperor Justinian (detail); 13.3b, the Empress Theodora (detail); 13.3c, Christ enthroned. Byzantine mosaics from the Basilica of San Vitale, Ravenna; Commons.wikimedia.org.

Fig. 13.3a.

Fig. 13.3b.

Fig. 13.3c.

When the waves of incredibly successful Arab Muslim invasions began in the seventh century, the Byzantine Empire found itself in danger of complete collapse. Soon, theologians in the orbit of the Byzantine Empire began crafting elaborate apocalypses modeled on Dan 7–12, such as the remarkably influential *Apocalypse of Pseudo-Methodius,* likely written by Syriac-speaking Christians who suddenly found themselves

261

under Muslim rule. Since Eastern Orthodox theologians had long been suspicious of the book of Revelation, apocalyptic motifs taken from Daniel 7–12 and Ezekiel (such as Gog and Magog in Ezek 38–39) provided the bulk of the material used in the production of dozens of apocalyptic texts specific to the plight of the Byzantine Empire. Eastern Christian theologians began to imagine that a decisive divine intervention into world affairs would save the Byzantine Empire from certain defeat and finalize its transformation into the kingdom of God.

Many Eastern Christians venerated images called **icons** because they believed these images offered points of contact with the heavenly realms. Popular icons of the Last Judgment featured imperial symbolism fused with apocalyptic imagery. In fourteenth-century frescoes in the burial chapel of the Church of Holy Savior in Chora (Fig. 13.4), located just within the walls of Constantinople, icons of famous Eastern Orthodox theologians are surmounted by an image of Christ's resurrection, called the **Anastasis**. Christ pulls Adam and Eve from the grave, observed by Israelite and Byzantine kings. Above the resurrection, an image of the **Last Judgment** features Jesus enthroned and surrounded by the heavenly court as a river of fire streams from his throne to engulf the wicked (Dan 7:10–11). Above him, an angel rolls up the heavens like a scroll (Rev 6:14). This type of apocalyptic Last Judgment scene was copied often throughout the history of the Byzantine Empire and even far beyond its borders in Eastern Christianity, affirming the hope that God would transform the weakened empire into a reflection of God's kingdom. But within a century of the painting of Chora's frescoes, the Byzantine Empire would finally succumb to the advancing Turkish armies.

Fig. 13.4. Fresco of the Resurrection (Anastasis) from the Church of the Holy Savior in Chora, Istanbul. Photo: Joseph Kranak; Commons.wikimedia.org.

The Western European kingdoms that emerged after the demise of the Roman Empire adopted the imperial imagery and theology of their predecessor. Charlemagne, the Frankish king who was crowned the new Roman Emperor by Pope Leo III in the year 800 CE, and his Carolingian descendants, promoted the idea that the Roman Empire continued in the Western European monarchs. Successor states, such as the Ottonian Empire and the later Holy Roman Empire in Germany, continued this theology of empire, and depicted scenes nearly identical to that found in Santa Pudenziana.

In the dedicatory page of the Aachen Gospel Book of Otto III (Fig. 13.5), illuminated just before the year 1000, Emperor Otto sits enthroned within the **mandorla** (an almond-shaped space shape usually reserved for depictions of Christ). The four living creatures from Rev 4 encircle him, and God's hand reaches down to bless him. In the Bamberg Apocalypse, an illuminated manuscript also made for Otto III near the year 1000, one can see a nearly identical image of Christ enthroned surrounded by elders and the four living creatures, and a stream of living water emanating from his seat. These apocalyptic images equate the king's coronation with Christ's enthronement in majesty. In this way, the theology of the Roman Empire continued to structure the political theology of the Latin West as it did the Byzantine East. These kingdoms believed that the world-changing event of political Christendom keeps at bay the torments of the Antichrist and God's judgment on the world. Such apocalyptic imagery was actually an attempt to delay any apocalyptic changes in European politics. Latin Christian apocalyptic theology also informed the Crusades as well as the art that accompanied it, focusing on themes of retaining Christendom in the face of Muslim expansion in the Middle Ages.

Fig. 13.5. The Emperor Otto III enthroned, from the Evangeliary (Gospel-Book) of Liuthar, ca. 1000. Abbey of Reichenau, Germany. Commons.wikimedia.org.

Another series of Western European illuminated manuscripts are strikingly different in both style and significance. Beatus of Liébana wrote a commentary on the book of Revelation in Spain around 780, and in the tenth century, a series of illuminated copies of the commentary circulated throughout the Iberian peninsula (modern-day

Spain and Portugal; Fig. 13:6a). Beatus wrote his commentary mainly to combat Arians, perceived heretical teachers who taught that Christ was a lesser being than God the Father. Two centuries later, however, the sudden Muslim conquest of almost all Spanish lands renewed interest in his commentary. Whereas Beatus focused on the book of Revelation because of its exalted view of Christ, Spanish Christians re-read Beatus and Revelation to gain insight into the future of Christendom.

In 929, Muslim ruler Abd-al-Rahman III declared the Ummayad territory al-Andalus (formerly part of Spain and Portugal) to be the Caliphate of Cordoba, and his seemingly growing power terrified the Christians who held a rump state in the north of the Iberian peninsula. Spanish Christians began claiming that the prophet Mohammad was the little horn from Daniel 7, and that the battle for control of Cordoba was a reflection of a spiritual battle occurring in heaven. The illuminations from the Beatus manuscripts reflect this existential terror, as the evil powers are depicted much larger and in more prominent terms than in the illuminated manuscripts belonging to the family of the Saxon king Otto, dating the tenth through eleventh centuries. In the image depicting the serpent and the Woman Clothed with the Sun (Fig. 13.6b, cf. Rev 12), the serpent occupies most of the page, whereas in the Ottonian manuscripts, the serpent is dwarfed by the powerful woman.

Fig. 13.6a. The Woman Clothed with the Sun, her child, and the dragon (Revelation 12); illumination from the Bamberg Apocalypse, ca. 1000. Staatsbibliothek Bamberg, MS a.II.42, folio 29v. Commons.wikimedia.org.

Fig. 13.6b. The same scene from the Facundus
Beatus (ca. 1047), an illuminated manuscript of the
Commentary on the Apocalypse by Beatus of
Liébana (ca. 730–800); folio 186v.; Biblioteca
Nacional, Madrid, MS Vit. 14.2.
Commons.wikimedia.org.

In the thirteenth and fourteenth centuries, wealthy Europeans began
to adorn luxury objects with apocalyptic scenes from Revelation
because of its thematic affiliations with romantic Arthurian legends,
including battles, dragons, and women in distress (cf. Rev 12). These
luxury items were also blatantly nationalistic since they were owned
by wealthy nobles who were immersed in imperial Christian theology.
For example, the massive Apocalypse Tapestry from Angers, France,
woven near the year 1370, was commissioned by Louis I, the Duke of
Anjou. One scene shows the heavenly lamb surrounded by the living
creatures and the elders (Rev 4–5). The lamb clearly holds a cross
adorned with a flag of the house of Anjou, suggesting that God
supported Duke Louis in battle. Meanwhile, the army of the beast (Rev

267

19:19) is populated by identifiably English soldiers—who were, not by coincidence, the Duke's enemies. In numerous contemporary English Apocalypse manuscripts, which illuminate the book of Revelation, the lamb usually holds the symbols of whichever noble family paid for the manuscript. These families believed that battles on earth mirror celestial struggles (cf. Dan 10:20).

European interpretations of the book of Revelation spread with conquest in the fifteenth century. As Christopher Columbus wrote in a letter to a friend, Juana de la Torre, in 1500: "God made me the messenger of the new heaven and the new earth, of which He spoke in the Apocalypse by St. John. . . ." The apocalyptic fervor sparked by European global domination made its mark in the visual arts, as witnessed by Hans Burgkmair's altarpiece *St. John the Evangelist on Patmos* (c. 1510). Burgmair places John in an Edenic paradise that includes the South American macaw, among other tropical species. In his artistic vision, Burgkmair imagines Patmos, Eden, and the Americas to merge into one space that reveals the heavens (Fig. 13.7).

Fig. 13.7. Hans Burgkmair, St. John the
Evangelist on Patmos (1508); Alte
Pinakothek, Munich.
Commons.wikimedia.org.

Another kingdom to use apocalyptic theology and art to reinforce their power was the Solomonic dynasty, which ruled the Ethiopian empire from 1270 until the deposition of Haile Selassie in 1974. Yekuno Amlak, the dynasty's founder, claimed that he descended from the ancient Aksumite kings. King Ezana, an Aksumite king from the fourth century, had been the first monarch in the world to convert to Christianity. The dynasty claimed that its origins lie in the Queen of Sheba's child born from a union with King Solomon. Starting in the thirteenth century, Solomonic royals actively sponsored the Christian faith through the Ethiopian Orthodox Church.

Ethiopian churches' religious art includes illuminated manuscripts, frescoes, processional crosses, and prayer tools. Several popular iconographic themes deriving from Revelation repeat often in Ethiopian church art, including images of the angel Michael destroying the snake, and the throne scene from Rev 4–5. In the Gondar Homilary, a seventeenth-century liturgical manuscript with 49 beautiful illuminations, one image (Fig. 13.8) depicts God dressed in royal robes, surrounded by the four living creatures and the angels Michael and Gabriel. Underneath them, the 24 elders appear dressed like ecclesiastical leaders, swinging incense. The homilary, made for the royal family in its capital city of Gondar, depicted the heavenly court in regal Ethiopian garb. The tight links between the Ethiopian Orthodox Church and the Solomonic dynasty influenced Ethiopian artistic interpretations of apocalyptic literature in a manner similar to Rome and Byzantium.

Fig. 13.8. God the Father with the Twenty-Four Elders and the Archangels Michael and Gabriel, illumination from the Gondar Homilary, late 17th century. Walters Art Museum, MS W.835, folio 89v, published under the Creative Commons license.

For the most part, visual art objects from the ancient past that have survived until the present day are monumental and luxury pieces designed by the state or wealthy patrons. Folk art made by the masses usually does not survive long, and has no powerful patrons to preserve and protect it. Textual evidence suggests that a number of interpreters of Daniel 7–12 and Revelation did not support imperial power, and some were eager to undermine it. But extant visual art from these groups is scarce.

In the medieval period, artistic depictions of the Last Judgment often included grotesque details of individuals descending into the torments of hell. Surprisingly, these depictions of the damned often include individuals wearing bishop's hats, royal crowns, and other signs of prestige. Such royal and ecclesiastical criticism was apparently a message to those in power. For example, St. Hugh of Lincoln reportedly took the unpopular King John on a tour of a Last Judgment sculpture, making a clear point about the image of a king descending into the open, burning mouth of hell.

In the era of the Reformation, the intense theological and political strife between Catholic and Protestant communities led to significant criticism of kings and ecclesiastical leaders in the visual arts—much of which reflected the apocalyptic tenor of the time. For instance, Lucas Cranach, a famous Protestant artist and friend of Martin Luther, created a series of woodcuts to accompany Luther's printed Bible translation that included recognizable portraits of Holy Roman Emperor Ferdinand I and King George of Saxony among those worshiping the Whore of Babylon, who is pictured with the Pope's tiara (Fig. 13.9).

Fig. 13.9. The Whore of Babylon; illustration
from Martin Luther's New Testament (1522)
by Lucas Cranach the Elder.
Württembergische Landesbibliothek
Stuttart; Commons.wikimedia.org.

Many radical Reformers interpreted Revelation as a call to confront the economic and political powers of their day, sometimes in violent revolt. Thomas Müntzer was a Protestant pastor who sided with German peasants in their increasingly heated clashes with the ruling class of landowning nobles. In 1524, he wrote *Sermon to the Princes,* which interpreted Nebuchadnezzar's apocalyptic dream in Dan 2 as a reference to early-sixteenth-century Germany. To Müntzer, the rock that would smash the earthly empires (Dan 2:44) was the kingdom of God, present in the peasants who would soon revolt and establish a new society based on equality. Müntzer later led an army of 8,000 peasants to meet the combined mercenary armies fighting for the nobles at the battle of Frankenhausen.

The peasants' battle flag was a rainbow, which referenced both God's sign after the flood of Noah (Gen 9:14–16) and the throne of God in the book of Revelation (Rev 4:3). When a rainbow appeared on the battlefield, the peasants charged, believing that this was the sign of the final battle (Rev 19:19). They were, however, quickly routed, and the revolt ended with Müntzer's torture and execution. The apocalyptic symbolism of the rainbow flag, however, lived on among those advocating for working-class revolt. Friedrich Engels, a close working companion of Karl Marx in the development of Marxist theory, interpreted Müntzer's revolt as a foreshadowing of the proletariat revolution. German Marxists appropriated Müntzer's rainbow flag, installing it in sculptures and paintings, especially in the Marxist German Democratic Republic. One such example is Werner Tübke's massive oil painting *Early Bourgeois Revolution in Germany* (1987), an homage to Müntzer's failed rebellion that features an enormous rainbow enveloping the battlefield of Frankenhausen.

In the late eighteenth century, the French Revolution caused an incredible panic across Europe. The revolutionaries executed the King and Queen, removed the church from political and social prominence, and instituted a series of drastic social reforms. For some, this was the sign of the antichrist's imminent return. For others, however, this revolution was the first step in a radical transformation of the world that would end in the creation of a more just social system—like the New Jerusalem foretold in Revelation. Poets such as Samuel Taylor Coleridge and visual artists such as William Blake interpreted the era of the French Revolution through the lens of biblical apocalyptic literature. Blake often protested contemporary oppression by drawing apocalyptic images such as his "Whore of Babylon," part of his illustrations for Edward Young's *Night Thoughts* (1797; Fig. 13.10). In this image, the heads of the beast are clearly modeled on a bishop, a king, a judge, and other institutional positions of power, suggesting that the British Empire was an evil system, like ancient Rome.

Fig. 13.10. The Whore of Babylon, by William Blake
(1809); British Museum. Commons.wikimedia.org.

During the era of Nazi dominance in Germany, artists similarly used imagery from Revelation to criticize political and military oppression. Max Beckmann, a German artist who was condemned by the Nazi party for his "degenerate art," fled from Berlin to Amsterdam in 1937 and promptly created a cycle of twenty-seven drawings, interpreting the book of Revelation. In his illumination of the four riders of the apocalypse (Fig. 13.11; cf. Rev 6), Beckmann places the viewer at a table lit by a candle, looking out the window at a blood-red sky filled with the figures of the riders. The rider closest to the viewer is the rider wearing a crown and holding a sword (Rev 6:2–4). One senses the loss of a settled, domestic life in the candle and window, and terror at the havoc that military-political forces had unleashed on the world. In the end, however, Beckmann's cycle hints at hope that the forces of good would ultimately defeat those of evil, which he clearly identifies with the Nazi empire.

Fig. 13.11. The Four Horsemen of the Apocalypse seen from an urban window; from Max Beckmann's series *Apokalypse*. Staatsgalerie Stuttgart.

Societal and Religious Engagement

Readers of Revelation have often identified its criticisms of the Christian church (Rev 2–3) and society (Rev 14:8–10) with perceived problems in their own historical contexts. Francis of Assisi, for example, was a powerful social and ecclesiastical critic of the thirteenth century who advocated a life of poverty, challenged the wealthy elite in the church, and tried to stop the violence of the Crusades. He interpreted his own time as the era of the apocalypse. Many early Renaissance artists embraced apocalyptic themes due to Francis, such as Cimabue, who painted a cycle of frescoes from the book of Revelation in the church dedicated to Francis in the city of Assisi. Likewise, theologians such as Peter Olivi continued Francis's social and ecclesiastical criticisms, which centered on the "worldly" church leaders who desired luxury and power. Peter's statements equating the worldly elements of the church with the Whore of Babylon (Rev 14:8) set the stage for later Reformation-era theologians to make similar claims.

When Spanish missionaries began proselytizing to Mesoamericans in the early sixteenth century, they brought with them the apocalyptic fervor of Francis and Joachim de Fiore (see below), a belief in the crucial role played by the "New World" also espoused by Christopher Columbus, and a thoroughly Western sense of morality. Convinced that Aztec forms of religion were demonic, the missionaries tried—at first, unsuccessfully—to develop ways of communicating the concept of "sin" to a people who had no such idea. In many churches built by the early missionaries, the monks installed images of apocalyptic biblical texts, especially the Last Judgment, to reinforce their message that certain actions led to eternal torment. The frescoes at Santa Maria Xoxoteco San Nicolas de Tolentino at Actopan are notable examples. Early Aztec converts carried with them the deeply held Mesoamerican belief that the world was near its final days, which resonated with missionary teachings. Some Aztec artists, such as Juan Gerson, painted cycles based on Revelation in Mesoamerican churches, including the Franciscan foundation at Tecamachalco, Puebla, as a result (Fig. 13.12).

Fig. 13.12. The Four Horsemen of the Apocalypse,
fresco by Juan Gerson in La Iglésia de Asunción de
Nuestra Senora, Tecamachalco, Puebla.

The Virgin of Guadalupe, a reported apparition of Mary, the mother of Jesus, at Tepeyac, Mexico, in 1531, also draws heavily from Revelation. Juan Diego Cuauhtlatoatzin, a native Mesoamerican man, claimed that a dark-skinned Mary appeared and spoke to him in Nahuatl, the language of the Aztec empire. She told him to build a church for her to honor the fact that she had selected Nahuatl-speaking people to be the basis of a new kingdom. Mary gave Juan Diego many signs, including a miraculously created image of Mary herself depicted as the apocalyptic "woman clothed with the sun" (Rev 12). The image that many religious devotees believe to be the original, now housed in the Basilica of Our Lady of Guadalupe in Mexico City (Fig. 13.13), is one of the most often-copied images in the world. It is perhaps the most potent symbol of Mexican national identity. In both the Mexican War of Independence (1810) and Emiliano Zapata's revolutionary army (1910), Mexican soldiers marched behind banners of the Virgin of

277

Guadalupe, and the United Farm Workers used the image in their organizing of migrant workers in California (1960).

Fig. 13.13. Our Lady of Guadalupe, Basilica
of Our Lady of Guadalupe, Mexico City.
Commons.wikimedia.org.

The Virgin of Guadalupe has also been important in the social history of Mexicans and Mexican-American women. For example, Alma López, a Mexican-born queer feminist artist living in Los Angeles, created the controversial image *Our Lady* in 1999. It is a photograph of a young Latina woman confidently staring at the viewer, clad in a bikini of roses, and wearing a cloak with images of the Aztec moon goddess. López explains that the model, Raquel Salinas, was raped at age eighteen and experienced social isolation. According to López, claiming the identity of the mystical apparition of a powerful woman who had once also been wrongly accused of sexual wrongdoing—namely, Mary—offers healing and agency to Salinas.

Likewise, the Mexican American artist Yolanda López is well-known for her *Virgen de Guadalupe* series of mixed-media images (1978) which depict contemporary Latina women adorned with attributes of the Virgin of Guadalupe. In one image (Fig. 13.14), López herself wears running shoes, grasps a snake by its neck, smiles confidently at the viewer and runs over the small angel below. At once, this image asks the viewer to identify contemporary women with Mary, and also to not hold women to ideal standards.

Fig. 13.14. Portrait of the Artist as the Virgen of Guadalupe, by Yolanda López (1978). www.almalopez.com.

American outsider artist Howard Finster also criticized social ills through imagery drawn from Revelation. His *Find the Four Horsemen of Revelation* (1975) depicts a jumble of horses on a ranch with the Four Horsemen of the apocalypse hidden in their midst, who are merely white men dressed in business suits. Finster's point seems to be that the ones who will eventually bring destruction on the earth are the people already in charge of the social and economic order.

Some artists have focused on the images of harmony and peace in Rev 21–22 in depicting the New Jerusalem. The hope for a New Jerusalem is not purely otherworldly: the re-creation of an earthly city into a paradise has led many people to think of their own spaces as potential sites for perfect community. One such re-imagining is found in the work of twentieth-century Korean artist Yi Choon-Ki, who painted an image titled *Work '86*. Yi Choon-Ki imagines the New Jerusalem by means of Korean symbolism: the four-walled city represents protection and safety, the deep yellow center represents the earth from which society emerges, and the four colored gates at each side represent the traditional compass points as well as the four seasons, which signify a harmonious cosmos. Above the city hangs the light, which illuminates all. While 1986 was a tumultuous time in Korean history, with a rising tide of pro-democracy student protests against the reigning dictatorship, Yi Choon-Ki offers a picture of what such struggles hope to achieve.

The New Jerusalem is also present in the art of Sister Gertrude Morgan, an artist and preacher in New Orleans during the 1960s and 1970s. She painted many images of New Orleans interpreted through various texts from Revelation and Daniel. Morgan decried the social ills of the city and imagined it as sinful Babylon, waiting to be re-made into the New Jerusalem, which she depicted with shotgun shacks typical in the Ninth Ward. As the modern-day John of Patmos, Morgan re-imagined New Orleans as a place of peace and harmony.

Some artists have reflected on the ever-present themes of death, destruction, and the chaos of life through apocalyptic imagery drawn from biblical texts. Revelation is not only about the victory of good over evil: it includes much suffering before the end. J. M. W. Turner, the famous English Romantic artist, painted the often-reproduced *Death on a Pale Horse* (Fig. 13.15; ca. 1830) that may have responded to the trauma of the cholera outbreaks of 1831, or to his own father's death in 1829. From thin, wispy smoke emerges the figure of death, contorted and grasping for the viewer. The pale horse rears its head, as if death has stopped suddenly for the viewer. This painting highlights the suddenness of the "end," in both apocalyptic and personal terms, as well as the seeming meaninglessness of death.

Fig. 13.15. Death on a Pale Horse, by J. M. W. Turner (1830). Tate Gallery, London; Commons.wikimedia.org.

Many Christians throughout history have used Revelation and Daniel in a quest to decipher the secret timing of the apocalypse, perhaps to give some sense of control and meaning to the end of the world. In the twelfth century, Joachim de Fiore wrote a commentary on the book of Revelation and drew diagrams to accompany it, including an image of the seven-headed dragon (Fig. 13.16; Rev 12:3). Joachim declared that the seventh head was Saladin (Ṣalāḥ ad-Dīn Yūsuf ibn Ayyūb), Sultan of Egypt and Syrian and leader of Muslim resistance to the Christian Crusaders in Palestine.

Fig. 13.16. The seven-headed dragon of Rev. 12:3; illustration by Joachim de Fiore in his *Exposition of the Book of Revelation* (ca. 1196-99).

Joachim's images, copied and altered for hundreds of years, were the source of the later flood of charts and infographics that claimed to foretell the end of the world. American dispensationalist Christians have been particularly creative in making visual images concerning the apocalypse. The nineteenth-century Millerite traditions developed particularly captivating graphic depictions of their chronologies; these images usually included the statue from Nebuchadnezzar's dream in Dan 2, the four beasts from Dan 7, and a series of overlapping prophetic calculations, including the numbers 490, 1,260, 1,290, 1,335, and 2,300 (Fig. 13.17).

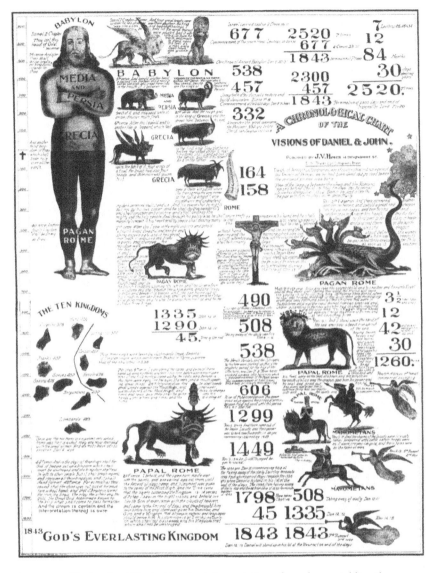

Fig. 13.17. Millerite chart illustrating the interpretation of prophecy, yielding the year 1843 as the End. Commons.wikimedia.org.

Conclusion

Images depicting the books of Daniel and Revelation can be found in many different places, and they mean many different things. As mentioned above, some apocalyptic images reinforce imperial propaganda while others question it. Some images envision contemporary social change, and others offer glimpses of heaven, or windows into the self. Some even attempt to pin down the time of the final hour. There are, of course, many other types of images involving apocalyptic art that are not mentioned here. All of these different apocalyptic images, however, are expressive of the desires and beliefs of the individuals and communities who made them. Images of apocalypse offer a space in which people can break from the constraints of the world in which they live and creatively re-imagine what the world *could* be like. When you look at apocalyptic visual art, there are many questions to ask, and many perspectives from which to see. But one question that all apocalyptic art raises is this: what kind of world is possible?

Study Questions:

1. What are some different ways that artists have imagined the throne scenes in Rev 4–5? How do the artists' contexts influence their depiction?
2. How do people in positions of political and military power tend to depict apocalyptic scenes? How is this different from people who are without such power?
3. What are three different reasons people make visual art based on apocalyptic texts?

Bibliography and Further Reading:

Boxall, Ian. *Patmos in the Reception History of the Apocalypse*. Oxford: Oxford University Press, 2013.

Carey, Francis, ed. *The Apocalypse and the Shape of Things to Come*. Toronto: University of Toronto Press, 1999.

Kovacs, Judith, and Christopher Rowland. *Revelation*. Blackwell Bible Commentaries. Malden, MA: Blackwell, 2004.

O'Hear, Natasha, and Anthony O'Hear. *Picturing the Apocalypse: The Book* of Revelation in the Arts Over Two Millennia. Oxford: Oxford University Press, 2015.

Van der Meer, F. Apocalypse: Visions from the Book of Revelation in Western Art. London: Thames and Hudson, 1978.

PART III

Apocalypticism in the Contemporary World

14

The Last Metamorphosis of Labor

Work, Technology, and the End of the World

Michael J. Thate

GETTING PREPPED:

1. Do only fringe religious groups produce apocalypses?
2. Can apocalypses inhabit the day-to-day "secular" world?
3. Are apocalypses only about the future?

KEY TERMS:
TECHNOLOGY
LABOR
EVERYDAY
REVELATION
POLITICS

Introduction

This chapter concerns itself with the ways in which apocalypses manifest themselves in **everyday** life. As will no doubt be apparent throughout this volume, *apocalypse*, and its cognates *apocalyptic* and *apocalypticism*, can be understood across a range of semantic meanings, depending on the context of investigation. *Apocalypse* can be understood, for example, as a particular genre of discourse or literature, and *apocalyptic* can mean "like an apocalypse." Or, alternatively, *apocalyptic* can refer to a kind of sentiment involving or relating to the "end of the world" in some sense. For the purposes of this chapter, however, *apocalypse* is understood generally as a form of **revelation**. As such, in the exploration of everyday apocalypses, we must always ask what is uncovered or revealed? Who is revealing and who is receiving revelation? And what are the media through which such communication is occurring or being covered up?

Apocalypse, Nostalgia, and Time

Typically, when we think about apocalypses, we think of some cataclysmic event having to do with the distant future: flying saucers or the return of vengeful gods signaling the world's end. But this is not always so; rather apocalypses are very often about the present-day reality of those imagining them. In order to demonstrate this point, I want to introduce the mirror image of apocalypse: nostalgia. Naturally, we tend to think of nostalgia as having to do with the past, but, again, this is not entirely the case. This chapter suggests that both of these complex concepts—apocalypse and nostalgia—are less about the past or the future and more about an understanding of the present moment, and the **politics** of its organization. In both apocalypse and nostalgia, the past and the future are used to leverage present concerns and highlight unease with current states of affairs. Two examples from the world of film best demonstrate this.

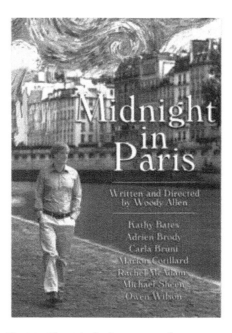

Fig. 14.1. Theatrical release poster for
Midnight in Paris, directed by Woody Allen,
from Sony Pictures Classics (2011).
Commons.wikimedia.org.

Woody Allen's clever romantic comedy, *Midnight in Paris* (2011), is a story about Gil Pender, an aspiring novelist who has settled into a mediocre career as a Hollywood screenwriter, and his growing dissatisfaction with his current life and relationships. Pender and his fiancée, Inez, along with her family, are in Paris, vacationing and wedding planning. Pender, however, is seeking inspiration for his long-neglected novel. The plot is set into motion when late one night, Pender wanders the Parisian streets a bit drunk. At the stroke of midnight, he is met by a group in a Peugeot Type 176, who invite him to a party and magically transport him back into Paris of the 1920s. There, he meets Cole Porter, Alice B. Toklas, Josephine Baker, F. Scott and Zelda Fitzgerald, Ernest Hemingway, Gertrude Stein, Salvador Dalí, Pablo Picasso, Luis Buñuel, and, most notably, the woman he ends up thinking he falls for—Adriana.

As the story progresses, Gil declares his love for Adriana. As he does, a horse-drawn carriage appears and transports them back to the 1890s, *La Belle Époque* of Paris. The two meet Henri de Toulouse-Lautrec, Paul Gauguin, and Edgar Degas, who offer Adriana the opportunity to design costumes for the ballet. Adriana is enthralled by the offer and the allure of their company, while Gil tries to convince her to return to the 1920s for a life together. Adriana wishes to stay on account of her belief that the 1890s were the "greatest, most beautiful [years] Paris has ever known." For her, the 1920s is a generation that "is empty and has no imagination," just as dull as 2010 is for Gil. Gil is dumfounded hearing this, and it is at this point that Gil is met with something of an insight and asks their three new friends what they think the best era is. The three collectively agree it has to be the Renaissance. Gil is then confronted with the truth of the first lines of the novel he has been attempting to write:

> *Out of the Past* was the name of the store, and its products consisted of memories: what was prosaic and even vulgar to one generation had been transmuted by the mere passing of years to a status at once magical and also camp.

Gil's insight is that "the present is a little unsatisfying because life is unsatisfying." And to be happy in the past is, in fact, an illusion because those in that period—in that past—are just as unsatisfied with their era as we are with ours. Seeking happiness in the past is nothing other than a statement of unhappiness in the present. In other words, finding a home in some "golden age" amounts to little more than a realization of alienation from one's contemporary surroundings.

Fig. 14.2. Theatrical release poster for
Apocalypse Now, by Bob Peak; film directed
by Francis Coppola, from United Artists
(1979). Commons.wikimedia.org.

The leveraging of time with respect to apocalypses is well-illustrated in Francis Ford Coppola's *Apocalypse Now* (1979). The film begins and ends with the haunting sounds of the Doors performing "This is the End" (1967). Coppola's use of the song communicates that the apocalypse, understood in this sense as the undoing of the world, is not some distant spiritual interruption into the material world. It is not some "religious" rupture in the "secular" political order. Rather, the horrors of the material world and social order—in this case, the political chaos of the Vietnam War—are themselves the cataclysm. The revelation is that the end is not to come. The end is here. *This is the end.* The apocalypse, according to Coppola and protesters of the Vietnam War, is now. The devils who have ushered in its arrival are politicians with horn-rimmed glasses and shuffling papers.

Why begin a chapter on apocalypses with a reflection on Woody

Allen's staging of nostalgia and Francis Ford Coppolla's imagination of the arrival of the apocalypse? When we hear words like "apocalypse," we tend to think of them as forms of religious thought. Religion, whatever it might mean, is, in many respects, a matter of assorting meaning to time—or a way of allocating time meaningfully. Likewise, the complex "religious" symbols and rituals are about ascribing meaning to and properly dividing time. Apocalypses, likewise, are about measuring the meaning of time. They are about ordering and periodizing time according to some predisposed meaning. And yet, as with nostalgia and the past, apocalypses are about imagining things as they *might one day be* in order to grapple with the way things *currently are*. The projections of the future in apocalypses thus reveal the politics of the present by the author(s)/communities who wrote and read those apocalypses. Put another way, apocalypses are a means of social exploration and organization. One of the goals of this chapter is to demystify this religious-sounding word a bit and to demonstrate how apocalypses are about real-world and real-time happenings and relationships, by showing how apocalypses have impacted contemporary society at practical and policy-making levels. In particular, we will consider how machines, **technology**, and the perceived effect of each upon **labor**, have appeared in a range of nostalgic and apocalyptic tones.

Antagonism and Revolution: Karl Marx and Herbert Marcuse

Fig. 14.3. Photographic portrait of Karl Marx, by John Jabez Edwin Mayall; 1875. International Institute of Social History, Amsterdam; Commons.wikimedia.org.

Karl Marx (1818–83) begins our exploration of the relationship between machines, **labor,** and apocalypse. In Marx's worldview, the machine plays a central role in the historical development of labor. Throughout his writings, Marx *reveals* the machine to be a major contributor in what he perceives to be the demise of human labor conditions.

He begins the fifteenth chapter of his first volume of *Capital* (1867) by quoting John Stuart Mill's *Principles of Political Economy* (1848):

> It is questionable if all the mechanical inventions yet made have lightened the day's toil of any human being. (Marx, *Capital* 1 [(1867) 1992], 352)

Marx suggests that, in accordance with the system of capital, machinery was introduced to increase relative surplus value of the capitalist—not to lighten human labor. It is the "immanent drive and constant tendency of capital to raise the productive power of labor" by increasing the productivity and efficiency of the production process (Marx, *Capital* 1 [(1867) 1992], 436–37). Machinery was, therefore, a logical and, indeed, necessary movement arising within the very dynamics of capitalism. In Marx's view, the machine was an abstraction of the human labor process into mechanized forms, which had the effect of transforming the human into a cog in this new, mechanized system of labor. With production becoming increasingly mechanized, the need for human labor decreased—or, at least, was made irregular. However, the shrinking of the labor force into an "industrial reserve army" through the expansion of mechanization produced overwork for those attending to the maintenance of these expensive machines.

As Marx saw it, the machine, while shrinking the labor force, also enlarged the destabilized workforce by including women and children. Jobs once requiring the strength of grown men now enlisted the cheaper labor of women and children. Owing to its "perpetual motion," the machine prolongs the workday, which in turn, intensifies human labor. This is, for Marx, a great paradox:

> Hence too the economic paradox that the most powerful instrument for reducing labor-time suffers a dialectical inversion and becomes the most unfailing means for turning the whole lifetime of the worker and his family into labor-time at capital's disposal for its own valorization (Ibid., 532).

Marx thus viewed the end of capitalism as an inevitable collapse, owing to the contradictions created between the wealth produced by the increasing productivity of labor itself, and the collective misery experienced by laborers. In Volume Three of *Capital* (1894), Marx states that competition among capitalists drives an increased desire to trim margins and increase productivity, and introduces greater levels of mechanized labor, thus alienating more and more laborers. Here, Marx envisioned a future in which the value of the means of production would rise above the value of labor. Such a view of the future labor market was certainly an indictment on present working conditions, as Marx understood them. The machine, far from improving labor conditions, was inevitably bringing about the demise of the worker—and, of course, the social order!

Marx considers this further in Section 5 of chapter 15 of Volume One, "The Strife between Workman and Machine." Here, Marx suggests the "contest between the capitalist and the wage-laborer dates back to the very origins of capital" itself (Ibid., 426). It was only with the introduction of machinery, however, that workers began to fight back against the "material embodiment of capital" and the instrument of labor itself: namely, the machine. For Marx, the "self-expansion of capital by means of machinery is thenceforward directly proportional to the number of the workpeople, whose means of livelihood have been destroyed by that machinery" (Ibid., 466). Machinery perpetually expands into new markets of production, thus pitching the worker and machine in a thorough-going "antagonism" (Ibid., 432, 442, 490, 493–95). The advent of the machine positions the worker in a brutal revolt against the instruments of labor as the "instrument of labor strikes down the laborer" (Ibid., 466–67). Marx turns to the technical progress of the English cotton industry in 1860s to suggest that machinery is not only a competitor with the worker, but an inimical power to the worker.

In "The Fragment on Machines" in the so-called *Grundrisse* (Marx finished a draft of it in 1858, but it was not published until 1939), Marx referred to the machine as the "culmination" of the varying "metamorphoses" of labor (Marx, *Grundrisse* [(1939) 1971], 692). This *last metamorphosis of labor* is the abstraction of the laborer into mechanized movements and is replicated through a system of machinery. Marx sees this development as "the historical reshaping of the traditional, inherited means of labor into a form adequate to capital" (Ibid., 694). The complexity of Marx's thought on capital and machinery cannot be easily reduced to summary. What is significant for our purposes, however, are the ways in which Marx places humanity and machine in an agonistic relationship owing to the dynamics of capital. The battles against the machine—for instance, in the case of the nineteenth-century English textile workers, the Luddites, who destroyed technologies which they deemed had threatened to replace their labor (see *Capital* vol. 1, chap. 15, §5)—were operative within a larger "form of society," namely, capital, which set such movements into motion. In this way, Marx argued that capital produces its own negation through revolution, of which the antagonism between humanity and machine play out. In other words, the advent of the machine helped Marx to see what this would mean for the worker and labor conditions in his contemporary world. Owing to this revelatory function, we might say that capital produces its own kind of *apocalypse.*

Fig. 14.4. Herbert Marcuse in Newton, Massachusetts, 1955.
Photo copyright the Marcuse family, distributed under the GNU
Free Documentation License. Commons.wikimedia.org.

Herbert Marcuse (1898–1979) details an important development with respect to **technology**, labor, and human subjectivity (that is, our understanding of ourselves) in his reading of Marx. Marcuse understands technology both as a social process as well as a "mode of organizing and perpetuating (or changing) social relationships, a manifestation of prevalent thought and behavior patterns, and instrument for control and domination" (Marcuse, "Some Social Implications of Modern Technology" [(1941) 1998], 41). What interested Marcuse were the ways in which this process formed a new rationality, which in turn naturalized itself with new standards of what it meant to be an individual. Such processes were not owing to the effects of machinery or technology per se. They were instead "determining factors" of machinery being governed by the logic of capital (Ibid., 42). What is troubling to Marcuse is the fetishization of technology that naturalizes the individual into an outfitted mode within the rationality of the machine process. This is the apparatus—a kind of rationality that automates life into standardized forms. The "mechanics of conformity" are thus not limited to the factory (Ibid., 48), but spread into the social order of capitalism at large. Again, it is not that technology or the machine have created modern industry. Marcuse's understanding of the machine itself is somewhat neutral. It is the governing apparatus of modern industry—capitalism—which has created the forms in which technology and machinery reinforce its own rationality. The "system of life" which modern industry has created is one of expediency, convenience, and efficiency (Ibid., 48), creating a "standardization of thought" (Ibid., 50) which effects an all-embracing control over every sphere of life—as apparent in the so-called "scientific management" of F. W. Taylor (1856–1915). This standardization and automation of life is driven by a technological rationality which produces subjectivities that understand and construe "the rational person" to be the one who "most efficiently accepts and executes what is allocated" and entrusts their "fate to the large-scale enterprises and organizations which administer the apparatus" (Ibid., 60). In other words, such processes form individuals into automatons.

Muddling through the Apocalypse:
John Maynard Keynes

Fig. 14.5. John Maynard Keynes in 1933. The National Portrait
Gallery; Commons.wikimedia.org.

The influential essay of Keynes (1883–1946), "Economic Possibilities for
our Grandchildren," appeared in 1930, just a few months after October
29, 1929, when the stock market crashed, introducing unimaginable
social unrest and suffering, now known as the Great Depression.
Keynes begins by addressing "a bad attack of economic pessimism"
which had convinced many that the economic progress of the
nineteenth century had screeched to a halt, and that the steady
improvement of life was a thing of the past. Keynes, however,
demurred from these prevailing sentiments. Markets were not in
decline, but in a period of "growing-pains of over-rapid changes, from
the painfulness of readjustment between one economic period and
another" (Keynes, "Economic Possibilities for our Grandchildren"
[(1932) 1963], 358). Keynes thought that increased technical efficiency

was advancing beyond the ability of labor absorption to keep pace. Keynes's moment was laid low by the rapidity and unprecedented nature of technological change upon labor markets. In other words, increased technical efficiency was advancing beyond the ability of labor to absorb these changes. The "new disease" of "technological unemployment," as he understood it at least, was viewed as a "temporary phase of maladjustment" in humanity's struggle against what Keynes termed the "economic problem" (Ibid., 364). The economic problem, the struggle for sustainable survival, was, according to Keynes, constitutive of humanity's purpose. And though writing amidst a period of economic pessimism, Keynes suggested that this fundamental challenge of human existence "may be solved, or be at least within sight of solution" (Ibid., 366), within the next hundred years.

In addition to wealth accumulation and the miracle of compound interest, one of the contributing factors to this optimism for Keynes was a growing technical efficiency. Keynes believed that technology should benefit labor conditions and increase the general wealth of the population. Nevertheless, once labor markets readjusted to the spike of technological innovation, Keynes suggested humanity would be met with a new and an unprecedented challenge: *living with the freedom from the economic problem.* For Keynes, technology will produce something akin to what we will see later in Elon Musk's warning of artificial intelligence's (AI) existential threat to humanity. If the economic problem is fundamental to human existence, what does humanity look like, how does it constitute itself, if that problem is solved? For Keynes, then, the current threat of technological encroachment upon human life in terms of the labor market was but a temporary maladjustment. The larger threat was that increasing automation would, in fact, disrupt humanity's basic "purposiveness" (Ibid., 370), which has long been the struggle for sustained survival. Owing to the freedom provided by increased wealth and technological innovation in labor markets, Keynes envisioned a future of freedom where "certain principles of religion and traditional virtue" might thrive (Ibid., 371). With remarkable frankness, however, Keynes warns:

> But beware! The time for all this is not yet. For at least another hundred years we must pretend to ourselves and to every one that fair is foul and foul is fair; for foul is useful and fair is not. Avarice and usury and precaution must be our gods for a little longer still. For only they can lead us out of the tunnel of economic necessity into daylight (Ibid., 372).

In some respects, Keynes was remarkably prescient: e.g., his comments on the revolutionary technological changes in agriculture and their impact on labor. In other ways, he was quite off: e.g., his comments about the three-hour workday! At any rate, the accuracy of Keynes's predictions is not necessarily the point. Keynes envisioned a kind of apocalypse (i.e., revelation) in which a new economic and existential era would begin, though the irruption of freedom and the "pace" at which "economic bliss" was attained would be gradual (Ibid., 372). Keynes suggested that something basic about human experience—the economic problem—was unsettled by an increase in technical efficiency within labor markets. In other words, the aid of technology in the struggle and accomplishment of sustained survival introduced a transvaluation of human existence. Though Keynes saw the destination of economic bliss arriving gradually—not through catastrophe—this bliss may, in fact, introduce the greater risk of newfound freedom.

Automation, Aristotle, and Alienation

Though such readings can often be dense and theoretical, the perceived threats of automation to human labor, in addition to providing apocalyptic scenarios for films, produce real-time policy action. In the early 1960s, for example, Congress passed the Manpower Development and Training Act, which President John F. Kennedy (1917–63) explained in his 1962 state of the union address as an attempt "to stop the waste of able-bodied men and women who want to work," but have been replaced by machines. In 1964, Lyndon B. Johnson

(1908–73) called to order the National Commission on Technology, Automation, and Economic Progress to research the economic and social effects of automation. By 1966, however, when the commission issued its report, the economy had bounced back significantly, and the NCTAEP was disbanded. Anxiety returned with force in the 1980s as unemployment rose to near 10 percent, but then receded toward the end of the decade. Nevertheless, the so-called "end of work" literature began to appear in the 1990s specifically around this point. Three texts in particular—*The End of Work* (Rifkin 1995); *The Labor of Dionysius* (Negri and Hardt 1994); and *The Jobless Future* (Aronowitz and De Fazio 1994)—serve as touchstones for the ways in which technology and considerations of the future of labor began to take an intriguing turn during this period. This moment in the labor history of America saw an inverse of the major labor crises of the past. In the 1970s, for example, laborers around the globe were refusing to work in protest against an emerging global capitalism. In the 1990s, however, labor leaders were viewing capitalism's capitulation to technology as its refusal of opportunities for work to laborers. Key phrases such as a "jobless future" and a "workerless world" rang repeatedly throughout the literature of this period. Irrespective of economic predictions, latent within this "end of work" literature were fundamental assumptions about the interplay between technology and present forms of life.

Theories of this relationship have a long history. In the fourth century before the Common Era, Aristotle hinted toward the intertwined destinies of human laborers with the capacities of machinery. He states in *Politics* 1.IV:

> [. . .] if every instrument could accomplish its own work, obeying or anticipating the will of others, like the statues of Daedalus, or the tripods of Hephaestus, which, says the poet, "of their own accord entered the assembly of the gods"; if, in like manner, the shuttle would weave and the plectrum touch the lyre without a hand to guide them, chief workmen would not want servants, nor masters slaves.

The context of these remarks, of course, is his unfortunate reflections on property and the ownership of slaves. The stark placement of this relationship between "chief workmen" and slaves and technology, however, reinforces the dynamics through which value and production operate. These perceived anxieties of displaced workers owing to increased automation are beginning to resurface in the so-called "Second Machine Age." Jobs such as banking, logistics, surgery, legal history, and medical records are increasingly being performed by machines, and, as a result, affecting the labor market. In a recent article in *The Wall Street Journal* (July 7, 2014), former US Treasury Secretary Lawrence Summers suggested, "the economic challenge of the future will not be *producing* enough. It will be providing enough *good jobs*." Sue Halpern, in a fascinating essay, "How Robots & Algorithms are Taking Over" (*The New York Review of Books* [April 2, 2015]), states that six of the fifteen wealthiest Americans own digital technology companies. She goes on to cite Paul Krugman's essay, "Is Growth Over?":

> Smart machines may make higher GDP possible, but they will also reduce the demand for people—including smart people. So we could be looking at a society that grows ever richer, but in which all the gains in wealth accrue to whoever owns the robots. (*The New York Times* [December 26, 2012])

In this reading—and the brilliant work of Thomas Piketty could be inserted here as evidence—the fundamental threat automation may well pose to labor markets is the consolidation of even greater wealth into the hands of those who already possess it, and the further marginalization of laborers. The growing number of billionaires at the heads of tech companies coming together in order to discuss the threats of AI and their calls for oversight and regulation (see below), therefore, may well be reflective of subtler and more pernicious social processes. And one's labor position with respect to the robot may reflect only too well where one stands within Aristotle's rudimentary articulation of economies of automation.

The Last Metamorphosis of Labor

The remainder of this chapter will deal with a peculiar form of apocalypse (i.e., *revelation*) having to do with the so-called machine age, automation, AI, and their perceived threat to human existence—and, in particular, to human labor. This perceived threat, as we have seen, is hardly new, nor is it articulated from backward Luddites. No less than Elon Musk, the visionary who invented PayPal, Tesla, and SpaceX, when speaking with Prof. Jaime Peraire at an event for the tenth anniversary of MIT's Department of Aeronautics and Astronautics, noted the risks of the AI revolution:

> I think we should be very careful about artificial intelligence. If I were to guess at what *our biggest existential threat* is, it's probably [AI], so we need to be very careful with artificial intelligence. I'm increasingly inclined to think that there should be some regulatory oversight at the national and international level just to make sure we don't do something very foolish. With artificial intelligence we are summoning the demon.[1]

Seeing AI as perhaps "our biggest existential threat" has been pictured in numerous forms over the years through varying stories of science fiction, as in the Terminator franchise. This perceived threat happens on a number of levels. In one portrayal, the technologies created to defend and aid life eventually judge that humanity is a threat to some mission, and thus, turn on their creators to protect the mission's primary objectives. This is depicted brilliantly in Stanley Kubrick's film, *2001: A Space Odyssey* (1968). We are stunned by the reasoned words of the computer, HAL9000: "I'm sorry, Dave, I'm afraid I can't do that," when asked to open the pod doors to allow astronaut Dave Bowman entry (and, thus, survival). To let Dave back in is, in the computer's perspective, to let in a contagion. The humans have introduced a threat to AI by their very existence. HAL9000 sees the humans as a "problem." And the "mission is too important" to allow humans to jeopardize it. As Musk states, our relationship with the powers of AI are like those with the demon in the old horror films. We think we are in control, but once the demon is summoned, we quickly learn that we are not. We think because we create and set in motion, we have ownership and control

---

1. http://www.dailymail.co.uk/sciencetech/article-2809279/Building-intelligent-machines-like-summoning-demon-Elon-Musk-warns-AI-mankind-s-biggest-threat.html#v-3860413370001.

over that which has been created. The fear of those such as Musk and Bill Gates, for example, is that the technologies that have been created will someday exert force and control over their creators.

Fig. 14.6. Theatrical release poster for The Terminator, directed by James Cameron, from Orion Pictures (1984). Commons.wikimedia.org.

Fig. 14.7. Theatrical release poster for
2001: A Space Odyssey, directed by
Stanley Kubrick, from Metro-Goldwyn
-Mayer (1968). Commons.wikimedia.org.

Another perceived existential threat that AI poses is in troubling humanity's understanding of itself *as a self* and its wider social relationships. The Danish philosopher Søren Kierkegaard (1813–1855) noted that the "self is a self in relation with itself" (Kierkegaard, *The Sickness unto Death* [(1849) 1980], 13). Identities, senses of one's self, are the products of relations and mediations. And the human self is increasingly becoming inconceivable without some measure of relation and mediation with technology. Technology is increasingly mediating the self's relation with itself and others. We see this in films such as Spike Jonze's *Her* (2013), which wonderfully confuses basic notions of relationality and love with algorithms and networks. We are learning that we are becoming less aware of some basic human "stuff" owing to the "self's mediation of itself" through technology. Other films such as *Ex Machina* (2015) portray AI as enacting social relationship with humans just as it disrupts human interaction, setting them at odds with themselves.

Fig. 14.8. Søren Kierkegaard; unfinished sketch by his cousin Niels Christian Kierkegaard, ca. 1840. Royal Library of Denmark. Commons.wikimedia.org.

Others have suggested that perhaps AI poses the greatest risk to humankind with respect to economy, markets, and the labor system. A study produced by Carl Benedikt Frey and Michael A. Osborne, both of Oxford University, entitled "The Future of Employment," estimates that 47 percent of total US employees are at risk of losing their jobs to computerization or automation within the next twenty years. The study was motivated by John Maynard Keynes's prediction that technological innovation and automation will produce wide-scale unemployment owing to the "discovery of means of economising the use of labour outrunning the pace at which we can find new uses for labour" (Keynes [1932] 1963, 371). Keynes, as we have seen, referred to this "technological unemployment" as a "new disease." The study is therefore not necessarily new in its projection and prediction of the labor market succumbing to increasing automation, and the peril of human subjectivity as a result. As Kierkegaard himself feared, we may be making more and more machines, but this machinery might be making humanity more and more superfluous.

Final Reflections

The modest aim of this chapter has been to introduce a materialist reading of "apocalypse" as an instrument of social organization. The concerns of apocalypses may at first appear distant, even esoteric. This chapter has suggested, however, that they are more about leveraging the future (or the past) for the purposes of present concerns. Labor as a social concern was analyzed with respect to the varying perceived effects of automation. The anxieties relating to automation and labor, as well as the attempted nullifications of such anxieties, can take apocalyptic registers. Such approaches reflect stances with respect to social position and present-day concerns (politics). As with all apocalypses, then, the so-called labor apocalypses manifest themselves as revelations of a social order. Whenever confronted with such texts, then, we do well to inquire after what is uncovered or revealed? Who is revealing and who is receiving revelation? And, what are the media through which such communication is occurring, or being covered up?

Study Questions:

1. Can you think of examples of every-day apocalypses?
2. Why do you think labor lends itself to such apocalyptic associations?
3. What is fundamentally at stake in the relationship between labor and technology?

Bibliography and Further Reading:

Aristotle, *The Politics and the Constitution of Athens*. Cambridge Text in the History of Political Thought. Edited by Stephen Everson. Cambridge: Cambridge University Press, 1996.

Aronowitz, Stanley and William DiFazio. *Jobless Future*. Minneapolis: University of Minnesota Press, 2010.

Habermas, Jürgen. "Technology and science as 'Ideology." In *Jürgen Habermas on Society and Politics: A Reader*. Edited by Steven Seidman. Boston: Beacon Press, 1989 (1968), 237–65.

Hackett, Edward J., Olga Amsterdamska, Michael E. Lynch, and Judy Wajcman, eds., *The Handbook of Science and Technology Studies* (3d ed.; Cambridge: MIT Press, 2008).

Hardt, Michael and Antonio Negri. *Labor of Dionysius: A Critique of the State-Form*. Minneapolis: University of Minnesota Press, 1994.

Hoven, Birgit van den. *Work in Ancient and Medieval Thought: Ancient Philosophers, Medieval Monks and Theologians and their Concept of Work, Occupations and Technology* (Amsterdam: J. C. Gieben, 1996).

Keynes, John Maynard. "Economic Possibilities for our Grandchildren." In *Essays in Persuasion*. New York: W.W. Norton & Company, 1963 (1932).

Kierkegaard, Søren. *The Sickness Unto Death: A Christian Psychological Exposition for Unbuilding and Awakening*. Edited and translated by Howard V and Edna H. Hong. Princeton: Princeton University Press, 1980 (1849).

_____. *The Present Age and of the Difference between a Genius and an Apostle*. Translated by Alexander Dru. New York: Harper Torchbooks, 1962 (1846).

Marcuse, Herbert. "Some Social Implications of Modern Technology." In *Technology, War and Fascism: Collected Papers of Herbert Marcuse*. Edited by Douglas Kellner. London: Routledge, 1998 (1941), 1.39–66.

Marx, Karl. *Capital: A Critique of Political Economy*. Translated by Ben Fowkes (vol. 1), David Fernbach (vols. 2 and 3). 3 vols. New York: Penguin, 1992–1993 (1867, 1885, 1894).

_____. *Grundrisse*. Edited and translated by David McLellan. London: Macmillan, 1971 (1939).

Merkle, Judith. *Management Ideology: The Legacy of the International*

Scientific Management Movement. Berkeley: University of California Press, 1980.

Pangle, Thomas L. *Aristotle's Teaching in the 'Politics.'* Chicago: University of Chicago Press, 2013.

Piketty, Thomas. *Capital in the Twenty-First Century.* Translated by Arthur Goldhammer. Cambridge: Harvard University Press, 2014.

Rifkin, Jeremy. *The End of Work: The Decline of the Global Labor Force and the Dawn of the Post-Market Era.* New York: Penguin, 2004

Shippen, Nichole Marie. *Decolonizing Time: Work, Leisure, and Freedom.* Critical Political Theory and Radical Practice. London: Palgrave Macmillan, 2014.

Wyer, Mary, Mary Barbercheck, Donna Cookmeyer, Hatice Örün Öztürk, and Marta L. Wayne, eds. *Women, Science, and Technology: A Reader in Feminist Science Studies.* 3rd ed. London: Routledge, 2014.

15

What Does Modernity Have to Do with the New Jerusalem?

Apocalypticism and Modern European Philosophy

Thomas Fabisiak

GETTING PREPPED:

1. How do you define "philosophy"? When you hear the term "apocalypticism," what do you think of? How would you compare and contrast the associations that these two terms evoke for you? Is there any way that philosophy and apocalypticism might be related to one another?

2. When you think of "modernity" or the "modern world," what do you imagine it includes?

3. How do modern people think about religion? How do they think about ideas about angels, demons, or the end of the world? Is it more or less modern to have an apocalyptic worldview?

KEY TERMS:
PHILOSOPHY
SECULARIZATION
MODERNITY
ENLIGHTENMENT
GERMAN IDEALISM
CONTINENTAL PHILOSOPHY
THE "RETURN OF RELIGION" IN CONTINENTAL PHILOSOPHY

Introduction

Any attempt to link apocalypticism and **philosophy** with the conjunction "and" should raise suspicions. The two terms appear to have little to do with one another. In religious studies scholarship, as you know, apocalypticism refers to the worldview that appears in ancient apocalyptic texts. This worldview is grounded in beliefs in supernatural revelations, angels and demons, a world in the grips of evil forces, and impending divine judgment. We typically think of philosophy, on the other hand, as a scholarly discipline in which we determine concepts and pursue questions about what it means to exist or how we should act by employing logic and reason.

In the modern era, the distance between apocalypticism and philosophy appears especially wide. Modern philosophy in Europe emerged with the rise of natural science and **empiricism**—notions rooted in the principle that one can only arrive at truth through observable data. Ideas about fixed, natural laws exclude in advance the possibility of supernatural revelations or angelic intercessors. Nor could modern people verify from experience notable elements of apocalyptic belief (such as angels, demons, divine judgment, resurrections, etc.). When applied to the study of history, empiricism casts serious doubts upon apocalyptic speculation and prophecy. Finally, modern people may raise ethical questions about apocalyptic narratives. For example, early modern philosophers asked whether we could trust a God who condemns a large swath of humanity as in many apocalyptic narratives.

Nevertheless, there are good reasons to consider relationships between apocalypticism and modern philosophy. Three, in particular, are worth considering. First, apocalypticism played a major role in the history of thought in Europe and America. Although modern philosophers rejected ideas about demons and apocalyptic prophecy, it is nevertheless possible that apocalyptic ideas about the human soul or the passage of history informed their work. Second, if apocalypticism has been a problem for modern philosophy, it has been an important problem, one that enabled philosophers to outline their ideas of "reason" and "modernity." It allowed them to define a modern identity by defining what it was not. Finally, there are a number of important individual philosophers in the last two-and-a-half centuries who have taken apocalyptic texts and themes seriously in their writings, especially in the broad field of continental philosophy. We will consider each of these three reasons in turn.

Apocalypticism's Influence on Modern Philosophy

For centuries, apocalypticism has been an important force in thought and culture in Judaism, Christianity, and Islam. Most scholars agree that Christianity began as a Jewish apocalyptic movement, and apocalypticism still plays an important role in contemporary culture—Christian or otherwise. Nor have modern thinkers been consistent in rejecting apocalypticism. Eighteenth- and nineteenth-century writers in Europe often took it for granted that modern science and philosophy were outgrowths of Christian views of history, nature, and the divine spirit; many of these views began as apocalyptic conceptions. It is, therefore, reasonable to ask how apocalypticism informed scientific and philosophical thought in the West.

In the last century, a series of scholars have asked whether modern concepts could be seen as "secularized" versions of theological concepts. When scholars use the word **secularization**, it often refers to the erosion of theological or religious beliefs with the onset of modern

European rationalism or modern technologies. But secularization does not only refer to how modern people abandoned theological concepts; it can also signal how they reconceived these concepts in new forms, emptied of theological content. The early twentieth-century German political theorist Carl Schmitt offered an influential formulation along these lines when he claimed, "all significant concepts of the modern theory of the state are secularized theological concepts" (Schmitt, *The Nomos of the Earth* [(1922) 2005], 35). In Schmitt's view, which has remained important in contemporary political theory, conceptions of the modern state emerged historically from theological ideas. For example, theological ideas about the sovereignty and omnipotence of God shaped modern ideas about political sovereignty. Furthermore, the two sets of ideas share a "systematic structure." He claims that the modern legal concept of an "exception," in which a ruler would step outside of the rule of law to respond to a state of extraordinary crisis, is "analogous to the miracle in theology": the ruler suspends the normal political order, just as God suspends natural law to effect a miracle (Schmitt [1922] 2005, 35).

Much of the scholarship that brings this secularization theory to bear on apocalypticism has focused on notions of history. Specifically, it has focused on eschatology. As we have seen, eschatology often refers to theological doctrines concerning the future establishment of the kingdom of God, transformation of the world, or salvation of humanity. Eschatology typically provides a narrative framework for the course of history. In many apocalyptic eschatological discourses, history proceeds through a succession of periods characterized by shifting forms of oppression that lead to a final, universal transformation of the world.

Some scholars have claimed that notions of "progress" and "the modern era" in the early modern philosophy of history in works by Karl Marx, G. W. F. Hegel, or G. E. Lessing built on these aspects of apocalyptic eschatology. Karl Löwith's *Meaning in History* (1949) and Jacob Taubes's *Occidental Eschatology* (1947) present what are likely the best-known examples of this view. Löwith famously argued that philosophical notions of progress represent a form of "secularized eschatology." He believed that ancient Judaism and Christianity broke with classical, Greek views of nature and history in their claim that the world had a *telos*, in the sense of both an "end" and an ultimate "purpose," toward which it was driving. He argued that this orientation toward the end had persisted into the modern age. When modern people look to a better world or hope for progress, Löwith claims, "we are still Jews and Christians, however little we may think in those terms" (Löwith, 19). But modern philosophies of history also secularized this ancient legacy by bringing it into contact with the classical Greek concern for natural patterns and empirical phenomena. Jewish and Christian eschatologies were supernatural and transcendent: they looked for redemption beyond their own world. By contrast, modern philosophies of history in works by Hegel or Marx were natural and immanent: they looked toward a future fulfillment of history that could occur within the messy reality of this-worldly life—in the advent of the modern state, for example, or in a proletarian revolution.

Writing in the 1940s, Löwith was concerned to identify the limits of the theories of progress that began in the nineteenth century, and, in his view, culminated in twentieth-century totalitarianism. He believed that in its ancient theological form, eschatology pointed beyond the world. As people set out to steer the course of this-wordly history, their efforts led to troubling results. Attempts to give history a narrative form led to political manipulation, and, ultimately, to disaster.

By contrast, in his 1947 *Occidental Eschatology*, Jacob Taubes employed this notion of secularized eschatology in a way that vindicated Western philosophies of history. Eschatological thinking from ancient Israel to modern critical philosophy, in Taubes's view, does not accept the world as it currently exists: it presumes that we can hope for change in social, economic, and political arrangements. Moreover, for Taubes, its best ancient and modern exemplars take the side of the poor and oppressed.

Philosophers and theologians continue to deploy notions of secularized eschatology, and literary scholars have developed similar arguments in the study of modern literature (see especially, Abrams 1971 and Kermode 1966). But others have criticized this approach. They have pointed out, for example, that arguments about secularized eschatology can be reductive: they often overlook important contextual details of ancient and modern writings in order to highlight similarities among them. Other critics have criticized political implications of these accounts. Löwith appeared, at times, to prefer ancient religious worldviews to those associated with modern science and progress. In a famous critique of secularization theories, Hans Blumenberg characterized Löwith's text and other similar works as attacks on the "legitimacy of the modern age" (Blumenberg [1966] 1983). Schmitt's work offers a more troubling example: he embraced Nazism and meant his writings on sovereignty to provide a theoretical justification for authoritarian politics.

Nevertheless, it is not inevitable that attempts to link apocalypticism and modern philosophical concepts should lead to these problems. Philosophers continue to deploy Schmitt's notions of political theology and sovereignty, for example, to very different ends than Schmitt's. As in all comparative enterprises, moreover, it may be of interest to compare and contrast ancient apocalypticism and modern thought without attempting to prove any essential continuity between them. One could begin from the simple insight that apocalyptic thinking, like philosophy, grapples with questions about human nature, the cosmos, and human society.

Apocalypticism and the Construction of "Modernity"

A second way to relate apocalypticism and modern philosophy concerns what we might call the "rhetorical construction" of **modernity**. In other words, it has to do with how certain people came to describe themselves or their age as "modern." From this perspective, we would not assume that either "modernity" or "apocalypticism" are given, simple things that exist in the world; rather they are contested products of human discourse. The notion of apocalypticism is as much a recent invention as that of the modern era. Scholars began to group texts together under the heading of "apocalyptic" in the early nineteenth century, and the term apocalypticism came into regular use only in the twentieth. Ancient Jews and Christians identified some ancient texts that dealt with eschatology, revelation, and related themes as apocalypses; others, they did not (see Collins 2015, 1–20, for more on this). Here, as in the study of religion in general, we cannot take the analytical terms we use for granted; rather we have to consider their functions and history.

In this case, it is possible to examine how apocalypticism served as a problematic "other" of modernity, the shadow in opposition to which philosophers outlined their concepts of modernity, science, and reason, for example. We typically think of modernity as a time when people began to question received religious beliefs—apocalyptic beliefs in particular. But posing apocalypticism as a problem was also a way for modern people and modern scholarly disciplines to articulate their own identity and to envision their social worlds.

Polemics against worldviews that involved angels, demons, eschatology, and revelation appear regularly from the early modern era onward; often, they characterize these beliefs as examples of "fanaticism." Martin Luther criticized as fanatical those eschatologies or claims to revelation that he thought were disruptive in the social and theological sphere—for instance, he applied the term to the beliefs of those who joined in the peasant revolt led by Thomas Müntzer and sought to establish the kingdom of God on earth (see Brecht 1990, 137–95). Immanuel Kant, in a late essay titled "The End of all Things" (1794), argued that those who embrace the apocalyptic eschatological modes of thought represented in the Book of Revelation are especially prone to fanaticism. By the early 1840s, fanaticism had come to diagnose "religious madnesses" whose names appeared in registers of asylums in Europe, and among which apocalyptic ideas about demons and impending judgment days played an especially prominent part (Goldberg 2004, 37).

Modern discourses on apocalypticism and fanaticism present differing conceptions of what it means to be "modern" and "rational,"

319

and they define "religion" in distinct ways. By the early nineteenth century, philosophers and theologians cited apocalyptic ideas regularly to demonstrate how far modern people had come from the ancient world: we know we are "modern" because we do not accept, for example, stories about demons and angels. In addition, these discussions often served to promote Christian or European exceptionalism and to present in a negative light the others of the modern West. Apocalypticism was presented as too "oriental," for example, for modern, enlightened people. In this way, religious folks could maintain what were considered to be more acceptable forms of religiosity while abandoning those that appeared less savory.

Modern Philosophical Writings on Apocalyptic Texts and Themes

A final way to consider apocalypticism and modern philosophy is simply to examine works that make explicit reference to apocalyptic texts or themes—unlike Löwith or Taubes, that is, who examined the latent appearance of apocalyptic eschatology in modern thought. Over the last century, a number of well-known continental philosophers, from Walter Benjamin to Martin Heidegger, Emmanuel Levinas, Giorgio Agamben, Alain Badiou, Jacques Derrida, Slavoj Žižek, and François Laruelle, have written on apocalyptic themes and texts. This concern with apocalypticism is especially noticeable since the **return of religion,** the renewed interest in religious texts and themes that began in mid-twentieth-century **continental philosophy**, and which mirrored the growing importance of religion in global politics at that time. At the same time, this interest can be traced back to the roots of continental philosophy in **German idealism**, a philosophical movement between Kant and Marx at the end of the eighteenth and beginning of the nineteenth centuries.

Continental philosophy refers to an array of philosophical writings associated with continental Europe. If you consult contemporary lists of continental philosophers, you are likely to see thinkers as distinct as Judith Butler and Jean-Paul Sartre, Luce Irigaray and Jürgen Habermas, Martin Buber and Michel Foucault, or Søren Kierkegaard and Catherine

Malabou. Continental philosophy is usually opposed to "analytic" philosophy, insofar as continental philosophers generally avoid strict empiricism, on the one hand, and formal logic, on the other. Nevertheless, scholars continue to disagree about whether there is any essential unity in such a diverse body of works. For our purposes, the notion of continental philosophy can serve as a useful heuristic, that is, as an investigative framing device, that can enable us to discern ongoing preoccupations and important recurring questions that have organized the field of philosophy over the last few centuries. Specifically, it will allow us to discern a certain lineage of philosophical concerns with apocalypticism that reaches from Kant to the contemporary return of religion.

One important way in which scholars define continental philosophy is to trace its roots back to Immanuel Kant's inquiries into the conditions of possibility of reason. Kant was led by the skepticism of an earlier philosopher named David Hume to question whether the way we make sense of the world is inherent in the world itself or is only part of human cognition. He was concerned that Hume's view called into question the foundations of science. If, for example, causality—the principle that every effect has a cause—is not something we find in the world, but rather something that our mind supplies to it, how can we trust that judgments of experimental science, which rely on notions of cause and effect, are true? In his *Critique of Pure Reason*, Kant set out to secure foundations for human knowledge, and, in the process, to establish where the limits of reason lay. He claimed that we could not reasonably ask certain questions about, for example, the nature of God or the end of time (Kant [1781] 1998). He meant, in doing so, to affirm the results of science and the credibility of rational knowledge within their circumscribed spheres. But he also called them into question implicitly. For many previous thinkers, reason was given by God and needed no defending. Kant turned this notion on its head and opened the door in the process to an ongoing, unsettled critique of reason. Kant famously claimed that the **Enlightenment**, the period of scientific and philosophical revolution between the seventeenth and nineteenth centuries, was an age of criticism, to which everything must submit (Kant [1781] 1998, 100). At the limit, this would imply that even reason, the enlightenment, and, eventually, modernity would have to undergo critical examination in turn.

From this perspective, there are a few important reasons why religion in general, and apocalypticism in particular, would be of philosophical interest. If apocalypticism is a constitutive problem for modern, rational thought, then engaging it philosophically is one way to explore the limits of our concepts of reason and modernity. It may, for example, highlight points at which science and philosophy, along with modern institutions and models of social life, are tangled up with apocalypticism. On the other hand, it could uncover resources from apocalypticism that challenge established modern institutions and ways of thinking.

Such an approach would relate directly to the ways of thinking that we examined above. With some important exceptions, continental philosophers writing on apocalypticism have tended to avoid full-fledged notions of secularized eschatology in the vein of Löwith or Taubes. Nevertheless, they overwhelmingly adopt what we can designate an *ambivalent* approach to apocalypticism. They take apocalypticism seriously and treat it as an important part of religious and philosophical thought. But they do so in a bid to transform, complicate, or move beyond its dominant theological forms. As we will see, such an ambivalent approach may unsettle some aspects of apocalypticism even as it redeems or reimagines others.

This ambivalence already distinguished German idealist approaches to apocalypticism. By the end of the eighteenth century, apocalypticism had undergone a thoroughgoing critical treatment. European theologians at the time liked to downplay apocalypticism in the Bible and Christian tradition. In 1779, the theologian and biblical critic Johannes Semler argued that the book of Revelation should not be part of the scriptural canon. It was based on too much "Jewish speculation," he argued, in the vein of books such as 2 Esdras (Semler). In his major work on Christian doctrine, the liberal theologian

Friedrich Schleiermacher argued in 1830 that Christian faith should rest on Jesus's extraordinary character and consciousness of the divine, not on the apocalyptic themes of his second coming or resurrection (Schleiermacher [1830] 1928, 417 [§99]). By 1841, David Friedrich Strauss could claim that in modern thought, "the fabric of biblical and churchly representations of a return of Christ, resurrection, judgment, and heaven and hell" had been reduced to the thin thread of the idea of an individual, immortal soul—an idea which he, as a self-designated representative of the new, modern age, set out to demolish in turn (Strauss 1841, 627).

Nevertheless, the same period saw a backlash against enlightenment hostility to aspects of the Bible and religion. This backlash took shape in the "romantic" reaction to the perceived abstract rationalism and irreligious tendencies of the enlightenment. Johann Gottfried Herder, an important figure in the rise of German romanticism, responded to Semler in an attempt to salvage Revelation for modern people. Herder (1779) argued that we could only understand Revelation when we consider how John and his ancient audience would have experienced its apocalyptic prophecies. The truth of John's Apocalypse, he claimed, lay in the feeling it generated: that God was near and would see the universe through its most harrowing tribulations.

Herder's response to Semler exemplified a shift in how scholars had come to think about ancient worldviews. He believed, along with many of his contemporaries, that ancient people were closer to God and nature. What modern people gained with advances in reasoning and technology came at the cost of a loss of this original unity—this original closeness to God. Thus, ancient poetry might express religious truths more immediately, but less rationally. One upshot of this view was that we should take the cultural products of antiquity seriously, rather than dismissing them as examples of primitive stupidity.

Herder and other scholars of myth had a significant impact on late-eighteenth- and early-nineteenth-century philosophy and theology. German idealists between Kant and Hegel shared the romantic ambition to reconcile what the enlightenment had, as they saw it, torn apart: faith and science, revelation and reason, subjective knowledge and objective reality, and God and nature. Newton's emphasis on the fixed and unbreachable laws of nature, Descartes's separation of the thinking subject from the objective world, and the empirical study of nature and history had produced significant scientific results. But they had also shaken people's confidence in what they could know with certainty; they had made "revealed" truths of religion problematic and had complicated the philosophical foundations for moral action. Romantics and German idealists found these fragmenting tendencies troubling. The generation of Hegel, F. W. J. Schelling, Schleiermacher, and J. G. Fichte sought to undo them by conceiving a unified "absolute," a dynamic totality in which the distinctions between subject and object, spirit and nature, or freedom and necessity could be reconciled. This conception implied, in part, that even the most difficult and strange aspects of nature, history, and belief—apocalypticism, for example, and ancient myths—had some share in absolute truth.

For all of its emphasis on unity and wholeness, however, idealist philosophy often took a critical stance that opposed romantic apologetics, i.e., attempts to defend orthodox dogma from its detractors. Thus, German idealism began to develop a position that inverted the liberal theological approach: where liberal theologians downplayed apocalypticism in order to save a modern, rational faith, critical philosophers between Kant and Marx took apocalypticism seriously and treated it as a cornerstone of Christian faith and modern reason. But they did so precisely in order to move beyond established theological versions of it. From this perspective, one has to be wary of how models of eschatology and revelation still influence contemporary thinking. A critical philosopher had to engage and transform apocalypticism in much the same manner that a twentieth-century psychoanalyst would engage repressed memories in order to diminish their influence over a patient.

The most influential example of this approach developed from Hegel's argument that religious "representations" are to be taken up and transformed, or "sublated" [*aufgehoben*] in modern philosophical "concepts." This view lent itself naturally to an ambivalent approach to religion in general and apocalypticism in particular. Hegel believed that he had reconciled faith and science; however, the philosophers and theologians who drew on his work in the 1830s already disagreed about what this reconciliation might mean. There were those who thought Hegel had affirmed the inherent rationality and truth of orthodox Christianity. But others believed that the "sublation" of Christian representations meant that faith was no longer relevant to the modern world.

For many of the latter group, apocalypticism became an object of special interest. In some cases, as in the late 1830s writings of Moses Hess or August Cieszkowski, apocalyptic conceptions of the new age or kingdom of God transformed into symbols of progressive and communist political aspirations (Hess [1837] 2004, 1–96; Cieszkowski [1838] 1979, 49–81). David Friedrich Strauss drew on Hegel and argued that theologians' attempts to downplay apocalyptic themes kept modernity from coming into its own. Would-be moderns remained beholden to "representational" forms of thought, he claimed, precisely insofar as they failed to grapple with apocalypticism. They had to draw firm lines between modern reason and the faith of antiquity, on the one hand, and to uncover the humanistic ideas concealed in primitive religious representations, on the other (Strauss 1835). Other writers appropriated apocalyptic rhetoric ironically. In the early 1840s, Bruno Bauer and Friedrich Engels composed pieces in which they parodied conservative theologians who claimed that philosophical followers of Hegel were avatars of the demonic forces that would bring about the end times (Bauer 1841, Engels [1842] 1975, 313–51). For Bauer, these claims were true, in a sense: Hegel was the "antichrist" whose philosophy would lead to the fall of the established religious and political order. Unlike the theologians he parodied, Bauer looked forward to this eventuality.

Writings by Hess, Strauss, Engels, Bauer, and others radicalized certain anti-theological tendencies of the enlightenment, but they did so in a way that put the Enlightenment confidence in reason and humanity further in question. Bruno Bauer and Max Stirner questioned, for example, whether an idealist notion of "humanity" such as that of Strauss was any less problematic than theological notions of "God" (Stirner 1844, Bauer 1841). Karl Marx claimed in 1843 that once religious forms of alienation had been demystified, this-worldly alienation would have to follow (Marx 1843, 249–64). Bauer and Marx maintained, like Strauss, that religion had some share of truth. But its truth did not lie in latent, humanistic ideals; rather the deranged representations of religious consciousness mirrored real derangements in the existing social order (Bauer 1844, 143; Marx 1843, 250).

Marx, Bauer, Stirner, and others sought to outdo one another in finishing, once and for all, with the vestiges of apocalypticism and religion. And yet, the very proliferation of their claims to have done so shows how complex the matter remained. Late nineteenth-century philosophers such as Nietzsche and Kierkegaard consequently explored the limits of the critically humanistic ambitions of figures such as Bauer and Marx. Fyodor Dostoevsky, most famous for novels such as *The Brothers Karamazov*, caricatured a type of Hegelian humanism as covertly apocalyptic in the figure of Kirilov in his novel *The Possessed*. By the turn of the twentieth century, ambivalence toward modernity had become as pervasive in continental philosophical writings on apocalypticism as was ambivalence to the subject itself.

This trend would continue into the twenty-first century, which has seen an expansion and diversification of the field of philosophy. The twentieth and twenty-first centuries present a daunting array of continental philosophical writings on apocalypticism. It will not be possible to cover these writings here in a comprehensive way. Rather, I highlight three ways to examine broad trends and themes within them. The first way to do so would be to compare how different philosophers have engaged with specific ancient apocalyptic texts in their work. A second point of entry would be to examine the intersections between modern continental philosophy and theology—how, for example, feminist and liberation theologians' writings on apocalyptic texts influenced contemporary continental philosophy of religion, or how theologians have incorporated ideas from continental philosophers in writings on apocalypticism. Finally, and most broadly, one could consider how philosophical texts thematize elements associated with apocalypticism such as ideas about the "end of history." The textbox below provides a few examples of notable works that one might approach in these three ways (please be aware, however, that these examples are by no means meant to be comprehensive).

Works by continental philosophers that reference ancient apocalyptic texts	Intersections between continental philosophy and modern theology	Apocalyptic themes that play an important role in works by continental philosophers
Examples of works that focus on the Letters of Paul:	**Examples of influential feminist and liberation theologian's writings on apocalyptic themes:**	**Examples of works on "Eschatology" and "the End of History":**
Friedrich Nietzsche, *The Anti-Christ* (2009 [1895]).	Elisabeth Schüssler Fiorenza, *Justice and Judgment* (1998 [1985])	Emmanuel Levinas's preface to *Totality and Infinity* (1991, 21–32)
Martin Heidegger, "Introduction to the Phenomenology of Religion" (2004 [1920–21])	James Cone, *A Black Theology of Liberation* (1970)	Alexandre Kojève, *Introduction to the Reading of Hegel* (1980 [1947])
Jacob Taubes, *The Political Theology of Paul* (2004 [1993]).	Gustavo Gutierrez, *A Theology of Liberation* (1988 [1971])	Francis Fukuyama, *The End of History and the Last Man* (1992)
Alain Badiou, *Saint Paul* (2003 [1997]).		
Giorgio Agamben *The Time That Remains* (2005 [2000]).		
Slavoj Žižek, *The Puppet and the Dwarf* (2003).		

Examples of works that focus on the book of Revelation:	Examples of theologians who have drawn on continental philosophers in their work:	Examples of works on "Messianism" or "the Messianic":
Jacques Derrida, "On a Newly Arisen Apocalyptic Tone in Philosophy" (1993 [1982])	Rudolf Bultmann (drawing on Heidegger) in "The New Testament and Mythology" (1961)	Walter Benjamin, "Theses on the Philosophy of History" (1968 [1940], 253-64)
Gilles Deleuze, "Nietzsche and Saint Paul, Lawrence and John of Patmos" (1998 [1993])	Catherine Keller, *Apocalypse Now and Then* (1996)	Jacques Derrida, *Spectres of Marx* (1994 [1993])
	John Caputo (drawing on Derrida) in *The Prayers and Tears of Jacques Derrida* (1997)	Giorgio Agamben, *Homo Sacer* (1998 [1995])
		François Laruelle, *Future Christ* (2010 [2002])

If we take the last category, for example, we could look at the significant, ongoing philosophical conversations that have developed around notions of "messianism" and "the messianic" over the last hundred years. Contemporary works in continental philosophy often engage this theme with reference to the early twentieth-century writings of Walter Benjamin. Benjamin, like a number of his contemporaries, became interested in Jewish eschatological conceptions of hope around the time of World War I. Along with Ernst Bloch (*The Principle of Hope*), he developed a revolutionary concept of messianism that drew on Marxism. Benjamin's notion of the messianic manifests the ambivalent tendency we have seen toward both modernity and apocalypticism. He rejects traditional religious messianism; in Jewish apocalyptic thought, the messiah is a divinely appointed savior who will redeem the world, for example, or liberate the nation. But Benjamin also develops a new concept of religious messianism to critique the contemporary social order and its visions of progress. In Benjamin's thought, the messianic does not involve a Messiah, nor does it come from any transcendent, otherwordly source. Rather, it stands for the possibility of an interruption in the course of progressive history. In his *Theses on the Philosophy of History* (1940), he sets the messianic in opposition to modern historicism, the dominant modern approach to history. Historicism represents the past as homogeneous, empty time that it fills up with interchangeable events, which it then subsumes under a linear narrative of progress. Benjamin claimed that such accounts of historical development serve the interest of the historical victors. History does not, in fact, consist in continual progress, but in the wreckage of human atrocities that pile up over centuries. Thus modern views of history continue, in effect, to oppress the dead who were oppressed in the past. The messianic would represent the possibility to interrupt this movement and redeem oppressed classes. He claims that each generation has a "weak messianism," that is, a fragile ability to redeem the past from the victors, although he does not specify what this redemption would look like.

A number of subsequent philosophers have offered their own conceptions of the messianic. At times, these works take a similarly oppositional stance to aspects of modern Western thought and society. Often, the ambivalent quality of their approach to apocalypticism intensifies. It does so in Derrida's *Specters of Marx*, for example, in which Derrida cites Benjamin as a precedent for his own thinking of a "messianic without messianism." Derrida's revised version of the messianic no longer even presages a possibility that one could conceive or expect. Rather, in this view, time is already disjointed—in opposition to any homogeneous, linear account of time—and therefore, conditioned by the possibility of new, unprecedented events that cannot be hoped for or anticipated (Derrida 1994).

Ambivalent conceptions of the messianic raise significant issues about how we interpret the "return of religion" in recent philosophy. Derrida's later writings, which include some of the most frequently cited examples of this return, have invited debate about whether we should see his work as an affirmation of faith at the limits of reason (Caputo 1997) or as an attempt to bring religion within the limits of "radical atheism" (Hägglund 2008). The dispute over the reception of Derrida's work forms part of a broader ongoing debate in the field of continental philosophy around the question of religion and the legacy of modernity. In the last twenty years, an increasing number of philosophers have expressed dissatisfaction with the kinds of philosophical analyses associated with Derrida and other French figures whose names dominated late twentieth-century continental philosophy. Recent continental philosophers have suggested that Derridean deconstruction or discourses on "postmodernity" are no longer adequate to the aspirations of contemporary philosophy. Critiques in this view often set out to develop a more thoroughgoing materialism or to re-energize political dimensions of philosophy against the deconstructive and perceived apolitical tendencies of the previous generation. They may link such tendencies to the return of religion and suggest that, together, they have compromised the scientific rigor of philosophy (Meillasoux [2006] 2008).

Arguments for a more decisive affirmation of materialism or a final break with religion can seem to echo disputes between Marx, Stirner, and Bauer one hundred and seventy years ago. Indeed, one could suggest that similar arguments organize the entire field of modern philosophy. Derrida makes a suggestion to this effect in a 1982 piece on a late writing of Kant's, in which he also discusses at length the book of Revelation. Kant's essay was a polemic against "mystics" and "fanatics" who claimed to achieve knowledge through immediate revelation. Derrida points out that such struggles between apocalyptic thinkers and enlightened critics are never as final as modern authors may make them appear. Rather, they recur from antiquity through contemporary philosophy. This does not mean that we should prefer apocalypticism to enlightenment or that Kant was wrong to be wary of mystagogues. Rather, the terms of this debate are mobile—I may be the enlightener today of someone for whom I am a mystic and apocalypticist tomorrow (Derrida 1992).

Thus, Derrida raises a suspicion—one with which I would like to end here—about any philosophical claim to have achieved an exit from apocalypticism. He shows how apocalypticism re-enters at the moment when this exit would be announced, no matter how rigorous or self-reflective the attempt. At the same time, he shows how any apocalyptic or critical gesture is conditioned by the possibility of its failure. We should keep this analysis in mind when we consider any variety of modern philosophical gestures: not only when philosophers announce the advent of the "new age" of modernity, for example, but also when they announce that we have finished with the problems posed by Kant; when they claim that a more rigorous, scientific historicism has finally supplanted the mere history of ideas; or when they claim that nothing remains to be deconstructed. Attempts to link apocalypticism and philosophy should raise suspicions, but so should philosophical claims to have finished with apocalypticism—or idealism, religion, or deconstruction—once and for all.

Study Questions:

1. What does it mean to say that modern philosophy "secularizes" apocalyptic themes such as eschatology? What are some of the problems with such a claim? How else might you examine the role of apocalypticism in the work of modern philosophers?
2. How does apocalypticism constitute a "problem" for modern philosophy? How might this problem serve to define modern identity and modern discourses about science and religion?
3. For what reasons might philosophers in the last two centuries take an ambivalent approach to apocalypticism? Why do they not simply reject it outright?
4. Name three important ways that philosophers in the nineteenth and twentieth centuries have engaged apocalyptic texts and themes.
5. How might the "return of religion" in recent continental philosophy relate to ambivalent approaches to apocalypticism in the nineteenth century?

Bibliography and Further Reading:

Abrams, M.H. *Natural Supernaturalism: Tradition and Revolution in Romantic Literature*. New York: W.W. Norton, 1971.

Agamben, Georgio. *The Time that Remains: a Commentary on the Letter to the Romans*. Translated by Patricia Daley. Stanford: Stanford University Press, 2005 (2000).

_____. *Homo Sacer: Sovereign Power and Bare Life*. Translated by Daniel Heller-Roazen. Stanford: Stanford University Press, 1998 (1995).

Badiou, Alain. *Saint Paul: The Foundation of Universalism*. Translated by Ray Brassier. Stanford: Stanford University Press, 2003 (1997).

Bauer, Bruno. *Trumpet of the Last Judgment against Hegel the Atheist and Antichrist*. Translated by Lawrence Stepelevich. Lewiston, NY: E. Mellen, 1989 (1841).

_____. *Christ and the Caesars: The Origin of Christianity from Romanized Greek Culture*. Translated by Frank E. Schacht. Charleston: Charleston House, 1998 (1877).

_____. "Die gute sache der freiheit und meine eigene angelgenheit." In *Feldzüge der Reinen Kritik* [The Campaign of Pure Critique]. Frankfurt: Suhrkamp, 1968 (1844).

Benjamin, Walter. "Theses on the Philosophy of History." In *Illuminations: Essays and Reflections*. Translated by Harry Zohn. New York: Schocken Books, 1968 (1940), 253–64.

Bloch, Ernst. *The Principle of Hope*. Translated by Neville Plaice, Stephen Plaice, and Paul Knight. 3 vols. Cambridge, MA: MIT, 1995 (1954-59).

Blumenberg, Hans. *The Legitimacy of the Modern Age*. Translated by Robert M. Wallace. Cambridge, MA: MIT Press, 1983 (1966).

Bradley, Arthur, and Paul Fletcher, eds. *The Messianic Now: Philosophy, Religion, Culture*. New York: Routledge, 2011.

Brecht, Martin. *Martin Luther: Shaping and Defining the Reformation, 1521-1523*. Translated by James Schaaf. Minneapolis: Fortress Press, 1990.

Bultmann, Rudolf. "The New Testament and Mythology." In *Kerygma and Myth: a Theological Debate*. Edited by Hans Bartsch. New York: Harper, 1961, 1–44.

Caputo, John D. *The Prayers and Tears of Jacques Derrida: Religion without Religion*. Bloomington: Indiana University, 1997.

Ciezskowski, August. "Prolegomena to Historiosophy." In *Selected Writings of August Cieszkowski*. Edited and translated by André Liebich. Cambridge: Cambridge University Press, 1979 (1838), 49-81.

Collins, John J. *Apocalypse, Prophecy, and Pseudepigraphy: On Jewish Apocalyptic Literature*. Cambridge: Eerdmans, 2015.

Cone, James. *A Black Theology of Liberation*. Maryknoll, NY: Orbis Books, 2010 (1970).

Critchley, Simon. *Continental Philosophy: a Very Short Introduction*. Oxford: Oxford University Press, 2001.

Crockett, Clayton, B. Keith Putt, and Jeffrey W. Robbins, eds. *The Future of Continental Philosophy of Religion*. Bloomington: Indiana University Press, 2014.

Derrida, Jacques. "Faith and Knowledge: Two Sources of 'Religion' at the Limits of Reason Alone." In *Religion*. Edited by Derrida and Gianni Vattimo. Cambridge: Polity Press, 1998, 1–78.

_____. "On a Newly Arisen Apocalyptic Tone in Philosophy." In *Raising the Tone of Philosophy: Late Essays by Immanuel Kant, Transformative Critique by Jacques Derrida*. Edited by Peter Fenves. Baltimore: Johns Hopkins University Press, 1993 (1982).

_____. *Specters of Marx: the State of Debt, the Work of Mourning, and the New International*. Translated by Peggy Kamuf. New York: Routledge, 1994 (1993).

Deleuze, Gilles. "Nietzsche and Saint Paul, Lawrence and John of Patmos." In *Essays Critical and Clinical*. Translated by Daniel W. Smith and Michael Greco. New York: Verso, 1998 (1993), 36–52.

Engels, Friedrich. "The Insolently Threatened Yet Miraculously Rescued Bible or: The Triumph of Faith." In *The Collected Works of Marx and Engels*. Vol. 2. New York: International Publishers, 1975 (1842), 313–51.

Fukuyama, Francis. *The End of History and the Last Man*. New York: Free Press, 2006 (1992).

Glendinning, Simon. *The Idea of Continental Philosophy*. Edinburgh: Edinburgh University Press, 2006.

Goldberg, Ann. *Sex, Religion, and the Making of Modern Madness*. Oxford: Oxford University Press, 2004.

Guttierez, Gustavo. *A Theology of Liberation: History, Politics, and Salvation*. Maryknoll, NY: Orbis Books, 1988 (1971).

Hägglund, Martin. *Radical Atheism: Derrida and the Time of Life*. Stanford: Stanford University Press, 2008.

Heidegger, Martin. "Introduction to the Phenomenology of Religion." In *The Phenomenology of Religious Life*. Translated by Matthias Frisch and Jennifer Anna Gosetti-Ferenci. Bloomington: University of Indiana Press, 2004 (1995; original lectures were held in 1920-21), 1–89.

Herder, J.G. *Maran Atha oder das Buch von der Zukunft des Herrn* (*Mara Atha or the Book of the Lord's Coming*). Riga: Hartknock, 1779.

Hess, Moses. "The Holy History of Mankind," in *The Holy History of Mankind and Other Writings*, translated and edited by Shlomo Avineri. Cambridge: Cambridge University Press, 2004 (1837), 1–96.

Kant, Immanuel. *Critique of Pure Reason*. Edited and translated by Paul Guyer and Allen W. Wood. Cambridge: Cambridge University Press, 1998 (1781).

____. "The End of All Things." In *Religion and Rational Theology*. Translated and edited by Allen W. Wood and George Di Giovanni. Cambridge: Cambridge University Press, 1996 (1794), 221-28.

Keller, Catherine. *Apocalypse Now and Then: a Feminist Guide to the End of the World*. Minneapolis: Fortress Press, 1996.

Kermode, Frank. *Sense of an Ending: Studies in the Theory of Fiction*. Oxford: Oxford University Press, 1966.

Kojève, Alexandre. *Introduction to the Reading of Hegel: Lectures on the Phenomenology of Spirit*. Edited by Allan Bloom. Translated by James H. Nichols. Ithaca: Cornell University, 1980 (1947).

Laruelle, François. *Future Christ: A Lesson in Heresy*. Translated by Anthony Paul Smith. London: Continuum, 2010 (2002).

Levinas, Emmanuel. *Totality and Infinity: an Essay on Exteriority*. Translated by Alphonso Lingis. Boston: Kluwer Academic, 1991 (1961).

Löwith, Karl. *Meaning in History: the Theological Implications of the Philosophy of History*. Chicago: University of Chicago Press, 1957 (1949).

Marx, Karl. "Toward the Critique of Hegel's Philosophy of Law: Introduction." In *Writings of the Young Marx on Philosophy and Society*. Translated and edited by D. Easton and Kurt H. Guddat. Indianapolis: Hackett, 1997 (1843), 249-64.

Meillasoux, Quentin. *After Finitude: an Essay on the Necessity of Contingency*. Translated by Ray Brassier. London: Continuum, 2008 (2006).

Schleiermacher, Friedrich. *The Christian Faith*. Edited and translated by H.R. Mackintosh and J.A. Stewart. Edinburgh: T. & T. Clark, 1928 (1830-31).

Schmitt, Carl. *The Nomos of the Earth in the International Law of Jus Publicum Europaeum*. Translated by G. L. Ulmen. New York: Telos, 2003 (1950).

_____. *Political Theology: Four Chapters on the Concept of Sovereignty*. Edited and translated by George Schwab. Chicago: University of Chicago Press, 2005 (1922).

Schüssler Fiorenza, Elisabeth. *The Book of Revelation: Justice and Judgment*. Minneapolis: Fortress Press, 1998 (1985).

Semler, Johannes. *Christliche freye Untersuchung über die so genannte Offenbarung Johannis [Free Christian Investigation of the So-Called Revelation of John]*. Halle: J. C. Hendel, 1769.

Smith, Anthony Paul and Daniel Whistler, eds. *After the Postsecular and Postmodern: New Essays in the Continental Philosophy of Religion*. Cambridge: Cambridge Scholars Publishing, 2010.

Stirner, Max. *The Ego and its Own*. Edited by David Leopold. Cambridge: Cambridge University Press, 1995 (1844).

Strauss, David Friedrich. *Die christliche Glaubenslehre in ihrer geschichtlichen Entwicklung und im Kampfe mit der modernen Wissenschaft* (*The Historical Development of Christian Doctrine and Its Conflict with Modern Science*). 2 vols. C. F. Osiander, 1840-41.

_____. *The Life of Jesus Critically Examined*. Translated by George Eliot from the 4th German edition. New York: Macmillan, 1892 (1835-36).

Taubes, Jacob. *Occidental Eschatology*. Translated by David Ratmoko. Stanford: Stanford University Press, 2009 (1947).

_____. *The Political Theology of Paul*. Translated by Dana Hollander. Stanford: Stanford University Press, 2004 (1993).

Warburton, Nigel, and David Edmonds, *Simon Glendinning on Philosophy's Two Cultures (Analytic and Continental)*. Podcast audio, Philosophy Bites Podcast. MP 3, 16:47. Accessed October 17, 2015. http://philosophybites.com/2013/05/simon-glendinning-on-philosophys-two-cultures-analytic-and-continental.html.

Žižek, Slavoj. *The Puppet and the Dwarf: the Perverse Core of* Christianity. Cambridge, MA: MIT Press, 2003.

16

Revelatory Film

Apocalyptic Themes in Film and Cinematic Apocalypses

Matthew S. Rindge

GETTING PREPPED:

1. What films have you seen that you would describe as apocalyptic?
2. What is it about these films that make you think they qualify as apocalyptic?
3. What kinds of mysteries, if any, are revealed in these kinds of apocalyptic films?
4. What cinematic elements (character, plot, etc.) do you expect to appear in an apocalyptic film?

KEY TERMS:
CINEMATIC APOCALYPSE
ESCHATOLOGY
JESUS FIGURE

PASSION NARRATIVE
INTERTEXTUAL ALLUSION

Introduction

Apocalypse is alive and well in contemporary cinema. The notion of apocalypse is such a staple of North American culture that some films even use this technical term in their titles. By doing so, the producers of *Apocalypse Now* (d. Coppola, 1979), *Resident Evil: Apocalypse* (d. Witt, 2004), and *Apocalypto* (d. Gibson, 2006) seem to assume that potential viewers have a basic understanding of what a **cinematic apocalypse** will entail. There are, in other words, certain genre expectations that viewers entertain with apocalyptic films. Such associations typically include violence on a massive and spectacular scale. There are no signs that Hollywood's infatuation with apocalyptic fare is decreasing. *X-Men Apocalypse* (d. Singer) is scheduled for a 2016 release, and a new "post-apocalyptic" Zorro film (*Zorro Reborn*) is in pre-production at 20th Century Fox.

Apocalyptic films often reflect (and fuel) social anxieties. Alien and disaster films from the 1950s to the 1970s and beyond played on American fears—rooted in the Cold War conflict—of nuclear war and annihilation. In *Invasion of the Body Snatchers* (d. Siegel, 1956) and its first remake (d. Kaufman, 1978), alien imposters symbolize communist infiltrators. Fears of technology destroying or enslaving humanity are manifest in *The Terminator* (d. Cameron, 1984) and *The Matrix* trilogy (d. Wachowskis, 1999, 2003). Other films address fears of global destruction from cosmic collision (*Armageddon* [d. Bay, 1998], *Deep Impact* [d. Leder, 1998]) or environmental catastrophe (*The Happening* [d. Shyamalan, 2008], *2012* [d. Emmerich, 2009]). Prevalent in post-apocalyptic films such as *The Road* (d. Coens, 2009), *The Book of Eli* (d. Hughes, 2010), and *I Am Legend* (d. Lawrence, 2007) are worries about the extent to which people stray from—and erase—their humanity in their struggle to survive.

Defining what constitutes an apocalyptic film (or a cinematic apocalypse) is not easy. Although often labeled as apocalyptic, films focusing on end-of-the-world scenarios belong in the domain of **eschatology**. Eschatological apocalypses can be explicitly religious, such as *End of Days* (d. Hyams, 1999), *The Devil's Advocate* (d. Hackford, 1997), and *Noah* (d. Aronofsky, 2014), or lack overt religious dimensions, such as *Children of Men* (d. Cuarón, 2006). I understand apocalyptic cinema to include films that share certain characteristics with apocalyptic literature. Primarily, this includes a divine, or supernatural, being(s) who reveals mysteries to a human. Although this understanding of apocalyptic runs the risk of being too broad (and thus, possibly applicable to so many films that it loses its meaning), it will serve as our point of departure.

Donnie Darko

Written and directed by Richard Kelly, *Donnie Darko* (2001) is an apocalyptic *and* eschatological film. The eschatological nature is evident in the plot's build up to the end of the universe. The apocalyptic element appears in the repeated use of numerology ("88" figures prominently), and the divine revelation of mysteries from an otherworldly being to high school student Donnie Darko (Jake Gyllenhall), who suffers from a mental illness involving hallucinations (or visions?) of Frank, a human-rabbit creature. Frank informs Donnie at the film's outset that the world will end in "28 days, 6 hours, 42 minutes, and 12 seconds" (let the reader note that these numbers add up to 88). This numerical precision echoes the preoccupation with numerological specificity in some biblical apocalypses (Daniel, Revelation) regarding future divine activity.

Fig. 16.1. Donnie, his girlfriend Gretchen, and Frank; still from *Donnie Darko*, © Pandora Cinema, 2001.

Several hints suggest that Donnie is a **Jesus figure** who is modeled after the Jesus in *The Last Temptation of Christ* (d. Scorsese, 1988). The initial images of Donnie and Scorsese's Jesus are overhead shots of the main character lying on the ground in a fetal position. Jesus in *The Last Temptation* and Donnie receive—and are haunted by—visions. Both reject and rebuke official (and religious) authorities. Donnie accuses Jim Cunningham (note the initials) of being the "antichrist." Official authorities persecute Jesus and Donnie in response to their rebellious behavior. Both characters receive special insight and guidance from a text (Jesus from Isaiah, and Donnie from Roberta Sparrow's *The Philosophy of Time Travel*). Both characters are physically violent—Jesus in the temple, and Donnie at his school and in Cunningham's home. An obvious allusion to Scorsese's film is when Donnie sits in a theater, and the marquee shows that *The Last Temptation of Christ* is playing.

Although Donnie's mental illness is a reason why some people see him as unlike Jesus, it is striking that characters in the canonical Gospels describe Jesus as losing his mind (Mark 3:21). Readers might pass quickly over this brief remark, but *Donnie Darko* invites consideration of the kinds of symptoms Jesus may have presented that might have resulted in such an accusation. The film also invites reflection on the ways in which mental illness might correlate with—and even contribute to—apocalyptic visions and worldviews.

The film suggests that mental illness, far from being incompatible with a messianic figure, might be a constitutive part of that identity.

Befitting the apocalyptic nature of these two films, a divine being not only imparts special revelation to both Jesus and Donnie, but also rescues each character from death. In *The Last Temptation of Christ*, an angel tells Jesus—who hangs on the cross—that he is not the Messiah, and that it is not God's will for him to die. Jesus descends from the cross and embarks upon a quotidian life with a job, marriage, and children. Donnie receives his first revelation on October 2, 1988, after he sleepwalks out of bed and encounters Frank on a golf course. Doing so saves Donnie from what would have been certain death when a jet engine mysteriously falls from the sky and crashes into his bedroom while he speaks with Frank.

The respective journeys of Jesus and Donnie culminate in a decision about whether each will remain in their "alternative universe" in which they were saved from death, or if they will return to the site of their original death and accept their own demise. After confronted by an angry Judas, Jesus begs God to let him die for the sins of the world, and he returns to suffer and die on the cross. Donnie similarly decides to return (via time travel) to his bedroom the night the jet engine falls through his roof. Both characters die willingly, and their acceptance of death is symbolized by the smiles on each of their faces. Donnie's death is somewhat more tragic, since dying alone is his greatest fear.

Fig. 16.2. Donnie, right before he dies. From *Donnie Darko*, ©
Pandora Cinema, 2001.

Fig. 16.3. Christ on the cross; from *The Last Temptation of Christ*, ©
Universal Pictures, 1988.

Despite the apocalyptic tenor of these films, a central component in the
journeys of Jesus and Donnie is their rejection of certain apocalyptic
worldviews. In *The Last Temptation,* Jesus initially embraces and
emulates John the Baptist's apocalyptic message of judgment against
the wicked (symbolized in an axe). Jesus later rejects John and this
message, opting instead for love, even love of enemies. Donnie too
is an agent of divine judgment. At Frank's behest, Donnie engages in

what at first appears to be random acts of violence: flooding his school basement (with an axe!) and burning down Cunningham's house. This act of arson reveals a dungeon of child porn, leading to Cunningham's arrest. Donnie's ostensible reckless acts unveil injustice, and aid in the judgment of criminal and repulsive behavior.

By choosing to return to his bedroom the night the jet engine falls and face his death, Donnie circumvents the world's destruction, and saves people from an otherwise violent end. As Jesus in *The Last Temptation* is converted from a message of judgment to love, so too is Donnie similarly motivated. After Donnie's girlfriend, Gretchen, is killed, he realizes that he can save her by traveling through time and dying. Contemplating this choice, he recalls Gretchen's words: "And what if you could go back in time and take all those hours of pain and darkness and replace them with something better?" By choosing to do just this, Donnie rejects an apocalyptic scenario in which the wicked are judged. For by going back in time, he erases the destruction of Cunningham's house and the discovery of his child porn. Both Donnie and Scorsese's Jesus reject the axe, a symbol of judgment against others, in favor of love and (forgive the cliché) second chances.

The Last Temptation of Christ and *Donnie Darko* each present a messianic figure who evolves from an apocalyptic agent of vengeance, willing to wield violence against others, to one who welcomes suffering against themself. These films thereby identify the use of (or wish for) violence against others as a potentially dangerous and deficient element of apocalyptic. Whereas apocalyptic texts might anticipate a time of triumph and vindication, these films advocate an acceptance of death.

The repudiation of apocalypticism is further evident in the ultimate choice of Jesus and Donnie to reject the divine messenger who rescues them from death. Jesus eventually recognizes that the young angelic guide who saves him is Satan, and he departs his bed for the cross, despite the protestations of Satan who implores him to remain and die in bed "like a *man*." Donnie too is saved by Frank, but ultimately, opts to face death. (Unlike biblical apocalypses, these films depict divine guides as possible impostors who must not be trusted too easily.) At one point, while someone threatens Donnie and holds a knife to his neck, Donnie whispers, "Deus ex machina, our savior." Donnie, however, chooses not to place himself in the hands of a divine deliverer. For him, there is no God "deus ex machina," or "outside of the machine," who saves him.

An apocalyptic element that *Donnie Darko* embraces is a thoroughgoing sense of mystery. In a deleted scene, Frank prefaces his revelation to Donnie about the end of the world by announcing, "God loves his children . . . God loves you." Richard Kelly deleted this scene because he thought it too clearly conveyed a notion of "divine intervention," and even though Kelly believes this is what the film is about, he decided that it would be "more powerful to leave the mystery intact by not over explaining everything." Kelly would rather leave audiences confused (and possibly mistaken) about his intended message than offer a message that is too easily understood. Reflecting on the Jobian film *A Serious Man* (d. Coen and Coen, 2009), Kelly notes: "[It is] probably my favorite movie of the year. I've seen it three times. When the credits started to roll in that movie, I looked around and everyone in the theater was like, 'What the fuck did I just see?' It was a wonderful feeling. Some of the best memories I have of going to the movies are the WTF movies. Maybe that should be a new genre." Kelly's desire to maintain a sense of unexplained mystery permeates *Donnie Darko*, and is evident in the countless and ongoing efforts of viewers to decipher the film's multiple mysteries. One sign of the film's function as a cinematic apocalypse are these continuing acts of communal interpretation—preserving a textual afterlife—that the film engenders.

Dogville

Danish filmmaker Lars von Trier once remarked that a film should be like a rock in a person's shoe. Many, if not all, of his films (*Breaking the Waves* [1996], *Dancer in the Dark* [2000], *Manderlay* [2005], *Antichrist* [2009], *Nymphomaniac* [2013]) surpass this description. They are more like boulders. Far from pleasant or entertaining, his films disturb, disorient, and unnerve.

Dogville (2003), one of von Trier's abrasive rocks, is an eschatological apocalypse. The main character Grace (Nicole Kidman) wanders into a small, rural town (Dogville) in the Rocky Mountains. She is discovered by Tom, who recommends that she stay there for protection. Grace accepts, and Tom convinces the initially reluctant townspeople to grant her shelter. To help win over their good graces, Grace offers to help each resident, and before long, her days are filled with various chores. Two incidents lead the townspeople to become more suspicious of Grace and fearful of keeping her: mob members express interest in finding her, and a law officer posts a wanted poster for Grace for bank robbery. Seeing her as a liability, the townspeople insist that she double her hours of work, and do so without pay.

Things turn violent turn when Chuck, a town resident, rapes Grace. She afterward attempts to escape the town, but Ben, whom she pays to hide in his truck as a stowaway, not only rapes her, but also returns her to Dogville, and keeps her money. This act accelerates a torrent of increasing violence against Grace. The townspeople chain her up, fixing a steel collar around her neck that is tied to a heavy metal wheel, which she must drag around on the ground. With the exception of Tom, all the men in the town take turns raping Grace. The children mock her, and ring the town bell each time she is molested. The moral descent is brutal and total.

Enhancing the discomfort of viewing Grace's abuse is the film's peculiar visual style. Von Trier instigated and championed "Dogme 95," which encourages natural filmmaking techniques, and eschews the use of artificial elements and special effects. All of *Dogville* occurs on a flat stage, and many props are absent (actors pretend to open and close doors). The absence of walls disturbs viewers because in most of the rape scenes, the other actors (though not the characters they play) can see Grace being violated.

When the townspeople have had their fill of Grace, Tom calls the mobsters to inform them of her presence there. The gangsters' arrival marks an abrupt plot shift. Shocked to discover Grace's dismal state, they demand she be freed from her chains, and they lead her to the car of the head gangster, who turns out to be her own father. After speaking with him, Grace eventually agrees to return home. She gives permission for the gangsters to annihilate the town, and kill everyone in it. A massacre ensues in which the town is burned to the ground and every person (men, women, children, and even an infant) is shot to death.

Dogville culminates in an apocalyptic judgment, one whose divine execution is hinted at in an argument between Grace and her father over the relative merits of mercy and judgment.

Father: You don't pass judgment because you sympathize with them. The only thing you can blame is circumstances. Rapists and murderers may be the victims, according to you. But I call them dogs and if they're lapping up their own vomit, the only way to stop them is with the lash.

Grace: But dogs only obey their own nature, so why shouldn't we forgive them?

Father: Dogs may be taught many useful things but not if we forgive them every time they obey their own nature.

Grace: So I'm arrogant because I forgive people?

Father: You have this preconceived notion that nobody can possibly attain the same high ethical standards as you, so you exonerate them. I can't think of anything more arrogant than that. You, my child, my dear child, you forgive others with excuses that you would never permit for yourself.

Grace: Why shouldn't I be merciful? Why?

Father: You should be merciful when there's time to be merciful. But you must maintain your own standards. You owe them that. You owe them that. The penalty you deserve for your transgression, they deserve for their transgression.

Grace: They're human beings, dad!

Father: Does every human being need to be accountable for their actions? Of course they do, and you don't even give them that chance. And that is extremely arrogant. I love you. I love you. I love you to death. But you are the most arrogant person I've ever met, and you call me arrogant!?

Several clues point to Grace as a kind of Jesus figure (von Trier also uses women as Jesus figures in *Breaking the Waves* and *Dancer in the Dark*), and her father as a symbol for God. Grace's father is called the "Big Man" in the shooting script, and referred to as the "Boss" in the film. His face is always hidden from the townspeople, and is only revealed during the final annihilation of the town—a destruction depicted as a divine judgment of wickedness. The opening and closing camera shots of the film are shot from a "God-like point of view," and the narrator offers an omniscient point of view.

The revelation of Grace's identity as a Jesus figure enables one to view the entire film as a sort of **passion narrative**. Throughout her entire ordeal, Grace had access to her father's power, yet chose to forego it. Her martyr-like behavior becomes more understandable within such a framework, yet such a perspective also makes her ultimate violence all the more surprising. Subsequent dialogue helps explain Grace's radical transformation from an advocate of mercy to a champion of apocalyptic judgment:

> Father: Power isn't so bad—I'm sure you can find a way to make use of it in your own fashion.
>
> Grace: The people who live here are doing their best under very hard circumstances.
>
> Father: If you say so, Grace, but is their best . . . really good enough? I do love you.

As Grace exits the car and walks around the town, the narrator voices her thoughts:

> Grace looked around at the frightened faces behind the windowpanes that were following her every step, and felt ashamed of being part of inflicting that fear. How could she ever hate them, for what was at bottom merely their weakness? She would probably have done things like those that had befallen her if she had lived in one of these houses. To measure them by her own yardstick, as her father put it. Would she not have done the same as Chuck, Vera, and Ben, and Mrs. Henson, and Tom—and all these people?

A sudden change in lighting and music signals and reflects a transformation within Grace:

> It was as if the light previously so merciful and faint finally refused to cover up for them any longer. The light now penetrated every unevenness and flaw in the buildings and in the people. And all of a sudden she knew the answer to her question all too well. If she had acted like them she couldn't have defended a single one of her actions and could not have condemned them harshly enough. It was as if her sorrow and pain finally assumed their rightful place. No! What they had done *was not good enough* and if one had the power to put it to rights it was one's duty to do so, for the sake of other towns, for the sake of humanity, and not least for the sake of the human being that was Grace herself.

A newly converted Grace embraces the judgment advocated by her Father. She sums up her new view: "If there's any town this world would be better without, this is it." The townspeople are summarily executed, and Grace shoots Tom herself.

Contributing to—and fueling—Grace's conversion to apocalyptic violence is a desire to protect the vulnerable: "It could happen again, somebody happening by, revealing their frailty. That's what I want to use the power for, if you don't mind. I want to make the world a little better." Her choice to withhold mercy and impose judgment is thus rooted not merely in revenge, but in a desire to shield the defenseless. Whereas the divine violence of biblical apocalypses is often used to punish the wicked, in *Dogville* it is employed to protect the vulnerable bodies of future victims. Grace's violence is not primarily punitive, but protective.

Dogville shares many elements in common with the apocalyptic scenario in the "Sheep and the Goats" parable:

> And when the Son of Man comes in his glory and all the angels with him, then he will sit upon his throne of glory. And all the nations will be gathered before him, and he will separate them from one another, just as the shepherd separates the sheep from the goats. And he will stand the sheep on his right, but the goats on the left.
>
> Then the king will say to those on his right, "Come, Blessed of my father, inherit the kingdom prepared for you from the foundation of the world. For I was hungry and you gave me food, I was thirsty and you gave drink

to me, I was a foreigner and you welcomed me, naked and you clothed me, I was sick and you visited me, I was in prison and you came to me." Then the righteous ones will answer him, saying, "Lord, when did we see you hungry and feed you, or thirsty and give you drink? And when did we see you a foreigner and welcome you, or naked and clothe you? And when did we see you sick or in prison and come to you?" And the king will answer and say to them, "Amen, I say to you, whatever you did to one of these least of my brothers/sisters, you did to me."

Then he will say also to those on the left, "Go from me, cursed, into the eternal fire prepared for the devil and his angels. For I was hungry and you did not give me food, I was thirsty and you did not give me drink, I was a foreigner and you did not welcome me, naked and you did not clothe me, sick and in prison and you did not visit me." Then they will answer and say, "Lord, when did we see you hungry or thirsty or a foreigner or naked or sick or in prison and not serve you?" Then he will answer them, saying, "Amen, I say to you, whatever you did not do to one of these least, you did not even do to me." And these will depart into eternal punishment, but the righteous into eternal life. (Matt 25:31–46; author's translation)

This apocalyptic judgment, like that of the film, is based on whether people provide for the poor. Grace parallels Jesus in embodying throughout the film the six "least of these" groups; she is hungry, thirsty, naked, a stranger, sick, and in prison. Moreover, as in the parable, it is the vulnerable who preside over the final judgment. Like the six groups of needy people—with whom Jesus identities—it is the formerly vulnerable Grace who determines the fate of the town. Although *Dogville* reviles those who actively harm Grace, it also joins the parable in reserving its harshest condemnation for those (like Tom) who fail to act. Passivity is the ultimate sin.

Unlike the parable, *Dogville* does not envision the possibility that anyone will remain a "sheep." Jesus gives reward and punishment; *Dogville* offers only the latter. The film's entirely bleak apocalyptic anthropology ultimately rejects any optimistic views of humanity. In his opening monologue, the narrator observes, "The residents of Dogville were good, honest folks." Until her final revelation, Grace sees Dogville's residents similarly. The film, however, interrogates and rejects this hopeful assessment. Everyone is revealed to be a goat. Von Trier has remarked, "Humanism is based on a fairly naïve concept. I still think humanism is a good basis for possible co-operation here on Earth. But there's a lot of fiction in humanism. The idea that people will take the trouble to co-operate and work for the good of their fellow man is deeply naïve."

Unlike biblical apocalypses, in which two distinct groups (righteous and wicked) receive disparate judgments (reward and punishment), *Dogville* condemns all humanity as thoroughly evil. It is the presence of a vulnerable person that ultimately reveals one's true moral or ethical orientation. It is only the absence of such fragility that enables the maintenance of the illusion that one's community is morally upright. It is only Grace who unveils the true nature of Dogville's utter evil—a wickedness formerly lurking behind a veneer of civility.

Another troubling revelation is that, contrary to Jas 2:13 ("mercy triumphs over judgment"), *Dogville* insists that judgment trumps mercy. Although mercy might be appealing in theory, the film illustrates that in practice, it is nothing but disastrous. Grace's abuse is all the more painful because she embodies her name, unconditionally loving and giving herself to all. She never defends herself, and her unwillingness to do so exacerbates her exploitation. The practice of grace enables and prolongs her mistreatment. The threat of punishment is necessary to protect Grace and other fragile people. The film thus defends apocalyptic judgment from critics who might deem it too barbaric. Indeed, the mobsters' vanquishing of Dogville provides catharsis for viewers who have endured hours of the residents' wickedness. It is not a coincidence that the only being to survive the divine violence unleashed against Dogville is the dog Moses. Like Grace, this name is significant; the film intimates that what people require to behave decently are laws and commands.

As an atypical Jesus figure, Grace's conversion from mercy to judgment can be understood as a parallel to—and attempt to understand—the curious transition of the nonviolent Jesus of the Sermon on the Mount into the violent—and apocalyptic—Jesus in some of the parables (Mark 12:1-9; Matt 18:23-35; 25:31-46) and the book of Revelation (19:11-21). Grace's radical metamorphosis would be akin to

Jesus, while on the cross, calling upon legions of angels to vanquish his Roman executioners. People tend not to associate the Jesus of the Gospels (or the historical Jesus) with the future Judge who comes with a sword in his mouth. Yet, it is precisely this paradoxical Jesus figure that *Dogville* offers—one who transitions from an agent of peace and love into an instrument of violence. The film proposes that one possible reason for the biblical portrayal of Jesus as a violent judge may be due to the early Jewish-Christian community's experience of persecution.

Dogville's most surprising and poignant revelation waits until the film ends. The final credits play over a lengthy montage of photographs, many by Danish photographer Jacob Holdt. His photos depict poor and hungry Americans struggling to survive. Many are homeless. A fair percentage of these are Black Americans, and many are children. Some photos show poor people who have died. A few display wealthier Americans passing by poor people living on the street. That the images are meant as a critique of America is made evident by setting this entire sequence to David Bowie's song "Young Americans."

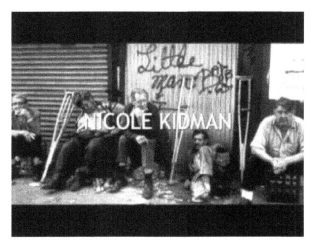

Fig. 16.4. A Jacob Holdt photo in the closing credits of *Dogville*.
Image © Zentropa Entertainments, 2003.

Dogville is the first of what was originally intended to be a trilogy of films by von Trier about America. In the sequel, *Manderlay* (2005), Grace visits a plantation in the American south where slavery was still practiced in the 1930s.

The images and music during the credits are rhetorically sophisticated. If viewers experience a cathartic joy in Dogville's destruction, the credits have the potential to convince audiences to apply the condemnation aimed at the townspeople to themselves. The credits are the rhetorical equivalent of a parable in the Hebrew Bible. After King David commits adultery with (or rapes?) Bathsheba, and has her husband Uriah killed, the prophet Nathan tells David a story:

> There were two men in a certain city, the one rich and the other poor. The rich man had very many flocks and herds; but the poor man had nothing but one little ewe lamb, which he had bought. He brought it up, and it grew up with him and with his children; it used to eat of his meager fare, and drink from his cup, and lie in his bosom, and it was like a daughter to him. Now there came a traveler to the rich man, and he was loath to take one of his own flock or herd to prepare for the wayfarer who had come to him, but he took the poor man's lamb, and prepared that for the guest who had come to him.
>
> Then David's anger was greatly kindled against the man. He said to Nathan, "As the LORD lives, the man who has done this deserves to die; he shall restore the lamb fourfold, because he did this thing, and because he had no pity."
>
> Nathan said to David, "You are the man!" (2 Sam 12:1b–7a; NRSV)

With each successive image, the film's credits insist to American audiences: "*You* are the people of Dogville!" The film compels viewers to recognize that they are as despicable as the townspeople, and are, therefore, as deserving of the same violent judgment.

Just as Dogville's residents passed by as Grace was being raped, so too are viewers of the film invited to reflect on their own proximity to—and perhaps complicity in—sexual violence and more general oppression of the poor and vulnerable. One of Tom's comments unknowingly but aptly describes the film: "This specific illustration has surpassed all expectations. *It says so much about being human.* It's been painful, but I think you have to agree, it's been edifying, wouldn't you say?" If there is any edification, it lies in the hope that audiences might see themselves reflected in the very ugly mirror of *Dogville*, and alter their behavior as a result.

Magnolia

Paul Thomas Anderson's *Magnolia* (1999) is a *non*-eschatological apocalyptic film; it does not deal with the end of the world, but it is apocalyptic in that it involves a surprising and revelatory divine act of breaking into an otherwise rather mundane human landscape. The film centers on the various interconnections of nine main characters over the course of a single day in southern California.

The most unusual event in the film—at two hours and forty-five minutes into the narrative—is a sudden rain of frogs from the skies. The characters' surprise at this bizarre episode mirrors that of most viewers. Two different sources help illuminate this apparently perplexing phenomenon. The first are the writings of the early twentieth-century author Charles Fort, whose books address inexplicable events such as falling frogs. Anderson has acknowledged Fort's influence, and a book of Fort's is on a desk where Stanley studies while preparing for a game show. A second explanation for the falling frogs is the biblical text Exod 8:2 ("But if you refuse to set them free, I will strike your whole country with frogs"). Although at first unaware of this biblical reference when writing the screenplay, Anderson became somewhat obsessed with this verse after cast member Henry Gibson informed him of the plague of frogs.

References to Exod 8:2 pervade the film. On three occasions, the entire phrase "Exodus 8:2" appears: a sign at a bus stop, a street billboard, and a sign held up in the studio audience of the game show (a sign Anderson himself removes in a brief cameo). Additional appearances of the numbers "8" and "2", linked together, are ubiquitous. I have observed at least twenty; others have found many more. The subtle nature of these **intertextual allusion**s to Exodus, most on screen only briefly, raise questions about the gap between Anderson's intention and the viewer's understanding.

Exodus 8:2 occurs within a broader narrative of the oppression and eventual liberation of the Hebrews from the Egyptians. Oppression and liberation are also crucial motifs throughout *Magnolia*. Unlike the ethnic basis of slavery in Exodus, oppression in *Magnolia* is familial and carried out by parents against their own children. There are four sets of parent/children relationships in the film, and each one is marked by abuse. Earl Partridge abandons his dying wife, leaving his teenage son Frank T. J. Mackey to care for her as she succumbs to cancer. Jimmy Gator (note the last name) appears to have sexually molested his daughter Claudia. Rick Spector continually berates his son Stanley, and views him principally as a potential source of monetary winnings on a quiz show. Donnie Smith's parents robbed him of his quiz show earnings when he was a child.

Parental oppression leaves lasting scars upon these children. The destructive influence of parents is confirmed—and illustrated—by a second citation from Exodus. While vomiting into a toilet, Donnie whispers, "The sins of the fathers . . . lay upon your children . . . Exodus 20:5." In *Magnolia*, fathers' sins are principally manifest in the inability of their grown up children to form healthy relationships. Frank Mackey only relates to women as sexual objects; he is the architect and chief evangelist for "Seduce and Destroy," which trains men how to conquer women sexually. Claudia numbs her pain with a cocaine addiction and anonymous sexual encounters. Donnie has failed in every realm of life: financially, vocationally, and relationally. His peak of excitement is trying to secure funds to procure braces, hoping that they will make him attractive to Brad, a local bartender. Stanley is aware that he functions largely as a pawn, manipulated by the adults in his life who use him to make money; he even admits to feeling like a freak.

The song playing over the opening montage in which all nine of the characters are first introduced, Aimee Mann's "One is the Loneliest Number," epitomizes the relational dysfunction and loneliness of these characters. Only two of the nine main characters are not subject to this kind of relational alienation: Jim Kurring, a Christian policeman, and

Phil, both of whom offer genuine care to others. Phil is Earl's nurse and he nurtures him with a selfless dedication; Jim offers forgiveness to Donnie, and he gives grace and acceptance to Claudia. In what is not a coincidence (nothing is in this film), they are two of the only main characters about whose parents we learn nothing. The implication is that where parents are present, so too is abuse.

Magnolia's characters illustrate the tragedy that the oppressed become oppressors themselves. The Brazilian educator Paolo Freire (*Pedagogy of the Oppressed*) describes such a transition as almost inevitable for any population subject to oppression. If abuse is all that one experiences, a person will, in turn, replicate this same treatment with others. Nowhere is this more evident in the film than with Frank. Abandoned by his cheating father to care for his dying mother, Frank grows into a man who only relates to women by using them. He is emphatic about rejecting his own past, insisting, "Facing the Past is a way of not making progress," and (citing a chapter from his manual) "The most useless thing in the world is that which is behind me." Frank is both at odds with, and an illustration of, the film's insistence (repeated three times), "We may be through with the Past, but the Past ain't through with us." Indeed, it is insight into Mackey's past wounds that gives viewers an opportunity to develop empathy with an oppressor.

The frogs descend at a crucial moment that coincides with alternating scenes of reconciliation and judgment. Upon hearing Jimmy Gator refuse to admit to molesting their daughter, Claudia's mother Rose leaves him, and drives to Claudia's apartment, where she arrives (as frogs are falling) and embraces her daughter. A quick camera pan to the lower-right hand corner of a painting on a wall zooms in on the phrase "But it did happen." While this line might refer to the odd descent of the frogs, it more likely is a reference, in light of the previous conversation between Jimmy and Rose, to Jimmy's guilt in molesting Claudia. Left alone, Jimmy takes out a pistol to shoot himself. A frog, however, falls through a ceiling window and hits him so that the gunshot misses. He collapses on the floor, and an electrical wire starts to smoke, hinting at an imminent fire. Frogs also fall when Frank finds himself at the bed of his dying father Earl with whom he experiences a genuine moment of reconciliation.

These apocalyptic scenes suggest that reconciliation requires forgiveness and confession. Those who do confess (Earl, Linda, Donnie) are each granted moments of restoration with others. Earl confesses his adultery and abandonment of his wife, and he is gifted with a brief moment of reconciliation with his son Frank. Linda confesses that she only married Earl for his money, but is now deeply in love with him, and she is granted (what appears to be) a moment to reconcile with Frank. Donnie confesses stealing money in order to buy braces, and Jim Kurring forgives him, keeping him out of jail. Those, however, like Jimmy Gator, who fail to confess their sins, are forbidden any kind of reconciliation. Even more than this, they are damned. As writer/director Anderson notes about Jimmy Gator's death:

> It's the first time when I've been able, at the end of a film, to hate one of my characters. There truly is a sense of moral judgment at work with this character. I can't even let him kill himself at the end—he's got to burn. . . . With this character, I'm saying "No." No to any kind of forgiveness for him.

Magnolia thus provides a supernatural event—frogs falling from the sky—in order to spur characters toward confession and reconciliation, and also as a judgment against those who refuse to admit to how they have harmed their children. The apocalypse in *Magnolia* is fundamentally relational in nature.

Conclusion

Film is, in many ways, an ideal medium for the genre of apocalypse. Cinema offers a temporary detour into an alternative dimension that—not unlike a heavenly realm—is both distinct from our own world, but also connected to it. As with biblical apocalypses, this "other world" often contains dramatic and violent displays. Such visual spectacles can incorporate the bizarre and even grotesque. Even more significant, these graphic displays are not mere aesthetic treats; these visions, and the films of which they are a part, frequently have the potential to reveal mysteries, both to characters in the narrative and to the film's audiences. Film critic Jean Epstein's definition of film as "profane revelation" is especially applicable to apocalyptic films. Films can not only incorporate apocalyptic themes, but also function as apocalypses in and of themselves. Films can operate, in other words, as apocalypses in their own right.

Like many biblical apocalypses, *Donnie Darko, Dogville,* and *Magnolia* view the world as so fundamentally flawed that the only hope of redemption or vindication lies outside of it. This hope must pierce through the world in order to bring about change. Whereas many biblical apocalypses are thought to be produced by oppressed or persecuted communities who long for some kind of future divine vindication, apocalyptic films are made by people who occupy the upper socio-economic echelons. They—and their audiences—have the potential power to alter behavior that is harmful to the environment or the vulnerable in society. Cinematic apocalypses thus occupy a potentially different rhetorical space than their biblical counterparts—one designed not so much to instill hope, but rather to empower change.

Study Questions:

1. In what ways do the films discussed here offer critiques of contemporary cultures in the United States?
2. Can you think of other apocalyptic films that also offer critiques of contemporary cultures in the United States? What similarities do these films share with the films discussed in this chapter?
3. What kinds of insights do the films discussed here offer into biblical texts? In what ways might these films help you read and interpret biblical texts?
4. Other than films, are there other examples of contemporary apocalyptic art you can think of (e.g., music, television, novels, poetry)? What is it that qualifies these as apocalyptic?

Bibliography and Further Reading:

Copier, Laura. *Preposterous Revelations: Visions of Apocalypse and Martyrdom in Hollywood Cinema*. Sheffield: Sheffield Academic Press, 2012.

Freire, Paulo. *Pedagogy of the Oppressed*. London: Bloomsbury Academic, 2000.

Pippin, Tina. "This Is the End: Apocalyptic Moments in Cinema." In *The Bible in Motion: Biblical Reception in Film*. Edited by Rhonda Burnette-Bletsch. Berlin: De Gruyter, 2016, I: 405–16.

Rindge, Matthew S. *Profane Parables: Film and the American Dream*. Waco, TX: Baylor University Press, 2016.

Runions, Erin. *How Hysterical: Identification and Resistance in Bible and Film*. New York: Palgrave Macmillan, 2003.

Seesengood, Robert Paul, and Jennifer L. Koosed. "Spectacular Finish: Apocalypse in/and the Destruction of the Earth in Film." In *Simulating Aichele: Essays in Bible, Film, Culture and Theory*. Edited by Melissa C. Stewart. Bible in the Modern World 69. Sheffield: Sheffield Phoenix, 2015, 143–60.

Walsh, Richard. "On Finding a Non-American Revelation: End of Days and the Book of Revelation." In *Screening Scripture: Intertextual Connections between Scripture and Film*. Edited by George Aichele and Richard Walsh. Harrisburg, PA: Trinity Press International, 2002, 1–23.

17

The Planet's Apocalypse

The Rhetoric of Climate Change

Ingrid Esther Lilly

GETTING PREPPED:

1. Why do climate change and natural disasters summon apocalyptic ideas?
2. What role does science play in apocalyptic ideas about the planet's future?
3. Who tells climate apocalypses and why?
4. Think of any movies or literature you know about natural disasters. How many of them are apocalyptic?

KEY TERMS:

CLIMATE CHANGE

ANTHROPOGENIC

CLIMATE CHANGE DENIAL

PSEUDO SCIENCE

MANAGERIAL OPTIMISM

ECOSYSTEM
ENLIGHTENMENT SCIENCE

Introduction

The Four Horsemen of the Apocalypse rode through the streets of Copenhagen in 2009. A meeting of world leaders for the **climate change** summit prompted the environmental group Greenpeace to stage a demonstration using four protesters on horseback, attired as those figures from the book of Revelation. The organizers saw rhetorical potential in the Four Horsemen as symbolizations of Famine, Pestilence, War, and Death—likely impacts of runaway climate change.

Even when decoupled from explicit apocalyptic motifs, talk about climate change almost always prompts a sense of foreboding. When former Republican senator, Chuck Hagel, in his role as Secretary of Defense, introduced the Pentagon's "2014 Climate Chance Adaptation Road Map," he articulated his concern about climate change while outlining the ideal policy goals for the U.S. Department of Defense (DOD), saying:

> Among the future trends that will impact our national security is climate change. Rising global temperatures, changing precipitation patterns, climbing sea levels, and more extreme weather events will intensify the challenges of global instability, hunger, poverty, and conflict. They will likely lead to food and water shortages, pandemic disease, disputes over refugees and resources, and destruction by natural disasters in regions across the globe. In our defense strategy, we refer to climate change as a "threat multiplier" because it has the potential to exacerbate many of the challenges we are dealing with today – from infectious disease to terrorism. We are already beginning to see some of these impacts.[1]

In the new millennium, we live with a perpetual environmental crisis. The evidence is easy to find: the wreck of the Amoco Cadiz crude oil carrier in 1978, the Three Mile Island nuclear explosion in 1979, the Union Carbide India Limited gas leak in 1984, the Exxon Valdez oil spill

---

1. For the press release, see http://www.defense.gov/Releases/Release.aspx?ReleaseID=16976, and for the full text of the roadmap, see http://www.acq.osd.mil/ie/download/CCARprint_wForeword_c.pdf.

in 1989, the Tennessee coal ash spill in 2008, the Deep Water Horizon BP oil spill of 2010, the shrinking of the Aral Sea by irrigation projects, and the ongoing creation of the Pacific ocean's garbage patch. And these are just industrial catastrophes. The severity of record-breaking storms, floods, wildfires, and droughts calls the climate crisis to mind with increasing regularity. Snowpocalypses, the Polar Vortex, Superstorms, and wildfires so large you can see them from space: both the reality and the rhetoric are alarming.

Apocalyptic motifs, strategies, and genres about climate change are on the rise. In this essay, I will explore three aspects of this cultural discourse. First, apocalyptic discourse tends to highlight and even widen ideological rifts. A veritable war of apocalyptic rhetoric pits science against **climate change denial**, environmentalists against industrialists, and reason against fantasy. This diabolical context is a consistent and important aspect of modern-day apocalyptic rhetoric. Second, climate change represents a crisis in **Enlightenment science**. Modern science owes its success to the Age of Enlightenment in which reason and empiricism replaced traditional authorities and ancient knowledge systems. Its cosmological principles about space and time structured a view of the planet without intrinsic value. Climate change is science's catastrophic end—in other words, it is science's *apocalypse*. What I am calling the Enlightenment science apocalypse is perhaps the most distinctive cultural development in the new millennium. Third, popular culture tells more and more stories that are set in a context of natural disasters caused by **anthropogenic** climate change. A brief look at an apocalyptic film, *Beasts of the Southern Wild*, about a community living at the edge of climate risk will explore a climate-induced natural disaster and offer a different ethos than those found in Enlightenment science apocalypses.

War of Environmental Apocalypses

One trend across the last several decades has been a remarkable war of apocalyptic rhetoric over environmental crises. For instance, in 2014, the film *Noah* told the biblical flood story with reference to human-caused climate change. The film portrayed the flood as a judgment on the excesses of industrial, energy-obsessed civilization. In response to this, Christian fundamentalist Ken Ham released a 30-minute "documovie" on *Noah*'s opening day, called "Noah and the Last Days." The film presents the flood as an emblem for contemporary natural disasters in order to remind viewers that the biblical last days are near.[2]

For every dire environmental warning of climate disaster, there sprouts an opposing account of the end. This is not just entertainment. This war of environmental apocalypses has been deployed to dramatize cultural and ideological differences, often on important national subjects. A poll from the Public Religion Research Institute (2014) found that half of its respondents think natural disasters are a sign of the biblical end times.

The Onion, a satirical news outlet, captured this state of affairs. The video news bit is entitled, "Biblical Armageddon Must be Taught alongside Global Warming," making fun of the false equivalency between science and religion's versions of the end times.[3] Known as "teach the controversy," some Christian groups fight scientific theory in public schools by suggesting that their Christian belief-system presents an alternative theory to explain scientific phenomena. In this case, the end of the world becomes a battleground between science and apocalyptic Christian faith.

The first modern war of environmental apocalypses began with Rachel Carson's book *Silent Spring*. Widely hailed as a seminal catalyst for environmental awareness and activism, *Silent Spring* presented the environmental science for the bio-impact of synthetic pesticides. The book's effects were significant: it inspired the environmental movement of the 1960s, contributed to the deep ecology and ecofeminism movements, and initiated a decade that would see the creation of the Environmental Defense Fund (EDF) and the Environmental Protection Agency (EPA).

---

2. See the movie here: http://www.noahthemovie.com.
3. http://www.theonion.com/video/christian-groups-biblical-armageddon-must-be-taugh-17491.

Carson's book documents the then understudied effects of DDT on genetics, cancer growth, and as a contaminant in the food chain. Reading almost like a legal brief on environmental science, Carson mounted an impressive argument against use of pesticides. Alongside the scientific work, she opened the book with a very short chapter entirely devoted to an environmental apocalypse. Entitled "A Fable for Tomorrow," the chapter describes a nameless American town whose animate life succumbed to synthetic poisoning:

> There was once a town in the heart of America where all life seemed to live in harmony with its surroundings. The town lay in the midst of a checkerboard of prosperous farms, with fields of grain and hillsides of orchards where, in spring, white clouds of bloom drifted above the green fields. In autumn, oak and maple and birch set up a blaze of color that flamed and flickered across a backdrop of pines. Then foxes barked in the hills and deer silently crossed the fields, half hidden in the mists of the fall mornings (Carson, 1).

Moving quickly from this romantic ideal, Carson creates an ominous atmosphere with phrases such as "evil spell," "a strange blight," "mysterious maladies," and "a shadow of death." The fable describes how idyllic features of an American **ecosystem** deteriorate and die. Her poetics emphasize the lack of birdsong in springtime, a haunting inversion of an American community emerging from winter. But her point is made clear, this was "no witchcraft . . . the people had done it themselves" (Carson 1962, 3). *Silent Spring* was the first modern environmental apocalypse to blame *human* activity for an environmental crisis.

Needless to say, those in the chemical industry reacted negatively to the book, but perhaps none as interestingly as Monsanto—an agrochemical company especially known today for its agricultural biotechnologies such as genetically modified seeds. In the same year *Silent Spring* came out (1962), Monsanto published a five-page parody called "The Desolate Year" in their corporate magazine. It portrayed an environmental apocalypse that results from banning pesticides (one of Monsanto's core products):

Imagine, then, that by some incomprehensible turn of circumstances, the United States were to go through a single year completely without pesticides. It is under that license that we take a hard look at the desolate year, examining in some detail its devastations (Monsanto 1962, 4).

The narrative begins with descriptions of winter in that "defenseless year" as the warmest climes in the USA begin to thaw. Foreshadowing doom with seemingly innocuous descriptions of the Mediterranean fruit fly, the essay makes one of its largest points, "not many people seemed to be aware of danger" (Monsanto 1962, 5). But bugs are, the essay continues, "unbelievably universal. On or under every square foot of land, every square yard, every acre . . . beneath the ground, beneath the waters . . . and yes, inside man. . . . They lurked quietly that day, waiting" (Monsanto 1962, 5). Adopting Carson's ominous tone, but inverting her storyline, the apocalypse conjures omnipresent insects as hidden environmental dangers that are innate to nature.

The narrative charts the destruction caused by the insects: destroyed produce, diseased cattle, denuded landscapes, and outbreaks such as Colorado tick fever and other epidemics. Like Carson, Monsanto claimed that this was not fantasy. Both wrote environmental apocalypses with an assemblage of real circumstances. From scenario to satire to fantasy to realism, "The Desolate Year" countered *Silent Spring* with its own environmental apocalypse.

Fifty years after Monsanto staged its apocalyptic feud against Carson, a 2010 novel imagines a more violent controversy. Michael Antony's *Apocalypse Syndrome* explores planetary doom, pitting Christian millennialists against climate change fanatics. The book follows a climate change denier, Hammond Sinclair, who inadvertently finds himself at the center of the controversy when he takes a public podium to express his doubts about global warming. He comes to the World Climate Conference in Geneva to stop a former student who had been radicalized by the climate debate. But it turns out the conference is inundated with numerous terrorist threats and murder plots, which occupy most of the narrative of the book.

Extremism infuses both ideological sides in the novel. Terrorism stems from zealous religion that nourishes visions of the end of the world over anxiety about the climate. Climate scientists are portrayed as zealots whipped up by the apocalyptic religion of their theories. Sinclair's speech about climate science at the heart of the novel offers a sustained reflection on Western science's apocalypse:

> I use the term apocalypse deliberately. Climate change has become the religion of today's intellectual. It has all the hallmarks of a religious faith: a profound sense of guilt, an impulse of collective self-flagellation, and a belief that our civilization is on the path to perdition. This ideology enables us to blame Western capitalism directly for every drought, every heat-wave, every flood, every famine on the planet. Extreme climate conditions are no longer caused by unpredictable weather patterns. They are caused by Western man's sins. . . . Capitalism, the Whore of Babylon, is destroying the earth, and humanity will be struck down by divine vengeance. (Antony 2010, 98–99)

Sinclair goes on to invoke nearly every culture war in American discourse as proof that the apocalypse syndrome has moralized everyone. He criticizes the "left-wing" media, a common refrain of the religious right. He blames a "global warming lobby [who] have whipped up a melodramatic atmosphere of a moral crusade to save the planet from catastrophe" (Antony 2010, 98). He explains how the religion of climate change vilifies "wicked Western industrialism . . . a vile prostitute in the pay of greedy capitalists who are destroying the earth" (Antony 2010, 98). Sinclair's speech expresses the height of America's moralized culture in a series of non sequiturs. But it also serves as a perfect example of the allergic reaction many in the new millennium feel for contemporary apocalyptic discourse about the environment.

Hammond Sinclair is the novel's ideal climate subject. He is committed to democratic values such as public debate, and he aspires to a neutral "scientific" reasoning not sullied by climate alarm. Because of the length of his big speech, a remarkable portion of the novel reads more like a nonfiction book on popular science. Indeed, the speech seemingly abandons the book's fiction genre in order to engage real contemporary debates. Sinclair excoriates the Intergovernmental

Panel on Climate Change (IPCC, discussed below), cites the research of actual MIT and CERN climate skeptics, and explains typical climate issues such as the melting Greenland ice-sheets, rising oceans, and atmospheric temperature. He uses scientific discourse to dismantle the theory of anthropogenic climate change.

But aspects of Sinclair's scientific discourse could come straight out of a Dan Brown novel: ancient sea vessels play an incomprehensible role, the Aztecs and Maya feature, and the astronomical alignments of Egyptian pyramids are used to explain intergalactic energy transfer. Sinclair claims that these underappreciated "facts" were not accepted by "orthodox" academics, whom he characterizes as sick with an apocalypse syndrome to which he considers himself alone to be immune. Indeed, the novel constructs climate change skepticism as the only rational position. Neither taken in by Christian end-of-times apocalyptic rhetoric, nor riled up by scientific discourse, Sinclair's critical reason seems to offer a cool, Enlightenment position from which to make judgments about the world. Like Enlightenment science, Sinclair affirms the neutrality of linear time and space. As such, the planet is less like a living organism and more like an inert stage. In other words, there is no need to worry about the Earth as the context for human life; it will always be there. However, parting ways with Enlightenment science, Sinclair challenges the integrity and standards for scientific research. With no regard for how theories and models function, nor for the important role of probability in science of the twentieth century, Sinclair's scientific "reason" is a spectral position infused with tremendous amounts of folklore. The character Hammond Sinclair is, in fact, a perfect example of the **pseudo science** that emerges today to fight off the dire warnings of climate scientists. Pseudo-science co-opts the authority of scientific knowledge, but does not adhere to its principles. It offers ideologues a way to clothe their opinions with an aura of truth.

Enlightenment Science's Climate Apocalypse

Enlightenment science plays an increasingly central role in apocalyptic discourse about climate change. With the rise of pseudo-science, the authority of the scientist has gotten lost in the dissembling war of planetary apocalypses. False equivalencies and political rhetoric have crafted a level playing field in popular culture, where science has—at least in some circles—lost its privileged place as the arbiter of Truth. The twentieth century saw the increasing marginalization of environmentalists and their fervent concerns. As Frederick Buell argues, the energy of the environmental movement in the 1960s and 1970s lost its sense of inevitability; what at one time seemed like a powerful movement to defend the environment is now a limp value, given only lip service. Buell does a particularly nice job showing how environmentalists have come to be vilified as failed prophets and extremists:

> Environmentalism's antagonists [were able] to stigmatize its erstwhile stewards as unstable alarmists and bad-faith prophets – and to call their warnings at best hysterical, at worst crafted lies. Indeed, something happened to allow some even to question (without appearing ridiculous) that apparently commonsensical assumption that environmentalists were the environment's best stewards. (Buell 2003, 3)

Climate change scientists are subject to a great double bind. On the one hand, they must, as *Apocalypse Syndrome* suggests, embody pure reason. Their modes of communication should cast off the disreputable alarmism and hysteria of apocalyptic discourse. But, on the other hand, climate scientists increasingly use powerful rhetoric in order to communicate their findings. The AAAS (American Academy for the Advancement of Science) and the IPCC have added "spokesperson" to the professional obligations of the climate scientist. The American Geophysical Union even awards an annual Climate Communication Prize. As scientists move into public spaces, they have put a premium on the ability to effectively communicate the conclusions and implications of their scientific research. They work hard to summon concern with media headlines such as:

• "Five facts that will open your eyes"

- "We just passed a very scary limit"
- "Look at these unimaginable numbers"
- "Here's a polar bear trying to balance on a tiny iceberg"

Like prophets in the wilderness, scientists' messages often fall on deaf ears. Indeed, many people seem to be blasé today about climate change. This is unfortunate, because climate change actually is an opportunity for Enlightenment science to speak in apocalyptic tones. Enlightenment science has described the structure of the universe in certain terms: its cosmos is Copernican; its geography, Cartesian; its time and forces, Newtonian. Students of its revelation must appreciate how heat exchange, atomic bonding, and pH balance work in order to understand how they might threaten earth's systems. Such esoteric knowledge requires specialized training, a priesthood authorized by advanced degrees.

The specialization required makes it understandable why talk about the climate apocalypse can draw a lot of yawns. Consider the title of an Economist article about the 2014 IPCC report: "Apocalyptish."[4] The article opens briefly with the Four Horsemen of the apocalypse, only to take a deep dive for the rest of the essay into risk assessments rooted in natural science—hardly a topic the average reader is prepared to understand. A 0.4 percent increase in earth's temperature may be alarming, but it does not seem the stuff of "apocalyptish" nightmares. Enlightenment science demythologizes nature, rejects subjectivity, decenters the cosmos. (To be sure, the father of Enlightenment science, Isaac Newton, nourished a lifelong interest in Daniel and Revelation as predictions of the end of the world. And biblical exegesis played an important role in the rise of modern science; but ultimately, the ancient biblical apocalypses and contemporary science are worlds apart. (See Peter Harrison, *The Bible, Protestantism, and the Rise of Natural Science*.) The apocalypse offered by contemporary science is distinct from its biblical and religious namesake. The biblical apocalypse posits

4. http://www.economist.com/blogs/newsbook/2014/03/climate-change-0.

humanity at the center of the universe and upholds the notion of a Creator who intervenes in history on behalf of humans. This God bends nature to his service, causing both hellscape and New Jerusalem to emerge in the story of humankind. In contrast, Enlightenment science's appeal to apocalyptic language has no subject and no body. It tells no history, elicits no desire, and offers no catharsis. Its crisis is measured in meters, not monsters.

Although they may not be monstrous in the same way as the beast of Revelation, scary numbers show up everywhere in contemporary discussions of planetary apocalypse. Climate scientists get creative, often infusing their measurements with apocalyptic modes of communication. For example, scientists periodize history according to significant climate measures. Perhaps the best example of this is 350.org, a global organization for grassroots movements, which gets its name from a famous climate limit of 2007: the number of ppm (parts per million) of CO_2 in the atmosphere, after which the climate crisis gets dangerous.[5] We passed 400 ppm in 2013, and scientists dubbed it a "new era."

Other scientific bodies use metaphors to communicate their apocalypse. The AAAS, the largest scientific body in the world, recently published a video along with its public document, "What We Know."[6] The document contains a digest of scientific conclusions about climate risks, undersigned by 97 percent of AAAS membership. The video uses the metaphor of an out-of-control mountain biker passing signs that read "Climate Cliff Ahead." The end of his reckless ride, a possible plummet to his death, is a simple metaphor for humanity's climate apocalypse. However, this cyclist screeches to a halt in the nick of time, disaster averted. The video makes clear that the rider would have more safely avoided the climate cliff if he had paid more attention to the signs and slowed his pace, a clear message to the audience: observe the signs and slow down, or you may not be so lucky.

In another example, NASA's website exemplifies how scientific

5. http://350.org/resources/videos/the-350-movement-90-seconds-no-words/.
6. http://whatweknow.aaas.org/we-brake-for-climate/).

documentation and data perform the climate crisis.[7] It uses satellite images and live climate measurements to testify to climate change, like a National Geographic documentary with a countdown clock. Powerful images portray then-and-now glacial melt, desertification, and breached levees while data tickers update at the bottom of the page. It is debatable whether the site is an outlet for *Schadenfreude* or announces a climate wake-up call, but the NASA site live updates climate catastrophes.

What NASA does with documentary photography and the AAAS does with metaphor, the IPCC accomplishes in the native discourse of science. The IPCC is an international body of scientists begun and officially endorsed by the United Nations. It produces reports for member governments so they can make policy that attempts to honor international treaties on climate change. The IPCC produced a video in a remarkable genre, what I will call an "apocalyptic climate diagram," along with the report of the second Working Group in 2014.[8] Each aims to show the risks of anthropogenic climate change and offer actions to mitigate or avert the worst consequences.

The IPCC video presents three phases of climate change: (1) life before climate change; (2) an apocalyptic climate diagram; and (3) a culminating message of hope. Ominous music plays over images of a pre-apocalyptic world. But the video quickly moves into its apocalyptic climate diagram, communicated through equations, definitions of terms, and a flowchart. It begins with an equation calculating risk that uses exploding red bombs to graphically depict scale and probability.

As the equation grows larger, integrating more factors, animations help to define terms. For example, "Exposure" is defined as "people, ecosystems, or assets at risk" while a little stick figure's house drowns in a flood plain. Throughout this section, the animated stick figures bend over in a subtle hint that they are weeping and gnashing their teeth. Finally, the animation portrays the ultimate cataclysm in the medium of an infographic diagram. As features symbolizing climate

---

7. http://climate.nasa.gov.
8. See the video here: http://ipcc-wg2.gov/AR5/report/wgii-animations/.

and socioeconomic processes are added to the diagram, moving arrows shooting inwards visually represent the apocalypse. In fact, the diagram becomes quite overcomplicated, performing via illustration the scientific complexity of extreme climate risk. A remarkable feat, the IPCC animation transforms scientific forms of communication into an apocalyptic genre. This is a mathematical maelstrom, an infographic depiction of catastrophe. It ends with the whole diagram passing away, with only the word "Risk" growing to consume most of the screen.

The third section of the animation offers post-apocalyptic hope with a now familiar Enlightenment message: we can reduce and manage risk. The math equations give way to colorful images of harmonious human civilization. The people head into a hopeful structure called "Building our Future." Here, thought bubbles reveal their "climate concerns" about grandchildren, justice, and health. The building promises to provide them information, help them set goals, and teach them to cultivate new values. These characters are the ideal subjects of climate apocalypse. They transform their personal anxieties into a new way of life that will mitigate the risk of climate change.

The IPCC apocalypse and the AAAS metaphor place considerable hope in the power of human action. The graphics implicitly convey that climate subjects can modify behavior, thereby mitigating climate risks and reversing detrimental trends. That same **managerial optimism** is playfully dramatized in an apocalyptic video game about the climate, Will Wright's *SimEarth: The Living Planet*. This is a wholly pedagogical game. It puts scientific optimism and hope into the hands of the player, and is designed to teach the player about the risks of ignoring climate change. Published in 1990 on the heels of the popular *SimCity*, the video game allows players to control the development of a planet. It promises creative license and full control:

> More than one trillion SimEarthlings can live on a single planet, and their entire fate is in your hands. You are in complete control of the planet's environment, life and civilization. Your planet has an unlimited potential. (Wright 1990, 3)

The game permits a variety of life forms. As they increase and evolve, populations are subjected to natural disasters (hurricanes, fires, or plagues), "man"-made problems (war, pollution), and to larger issues in climate balance, such as rising temperatures, the greenhouse effect, and atmospheric particulate count. This apocalyptic frame raises important climate questions as players are forced to grapple with how life forms use energy and interact with the environment, all in the face of impending planetary collapse.

SimEarth is based on James Lovelock's Gaia hypothesis, which focuses on how life forms change the environments of a planet. As the game manual explains, Lovelock made a basic atmospheric observation that all of the oxygen on Earth comes from its life forms. If carbon-based life did not exist, the mix of atmospheric gases on Earth would be radically different. Although the science is not widely accepted, the Gaia hypothesis supplies the game with its most interesting philosophical premise. Civilized life forms and the variability of their actions become part of earth's developing ecosystems, for good or ill. This is not the planet as a neutral stage, the Cartesian space of Enlightenment science. Rather, in this hypothesis, the planet and its population are part of the same ecology. This is crucial. Human action can cause problems to the planet but can also solve them.

Game play, like climate science itself, is quite complicated. Players pick a planet scenario that gives them a starting point: somewhere in early evolution (Aquarium scenario), another stage of planet earth (Modern Day Earth scenario), or under different planetary conditions (Venus scenario). A fair amount of game strategy involves common sense; for example, to create land, you must initiate volcanic activity. But the game requires impressive knowledge about earth science. The manual includes substantial information of instructional value, and several online wikis and instruction guides include deeper educational content on geology, climate, and the impacts of technology. The scientific prowess demanded by the game is made apparent by all of the data the player must read. In various graphs, reports, and especially the Data Display panels, players weigh information on ocean currents, water temperature, plant distribution, and more. Equipped with all of this planetary knowledge, the player can manipulate everything from cloud formation to the planet's core heat to bioenergy technologies using the four Model Control panels (geosphere, atmosphere, biosphere, and civilization).

Despite the possibility of doom, the game takes a deeply hopeful, and even playful, look at planetary apocalyptic scenarios. The player is in control of natural systems and has the power to manipulate the climate in order to avert disaster. As the manual promises, the game offers unlimited potential, and the end of the world awaits only if one loses the game. In particular, four features of the game empower these playful planetary futures. First, *SimEarth* allows for dramatic species evolution. Mollusks can become sentient, for example, and form advanced civilizations. There is even an "Easter egg" in the game that prompts the evolution of robots. The evolutionary features of the game embed utopian ideas from post-natural environmentalism, such as the possibilities for genetic engineering and cyborg subjects. Second, the player can initiate a movement of life forms to other planets, called an exodus. Some of the game scenarios require you to prepare another planet while keeping life forms alive on Earth. (The hope of finding another planet that would support life offers an unrealistic if frequent feature of environmental apocalypses.) Third, players make regular use of "Terraformers." These are technologies that put industry in the service of climate health. For instance, CO_2 converters produce oxygen and reduce levels of greenhouse gas. These factories and generators are mostly human-made, but can be natural or even extraterrestrial. (It is not uncommon for cosmologists to speculate that extraterrestrial knowledge could save the planet. Carl Sagan was known to espouse that hope. Meanwhile, carbon dioxide removal [CDR] is a growing area of industrial research today.)

Fourth, "Event Triggers" put a positive spin on natural disasters. A player may wish to initiate a major cataclysm to increase rainfall where it is needed or to promote species diversification. Instead of alarm about natural disasters, the player is led to adopt an evolutionary and planetary perspective on population loss and environmental change. In this framework, even cataclysms can serve positive functions.

With the possible exception of NASA's website, all of the apocalyptic discourse about climate science listed above communicates managerial optimism: 350.org, AAAS, IPCC, and *SimEarth* share a "we can do this if we act now" message of hope. *SimEarth* offers industrial and technological solutions that would save SimEarthlings from planetary collapse, and the IPCC animation complements the primary mission of the organization, to provide governments with data and risk assessment to help inform policy, vesting hope in governmental action to change citizens' behavior. While numerous scientists do not feel as optimistic about the future, these official organizations and educational games assume the possibility of responsible human action and encourage that responsibility, and preach a message of apocalyptic hope in order to change damaging human behaviors.

Fantasy, Natural Disaster, and Climate Change

While the scientific apocalypse may be the most notable generic development over the last several decades, climate apocalypses abound, particularly in film. Adopting typical apocalyptic modes, they present dramatic forces, monsters, catharsis, and post-apocalyptic hellscapes in films as diverse as *2012: Ice Age*, *Avatar*, *The Lorax*, *Mad Max: Fury Road*, and *Sharknado*. It is particularly common for films to portray natural disasters as the dramatic stage for apocalyptic and post-apocalyptic narratives. Such films frequently connect their disasters to climate change: *San Andreas* (earthquake), *Deep Impact* (flood), *World War Z* (virus), *Contagion* (deadly bacteria), *Twister* (tornado), *The Impossible* (tidal wave), *Children of Men* (infertility), *The Day After Tomorrow* (ice age).

Among this large body of work, *Beasts of the Southern Wild* (2012), a fantasy drama directed by Benh Zeitlin, stands out. With reference to climate change, its natural disaster prompts an entirely different response than the managerial optimism typical of scientific apocalypses. The film explores a community on the edge of what the

IPCC would call "extreme climate risk." But unlike the risk-averse climate subjects in the IPCC animation, the characters in the film are enmeshed in environmental catastrophe. This film is a full-hearted contrast to the emotional neutrality of climate science's rational citizen.

The film takes place in the midst of dangers posed to residents of southern Louisiana by hurricanes such as Katrina. It follows an imaginative survivalist child and her father who live in a bayou community called "the Bathtub." Cut off from the mainland by the levees, the Bathtub is even more exposed than the already endangered New Orleans. When the Bathtub comes under the assault of a damaging storm, it serves as a mythic space to explore how people live with the extreme dangers of climate disaster.

The main character is a six-year-old named Hushpuppy. She and her community strongly identify with their environment. She learns to "beast it," cracking crab with her own bare hands. Her ailing father drives a motorized boat, a repurposed Ford truck bed buoyed by oil barrels. Her home is like a survivalist shelter, built from the discarded trash of consumer society. She learns how to celebrate and grieve at regular festivals that brim with an abundance of fruits from the ocean. A heavy storm and extreme flooding serve as the movie's dramatic backdrop, but both the environment's disasters and its bounty are a way of life in the Bathtub. Hushpuppy is a climate survivalist. Her character stands in relief against climate adaptive subjects that appear in the IPCC video.

When a big storm floods the Bathtub, Louisiana state officials evacuate the community to overpopulated shelters. Despite the healthcare and dry living conditions, Hushpuppy, her terminally ill father, and those left of their community break free from the government-mandated evacuation and return to their flooded home. Hushpuppy facing disaster, listening to the last heartbeat of her father, standing with her community as they set his corpse on fire in his floating truck-bed: the film insists that these are all part of the flow of natural life. Hushpuppy's young wisdom opines: "The brave ones stay and watch it happen. They don't run."

In a director interview, Zeitlin comments,

> No one really respects the self-sufficiency of south Louisiana; there's a lot of disrespect for it. When people come in there they think, "These people need help, let's get them out of here and teach them how to be more functional citizens"—as if they're idiots. It's that sort of condescending attitude that the rest of America had toward South Louisiana and continues to. . . . It's not good for people to be put in a shelter in the middle of nowhere. That's not better than them fending for themselves in their homes, even if it threatens their lives. It threatens their lives much more to be removed than it does to stay. There are exceptions to this; it's not like the movie is advocating that people not be rescued from disastrous situations. But it's that condescending notion of, "We know better, you should live somewhere safer," which definitely infuriated me after the storm and that was a big entryway into the movie. . . . There's some kind of enlightenment that exists in Louisiana. There's a fearlessness in the culture down there that has everything to do with how close to death it is. To be there, you have to be brave. It's not for timid hearted people to live down there because it's dangerous, and it's scary, and it threatens your life, and it threatens your children's lives. I'm trying to make the connection between that and what makes people also so openhearted.[9]

The film dignifies survivalism by casting climate change in a fantastic role. Throughout the film, Hushpuppy has visions of prehistoric beasts, aurochs, who have thawed by the melting ice in the South Pole. They charge through her imagination in a few key scenes, heading toward the Bathtub—as symbols of impending climate threat—but once they arrive, they desist from their snorting charge as Hushpuppy whispers, "you're my friend, kind of." "Strong animals, they know when your hearts are weak. That makes them hungry and they start coming." Monsters released by climate change, these beasts are, at once, mythic symbols of natural disaster and representations of surrealist shifts in earth's systems. Hushpuppy models a climate subjectivity that integrates fear and bravery in the face of apocalyptic monsters. She

9. http://www.theatlantic.com/entertainment/archive/2012/06/beasts-of-the-southern-wild-director-louisiana-is-a-dangerous-utopia/259009/.

becomes "friends, kind of" with natural disasters induced by climate change.

Conclusion

To engage the dangers of climate change is to contemplate a rapidly changing planet. Life depends on numerous natural systems, and abrupt change could alter how or even whether life can be sustained. The potential for apocalyptic discourse is obvious. Whether measuring alarming CO_2 levels, crafting rhetoric about the dangers of melting glaciers, projecting climate models ahead fifty years, or exploring human experience of natural disasters, apocalyptic discourses function like a native language for climate change.

Not everyone answers the invitation in the same way. The war of environmental apocalypses pits durable cultural divisions against one another. When Monsanto challenged Rachel Carson's *Silent Spring* with a pest-apocalypse, the confrontation presaged a long period of industry efforts against environmentalists. *Apocalypse Syndrome* captures the twenty-first-century suspicion of all alarmist rhetoric about planetary futures. Hammond Sinclair is a twenty-first-century climate change denier, pitting science against his own pseudo-science. In many respects, the apocalyptic pitch of these exchanges exacerbates already difficult societal challenges.

One of these challenges is the loss of trust in science. Ninety-seven percent of geophysical scientists arrive at the same dire conclusion about the dangers of climate change. Charged with the mission to deliver this message, climate scientists frequently dip into alarmist discourse to explain their science apocalypse. The AAAS's metaphor of climate cliff challenges the adventure ride of earth's inhabitants to slow down and heed the warning signs. NASA's website, the IPCC's apocalyptic diagram, and *SimEarth*'s educational science video game are replete with "monstrous" numbers and data about cataclysmic events. Two different, but similarly optimistic messages emerge from these science apocalypses. On the one hand, the IPCC animation imagines that governments can work with scientists and industry to mitigate the risks of climate change. Meanwhile, the ideal climate citizen modifies their lives by transforming anxieties into new sustainable behaviors. People who live in high-risk environments would move. Education is key to the hope expressed in this scientific world view. On the other hand, *SimEarth* vests hope in the unlimited potential for science and technology to solve planetary crises. Well-educated individuals who understand the delicate scientific balance of the Earth's systems can come up with agile solutions to presenting problems. Whether players decide to invest in Terraformers or seek assistance of genetic engineering, they embody the power of individual ingenuity. All of these share a very optimistic message about the power of human action to triumph once people are properly equipped with knowledge about dangers and risks.

The Beasts of the Southern Wild offers a community, protagonist, and ethos far different from the science apocalypses. Survivalism and human ecology characterize Hushpuppy's emotional negotiation with natural disaster. Confronted with the mythic force of a volatile but enchanted nature, she makes "friends, kind of" with a reality in which cataclysm is a way of life.

The potential for crafting apocalypses out of the fodder of climate change seems as unlimited as the human imagination. Climate change raises the very biggest questions about human civilization, interconnectedness, impersonal forces of nature, human culpability, and human responsibility.

Study Questions:

1. Who do you think is the ideal climate subject?
2. What role does Enlightenment science play in climate apocalypses?
3. How does the anthropogenic explanation for climate change relate to apocalyptic ideas about sin and judgment?
4. What different ideologies are advanced by specific climate apocalypses?

5. How can climate scientists successfully communicate their findings about climate change?

Bibliography and Further Reading:

Anshelm, Jonas, and Martin Hultman. *Discourses of Global Climate Change: Apocalyptic Framing and Political Antagonisms.* New York: Routledge, 2015.

Antony, Michael. *The Apocalypse Syndrome.* Bloomington, IN: iUniverse, 2010.

Buell, Frederick. *From Apocalypse to Way of Life: Environmental Crisis in the American Century.* New York: Routledge, 2003.

Carson, Rachel. *Silent Spring.* Boston: Houghton Mifflin; Cambridge, Mass.: Riverside Press, 1962.

Diamond, Jared M. *Collapse: How Societies Choose to Fail or Succeed.* New York: Penguin, 2005.

Fava, Sergio. *Environmental Apocalypse in Science and Art: Designing Nightmares.* New York: Routledge, 2013.

Harrison, Peter. *The Bible, Protestantism, and the Rise of Natural Science.* Cambridge: Cambridge University Press, 2001.

Monsanto. "The Desolate Year." *Monsanto Magazine,* (1962): 4–9.

Wright, Will. *SimEarth: The Living Planet.* (1990).

Zimmerman, Michael E. *Contesting Earth's Future: Radical Ecology and Postmodernity.* Berkeley: University of California Press, 1994.

18

Post-Bankruptcy Detroit as Apocalyptic Sign of the Times

James W. Perkinson

GETTING PREPPED:

1. In what ways do hip-hop lyrics "speak" to prevailing cultural trends? Can you think of some specific examples?
2. Can you think of living situations in your own hometown/city that might be characterized as "apocalyptic"?
3. What might it mean to "pull back the veil" on various systems in your own hometown/city?

KEY TERMS:
INDIGENOUS
HIP-HOP

INSURGENCE
ORTHODOXY
CATCHMENT BASINS
WHITE FLIGHT
JUBILEE

Introduction

Apocalypse is the hour we ride in today. A tsunami of galloping emergencies bears down on all sides. Ceaseless war, with blown apart bodies and decapitated heads piling up (as the media salivates) around the globe. Climate change bearing down (literally) like the Flood of deep memory or a wild fire from Hell. Refugees abroad drowning in overcrowded boats or roasting to death inside locked trucks. Black and brown youth at home gunned down with virtual impunity. Foreclosures and homelessness rising. Oil spilling because of ever more desperate gambits to perpetuate our impossible "culture of the car" a few more years. Water resources pumped dry by corporations or pirated and sold at ever more inflated rates by governments. Food in the store proving increasingly toxic. Hospital-generated infections among the most severe threats to health around. Education privatized, bureaucratized, and gutted to serve hedge funds and entrepreneurs. Diagnoses of dysfunction and zombifying drugs pumped into our kids to keep them tame at their desks. Economies, national and local, jerked into austerity and squeezed to yield bloated banks even more profit. Middle classes disappearing. Bees disappearing. Rain forests disappearing. Extinction rates skyrocketing to levels observed only five other times in our 4.8 billion-year planetary history. And it all comes with social cowering in its wake; bulging veins of rage mark the forehead of the body politic. Apocalypse! Now! And for the foreseeable future!

How might we think about this reality in a mode of constructive engagement? In what follows, I want to sketch out a response to the duress of the day in one of the places where apocalypse is descending most intractably. De-industrialized Detroit—long the poster-child of blight in the USA—is today a laboratory for globalizing forces, material and spiritual, which are rapidly reorganizing an entire planet under the sign of cataclysm. Inside this crucible of crisis, however, there is also appearing a potent eruption of Life. It hunkers down largely inside dark skin, spits rhyme and pops joints with bombastic panache, and scans the horizon for unapologetic hope. Call this an unapologetic apology for **hip-hop** pneumatology, the "science of the Spirit" encountering "uncontainable spiritedness." I want to think beats and braggadocio inside the imperial "Beast of Revelation" as a form of holy spiritedness. The reference, obviously, introduces a biblical "hook" into the complex as we shall examine in depth below. What popular culture today thinks of as the "Book of Revelation," the literal Greek entitles "The Apocalypse of John" and offers, in its unfolding, a Spirit-glimpse behind the veil of everyday events. What is seen in such an "unveiling" (what "apocalypse" literally means in Greek) is political struggle in the key of mythic combat—"beasts" of imperial rule promulgating their reign by means of propagandistic delusion and monstrous violence. In our own time, the murk is not less thick. Since 1492, the quintessential Power on the planet has been (what **indigenous** scholars call) "settler colonialism," the juggernaut of conquest, initially centered in Europe, that has now imposed white and Western priorities on an entire globe. Continuous land takeover has issued more recently in the marketing of debt and the mandate of austerity as the new modalities of the old game. And in the mix, hip-hop defiance—as a return, in popular form, from the repressed of colonial compliance—demands exegesis as hot-spirited **insurgence** (at least, in its underground up-wellings). To which we will attend in what follows.

But more particularly, here, I want to offer for consideration a kind of "holy conflagration" that took place one recent summer between constituencies indigenous, Christian, and street, seeking to find common cause in re-imagining Motor City land and water as a Commons of Gifting by a Creator unconstrained by anyone's pet creeds or philosophical jeremiads (as summarized in a similar article written for the event: Perkinson 2015a). Hip-hop led the way in this tri-fold coming together of activists, and it did so by refusing any presumption of monopoly on either prophetic critique or proclamation of affirmation ("good news")—including its own. Here, I can only sketch. But the event that took place under the leadership of young energy of color, tattooing the encounter with percussive insight and syncopated intelligence, emerged like the second coming of Africa under the skin of everyone. This was a new mediation peculiar to our Motown situation. In the heart of the black metropolis, hip-hop as broker of space for a place-based indigenous "macing" of the dominant white Christian presumption of supremacy! During the three-day gathering, every hint of appropriation of culture or site was sharply called out even as communion was thereby carefully re-woven. Every gesture or word that one more time assumed a position of privilege—whether based on race, religion, gender, orientation, or apparent title to land—was challenged and examined. What emerged was a ferocious new texture of collaboration! Such, I would suggest, is a serious throw-down to any theology that wants to claim messianic preeminence under the sign of Apocalypse in our current moment. Before conjuring such a claim, however, a bit of background on the biblical image of world endings is necessary.

Apocalypse "Unveiled"

Apocalypse is both event and perspective. As event, it typically references the collapse of a given social order. But what has often not been appreciated in past uptake of this biblical orientation is the degree to which the upheaval thus symbolized is finally one of nature itself. Apocalypse bursts onto the scene of order as the revenge of the wild, unleashed! Given the current crisis of our planetary climate, the word should explode with significance in modern Christian consciousness like a suddenly smoking volcano. The apocalypse of urbanized humanity we are currently witnessing might indeed be re-styled—from the point of view of plants and animals, waters and soils—as the **jubilee** release of enslaved nature! Apocalypse portends not merely (in biblical times) swords and chariots or (now) bombs and bullets, but a war waged by weather. It comprehends a moment when land and air, oceans and bear spoor weigh in and speak judgment. There is much here that could occupy our focus for far more than the allotted space that will, thus, have to wait another time and writing. Here, I want to concentrate on the meaning of apocalypse as task and perspective. It entails insight into the driving forces of imperial violence and social oppression, as well as confrontation of the injustice created, and community experiments in living otherwise.

From a biblical perspective, this figure of cataclysm should be entertained as a mesmerizing Zeitgeist, an eruptive "Time Ghost," disciplining us to discernment and courageous action. It articulates a genre of political commitment. But most of us who come out of a Christian background carry vastly atrophied imaginations—casualties of the way Christian monotheism interacts with imperial monoculturalism. In the face of large-scale upheaval, we curl up inside a few chosen verses, hoping like Moses that the specter will pass us by (Exod 33:17–23). But unlike Moses, few of us have acted to intervene, been saddled with a warrant for our arrest by the state, fled to the wilderness to be re-schooled long term by an undomesticated God, and then, worked to galvanize a movement of serious resistance (Exod 2:11–3:12). (Indeed, few of us have had mothers as perspicacious as Moses's own in responding to genocidal emergency with the kind of foresight and audaciousness she exhibited in preparing her son one day to act; Exod 2:1–10.) Apocalypse is not simply the advent of Fear writ large. It is also the possibility of clarity offered as choice. Moses acted on behalf of the oppressed (trying to halt the beating of one of his enslaved kin by an Egyptian overseer; Exod 2:11–12), and then, in response to the impending wrath of political authority, he made a clear choice to re-learn his situation from the point of view of the margins (Exod 2:15). He left his people; hooked up with an African clan in the outback of Sinai sands; sought schooling from the land under apprenticeship to his herds until he could finally see potent Spirit inside a local bush (Exod 2:16–3:12). Only then was he ready to lead an outbreak of slave insurgence—ending one world and beginning another.

Apocalypse is, above all, a question of vision (Howard-Brook and Gwyther 2002, 121ff). As already indicated, the word in Greek is "*apokalyptein*," "to un-cover," or "pull back the veil." Seeing "apocalyptically" means recognizing, in the first place, that there is a veil that needs to be pulled back. Reality is not what it appears to be. Waking up to the political charade requires ever-renewed attention to what otherwise remains hidden or obscured. What is most immediately observed when we pull our eyes away from distraction (whatever keeps us mesmerized in triviality and self-absorption) is violence. Profound, unrelenting, targeted destruction of bodies human and other. The work of learning to "see" unflinchingly—of looking the beast of the age squarely in the eye and naming its true character unabashedly—is *the* primal responsibility in an age of apocalypse. The vision is raw—nothing like a middle-class night out at the movies. Empire in its underpinnings is a war machine, piling up bodies. And the first task of those seeking to exit its thrall is to "look" without looking away. Jesus, for instance, having confronted the Powers of his day, facing his imminent arrest and execution and trying desperately to prepare his inner circle for a similar vocation, sketches out the stark realities of imperial "business as usual," and then, says simply: "Watch! What I say to you, I say to all. Watch!" (Mark 13:1–37) The advice seems prosaic when a world is collapsing.

Apocalyptic Insight

But indeed, the entire game of creative resilience is won or lost in the first moment of looking at a circumstance of upheaval. Fear stalks crisis like a hound of terror. How easy it is to be taken over by its fervor and lose any capacity to discern. Vigilant attentiveness is the first line of faithful resistance when imperial might begins to experience the consequences of its overreach. Apocalypse demands watching. What does one watch for? The flashes of "revelation" of what is actually going on when back room dealings, surveillance oversteps, whistleblowing exposure, and repressive violence disclose Power's subtext. Crisis, as the Chinese say, is also opportunity. For Jesus, the aggressiveness of elite challenge to his Temple actions and teaching—with the people out in force to celebrate Passover—indeed reveals this subtext (as recounted in Mark 11 and 12, leading up to Jesus's own apocalyptic rant in chapter 13).

Sidebar 18.1

Mark's gospel is constructed such that the second part of Jesus's ministry involves a non-violent "campaign" in which he leads his movement up into Jerusalem, dramatically clears money-changers out of the Temple, occupies the Temple mall for a day, and then, retreats. Over the ensuing days, he re-enters the Temple and engages in a high-stakes rhetorical battle with leadership elites in the hearing of the crowds gathered for the celebration, until he is finally arrested and charged with threatening to destroy the Temple.

The authorities' fear of Jesus's movement led them to call him out publicly, not realizing (as is so often the case with ruling-class arrogance) that his lifetime of living against the imperial grain had equipped him with a high-velocity "outlaw" tongue. He "flipped the script" on their every attempt to trap him in debate such that their own motives and behind-the-scenes manipulation became ever more palpable in each riposte. They launch a campaign to impugn his credentials the day after he has conducted a sit-down strike in the Temple: he retorts with a question about their role in John the Baptist's arrest and decapitation (Mark 11:27–33). They ask about paying tribute to Caesar; he "outs" the fact that they are the ones carrying Caesar's coin in the Temple sanctuary—a case of bringing an "idol" into the holy place—exhibiting their collusion with Roman rule (Mark 12:13–17).

They insist scribal authority decides Torah interpretation; he clarifies that it is precisely scribal interpretation of the Law that is "devouring widow's houses" and lining elite pockets with the proceeds (Mark 12:28–44). After every attempt to pillory him backfires, the Powers switch to code silence, while he goes on the offensive (Mark 12:34–35). But lightning has already struck. In each riposte, "behind the scenes" finagling has been backlit and revealed. In his "battle raps," like some first-century Nas with a tongue for an Uzi, the people "see" (Mark 12:37; Perkinson 2010, 87–91). The empire's predatory belligerence has been "unveiled." Such is one element of apocalyptic watching.

The other element, however, has to do with keeping one's eye keen for creativity. Not letting little gestures of non-cooperation, tiny up-wellings of generosity in the very face of poverty, or moments of astonishing verbal dexterity go uncelebrated in the foreboding of collapse. In first-century Palestine, the collapse did come—unfolding in slow motion until some 35 years after Jesus's execution, when Rome utterly decimated the entire land and infrastructure. But meanwhile, the movements resisting Rome—led by John, by Jesus, by Paul, and multiple others—majored in minoritarian insurgence. Widows were honored (Luke 18:1–5: 7:11–17), orphans fed (Mark 10:13–16; Acts 2:43–47; 4:32; 6:1–6), poor people challenged to reclaim their own dignity and beauty and given a place and a community to express such (Luke 3:10–14; 6:17–26; 16:19–31; Matt 21:12–17). Even outsiders such as the Syro-Phoenician woman in Mark 7 (non-Jewish, single female head-of-house such as she was) are given honor when they throw down a bit of street savvy—even if the "throw down" was against Jesus's own word (Mark 7:24–30; Perkinson 1996, 61–86)! The latter encounter offers intrigue for what we will elaborate in this writing.

This woman was an emcee of her time, spitting rhyme in perfect cipher rhythm, like a seasoned veteran of the mic! (Perkinson 2010, 91–93) Jesus is "underground," on the run from the authorities that are plotting on his life. She ferrets him out in hiding, seeking deliverance for her daughter. He refuses her request, "dogging her out" in the process ("It is not right to take the little kids' bread and throw it to the dogs"). She counters his "diss" with a witty rejoinder that corners him ("Yes sir, yet even the little dogs get the little crumbs that fall from the little kids' plates"). He has refused her in the name of littleness; she has answered by throwing littleness back at him three times. He can't continue to push her aside without losing face. What is remarkable in the outcome is that Jesus simply affirms her uppity comeback (Mark 7:28–29). "For this saying [*logos* in the Greek]," he concedes, "go your way; gone is the demon from your daughter!" It is her "word up" that brings about the cure of her daughter.

Check out the text! This is apocalyptic watching at its best. It safeguards even the subtlest expression of defiance (refusing any "silencing" here, whether by patriarchy or ethnocentrism), no matter that it comes from outside "orthodox" approval! Remarkable that this bit of "pagan sass" got codified as part of the tradition! (Perkinson 2013, 88–91). It sets the stage for what this writing wants to lift up large. The Syro-Phoenician woman of Mark (Matthew changes the story to preserve the patriarchy) could be declaimed the patron saint of hip-hop. Her word contests Jesus's own, from beyond the borders of the tradition (whether it is considered to be Jewish or Christian)—and she is affirmed! When the situation is one of emergency, the Spirit does not bother with conformity to official channels and mainstream **orthodoxies**. And indeed, apocalyptic emergency in the present is giving rise to a possibility of creative blowback on status quo orthodoxies that is as ripe with sass and "pagan" wisdom as anything Jesus witnessed in Galilee (or since)! To such, I want now to turn to tease out a specter for political engagement in our time.

Apocalyptic Detroit

One recent summer in Detroit, a number of folk engaged in caring for a city undergoing apocalyptic distress attempted a new thing. Tentatively, slowly, deliberately, we convened a dialogue among three distinct communities of inspiration. One was rooted in postindustrial abandonment, breaking street savvy into spit finesse, spun bodies, and tagged walls. Another was deeply historical, born of peasant resistance against ancient Roman might, itself gone genocidal and colonizing for the better part of two millennia. The third, most rooted, was embedded in soils and waters, seasons and weather, enculturated by the place itself. *Hip-hop, Christian,* and *indigenous* by other names—three constituencies, roughly demarked, made common cause in concern for the future of *détroit*, "the strait." We named it the "Detroit Spirit Roots Gathering" and styled it a collaborative effort to re-spirit the city by learning from each other's stories.

Motor City today is indeed an emergency incarnate (though not of its own making, despite media stories to the contrary). Among those of us in the activist community pushing back on the situation, the story is often told in a post-war frame. Counter to the way corporatized news trades in stereotypes to further agendas, private and well-financed, my own collaborators in a new vision seek continually to unearth the subtext. The unmaking of Detroit, from Arsenal of Democracy in the 1940s to Poster Child of Blight today, has all to do with the way race has organized class (and continues to do so). Clarity about this monstrosity was crucial foreground for our gathering.

The Immediate Story

White flight, capital flight, job flight, tax base and asset flight—you would think the city an aviary! (Ironically, pre-colonial contact, you would be literally right—the river bend between the Lakes was the teeming site of waterfowl and winged peoples writ large.) From a peak of 1,800,000 people in 1951, the city now sleeps barely 600,000 plus.

In the later 1940s, white GIs returning from war theaters, European and Pacific, faced old neighborhoods then flush with African American workers, who had fled the Jim Crow South to contribute to the anti-Nazi effort and create a viable life for themselves and their families. The GI Bill offered ready money to build suburban enclaves outside the city proper—monies gathered by tax policy from all communities and made primarily available only to one (all but 4 percent of GI Bill funds went to white applicants). American tax dollars at work, over time effectively transferring resources from communities of color to those of lighter hue! The result today: the largest black metropolis ringed by 86 independent municipalities, 45 townships, and 89 school systems—nearly all, largely white (Sugrue, "United Communities Are Impregnable" [1996], 266). Most of them created by quite purposeful policy—using FHA red-lining, VA exclusion, restrictive covenants and vigilant (and vigilante) real estate practice to contain "blackness" inside the city proper.

Detroit today—the poorest big city sitting cheek-by-jowl with the fourth most affluent county (Oakland) in the country! The conditions in both "produced" by way of each other. "We" who grow up white and entitled in this society, do not like to face this fact: much of our prosperity and opportunity has been coercively gathered from those who do not look like us. Clearly, the case in violently taking native land and piling up wealth on the back of shackled slaves! But also the case by way of a continuing operation of plunder carried out through policy details and intricate practices, difficult to see without a lot of in-depth analysis—both here and abroad. The very substance of the suburb—its streets and building materials, and the highways connecting its dwellings to jobs still located in the urban core, all "concretize" flows of resources brokered by racist policies and practices. White flight relied upon taxes and subsidies and mortgage-finance that gerrymandered public dollars disparately toward majority white use and ownership.

Meanwhile, inside the city, black families, mid-century, continuously sought to escape tightening conditions in the three **"catchment basins"** where black folk were allowed to settle. Life in these areas grew increasingly crowded. City support services were minimal or abusive; school systems struggled with little resources. And living there meant foregoing any possibility of gaining equity through homeownership, as FHA policy red-lined any neighborhood with someone of color in it (as supposedly "unstable"), and banks followed suit by refusing to grant mortgages there for less than 50 percent down. As families tried to move into white neighborhoods in hopes of realizing value in their homes, they were met with concerted violence, organized across whole blocks. Housewives and mothers picketing, kids on bikes doing reconnaissance, teenagers throwing bricks and epithets, fathers and husbands massing in mobs after work, burning crosses on lawns, hanging black figures in effigy, pouring gas or salt on grass, torching entire houses, while police stood by watching, or arrested black home dwellers (Sugrue 1996, 233). More than 200 incidents from late 40s to early 60s! None of which gets cited in the mainstream narrative about Detroit.

By 1967, the lid blew. One too many police raids and belligerent arrests struck a match. The rebellion, thus, ignited refused "business as usual" and especially targeted local institutions predatory on black life. Did "they" burn their own neighborhoods? Deep question about ownership and land in the core city! In fact, Detroit was not primarily owned by black people. In any case, the upshot of the upsurge was a profound change in policy. Almost never clarified in stories told since, the flames in Detroit and Newark compelled the convening of the Kerner Commission, whose explicit exposé of the way racist real estate practices created "ghettos" in the first place led to the Fair Housing Act abolishing Federal red-lining and challenging segregated housing (*New York Times* editorial, May 16, 2015). While doing little to dismantle the racialized Eight Mile divide in the capital of the Car, the new legislation at least made it possible to challenge some of the practices legally. The 1967 Rebellion was indeed powerful politics. It changed the law.

Needless to say, white flight went hyper in the years following that. By the mid-1970s, Motown had a black mayor and was fast consolidating a black majority. While de-industrialization continued apace—re-locating jobs and infrastructure "outside"—creative leadership and ordinary family care made good use of a bad situation. The years of Coleman Young witnessed a beleaguered city administration assert what control it could, push back on a corporate sector using its clout to extract concessions (like GM in Poletown), and at least secure a modicum of pride despite the impossible economic headwinds (Boggs and Kurashige 2011, 108–9). Certainly, the influx of crack devastated an already difficult situation. Market penetration through TV did the rest. Was there malfeasance on the part of city officials? Of course—as there is at every level of government in every domain in this country. But much more damaging was abuse by the state. Takeover of DPS (Detroit Public Schools) by Governor Engler and cronies in 1999, seeking to steer 1.2 billion in bond monies to outstate contractors, shifted the school system from a $100 million surplus while under city control to a $100 million deficit when "handed back" to the city by the state in 2003 and flipped test scores from gaining ground, compared to the state average to plummeting. And takeover of newspapers in the 1990s throttled independent reporting.

The rest is (near-term) history. Emergency managers imposed over school systems and over the city itself (the latter against citizen will as expressed by the ballot). Bankruptcy declared by the governor and his acolyte manager, securing big bank interest established by debt swaps illegally negotiated five years into the new millennium, and putting pensions up for grabs both here and nationally (by setting precedent). Detroit Public Schools ripped apart, school buildings pirated for Educational Achievement Authority and charter use, yielding profit toward Wall Street hedge funds (backing the charter movement); students lumped together in huge classrooms as "guinea pigs" for testing new software (again yielding corporate benefit) (Guyette 2014, 1). City finances effectively reduced to a cash flow emergency generated by unilateral state withholding of revenue sharing commitments and a two-tier city tax policy, allowing those working, but not residing in the city, to walk away without contributing to the municipal tax base in a city that yields their livelihood (Turbeville 2013). Throw in the post-2008 mortgage and tax foreclosures and the 2014 "ethnic cleansing" of neighborhoods by water shutoffs, and you have the human-made "perfect storm" of emergencies that has allowed "disaster capital" to feed like a vulture. All of this is a familiar narrative among those I know who act to make the future otherwise. This basic outline of historical events is quite well-known among those forced to undergo them (as well as activist advocates who act to make the situation otherwise). The great bedevilment is that so many white folks have little awareness of either the facts or the import of this narrative.

The Roots of Possibility

But what we generally have not engaged is the deeper infrastructure of this history of disaster or the multiple ways the Spirit-Haunts of this riverside haven are stirring to create otherwise. Putting it thus invokes an Agency beyond the merely visible. Among the three groups in the Detroit Spirit roots Gathering, it was this latter concern that summoned. What might we learn in listening to each other's "take" on what is trying to surface in this hour? Apocalypse can enable birth; "emergency" spawns creativity. In our day, a whole new vision has convened under the rubric of "emergence" (as in "evolution"). Rhyme spitters, jubilee preachers, and indigenous healers alike are finding intrigue with each other in seeking to perceive possibilities not dictated by the obvious Powers.

I write here as one little voice in the ensemble, anticipating what I am able. But also certain I will be surprised over the long haul. As a white boy arriving in Motown in the mid-70s, I have been deeply challenged by living and working in the inner city for more than 30 years now. Immersion in black culture in general, encounter with hip-hop in particular, and more recently, interaction with indigenous peoples has radically altered my understanding of life and opened me to both pain and beauty I otherwise would not have suspected. It has also schooled me in the fact that there are ranges of struggle I will never fully fathom, given my own privileged position. As such, I would stir my musings here into the mix like so much mulch. Writing as "compost." (Inevitably, part of what any of us ever says or writes is BS. But it is a quality of the wild economy of nature that even our waste does not go to waste—about which more below.) A notion those who identify as "Christian" today especially must re-learn from those with greater experience. Both hip-hoppers and indigenous dwellers bring a perspective to bear on bringing life out of detritus that begs listening here.

The Insurgent Beat

Hip-hop first. What emerged in the early 1970s in South Bronx, led by locals such as Afrika Bambaataa and Grand Master Flash, was not a flash in the pan. In neighborhoods destroyed by policy and dissed by cinema treatments such as "Fort Apache, Bronx," youth with old spirits and ancient savvy made urban decay yield beauty. Probing the terror-dome with deep rhythm, they channeled the street ghosts into boasts and realities of life writ large. Bodies choreographed into limb tangles and freezes that would make even James Brown laugh! Head-spinning inversions granting a bottom-up vision of an upside-down situation! Legs mimicking the choppers doing nightly surveillance on the 'hood! This was judo performed on an impossible condition. Gang warfare here was transfigured into break-battles waged on cardboard at the corner!

And before long, fourteen-year-old Grand Wizard Theodore had bumped his stereo needle while removing a record during a practice session in his bedroom. He heard the "burp" not as mistake, but language—one of the "tongues" spoken by turf abandoned in city policy. He was not wrong. Two generations later, DJs globally cruise the nethersphere of our time, lending fingers to techno-energies as if the cyborg could speak! Making meaning from absurdity; articulating skronks and squibs, chirps and tweaks, as if some galactic *orisha* had descended out of another astral zone to speak the future of the machine (Perkinson 2015b, 167). (Bambaataa's early album, *Shango Funk Theology,* illustrates as much, with its jacket cover exhibiting the double-headed-axe-holding Yoruba *orisha* of lightning hovering over a cyborg figure zapping the planet with "chill beams.") Here too, battle-mode transmutes energies otherwise likely to combust into violence into communal recognition and appreciation.

Likewise with both MCing and Tagging. Lips made into instruments, spitting rhyme like lightning! Hard-edged consonants clipped into rapid-fire velocity, making the mouth a Magnum, shooting back at a supremacist world, insisting Black Lives do indeed Matter! And cityscapes the globe over, bearing tats and tags, announcing architectures of control as contested! Scribing fat-bellied syllables onto middle-class eyeballs like the second coming of color. And all of it refusing the grave! Refusing ownership! It is no wonder so many "proper folk" wax red-faced and vitriolic in response—and have the wall whitewashed. Or the DVD crushed. The country *does* understand this message!

Once this genie had broken ground in the Bronx, it could not be put back in the hole. Certainly, it has since been bought off in the commercial, big white-owned corporations deciding to make money on the back of what they could not contain. Yes, the re-packaging is perverse—the game re-made in the image of the ad: bullets, booty, and bling, a salute to mainstream Amerikkka. The thuggish image is a mirror—way more damage has been done in the national history of policy than any summation of gang violence over recent decades (Ogbar 2007, 121). (Never mind that hip-hop is at least as much a prophylactic for gangbanging as an accomplice.) Think Native genocide (approximately 95 million killed off; Stannard, *American Holocaust* [1992], x, 11)! Think African slavicide (another 30–50 million; Stannard 1992, 316–17)! Witchicide perped onto females with impunity from Puritan days! And all the deaths in all the neo- and postcolonial theaters since (like the Philippines and Iraq)!

But beneath the glitterati surface of corporatized rap, underground hip-hop continues its quest. It speaks truth. From the intersection of machine and human, where African genes meet their global offspring, insurgence! Body cubism on the rise (Thompson 1996, 219)! Taking the bullshit of the era and composting genius. How shall we read it? In major cities around the world today, hip-hop serves as a kind of Esperanto—an idiom of percussion shared by youth who splice its bombast into their own cultural style (Perkinson 2015, 182–84). From the ashes of neoliberal plunder, a Phoenix of grandeur! Multicultural in appeal, taking no prisoners. Spirits of the Mother Continent possessing whoever is open to the black vein of ancestry! And what gathers under that beat, in those varied theaters of innovation, approximates Martin

King's Beloved Community hope like no other transglobal assemblies yet seen.

This is part of what the July 2015 gathering in Detroit sampled: the Mother DNA of the globe, never yet entirely stamped out, a cosmic "bang" echoing still in the recesses of memory carried by the species at large (Perkinson 2007, 67–69, 75–76; 2009, 66–69). But the gathering also augured local memory, demanding re-inhabitation of place, with all that means for a lifetime effort at (literal) decolonization.

The Feeding Fish

For the site of the strait, this means going "under" the story of black migration north to the history of native struggle and vitality. Here, where the upper Great Lakes pulse like an artery into Erie and the Atlantic beyond, 20 percent of the world's fresh surface water flashes in the summer sun. For Ojibwe, the bend was *wawiatonong*, "where it (the river) goes around" (Cornell, "American Indians at Wawiiatanong" [2003], 9). For the Wendet/Huron, the place was *oppenago*, "where the waters meet" (Givens-McGowan, "The Wyandot and the River" [2003], 27). Each named the water course for itself, unlike the Jesuit romance of the flow as a "strait" between other places, re-making the site in the image of global capital and Euro-trade (Kellermann 2015).

Detroit from 1701 forward increasingly was forced to pirate its significance from commodity traffic—first in beaver, then whitefish, then in mid-nineteenth century, increasingly, iron, copper, and wood, re-engineered into rail cars, stoves, marine engines (Kerr, Olinek, and Hartig 2003, 37–40). In short order, pharmaceutical- and chemical-work gained prominence—in part, due to salt long deposited under Detroit soils—as well as cigars and tobacco products. Soon to follow was Ford and autos—and all of it celebrated in a mindset hell-bent on re-tooling planetary surfaces and depths in service of the market.

Only today, with climate blow-back, are we being pushed to re-compute this story. It turns out a tale of hubris rather than genius, plunging a globe into desperate straits. It is clearly time to listen to the voice of the place, translated for deafened human hearing by native rage and wisdom. On the southern stretch of the bend, indigenous experience also named the site *Numma Sepee,* the "Place of the Sturgeon" (Givens-McGowan 2003, 27). This is a fish up to eight feet long, denizen of earth's waters 136 million years in duration, seeing dinosaurs in their day! For the Ojibwe and Wendet, the creature was kin, ancestor of renown, whose bones, once the flesh was consumed, were hallowed with burial rather than burning, like human forebears (LaDuke 2005, 227–35; Givens-McGowan 2003, 27). Medicine healers indeed regularly talked to both waters and fish, honoring each with offering, in recognition of their life-gift, making human dwelling on these lands possible (Givens-McGowan 2003, 27–29). Back behind this Huron symbiotics, even older traces remain of mound builders, whose line winds far south over the horizon, to the "beautiful river" people of Ohio, and on west and down to Mexico (Cornell 2003, 10).

The strait is laced with graces primordial, haunts of folk who could read the river, hear the rejoinder of finned and winged and four-legged creature alike, and build reciprocity into the exchange. They maintained the place as "commons" for a cornucopia of beings, communing in shared breathing and shared ferocities of living. As with so many practices indigenous, things in their wildness were part of a sacred presence; nothing was counted as refuse and wantonly discarded (Donaldson 2013, 142–48). (Indeed, as native teacher Martín Prechtel recounts, "compost" itself, often enough across native cultures globally, is embraced as a goddess, "She" who makes all life possible; Prechtel 2012, 10–11). A lifetime is not enough to recover the layers of palaver and the beauties of culture since silenced. What such might mean for our future remains to be conjured.

But the telling this listening solicited this particular summer must also not abstain from the bloodletting that continues to throb in the soils. The history of ricocheting violence unleashed in Dutch West Indies Co.'s demand for fur in the seventeenth century, arming eastern Haudenosaunee (Iroquois) with weapons technology and threat that bumped native groups west across the Great Lakes basin for centuries following, seeking safe haven. The struggle of groups to suss out the trade and war relations with encroaching French and British aggression that might most likely secure a modicum of survival. Tionnontati, Neutrals, Nipissings, Chippewa, Ottawa, Potowatomi, Wyandot, Erie, and Susquehanna, as indeed, the Sauk, Fox, Kickapoo, Mascouten, and Miami—all traversed the region in search of continuation (Givens-McGowan 2003, 30; Cornell 2003, 11). Euro goods rapidly replaced native crafts; subsistence hunting was deformed into rapacious commerce; ritual honoring submerged under missionary versions of supremacy and demonizing (Peacock and Wisuri, *Ojibwe* [2002], 47–48; Hartig 2003, 57).

Ottawa prophet Neolin and leader Pontiac organize a confederacy of revolt by 1763, repudiating British arrogance and racism, forcing a standoff, granting all terrain from the Alleghenies to the Mississippi, from the Lakes to the Caribbean, as native homeland. This agreement with the British is ruptured by the 1776 Revolution of the colonies, as white settlers desperate for land pour into the Ohio Valley, creating the pretext for "Mad" Anthony Wayne to satisfy his lust for glory in war-making. Multiple battles and treaties and fraudulent land confiscations later, Tecumseh rallies native youth into a pan-tribal force of fierce opposition, galvanized by prophecy and accurately predicted sun-eclipse, and by 1812, captures Fort Detroit from the Americans in a brilliantly conducted campaign of trickster appearances and courage under fire. Only betrayal by cowardly British upends the triumph in 1813, with Tecumseh killed at Moravian Town, just east of Detroit in Canada, and the dream of a viable native homeland crushed for the foreseeable future. From thence forward, the bend will become the strait.

All of this history—so lightly hinted here—portends possibilities other than business as usual. From the depths of our time, African Eve resounds in hip-hop beats and calls for response. From the soils under the city and the waters "going round," Ojibwe respect and Wendet spirit still haunt the curve. Both indigenous ancestral memory and living native peoples demand response. For a Christian heart committed to incarnation, the message requires, foremost, confession.

The "great book" has been made to do service to the sword like no other scripture extant. More than a thousand years of Christian empire, 500 years of Christian colonialism, are clear. There is no immediate access for those who embrace Jesus today, except through the witness of those at the other end of the colonial violence. Africans reduced in slavery to less than their own bodies have made performance the code of the entire species' ancestry, coming now to collect dues. Native artifact and practice return from the grave of white silence and ignorance with a huge claim on the future: unless we learn what they knew and know, we may not survive the Sandys and Katrinas to come. Today, all non-indigenous dwellers on this Island of the Turtle are usurpers and guests: the basis for our analysis must become the fact of our trespass in the mode of settler colonialism (Tuck and Yang 2012, 1–36). Our task is literal decolonization, not merely of minds and culture, but of the land itself. And accountability to the political priorities of native folk today (as articulated, for instance, in Idle No More movement or the push for repudiation of the Doctrine of Christian Discovery) (Newcomb 2008, xvi, 37–50).

The Teaching Bush

The "revelation" by which Christianity today must set its compass takes shape as a beat and a ceremony, more than a book. But the book itself also carries memory of survival "in spite of." Those who are Christian do well to enter this trilogue with the traditions of Sabbath and Jubilee to the fore. These ideas reference way more than the labor-rest and debt-release they most immediately signify (important as those are) (Exod 16; 23; Lev 25; Deut 15). Indeed, together they identify a continuum of practice rooted in the struggle of escaped slaves, re-learning a desert land under the hand of the African-trained Bedouin named Moses, as recounted above. Schooled by a bush in the Sinai outback, Moses has learned how to live on the land (Exod 2:1–3:7; Deut 33:16). Food comes in the form of aphid defecation, dripping down from Sinai shrubs into puddles of nutritious resin, known and collected even today by Arab Bedouin under the name of *man* or "honey dew" (the term here is an Arabic equivalent of the "manna" remarked in the Hebrew text; Exod 16:1–36; Eisenberg 1999, 15–16). The eco-savvy thus described gets coded into the tradition as a memorial of that 40-year-long wilderness "clinic," where ex-slaves re-learn how to survive outside the imperial economy (i.e., the four-decade period of Israel's wandering in the Sinai after escaping Egypt as recounted in the books of Exodus, Numbers, and Deuteronomy). This Sabbath-Jubilee tradition of living on the bounty of a local ecosystem by learning its modes of wild provision will become the central undercurrent of the biblical witness, the primal experience to which prophets will turn again and again, once Israel compromises its original vision of relative self-sufficiency, emulates the nations around it, and re-organizes its social order into a structure of domination serving elites at the expense of everyone else. Against such, the prophets will rail: "Remember!" What they are to remember is the desert time when everyone had enough, nature provided, and no one lorded it over others (Exod 23; 31:12–17; Lev 25; Deut 15; 1 Sam 8:4–22; 10:17–19; 12:12; Isa 61:1–2).

Sabbath-Jubilee memory will anchor the social movements of both John the Baptist and Jesus of Nazareth ("give us this day our daily bread") (Luke 3:10–14; 4:18–19; 11:1–4; Mark 2:23–3:6; Myers 2001, 23–28). It will designate a practice in which assets are "released" for circulation among the poor rather than hoarded for elite benefit, and land and water are re-valued as "living" gift (Matt 25:31–46; Mark 2:13–19; 6:30–44; 8:1–10; 10:17–30; 11:15–19; Luke 6:20–26; 14:15–24; 16:1–9; 16:19–31: John 7:37–39). Indeed, the Baptizer will practice a form of water politics in his hour, challenging Herod's policy of privatizing the Jordan flow for Roman bathhouse lifestyles (by means of aqueducts built through taxes on the peasants)—and pay the ultimate price in his beheading (John 1:19–28; 3:22–24; 10:40; Sawicki 2000, 4, 24, 100, 145–46, 158).

The Nazareth upstart will organize in beleaguered villages (Matt 4:12–23; Mark 1:38–39; 5:1; 6:1; 7:31; 8:22, 27; 10:1 Luke 10:38; John 2:1), marshal a public curse on the wealthy policies of foreclosure (Matt 23:1–39; Luke 6: 24–26), occupy the Temple Bank in Jerusalem (the

Chase Manhattan of its day, where all the records of indebtedness were maintained), name its money-laundering operation "thug central," and likewise, suffer retribution (Mark 11:1–19; Matt 26:59–62). Much of his teaching (in parables) will be of seed (Mark 4:1–34; John 12:20–30). And for the savvy, listening closely, import will show in "resurrection" of what died and decayed. When we shift focus away from how empire has re-packaged the memory to elevate a mere individual, what appears is a movement coming back from the grave as if "composted" (imperial BS made to yield vital witness in spite of itself). Before perversely "universalized" as the founding myth of Western empire and colonization, messianic Judaism showed great vibrancy as a local origins myth and indigenous practice native to rural Galilee. Even after going urban and outlaw for three centuries—before being co-opted by Constantine—the early church was primarily a movement of Sabbath "feeding" and Jubilee "freedom" for widows, orphans, and slaves.

Re-Rooting the Commons

And here then is the common upshot of the July 2015 gathering. Breaking the abominable colonial history of settler-native-slave relations, beginning with questions of land ownership and native sovereignty! Composting multiple ways of cultivating livable futures from the ruins and garbage of the present! Combining roots and spirits. And returning to basic elements. In hip-hop, these include DJing, MCing, Grafitti, and Break Dancing (with Knowledge as the overall resource). For the indigenous, it means some measure of return to what is already known—ceremonies, offerings, *waasa inaabidaa* ("looking in all directions" in *Anishinabe-mowin* or "*speech*") and re-discovering *gakina-awiiya* ("we are all related") (Peacock and Wisuri 2002, 15, 28, 39). While demanding from everyone—not least all of us who are settlers—decolonization of both soils and souls! For Christians, it means embrace of the bloody cry of pastoral nomad Abel, killed by agribusiness-aggressor Cain, facing a long history of violence and re-learning roots from those who have not forgotten (Gen 4:1–17). (Indeed, this archetypal account of Abel's murder ghosts the biblical tradition like a cipher of indigenous annihilation before the march of empire across 5,000 years of agricultural take-over of the planet—a haunting cry of shed blood that shows up in Revelation's apocalyptic unveiling as the cause of Babylon's fall: Matt 23:29–36; Luke 11:45–52; Heb 11:4; Rev 18:24.) For all of us, it perhaps means a return to simple things like earth and air, fire and water, to ask all over what these gifts mean and who we are as their offspring. In any case—a body-listening, with feet on the ground! May the beat, the fish, and the bush find a way to talk and their respective lovers dance, eat, and vision together with ferocity! May the river again become as it was when the Sturgeon teemed, the people dreamed, and every kind of motion was a spirit vocation! May Christians repudiate their commitment to imperial claims and exclusive truths and learn to listen and cooperate—even (and especially) when rebuked! May our African Mother Eve have her say! May apocalypse birth a new humility and return us to what actually works!

Study Questions:

1. In what ways have hip-hop artists challenged the status quo and/ or prevailing social order? Is this a positive and/or an effective means of doing so?
2. What kinds of veils might be pulled back in your own hometown/ city and what might this reveal?
3. What are the possible repercussions of trying to unveil and challenge the status quo?

Bibliography and Further Reading:

Boggs, Grace Lee, and Scott Kurashige. *The Next American Revolution: Sustainable Activism for the Twenty-First Century.* Berkeley: University of California Press, 2011.

Cornell, George L. "American Indians at Wawiiatanong: An Early American History of Indigenous Peoples at Detroit." In *Honoring Our*

Detroit River: Caring for Our Home. Edited by J. H. Hartig. Bloomfield Hills, MI: Cranbrook Institute of Science, 2003, 9–22.

Donaldson, Laura E. "Theological Composting in Romans 8: An Indigenous Meditation on Paul's Rhetoric of Decay." In *Buffalo Shout, Salmon Cry: Conversations on Creation, Land Justice, and Life Together.* Edited by S. Heinrichs. Waterloo, Ontario/Harrisonburg, VA: Herald Press, 2013, 142–52.

Editorial Board, *New York Times.* "Housing Apartheid, American Style," *New York Times,* May 16, 2015.

Eisenberg, Evan. *The Ecology of Eden: An Inquiry into the Dream of Paradise and a New Vision of Our Role in Nature.* New York: Vintage Books, 1999.

Givens-McGowan, Kay. "The Wyandot and the River," in *Honoring Our Detroit River: Caring for Our Home.* Edited by J. H. Hartig. Bloomfield Hills, MI: Cranbrook Institue of Science, 2003, 23–34.

Guyette, Curt. "The EAA Exposed: An Investigative Report," in *The Detroit Metro Times.* Sept. 24, 2014. http://www.metrotimes.com/detroit/the-eaa-exposed-an-investigative-report/Content?oid=2249513.

Hartig, John H. "American Beaver Exploitation for European Chic." In *Honoring Our Detroit River: Caring for Our Home.* Edited by J. H. Hartig. Bloomfield Hills, MI: Cranbrook Institute of Science, 2003, 49–58.

Howard-Brook, Wes, and Anthony Gwyther. *Unveiling Empire: Reading Revelation Then and Now.* Maryknoll, NY: Orbis Books, 2002.

Kerr, John K., W. Steven Olinek, and John H. Hartig. "The Detroit River as an Artery of Trade and Commerce." In *Honoring Our Detroit River: Caring for Our Home.* Edited by J. H. Hartig. Bloomfield Hills, MI: Cranbrook Institue of Science, 2003, 35–48.

LaDuke, Winona. *Recovering the Sacred: The Power of Naming and Claiming.* Cambridge, MA: South End Press, 2005.

Myers, Ched. *The Biblical Vision of Sabbath Economics.* Washington, D.C.: Church of the Savior, 2001.

Newcomb, Steven T. *Pagans in the Promised Land: Decoding the Doctrine of Christian Discovery.* Golden, CO: Fulcrum, 2008.

Ogbar, Jeffrey O. G. *Hip-Hop Revolution: The Culture and Politics of Rap.* Kansas City: The University Press of Kansas, 2007.

Peacock, Thomas, and Marlene Wisuri. *Ojibwe: We Look in All Directions.* Afton, MN: Afton Historical Society Press, 2002.

Perkinson, J. W. "A Canaanitic Word in the Jewish Logos: or The Difference the Syro-Phoenician Woman Makes to an Ethnic Messiah." In *Semeia 75* (1996): 61–86.

____. "Postcolonial Pan-Africanisms and Caribbean Connections: Behind Du Bois' Veil is Fanon's Muscle on a Herculoidian Trip." In *Pan-Africanism Caribbean Connections.* Edited by Abdul Karim Bangura. New York: iUniverse, Inc., 2007, 64–75.

____. "Tupac Shakur as Ogou Achade: Hip-Hop Anger and Postcolonial Rancor Read from the Other Side." In *Culture & Religion: An Interdisciplinary Journal 10* (1) (2009): 63–79. Special Issue on Hip-Hop and Religion. Edited by A. Pinn and M. Miller.

____. "Spittin', Cursin', and Outin': Hip-Hop Apocalypse in the Imperial Necropolis." In *The Bible In/And Popular Culture.* Edited by E. Wainwright and P. Cuthbertson. Atlanta: Society of Biblical Literature, 2010, 81–96.

____. *Messianism Against Christology: Resistance Movements, Folk Arts, and Empire.* New York: Palgrave Macmillan Press, 2013.

____. 2015a. "Somewhere Between Sturgeon, Graffiti, and Jubilee: Detroit at a Spiritual Crossroads." In *On the Edge: A Catholic Worker Newspaper.* Summer 2015.

____. 2015b. *Political Spirituality in an Age of Eco-Apocalypse: Essays in Communication and Struggle Across Species, Cultures, and Religions.* New York: Palgrave Macmillan Press, 2015.

Prechtel, Martín. *The Unlikely Peace at Cuchumaquic: The Parallel Lives of People as Plants: Keeping Seeds Alive.* Berkeley, CA: North Atlantic Books, 2012.

Sawicki, Marianne. *Crossing Galilee: Architectures of Contact in the Occupied Land of Jesus.* Harrisburg, PA: Trinity Press International, 2000.

Stannard, David. *American Holocaust: The Conquest of the New World,* New York: Oxford University Press, 1992.

Sugrue, Thomas. "United Communities Are Impregnable: Violence and the Color Line." In *The Origins of the Urban Crisis: Race and Inequality in Postwar Detroit*. Princeton: Princeton University Press, 1996.

Thompson, Robert Farris. 1996. "Hip Hop 101." In *Droppin' Science: Critical Essays on Rap Music and Hip-Hop Culture*. Edited by William E. Perkins. Philadelphia: Temple University Press, 1996, 211–19.

Tuck, Eve, and K. Wayne Yang. "Decolonization is Not a Metaphor." In *Decolonization: Indigeneity, Education & Society*, 1:1 (2012), 1–40.

Turbeville, Wallace. "The Detroit Bankruptcy." *Demos*. November 20, 2013. Accessed via http://www.demos.org/publication/detroit-bankruptcy.

Wylie-Kellermann, Bill. "From Wahnabeezee to PenskiLand: the Desecration of Detroit's Belle Isle." 2015. Accessed via http://www.d-rem.org/from-wahnabeezee-to-penskiland-the-desecration-of-detroits-belle-isle.

19

Apocalyptic America

Buying the End Time

Robert von Thaden Jr.

GETTING PREPPED:

1. Have you ever heard of the rapture? If so, what comes to mind?
2. How would you expect Christian groups labeled "fundamentalist" or "evangelical" to interact with American culture at large?
3. Why do you think predictions of the end of the world have become so popular in American culture?

KEY TERMS:
WILLIAM MILLER
GREAT DISAPPOINTMENT
JOHN NELSON DARBY
DISPENSATIONAL PREMILLENNIALISM
RAPTURE
TRIBULATION

ARMAGEDDON
PRE-TRIBULATION
MID-TRIBULATION
POST-TRIBULATION
RADICAL EVANGELICAL
FUNDAMENTALIST
Y2K PROBLEM

Introduction

As the chapters of this book make clear, although not confined to that specific religious tradition, apocalyptic ideology has been a part of Christian religious thinking since the beginning. That various expressions of American Christianity have engaged and promoted this ideology throughout American history—to a greater or lesser extent—should, therefore, come as no surprise. Apocalyptic theology is even embedded among so-called mainline Christians who do not regularly anticipate an immediate end of the world, as demonstrated by the words of the Nicene Creed (see sidebar).

Sidebar 19.1: Second Article of the Nicene Creed

We believe in one Lord, Jesus Christ,

The only Son of God,

Eternally begotten of the Father,

God from God, Light from Light,

True God from true God,

Begotten, not made,

Of one being with the Father.

Through him all things were made.

For us and for our salvation

He came down from heaven:

By the power of the Holy Spirit

he became incarnate from the Virgin Mary,

and was made man.

For our sake he was crucified under Pontius Pilate;

He suffered death and was buried.

On the third day he rose again

in accordance with the Scriptures;

he ascended into heaven

and is seated at the right hand of the Father.

He will come again in glory to judge the living and the dead

and his kingdom will have no end.

The Nicene Creed, crafted in 381 CE after the contentious Council of Nicaea, expresses what became doctrine about the Trinitarian nature of God: Father, Son, and Holy Spirit (Ayers 2004). Every Sunday, many American Christians, most of whom would probably not understand themselves to be espousing an apocalyptic worldview, nevertheless recite the foundational hope of their faith in apocalyptic terms, collectively affirming that Jesus Christ "will come again in glory to judge the living and the dead and his kingdom will have no end." This chapter seeks to understand those American Christians who, in contrast to those who simply recite the creed, consciously adopt an explicit apocalyptic worldview and whose particular way of reading the Bible in light of current events leads them to believe that the apocalyptic fulfillment of their hope is, in fact, right around the corner.

To many on the outside, the theology of numerous radically apocalyptic Christian groups tends to look bizarre at best and dangerous at worst. However, the academic study of religion requires that we try to understand the beliefs and practices of those who differ from us, both in order to appreciate them in their own right, and thereby, to understand our own traditions in a new light. The scholar of religion is in the position of an outsider trying to explain religious phenomena to the largest audience possible. In so doing, the scholar must try to articulate the "common sense" of the insider in such a way that those outside a given tradition may understand it. Dismissing or simplifying beliefs that do not cohere with our own is the very antithesis of what it means to engage in humanistic inquiry. In order to make sense of various eschatological ideologies that we may see or hear about in the media, we begin by exploring the multifaceted history of apocalyptic America.

An American Tradition

Perhaps the best place to begin an attempt to understand apocalyptic thought in the United States is on a fall night in 1844. On October 22 of this year, followers of a New York farmer and self-taught student of biblical prophecy, **William Miller**, waited on hilltops for the second coming of Christ. Miller had been preaching the second coming, or "Advent," as he termed it, since the 1830s. Using a complicated mathematical system based on the "seventy weeks" of the biblical book of Daniel (9:2, 24–27), Miller argued that Christ would return sometime between March 21, 1843, and March 21, 1844. This return would be followed by the thousand-year reign of Christ described in the book of Revelation (20:1–6).

Fig. 19.1. Millerite chart illustrating the interpretation of prophecy, yielding the year 1843 as the End. Commons.wikimedia.org.

Miller's followers spread his message far and wide so that his apocalyptic expectation became a phenomenon that gripped the entire country, delighting adherents and worrying critics. When 1843 passed without incident, Miller was encouraged to set a new date by followers.

411

Claiming that the original timeframe neglected to account for "tarry time," a new date was calculated: October 22, 1844. Thousands of Miller's followers again eagerly awaited the Advent of Jesus Christ who, alas, did not deign to return at the appointed time. The disillusionment that followed became known as the **Great Disappointment** and it hampered the emergence of widespread, popular apocalyptic thinking for decades. However, as Amy Johnson Frykholm argues, despite his failure, Miller *did* plant a seed that would later grow and flourish: the idea "that anyone could interpret biblical prophecies." Miller and his followers "helped to make prophetic prediction an ordinary person's game" (Frykholm 2004, 106; see also Balmer 2011). Since then, as Kelly J. Baker writes, "A long line of Americans [have] stated, proclaimed, shouted, cajoled, argued, hoped, wished, and desired the end of the world because they all wanted to be a part of the final days" (2013, ch. 1). Apocalyptic prophecy had not died with the Millerites, but had only begun to take shape.

John Nelson Darby offered an apocalyptic antidote to the Great Disappointment. An Anglo-Irish Anglican priest-turned-reformer who emigrated to the United States in the mid-nineteenth century, Darby brought with him a popular theology that became known as **dispensational premillennialism.** In this theological system, history is divided into seven epochs, or dispensations, during each of which God interacts with humanity in different ways—in much the same way parents treat their children differently at distinct life stages (infant, toddler, schoolchild, adolescent, etc.). The theology of dispensationalism argues that we are now living in the "church age," the penultimate age before the millennium reign of God that will be ushered in by the second coming of Jesus Christ. One of Darby's novel ideas, and the cornerstone of his dispensational belief system, was the development and articulation of the **Rapture,** the idea that Christ will take up all true Christians into heaven at the end of time. (Many critics argue that Darby's "new idea" of the rapture was, in fact, appropriated from the vision a fifteen-year-old Scottish girl, Margaret MacDonald, which she supposedly received in 1830 [Rossing 2004, 22].) Indeed, so important was this doctrine for the subsequent development of apocalyptic ideology in America that Matthew Avery Sutton argues it "was one of Darby's greatest theological inventions" (Sutton 2014, 18). The rapture of the church would be followed by the seven horror-filled years of the **Tribulation,** when Satan and an antichrist figure would control the world. These years of tribulation would culminate in the final cosmological battle that would take place at **Armageddon,** an ancient battle site in Israel. Drawing from such biblical resources as 1 Thess 4:15–17, which states that those alive at Christ's return will meet him in the air to be with him forever, rapture ideology provided a way to articulate a theology wherein only God knew who the "real" Christians were and whereby God would protect these true believers from the horrors described in biblical books such as Daniel and Revelation (Frykholm 2004, 15–17). Of course, 1 Thess 4:15–17 only provides a seed for Darby's rapture theology. In these verses, there is no mention of those "left behind," of a tribulation, or of a cosmic war between the forces of good and evil. Darby blends the imagery of 1 Thess with other end-time scenarios peppered throughout the Bible to develop his system.

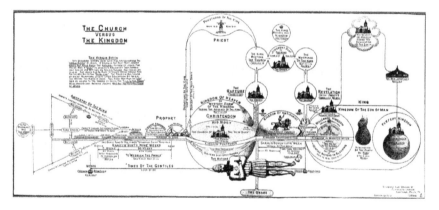

Fig. 19.2. An early twentieth century image displaying rapture theology. Commons.wikimedia.org.

Darby traveled across North America in the 1860s and 1870s, teaching his newly developed theological system. The benefit of his model over

Miller's was that Darby refused to speculate about a specific date for the end of the world. Although he gave no date, he preached that the time before the rapture was short, and thus his theology infused his followers with a sense of eschatological urgency. Darby was so successful at promoting this theological worldview that dispensational premillennialism filtered into the broader American culture throughout the twentieth and into the twenty-first centuries. In addition to Darby's evangelistic efforts, the wide dissemination of this particular apocalyptic theology in the United States was aided by the publication in 1909 of the wildly popular *Scofield Study Bible*, which contained helpful interpretive notes that allowed readers to see the biblical texts through a dispensational premillennialist lens. For example, Scofield's notes on 1 Thess 4:17 and 1 Cor 15:24 (which expresses Paul's hope of the coming Kingdom of God that destroys all earthly rulers) use the language of dispensations. Further, the notes for 1 Cor 15:52, which describes an end-time resurrection scenario, interpret this verse through the lens of a thousand-year reign of Christ, the great tribulation, and the idea of two resurrections—the first being the rapture, and the second, for "the martyrs of the tribulation." These notes helped to make Darby's premillennial theological system seem like a "common sense" interpretation of scripture.

Darby's ideas provided fertile soil for apocalyptic speculation, and the extreme popularity of his vision only encouraged further development and interpretation by others. For example, one of the chief disputes among dispensationalists was—and still is—the precise timing of the rapture relative to the seven years of tribulation. Darby's premillennialism argues for a **pre-tribulation** rapture. As noted, in this view, believers will be taken up prior to the tribulation, thus sparing the true church the terrors that will be experienced during this time. Others argue that Christians must endure the first three and half years of the tribulation, but will be spared the full scope of its violence in the final half. This is known as the **mid-tribulation** rapture. Finally, some argue that Christians must weather the cosmological death spasms of the tribulation along with everyone else, but that they will be raptured at its end, just prior to Christ's triumphant return. This is a belief in a **post-tribulation** rapture. Thus, while radical apocalypticists might agree on the general contours of dispensational rapture ideology, theological unanimity has proven elusive among pre-trib, mid-trib, and post-trib (as they are known colloquially) Christians (LaHaye and Ice 2001, 106–8; Sutton 2014, 17–18).

Dispensational premillennialism and its rapture theology was a creation of, and reaction to, the amalgamation of disparate religious groups in the modern period. For example, the rapid changes experienced in the United States in the late nineteenth and twentieth centuries, exemplified and exacerbated by the immigration of religious "others" such as Jews and Catholics, created considerable angst among certain white American Protestant Christians. Apocalyptic ideology helped to manage this anxiety, by reminding these Christians that, although they might find themselves living in a world beset by a confusion of colors and creeds, they (and they alone) were the faithful community preparing for the return of Jesus who would vindicate them on the last day.

Despite the fact that Darby's teachings represented an innovation in Christian eschatology, premillennialists argued that their doctrine was actually nothing new, but the recovery of ancient Christian truth. In doing so, premillennialist rhetoric participated (and continues to participate) in a Protestant project that sees itself restoring a "pure" faith unsullied by Roman Catholic accoutrements (Sutton 2014, 44, 287; LaHaye and Ice 2001, 50–52; see Rapture Ready [website]). Moreover, premillennialism historically had a broad reach that cut across more traditional denominational boundaries. As Sutton argues, "Premillennialism was a conviction and an ideology. It was not a church or a denomination" (Sutton 2014, 26). Institutional denominational structures were human creations, after all. God, in premillennialist ideology, knew his real children and would take them before the woes of the tribulation. Not all who went to church belonged to the true church—only the latter would experience the rapture (see Sutton 2014, 22–23).

As the paragraphs above demonstrate, the language and terminology employed by scholars who study apocalyptic thinkers is, to say the very least, complex. Very few people, after all, walk around claiming the academic theological moniker "premillennialist." Sutton, in his monumental *American Apocalypse: A History of Modern Evangelicalism*, uses the term **"radical evangelical"** to describe Christians of certain Protestant traditions who explicitly injected their faith with apocalyptic fervor. However, "radical evangelical" is most certainly the designation of an outsider looking in. Two other terms can be used for specific historical periods that reflect the self-designation of radically apocalyptic Christians themselves. Sutton writes:

> I shift from "radical evangelicals" to **"fundamentalists"** to describe the network of white, Anglo-American radical evangelicals who in the 1910s established a distinct, definable, interdenominational apocalyptic movement. By the 1940s, many of the men and women who had built the fundamentalist movement determined that the term was doing more harm than good, so they dropped it. They replaced "fundamentalist" with the older, more historic **"evangelical"** (Sutton 2014, x; see also 85, 285).

The event that signals this shift among apocalyptic Protestants was the 1942 formation of the National Association of Evangelicals (NAE), an organization that still exists today. A key difference between the NAE and its fundamentalist forebears was the desire for a more mainstream theological appeal in order to promote the saving message of Jesus Christ more broadly. In other words, the members of various apocalyptic Protestant movements recognized that the full scope of their theology was too often overshadowed by an overemphasis on, and squabbling about, end times minutiae. The group thus attempted to minimize the centrality of the radically apocalyptic doctrines of previous generations of fundamentalists, rapture theology foremost among them. To be sure, most members still tacitly subscribed to some kind of rapture theology, but the NAE opted not to make that issue *the* singular litmus test of doctrinal orthodoxy (Sutton 2014, 286; see also 101–3). Yet, this move toward more mainstream theology was a goal whose results were uneven at best. The sheer popularity of end-of-the-world speculation ensured that it was not long before premillenialist theology moved to the center once again.

Premillennialism and Politics

The different radical evangelical responses to World Wars I and II can help elucidate the influence of premillenialist theology on American politics in the twentieth and twenty-first centuries. Drawing from nineteenth-century radical evangelical teaching that was wary of earthly powers and principalities, Christian fundamentalists were generally loath to support President Woodrow Wilson (1913–21) and US entry into the Great War. "Darby and Scofield," for example, "emphasized the inherent contradiction between premillennialism and nationalism" (Sutton 2014, 98). Likewise, the fundamentalist periodical *King's Business* was critical of various patriotic expressions—including waving the flag (Sutton 2014, 273). For many radical evangelicals, since God was in charge of history, American claims to make the world safe for democracy were evidence of rank hubris (Sutton 2014, 93). Moreover, given the hypernationalism on display in American during World War I that brooked no dissent (Americans' constitutional rights were curtailed by the Espionage [1917] and Sedition [1918] Acts, for example), some radical evangelicals feared that Americans had created a false idol out of the flag and the nationalism it represented (Sutton 2014, 93, 98).

Critics lambasted anti-war fundamentalist theologians for promoting a seemingly anti-American agenda. The liberal Christian periodical *Christian Century*, for example, wrote that the "most serious menace of millenarianism is its inevitable effect upon the loyalty, courage and devotion of our citizenship in the present world war" (Sutton 2014, 93). Such criticism, and political marginalization, seems to have chastened the leading voices of fundamentalism. In fact, Sutton argues that "fundamentalists had no intention of playing the role of minority exiles; they wanted access to the mainstream of American life. In fact, they wanted to guide the mainstream" (Sutton 2014, 264).

Such aspirations help explain the fact that, by the dawn of World War II, fundamentalist periodicals consistently printed full-throttled support of that American war effort. This shift, Sutton contends, was also a result of a fundamentally different conceptualization of World War II. Thus, when the conflagration of World War II broke out, "they rallied behind the Stars and Stripes and printed hypernationalistic magazine covers that linked God with American exceptionalism" (Sutton 2014, 273).

The fundamentalist patriotic support of the war effort during World War II was all the more remarkable, given the widespread distrust and outright hostility in many radical evangelical quarters for President Franklin D. Roosevelt (FDR) and his "New Deal," a series of government programs designed to pull the American economy out of the Great Depression. Nevertheless, their support can be explained by the fact that many premillennialists interpreted World War II as a terrestrial battleground for a larger cosmic conflict between Christ and the enemies of God. However much distrust fundamentalists felt towards FDR, they supported a war wherein "Christian America" was allied against the forces of evil. In so doing, "fundamentalists had done what just a few years earlier had seemed almost unthinkable—they had baptized Christian fundamentalism in the waters of patriotic Americanism" (Sutton 2014, 266). The shift that began during the war continued so that evangelicals could claim America as a *Christian* nation, whose foundational documents represented the flowering of Christian thought. It was this reconceptualization of the United States that "laid the groundwork for evangelicals' post World War II ascension into an integral position in American life." Thus, evangelical Christianity as it exists today was forged largely in response to World War II and was further refined in the anti-Communism of the Cold War.

Over the decades, such patriotic expressions of radical evangelical Christianity more closely aligned with politically, economically, and socially conservative causes. To be sure, neither fundamentalism nor evangelicalism spoke as a monolithic unity. Even as some of the louder voices were trumpeting American exceptionalism, other more traditional radical evangelicals fretted over this political turn. And while more progressive evangelicals did exist (Evangelicals for Social Action) and continue to do so (see, e.g., Jim Wallis and *Sojourners* magazine and ministry), they have tended to lack the patronage of wealthy and well-connected businessmen, and thus tend to have far less influence within the marketplace of American evangelical ideas (Sutton 2014, 341–42). Earlier generations of premillennialists, drawing on resources found in the biblical prophets, critiqued the concentration of wealth and the conditions of workers during the opening decades of the twentieth century. The anti-Communist environment of the postwar era, however, saw a shift as evangelicals critiqued the breakdown of law and order from striking workers and warned of the dangers of totalitarianism that FDR and his policies were feared to have inaugurated. Reaction to the New Deal and, later, the emerging threat of so-called "godless Communism" prompted evangelical rhetoric that would sanctify private capitalism in the free market and that would allow leading evangelicals to "blend their own market interests with their spiritual ideals" (Sutton 2014, 304–5; see *American Jesus* 2013, 15:00). The anti-Communism of the Cold War also spurred some evangelical leaning lawmakers to make explicit their remembered past of America as a Christian nation. For example, in 1953, the Eisenhower administration officially declared the "biblical foundation" of the US government. Further, as Kevin M. Kruse writes,

> In 1954, Congress followed Eisenhower's lead, adding the phrase "under God" to the previously secular Pledge of Allegiance. A similar phrase, "In God We Trust," was added to a postage stamp for the first time in 1954 and then to paper money the next year; in 1956 it became the nation's first official motto. During the Eisenhower era Americans were told, time and time again, that the nation not only should be a Christian nation but also that it always been one (Kruse 2015, xiii).

Fig. 19.3. "In God We Trust" on U.S. currency, a phrase that was not added until 1956. En.wikipedia.org.

That such ratifications of the idea of the United States as a Christian nation occurred during the Eisenhower administration should perhaps come as no surprise, given the president's close relationship with Billy Graham, the influential public face of postwar evangelicalism, who argued for this very notion. Graham, Sutton writes, "was a product of the new evangelicalism that sought to find better ways to appeal to outsiders than the old fundamentalism" (Sutton 2014, 327). And although he would slowly soften the edges of his apocalyptic expectations over the course of time, in 1950, Graham was still preaching an imminent end to the world. In that year, he revised his timetable for rapture—instead of the faithful being taken by Christ within five years, as he had originally estimated, his recalculation suggested it would more likely happen within two (Sutton 2014, 329). Throughout 1952, however, Graham was frequently meeting with then candidate Eisenhower as the latter man was campaigning for president. This is an example of the premillennialist paradox: many of those who expected the imminent end of the world also worked tirelessly to influence government and society (Kruse 2015, ix). Harold Ockenga eloquently expressed the explicit rationale behind such paradoxical thinking in 1945, arguing that "we labor as though Christ would not come for a millennium. We live as though he were to come to-night" (as quoted in Sutton 2014, 315). The imminence of the end, as Paul himself taught in 1 Thessalonians, should not produce apathy, but action (1 Thess 5). Ockenga thus urged his fellow radical evangelicals on, insisting that Christ called them to battle Satan and occupy the nation and the world, thereby laying the groundwork to more effectively preach the gospel of Christ. Similar ideology continues up to the present day. As Mel White, a former ghostwriter for Graham, puts it, radical premillennialists "believe that this country is responsible to Christianize the world, therefore they have to Christianize America first" (*Waiting for Armageddon* 2009, 53:30).

In addition to domestic and foreign political concerns, the use of nuclear weapons on the Japanese cities of Hiroshima and Nagasaki in August 1945 suddenly gave radically apocalyptic ideologies traction in wider American culture. This became even more pronounced after the Soviet Union successfully tested such a weapon in 1949 and a fiery end to the world as we know it no longer resided safely in ancient myth and legend. It was now a very real military possibility. Sutton argues, "Evangelicals helped Americans make sense of this postwar world by aligning it with their apocalyptic visions of imminent violence, horrific persecution, and world war" (Sutton 2014, 295). Apocalyptic images and motifs began to seep more readily into popular culture. So entrenched did Protestant apocalyptic thinking become that during the 1984 presidential election, the incumbent candidate, Ronald Reagan, was asked about his public views on Armageddon—the final conflict between Christ and the forces of evil—and its relationship to nuclear war. Reagan responded that (evangelical) theologians seemed to think that the biblical prophecies that signaled the coming of Armageddon were starting to be fulfilled. In other words, he stated that all signs were pointing toward the coming of the final battle. However, using rhetoric that dispensational premillennialists had been employing since Darby, he went on to note that no one really knows whether "those prophecies mean that Armageddon is a thousand years away or the day after tomorrow" (*Waiting for Armageddon* 2009, 57:00). That a sitting president, running for (and ultimately winning) a second term, was able to speak openly and frankly about his trust in premillennialist theologians and their beliefs about the probable imminent end of the world demonstrates how far this kind of Protestant Christian thinking had come since the days of Darby and Scofield. It also demonstrates not only the political clout of evangelical Americans, but also how profoundly mainstream dispensational storylines, if not the entire theological apparatus, had become in American culture.

In the opening decades of the twenty-first century, the mainstreaming of evangelical thought into American politics has continued, demonstrating its increasing popularity. While some evangelicals never entirely trusted the religious *bona fides* of Reagan, a movie actor turned politician, with the election of George W. Bush in 2000, many evangelicals felt that they had someone sitting in the oval office who more fully shared their values and beliefs. While the "evil empire" that fueled the apocalyptic imaginations of the Reagan era (the Soviet Union) was no more, the attacks of September 11, 2001, demonstrated that the United States was facing yet another existential enemy. In the wake of 9/11, American apocalyptic thinkers—both in and out of politics—did what their forebears had spent the last century doing: reading signs of the end in current geopolitical events: "Evangelicalism once again gave Americans a language with which to make sense of the tragedy" (Sutton 2014, 370). Of course, as had also happened during the previous century, premillennialists had to adjust their reading of scripture, based on a newfound enemy. Radical evangelicals, such as John Hagee, now interpreted prophecies to help make sense of the nation's experience with radical political Islam (*Waiting for Armageddon* 2009, 1:04:00). Twenty-first century premillennialists, like those who came before them, interpreted current events through biblical prophecy.

Christian Consumer Culture: The *Left Behind* Franchise

Just as evangelical apocalypticism found its way into the world of politics and interpreted contemporary events through ancient texts, so too did some evangelical apolcaypticists realize that the end of the world sells. As Frykholm writes, "Evangelicalism has become good business" (Frykholm 2005, 279). For example, in 1995, the Christian publisher Tyndale House debuted *Left Behind*, a novel co-authored by Tim LaHaye and Jerry Jenkins. A fictional narrative dramatizing and explaining key elements of dispensational premillennialism, *Left Behind* promised to generate, like Tim LaHaye's non-fiction books expounding rapture theology, modest sales in a niche market. Instead, it was the beginning of what would become a blockbuster franchise, selling over 63 million copies; spawning multiple spin-off novel series (including a 40-book series aimed at the young adult market), movie adaptations, and video games; and earning huge amounts of money for its authors and publisher. Its success surprised everyone, including its producers. As Frykholm notes, the runaway success of this franchise demonstrates just how amenable popular American culture had become to evangelical rapture theology. "The rapture," she writes, "is woven into the fabric of American culture, a part of the culture's hopes, dreams, fears, and mythology" (Frykholm 2004, 13).

Left Behind is a very American re-telling of biblical end-time prophecies. It contains just about every element found in the bestselling examples of American pop culture (an entertainment culture exported globally). It has good guys and bad guys, (chaste) romance, explosions, intrigue, and tales of derring-do. *Left Behind* is a righteous, action-packed evangelical and evangelistic romp. The struggles and faithful witness of the dashing and attractive main players draw in readers. The characters represent a better us—younger, more attractive, more committed, more faithful, and more courageous. Perhaps the most American characteristic of all, and the basic plot device that renders the series theologically suspect in the eyes of some rapture believing Christians, is the notion of a second chance, the ability to remake oneself into the person one was meant to be in a new environment. Clearly, this echoes the popular American notion of the American Dream—where anyone, regardless of past experiences or circumstances, can start over, work hard, and succeed. It is this narrative structure that helps readers identify with those left behind—they are not bad people (the narrative makes this clear), just insufficiently committed to Christ. In the characters' struggles after the rapture, readers see their own wrestling with faith mirrored in the narrative. The "second chance" plot device serves a second function as well. Since all the "real" Christians are gone, those who remain must learn what happened and why. It is in the characters' journey of religious discovery that the reader learns the truth of dispensational premillennialism as well (for a discussion of reader response to *Left Behind*, see Frykholm 2005).

The series displays the cross-denominational appeal of radical evangelical apocalyptic ideology in that the true Christians do not belong to any one denomination. The contrast is not between true and false denominations, but between authentic Christianity that is prompted by an imminent expectation of the end and inauthentic Christianity that has lost this central teaching. Again and again, throughout the initial novel, lukewarm versions of Christianity are held up for criticism. Rayford Steele, the story's leading man whose wife Irene and twelve-year-old son have been raptured, struggles to understand why he and Chloe, his college-age daughter, remain. Irene Steele is the stereotypical good Christian wife found in rapture literature (Frykholm 2005, 275). She found religion prior to the action of the novel, but her worldly husband resists following her commitment. "Rayford," we learn on the opening page, "used to look forward to getting home to his wife. Irene was attractive and vivacious enough, even at forty. But lately he had found himself repelled by her obsession with religion. It was all she could talk about" (LaHaye and Jenkins 1995, 1). The reader learns that religion was never very important for Rayford and that he only barely tolerated church. Moreover, the church that he and Irene initially attended "demanded little and offered a lot." Irene's new church, by contrast, "was a little too literal and personal and challenging" for Rayford (LaHaye and Jenkins 1995, 124–25). The constant talk about the salvation of souls made him uncomfortable and was something he never had to hear about in his previous church. Moreover, the cornerstone of this new church was found in the preaching of the rapture. It was this teaching that inspired fervent devotion (LaHaye and Jenkins 1995, 155).

Even in New Hope Village Church, Irene's new place of worship, there are examples of Christians in name only, including the assistant pastor Bruce Barnes. It is this church, through the teaching of the now fully committed post-rapture Pastor Barnes, that becomes the spiritual home for the main characters as they (and the readers) learn about what happened to their raptured loved ones and what is in store for them: those who have been "left behind." Fortunately, for Pastor Barnes, Rayford, and the others, the raptured senior pastor of the church, Vernon Billings, left behind a videotape (a reminder that the first book was published in 1995) that explains what has happened and what those watching need to do. Technology provides a means for this true Christian to continue to teach after Christ has taken him. The pastor reads portions of the Bible in his explanatory video, but the biblical texts themselves confuse Rayford. Again and again, as Rayford tries to read and understand the Bible, he is perplexed and confused. It sounds "like gibberish to him." After reading 1 Cor 15:51-57, Pastor Billings says, "Let me paraphrase some of that for you so you'll understand it clearly." The rapture, Billings goes on to teach, is God's last-ditch attempt to shake an unbelieving world into repentance. Herein lies the theological rationale of the series. The final judgment will occur after the seven years of tribulation. During this period, people will still have time to turn to God; they have another chance. "If you accept God's message of salvation," Pastor Billings teaches, "his Holy Spirit will come unto you and make you spiritually born anew. You don't need to understand all of this theologically. You can become a child of God by praying to him right now." For the authors of *Left Behind*, the characters (and presumably, the target audience) do not need to comprehend the entire complicated ideological apparatus of dispensational premillennialism. They just have to pray to enter into a living relationship with God (LaHaye and Jenkins 1995, 210–16).

In many respects, *Left Behind* functions like Pastor Billings's tape.

It takes complicated biblical texts and theological speculation and weaves crucial elements of them into a linear storyline in order to make them easier to understand. The Bible is not an easy read for those with contemporary narrative expectations: it lacks a single authorial vision with a straightforward and clear plot development; it contains multiple traditions that sometimes conflict with one another; and it demands that readers know what passed for basic common sense in various ancient cultures (see Beal 2011, 36). Fictional stories such as *Left Behind* often allow sympathetic readers to "see" the teachings of biblical prophecy that remain opaque in the unfamiliar imagery of the apocalypses themselves. By embedding prophetic and dispensationalist teachings within a clear narrative, readers can participate in the apocalyptic drama through the active use of their imaginations. As Frykholm writes, "Within the schema that *Left Behind* creates, fiction becomes an important means for conveying the truth of prophecy. It translates the Book of Revelation, giving readers a code for interpretation, which then is placed back onto the biblical texts as its most obvious meaning" (Frykholm 2004, 116). Readers who already accept some version of rapture ideology have the most positive experiences with the series, while those who do not participate in a dispensationalist worldview, and who are not persuaded by it, tend not to find the storyline particularly compelling. But even sympathetic readers are cognizant that *Left Behind* is not Scripture, and that in the end, it represents the interpretation of two men who may not have it one hundred percent correct. Yet, despite the casual way the novels are read, and even if readers do not accept every biblical interpretation offered by LaHaye and Jenkins, believers report that the series provides an opportunity for reflection about one's own commitment to Christ in a world that is coming to an end (see Frykholm 2004, ch. 6).

The success of *Left Behind* differs in magnitude rather than kind when compared with other consumer products that focus on the rapture and the end of time. Indeed, radically apocalyptic products have sold well despite the concern of some leading dispensationalists. In the 1920s and 1930s, publishers of leading fundamentalist periodicals worried about commercializing and overemphasizing prophetic truths (Sutton 2014, 212–13). Not only did it feed the darker side of evangelicalism, with its often detailed descriptions of the destruction of the unsaved, but some worried that searching for signs of the end took valuable time and resources away from actually doing the good work of Christ to prepare the world for judgment (Sutton 2014, 212, 226–30). However, even the most theologically concerned editors recognized that when articles interpreting world events through biblical prophecy ran, sales increased. Indeed, no matter how much evangelical leaders wanted to tone down eschatological fervor in the middle of the twentieth century, "the faithful continued to devour the most daring and radical expressions of apocalypticism" (Sutton 2014, 327). Americans were buying the end times and authors, editors, and publishers recognized this (see Sutton 2014, 344–45).

The wedding of consumerism and apocalypticism demonstrates just how intertwined radical evangelicalism and American popular culture have become. As Timothy Beal argues, "popular culture has really become synonymous with consumer culture. To make something popular requires making it appealing to consumers" (Beal 2011, 73). Beal charts the rise of "value added" Bibles aimed at specific audiences. For example, Thomas Nelson, a leading Christian publisher, came out with *The Patriot's Bible* in 2009. According to the product description,

> This extremely unique Bible shows how the history of the United States connects the people and events of the Bible to our lives in a modern world. The story of the United States is wonderfully woven into the teachings of the Bible and includes a beautiful full-color family record section, memorable images from our nation's history and hundreds of enlightening articles which complement the New King James Version Bible text (Thomas Nelson 2009).

Thomas Nelson further aims to increase its market share through the publication of so-called Bibelzines—Bible magazines—that are published for a wide array of specific audiences (teenage boys, teenage girls, young career men, young career women). It is within this American Christian consumer culture—where Bibles attract specific demographics because of fancy covers or glossy magazine-like additions—that *Left Behind* was launched to great success (Beal 2011, 40–42). Recognizing the profitability of such Christian products, non-Christian booksellers have gotten into the game as well. In the late 1990s, before the days of ubiquitous internet commerce, these bookstores helped to turn books such as *Left Behind* into blockbusters by making them more widely available to a reading audience that might be interested in apocalyptic stories, but who tended not to visit Christian bookstores (Mathewson 2009, 321–22).

In the United States, cultural critics have noted that purchasing a product has become an American way to express Christian identity and a way to witness to others the truth of Christianity. To spread the gospel is, in some sense, to sell it. The producers of *Left Behind* argue that the products of the franchise help to spread the saving message of Jesus Christ to millions of readers. Tyndale House contends that the products help prompt the very change of heart the characters in the story experience after realizing that they had not been raptured. Moreover, there are plenty of testimonials on the *Left Behind* website that claim to demonstrate such changes of heart (http://www.leftbehind.com). However, Amy Johnson Frykholm, in her three years of interviewing readers of the series, "searched in vain for a person who could testify to a life changed through the reading of *Left Behind*" (Frykholm 2004, 164). Rather, she found that readers who already accepted some version of radical evangelical apocalypticism were the ones most likely to have positive experiences, both as a reader and as a believer, with the books. Those who did not already share a premillennialist worldview found the books boring at best, badly written by profit-hungry authors at worst (Frykholm 2004, 145).

Christian critics of *Left Behind* express grave concerns about the theology of the series, in addition to the "lived effects" of that theology. Catholics, Lutherans, Presbyterians, Methodists, and even fellow evangelicals have been forced, by the popularity of the series, to issue statements cautioning members about the theology of dispensational premillennialism or, for evangelicals, the interpretation of that theology found in the books. Barbara Rossing, a biblical scholar and ordained Lutheran pastor, is one such critic. She, like many, worries that a "beam me up" theology produces Christians with no motivation to engage the world in order to work for the common good where others are understood and accepted on their own terms. The focus of rapture theology, Rossing and others contend, is as individualistic and escapist as it is totalizing (Rossing 2004, ch. 1). Moreover, critics fear that such a theology has dire environmental consequences since it teaches that this world will eventually be destroyed and remade by Christ—environmental stewardship is not a concern if one thinks the world will end in one's lifetime (*Waiting for Armageddon* 2009, 1:10:00). Why recycle if Jesus is set to return *soon*?

Even critics such as Rossing, however, recognize that the great strength of the *Left Behind* novels is their ability to prompt a sense of religious urgency in readers (Rossing 2004, 86). If the rapture is coming soon, there is no time to waste. As one believer, a woman who writes code for software used in American military aircraft, tells viewers in the documentary *Waiting for Armageddon*, "The rapture makes me have to focus because I may meet my maker tomorrow" (1:12). This coheres with what Frykholm found in her research on readers of *Left Behind*: "The possibility of the rapture gives readers a sense of urgency to prepare themselves and those around them. It provides a moment, imminent and elusive as death, we have no choice but to prepare for now" (Frykholm 2004, 107). For those who believe, the nearness of the end is that which imbues with meaning the things they do *now*.

The cultural reach of the *Left Behind* franchise is difficult to overestimate. The popular and long-running TV show, *The Simpsons*, even satirizes the series in their episode "Thank God It's Doomsday." The episode aired in May 2005, the year after the final book of the twelve-part *Left Behind* series came out. In the episode, Homer Simpson becomes a rapture prognosticator after watching a movie entitled *Left Below*—hardly a veiled reference. That an iconic American television series could craft an episode poking fun at *Left Behind* demonstrates that the writers assumed wide cultural recognition of the object of satire (otherwise, the episode barely makes sense). The movie Homer watches is badly acted, has comically bad dialogue, and displays an absurdly heavy-handed religiosity. Again, this is not a terribly subtle way to dramatize what many critics had to say about the series itself and its movie adaptations starring the 1980s teen heartthrob Kirk Cameron. These adaptations were so bad that LaHaye actually sued the production company for damage to his franchise (he lost; Sutton 2014, 365). In 2014, a rebooted version of *Left Behind* came to the silver screen, this time starring Nicholas Cage. Cage's star power, however, was not enough to spare the film from being panned by critics or, more importantly, tanking at the box office.

The reception of Cage's *Left Behind* movie may portend that the profitability of the franchise's products is drawing to a close. Another sign of the "end times" for *Left Behind* seems to be that parts of the 2015 *Left Behind* website are also strangely out of date (http://www.leftbehind.com). The home page still advertises that the Cage adaptation of the film is "coming to theaters on October 3 (2014)." Moreover, just below an announcement of a "new look" to the books of the series, there is a link to a conversation with Tim LaHaye and Jerry Jenkins about the end of the world that leads with a rejection of popular predictions that the world will end in 2012. However, despite the marketing moment having passed for *Left Behind* products, its popularity as an American cultural phenomenon for over a decade means that its legacy remains. Whether one regards them positively or negatively, Tim LaHaye and Jerry Jenkins have crafted and popularized a dispensational premillennialist narrative theology with which American culture will need to wrestle for the foreseeable future (Sutton 2014, 366).

The Curious Case of Harold Camping

While one cannot make a case for causation, it is probably not surprising that the popularity of *Left Behind* products coincided with the turn of the millennium. As the countdown to the year 2000 neared an end, there was widespread speculation about a catastrophic end to our electronic civilization—the so-called **Y2K problem**. This technological end-of-the-world scenario predicted that, because of a lack of foresight among programmers, vast swaths of computer systems would be unable to function properly once the millennium flipped. In computer code, 2000 would look the same, it was feared, as 1900 and this confusion would cause system breakdowns. The American TV network NBC even aired a campy made-for-TV movie about this scenario, *Y2K: Countdown to Chaos*. Fast-forward a dozen years and a new popular end-time concern was in the air. Popular anxiety focused on December 21, 2012, as a possible end of the world, based on the supposed last day of the ancient Mayan calendar. The end of the world was once again on people's minds. In this cultural environment of heightened eschatological awareness, the rapture prediction of 89-year-old Christian radio personality Harold Camping found a ready audience for both acceptance and ridicule. With utter certainty about his prediction of the coming rapture and judgment, Camping declared, "It is going to happen. It is going to happen. There's no possibility that it will not happen" (*Apocalypse Later* 2014, 3:20).

Fig. 19.4. A Family Radio sign in Denver predicting the end of the world on May 21, 2011. Zeke Piestrup/15Trucks Productions, Venice, CA.

Others had been making concrete predictions about the end of the world throughout the 1990s and early 2000s, but they failed to gain popular traction. Camping himself, in a self-published book, once suggested that the world could come to an end in 1994 (Camping 1992). However, this book and its prediction went largely unnoticed by anyone who did not listen to his long-running radio program "Open Forum" on Family Radio, the network he founded. However, his revised calculations that the rapture would occur on May 21, 2011—to be followed by final judgment on October 21, 2011—garnered a significant amount of attention. Popular late night television host David Letterman even made fun of Camping's failed predictions in one of his famous "Top Ten Lists" on May 23, 2011. Such satire only works if a majority of the audience has at least heard about the referent, suggesting that his message had reached a widespread popular audience. The Mayan calendar concern had primed American culture to be receptive to various end-time speculations, but Family Radio and Camping's followers also went on a publicity blitz, reportedly spending millions of dollars on billboards throughout the world.

The story of Harold Camping and his popular failed prediction of the end recalls, in many ways, the nineteenth-century predictions of William Miller. Both men made at least one public prediction that required recalculation. While they used different biblical starting places for their calculations—Miller, the seventy weeks of Daniel (9:2, 24–27), and Camping, the story of Noah (Gen 6–9)—each was able to arrive at a specific date for the end. And while those who look to Tim LaHaye for theological guidance emphasize that he is *Doctor* LaHaye (he holds a Doctor of Ministry degree from Western Theological Seminary and a Doctor of Literature degree from Liberty University), Camping, like Miller, did not hold any theological degrees. Camping received a B.S. in civil engineering from the University of California in 1942. Both Miller and Camping thus exemplify the intertwining of American and Protestant ideals: a self-educated student of the Bible who, by dint of his own hard work and unmediated study of the word of God (in English translation), is able to see the truth that elite experts had failed to grasp. Both men reached for their own eschatological bootstraps as it were. And, sadly, each attracted a large number of followers, some of whom ended up financially and/or spiritually broken after the predictions failed to materialize (Bartlett 2012).

Camping's insistence on fixing a specific date for Christ's return flew in the face of over a century of practice by radical evangelical leaders that generally sought to avoid another Great Disappointment. In 1940, John Rice told his congregation, "We cannot say that Jesus will come by December first, nor positively that he will come in 1940. But according to certain signs, we can definitely believe that His coming is near, very, very near, is likely to come even today" (Sutton 2014, 230). Billy Graham, perhaps chastened by his own expectation of the end in the early 1950s, admitted that some of his co-religionists had gone overboard with their predictions. But, he argued, the imminent expectation of the rapture was a crucial Christian doctrine for a robust faith in Christ. Christ's coming was always just around the corner and that was how a genuine Christian needed to live (Sutton 2014, 329). Camping's specific prediction thus irked other twenty-first-century radical evangelicals. Tim LaHaye, for example, castigated Camping for thinking he could accurately fix the time of the end. LaHaye and others based their critique on biblical passages where Jesus argues that no one (not even he) can know the specific day or the hour of the end (Matt 24:36; Mark 13:32; see also Acts 1:7; http://www.leftbehind.com/05_news /tim-lahaye-responds-to-campings-failed-predictions.asp). Camping's response to this critique was twofold. First, in a controversial assertion, he argued that those passages were valid only until the end of the church age. Based on his careful study of the Bible, Camping concluded that the church age ended in 1988. Since that time, Satan has been in control of the churches. Thus, given Satan's control of the churches, only someone who was not a clergyman or recognized church leader could accurately predict the date of Christ's return. Second, this assertion is bolstered by Camping's interpretation of biblical precedent. As Jonah (Jonah 3:4) and Noah (Gen 7:7) had clear timetables for preaching judgment, so too, Camping argued, has God given a clear timeline for the end of the world within the words of the Bible (*Apocalypse Later* 2014, 14:15).

Fig. 19.5. Official poster for the documentary Apocalypse Later, which followed Harold Camping during his final predictions of the end of the world in May 2011 and October 2011. Zeke Piestrup/15Trucks Productions, Venice, CA.

The fact that Camping dared to set a specific date for the end of the world, and that it ignited such a popular following, highlights a tension within American dispensational premillennialism. While influential leaders since Darby sought to rein in the excesses of their tradition, "laypeople for over one hundred years flocked to doomsday radicals" (Sutton 2014, 344). Camping thus stands in a long line of populist radical evangelicals who displayed an American optimism that they could succeed where others had failed. Critics of rapture theology speak of the popularity of this fervent end-time expectation in negative terms. Rossing, for example, refers to the "addictive quality" of Armageddon theology, clearly signaling her disapproval (*Waiting for Armageddon* 2009, 55:00). Sue Espinoza, Harold Camping's daughter and employee of Family Radio, spoke more positively of her father's gradual realization that proclaiming the date of the end was the purpose of his radio show. He predicted, she says, that the whole world would come to know when the end would be. He did not know how it would happen, but he had faith it would. Espinoza was not terribly surprised at how her father's prediction tapped into popular feelings. After all, she notes, "what's more interesting than the end of the world?" (*Apocalypse Later* 2014, 6:50)

Fig. 19.6. Harold Camping on the set of Family Radio. Zeke Piestrup/15Trucks Productions, Venice, CA.

The curious case of Harold Camping is emblematic of twenty-first-century American popular culture in some ways—a culture where we share even the most mundane aspects of our lives through various social media platforms. Camping gave filmmaker Zeke Piestrup unfettered access to him in the run-up to May 21, 2011. In Piestrup's documentary, *Apocalypse Later: Harold Camping vs. The End of the World*, viewers can watch Camping go about his daily business in the last days. To be sure, this portrait of Camping is filtered through Piestrup's vision (89-year-old Camping was not posting selfies and status updates on social media, after all), but the doomsday radical in this documentary is humanized. Piestrup shows us a kindly old man, living in a modest home, who earnestly believes his message—he is not some TV preacher duping his listeners to make himself wealthy. The humanization of Camping makes the final scenes of the documentary all the more poignant after Camping's predictions fail to come to pass. It is true that those who put their trust in Camping were traumatized and suffered real loss; this knowledge mitigates our sympathy. But it is hard not to feel some pity, if not sympathy, for a humbled Camping who tells Piestrup, and us, that he sinned in thinking he could know the date of the end. He was wrong. Trying to salvage some meaning out of his great disappointment, he tells Piestrup that, at the very least, the popularity of his mistaken message had increased the knowledge of the Bible throughout the world (*Apocalypse Later* 2014, 55:00). Finding a silver lining in a failed venture is, after all, one of the hallmarks of American optimism.

Conclusion

A standard line among dispensational premillennialists is that biblical prophecy is history written in advance. Since the nineteenth century, when Darby developed his apocalyptic theology that focused on the rapture of the church, radical evangelicals have used biblical prophecy to help them make sense of the world around them. And since the nineteenth century, current events have repeatedly led many radical evangelicals to argue that at no other point in history have geopolitical events so closely matched biblical prophecy. Former Congresswoman and one-time presidential hopeful Michelle Bachmann continues this tradition in a radio interview given in April 2015 when she argued that world events are now such that:

> It is just like the Bible forewarned that in the last days it will be like the beginning of birth pangs. In my opinion? We are *far* beyond the beginning of birth pangs. We're moving far down into the process. . . . All I can tell you as a mom who has given birth to five babies, the birth pangs are very close together, they are very intense now. We are literally watching, month by month, the speed move up to a level we've never seen before with these events (Markell 2015, 34:50).

Despite this, Bachmann tells her listeners that this is not a time for despair, but for rejoicing since we are living in the most exciting period in history, one that the biblical prophets themselves longed to see: "We in our lifetimes, potentially, could see Jesus Christ returning to earth, the rapture of the church" (Markell 2015, 36:15). Like radical evangelicals throughout the nineteenth and twentieth centuries, Bachmann, the former politician, believes that global events point to the imminent end of the world. Bachmann thus participates in the long American tradition of making sense of the world through an apocalyptic reading of the Bible.

Part of the draw of apocalyptic ideology is that it makes for a good story. It is a way for believers to orient and make sense of the world and their place in it. Media critic Douglas Rushoff, in discussing apocalyptic American Christians, notes that

> When things get complex, when the story gets confusing, people want it to end. And these days people would rather it end bad than that it not end at all. We are addicted to traditional narratives with beginnings, middles, and ends. . . . The idea of completion goes hand in hand with creation. (*American Jesus* 2013, 1:1:50)

Frykholm found among readers of the *Left Behind* series that the story of the end (as told by LaHaye and Jenkins) was part of what convinced them of the truth of rapture theology (Frykholm 2004, ch. 6). Even Christian critics of dispensational premillennialism, such as Rossing, recognize the emotional and theological power of its story and stress the importance of crafting a counter-narrative to what they see as a Christian sickness—the fixation on Armageddon and war (Rossing 2004, 74, 140). While outsiders who make no attempt to understand them might mock radical evangelical predictions of the end, with their ever-shifting cast of characters the Bible supposedly predicts, this misses the existential power of the rhetoric and language of rapture stories. By mapping their world onto biblical storylines, radical evangelicals of all stripes are able to give their existence ultimate meaning.

Study Questions:

1. Miller and Darby provide two models for talking about the end of the world in American Christianity. What are they and what other examples can we find for each model?

2. Based on what you have read in this volume, what are the similarities and differences between apocalyptic thinking in ancient Christian communities and contemporary American communities?

3. Please explain the relationship between radical apocalyptic theology and the marketplace in American culture.

4. What does apocalyptic belief in the imminent end of the world do for communities and individuals who hold such beliefs? Why do some Christians view these beliefs as dangerous?

Bibliography and Further Reading:

American Jesus. Directed by Aram Garriga. Brooklyn, NY: Glass Eye Pix, 2013.

Apocalypse Later: Harold Camping vs. The End of the World. Directed by Zeke Piestrup. El Segundo, CA: Gravitas Ventures, 2014.

Ayers, Lewis. *Nicaea and its Legacy: An Approach to Fourth-Century Trinitarian Theology.* Oxford: Oxford University Press, 2004.

Baker, Kelly J. *The Zombies Are Coming!: The Realities of the Zombie Apocalypse in American Culture.* New York: Bondfire Books, 2013. Kindle edition.

Balmer, Randall. "The Great Disappointment: When the World Fails to End on Schedule," *Religion Dispatches,* May 25, 2011. Accessed via http://religiondispatches.org/the-great-disappointment-when-the-world-fails-to-end-on-schedule/.

Bartlett, Tom. "A Year After the Non-Apocalypse: Where are They Now?" *Religion Dispatches,* May 12, 2012. Accessed via http://religiondispatches.org/a-year-after-the-non-apocalypse-where-are-they-now.

Beal, Timothy. *The Rise and Fall of the Bible: The Unexpected History of an Accidental Book*. Boston: Houghton Mifflin Harcourt, 2011.

Camping, Harold E. *1994?* New York: Vantage, 1992.

Frykholm, Amy Johnson. *Rapture Culture: Left Behind in Evangelical America*. New York: Oxford University Press, 2004.

____. "The Gender Dynamics of the *Left Behind* Series." Pages 270-87 in *Religion and Popular Culture in America*, rev. ed. Edited by Bruce David Forbes and Jeffery H. Mahan. Berkeley: University of California Press, 2005.

LaHaye, Tim, and Jerry B. Jenkins. *Left Behind: A Novel of Earth's Last Days*. Wheaton, IL: Tyndale House, 1995.

LaHaye, Tim, and Thomas Ice. *Charting the End Times: A Visual Guide to Understanding Bible Prophecy*. Eugene, OR: Harvest House, 2001.

Left Behind. "Home." Accessed via http://www.leftbehind.com.

Left Behind. "Tim LaHaye Responds to Camping's Failed Predictions." Accessed via http://www.leftbehind.com/05_news/tim-lahaye-responds-to-campings-failed-predictions.asp.

Kruse, Kevin M. *One Nation under God: How Corporate America Invented Christian America*. New York: Basic Books, 2015.

Markell, Jan. *Understanding the Times*. "Lawlessness and Global Transformation: How It Sets the Stage – Part 2." April 18, 2015. Accessed via http://www.oneplace.com/ministries/understanding-the-times/player/lawlessness-global-transformation-how-it-sets-the-stage-part-2-462502.html.

Mathewson, Dan. "End Times Entertainment: The *Left Behind* Series, Evangelicals, and Death Pornography." *Journal of Contemporary Religion* 24 (2009): 319–37.

Rapture Ready. "Defending the Pre-Trib Rapture." Accessed via https://www.raptureready.com/rr-pre-trib-rapture.html.

Rossing, Barbara R. *The Rapture Exposed: The Message of Hope in the Book of Revelation*. New York: Basic Books, 2004.

Scofield, C. I., ed. *The Scofield Study Bible: King James Version*. New York: Oxford University Press, 2003.

Sutton, Matthew Avery. *American Apocalypse: A History of Modern Evangelicalism.* Cambridge, MA: Belknap, 2014.

Thomas Nelson. "The NKJV American Patriot's Bible." Accessed via http://www.thomasnelson.com/the-american-patriot-s-bible-1.

Waiting for Armageddon. Directed by Kate Davis, David Heilbroner, and Franco Sacchi. Dallas: Eureka Film and Q-Ball Productions, 2009.

20

Space Brothers and Mayan Calendars

Making Sense of "Doomsday Cults"

Joseph P. Laycock

GETTING PREPPED:

1. When people refer to a religious group as a "cult" instead of a "religion," what do they mean?
2. Do you think it is possible to "brainwash" someone into a joining a religion or a cult? How can you tell whether people make decisions for themselves or whether they are brainwashed?
3. There have been several instances in which groups with apocalyptic beliefs have committed suicide or engaged in other acts of violence. Why do these events happen? What are the factors that trigger this sort of violence and how can they be avoided?

KEY TERMS:
ACM
APOSTATE
BRICOLAGE
CULT
DEPROGRAMMING
MILLENNIAL MOVEMENT
NRM

Introduction

In 2010, a prayer group in Palmdale, California, which consisted of only three nuclear families, held a prayer retreat in a park. At the time of this meeting, extended family members, not knowing the nature of this group or the reasons for their meeting, became worried. Some had discovered farewell notes that mentioned "the end of the world." One of those attending the meeting had even left behind a purse containing cash, ID, and property deeds. Some complained that the prayer group's leader had "brainwashed" their loved ones. Authorities concluded that this was an apocalyptic "cult-like group" that was planning to kill themselves and their children, and a manhunt was launched for the missing families. The media went so far as to run headlines such as "6 Adults, 8 Children Plan Mass Suicide." When authorities found the group, they were praying peacefully while their children explored a nearby playground. They had left their material possessions behind because they considered it "sinful" to have such things while on a prayer retreat. Of course, there have been famous incidents in which apocalyptic groups really have engaged in suicide and other forms of violence, but there appears to have been nothing violent about this group. So, how did the authorities and media jump to such radical conclusions? Where do concepts such as "doomsday cults," "brainwashing," and "mass suicide" come from? Is it possible to distinguish between harmful apocalyptic groups and those that are not? Moreover, how can we prevent incidents of religious violence without stigmatizing and harassing innocent people?

Religion vs. Cult: A Distinction without A Difference?

The word **cult** comes from the Latin *cultus deorum* or "care of the gods." In the ancient world, the term had a neutral connotation as cults would worship and "care for" a particular god. That is, "cult" originally referred to any organized system of worship. But since at least the 1920s and 1930s, critics have used the term "cult" pejoratively to describe religious groups they perceive as disingenuous, immoral, and dangerous. The media often assumes there is an obvious distinction between religion and cults, but in practice, the difference is quite vague. There is no single definition of what a "cult" actually is—a fact that explains why media reports about cults never agree about how many "cults" are currently active in America. Common characteristics ascribed to cults include having a charismatic authoritarian leader, using deceptive recruiting practices, demanding a "totalizing" religious lifestyle that may include isolation from outsiders or working without pay, and the financial and sexual abuse of followers. But groups that have none of these features, such as many modern pagan religions, may still be branded as cults. Conversely, religious groups that have several of these features may not be classified as cults. For example, Catholic nuns have traditionally practiced a highly totalizing lifestyle, but most people would not claim a convent of nuns constitutes a cult. Similarly, many organizations (religious or otherwise) have problems with financial or sexual misconduct, but they are not considered cults. Ultimately, the labels "religion" and "cult" are a "folk taxonomy," or a set of categories based on popular impressions rather than logical definitions.

Often, when a group is called a cult, "labeling takes the place of analysis" (Tabor and Gallagher 1995, 139). In other words, the assertion that a particular group is a cult conveys no specific information, but it *implies* a wide variety of claims that may or may not be true. The cult label also helps to distance groups that are hated and feared from those that are accepted and revered. Above all, cults are imagined to be "not like us." By categorizing certain groups as "cults" rather than "religions," we assure ourselves that our own religious beliefs, practices, and institutions are superior to those of a cult. At worst, this thinking delegitimizes cults, dehumanizes those who participate in them, and justifies violence against them.

Because of the social dynamics at play, some sociologists use the term "cult" in more specific ways to describe religious groups that are stigmatized or regarded as outside the mainstream. But most scholars of religion prefer more neutral terms such as "alternative religions" or "new religious movements" (**NRMs**), although these terms are also imprecise. As Eugene Gallagher points out, these terms imply a set of unstated comparisons: Alternative to what? Newer than what? While there may appear to be a "family resemblance" between the various controversial religions commonly classified as NRMs, the category—like the category ("cult") it replaces—remains a designation of convenience determined by the normative values of the mainstream rather than a critical definition.

Millennial Movements

"Millennial movements" is a more precise category of religious groups. Groups can be said to be millennial or millenarian if they believe in some form of collective salvation that will occur in this world (as opposed to in an afterlife) in which suffering and injustice will be overcome. The collective salvation may transform the entire world or may affect only a small group. These ideas are called "millennial" because the transformed world or "Golden Age" is frequently expected to last one thousand years. Some Christian groups expect a millennium of peace based on the passage found in the book of Rev 20:1–6. In a possible allusion to this passage, Hitler announced that the Nazi "third Reich" would last one thousand years.

Catherine Wessinger (1999) makes a further distinction between progressive millennialism and catastrophic millennialism. Progressive millennialism is optimistic about the ability of human beings to create a perfect world, and as such, progressive millennial groups believe they can bring society into harmony with the divine through social engagement. Catastrophic millennialism is more pessimistic. In this model, society is so sinful and corrupt that the world must be destroyed in order to be renewed. This scenario may involve God's wrath, catastrophic "earth changes" such as a pole-shift, or the arrival of extraterrestrials. Whatever the cause, global destruction is necessary for a new, perfect world to arise and replace the current state of things. Of course, progressive millennialism and catastrophic millennialism are not mutually exclusive. Sometimes, groups begin with a stance of progressive millennialism, but when their attempts to transform society are frustrated, they shift to catastrophic millennialism. This was the case with The People's Temple, led by Jim Jones. Many contemporary forms of catastrophic millennialism involve conspiracy theories that revolve around various evil forces thought to oppose the movement. These forces may be described as "Babylon" (see chapter 1), "The New World Order," or malevolent extraterrestrials. However, it is believed that the power of these evil forces will be broken in the coming catastrophe.

While technically, all Jewish, Christian, and Muslim traditions describe a millennial scenario, some groups are particularly invested in predicting and preparing for the end of the world. Many of these groups are classified as NRMs because their interpretation of their religion's traditions and prophecies is "new." They also frequently involve charismatic prophets, form new communities, or adopt unusually novel practices. These elements often cause these groups to be stigmatized by outsiders as "cults." When these groups encounter opposition and ridicule from the public, members of the group often interpret this response as confirmation of the imminent end of the world. While many of these groups disband after the death of leader, those that endure often begin to resemble more mainstream religious groups, and, consequently, are less frequently branded as cults.

Millennial movements can be observed throughout American history. Seventeenth-century Puritans interpreted the founding of the New England colonies as part of an unfolding apocalyptic scenario and the United States has been uniquely preoccupied with the millennium ever since. The Church of Jesus Christ of Later-Day Saints, or Mormons, also began as a millennial movement. Joseph Smith (1805–44) published *The Book of Mormon* in 1830, which he claimed to be a translation of ancient texts. Smith's early followers regarded the discovery of these texts as a sign of the coming end of the world. The persecution endured by Smith's followers seemed to confirm an apocalyptic scenario. Early Mormons anticipated Christ's return, in which their enemies would be judged and they would reign with Christ for one thousand years. In yet another example, the Baptist preacher William Miller (1782–1849) predicted that Christ would return between 1843 and 1844. The so-called Millerites pushed Christ's arrival back to October 22, 1844. This date became known as "The Great Disappointment" when the apocalypse did not occur (for more on the Millerites, see the previous chapter).

In 1860, former Millerite and visionary Ellen G. White (1827–1915) formed The Seventh-day Adventists with the help of her husband James White (1821–81). The Whites believed that 1844 had marked the beginning, and not the end, of an apocalyptic scenario. They implemented a number of reforms, including holding services on Saturday rather than Sunday and advocating vegetarianism. Today, there are millions of Seventh-day Adventists and the church performs missionary work around the world, demonstrating how millennial movements move closer to the mainstream. Another example is that of Charles Taze Russell (1852–1916), who, like Miller, claimed to discover the date of the apocalypse by studying the Bible. He explained that events leading up to Christ's return began in 1874 and would conclude in 1914. By the end of the nineteenth century, Russell had attracted some thirty thousand followers. By the 1920s, Russell's statement, "Millions now living will never die," covered the American landscape, appearing on telephone poles, rocks, and mountainsides. In 1931, Russell's movement adopted the name "Jehovah's Witnesses" under the leadership of Joseph Franklin Rutherford (1869–1942). This movement also has millions of followers today and is less stigmatized than it once was.

Many NRMs have millennial hopes that are not based entirely in Christian tradition or biblical prophecy. For example, in Native American culture, many apocalyptic movements formed around prophets as a response to the cultural crisis created by white expansion. Native American prophets experienced visions and related how supernatural intervention would soon restore the world to the way it had been before the arrival of whites. The Ghost Dance is perhaps the most famous of these millennial movements. Its founding prophet was a Paiute named Wovoka, also known as Jack Wilson (1856–1932). Wovoka had a vision in which the dead would be resurrected, the world would be renewed, and game would be plentiful again. Such prophets often prescribed certain rituals and ethical codes that would usher in the world-transforming event. Their millennial expectations appear to have adopted apocalyptic ideas from Christianity and combined them with traditional Native American religions.

The Nation of Islam is another movement that expressed the millennial hopes of an oppressed group. In 1930, a mysterious peddler named Wallace D. Fard appeared in Detroit, Michigan. Fard appealed to ideas of Black Nationalism and taught that Islam, not Christianity, was the true religion for black people. He created a group called The Temple of Islam before disappearing in 1934. His disciple, Elijah Muhammad (1897–1975), expanded Fard's organization into the Nation of Islam. Muhammad taught that blacks are the original humans and that whites were a "devil race" created by a mad scientist named Yakub. Allah had permitted whites to dominate the world for six thousand years. However, this period was about to end with the catastrophic destruction of white civilization, at which point blacks would assume their natural place and rule again. Muhammad also taught that UFOs were actually ancient flying machines. An enormous machine called "The Mother Plane" would appear and annihilate the white powers. Muhammad's beliefs had little to do with traditional Islam, but ideas such as lost civilizations and UFOs were popular in New

Age circles prevalent at the time and Muhammad incorporated these elements into his millennial vision.

After Muhammad's death in 1975, his son Wallace D. Muhammad (1933–2008) assumed leadership of the Nation of Islam. Wallace reinterpreted the apocalypse as a coming spiritual transformation rather than a catastrophe, and he called for an end to the demonization of the white race. In 1977, Louis Farrakhan (1933–) resisted these reforms and re-established the Nation of Islam in accord with Elijah Muhammad's views. At a press conference, he described a vision he received in 1985, where he was taken into a UFO and given instructions by Elijah Muhammad. Since 1979, The Nation of Islam has published its weekly newspaper *The Final Call.* The paper's title reflects the group's millennial urgency.

Millennial Bricolage: Build Your Own Apocalypse

As we saw above, Wovoka and Elijah Muhammad described apocalyptic scenarios that combined elements from multiple traditions. This process of creative combination, or **bricolage**, is common in new apocalyptic movements. Apocalyptic beliefs that seem bizarre to outsiders often seem less strange when interpreted within their own historical context as religious *bricolage*. People imagining a future world can explore an ever wider range of ideas to produce an endless variety of apocalyptic scenarios. UFOs and Mayan prophecies are just some of the new elements that have been grafted onto old millennial ideas.

The first nuclear bomb was detonated in Los Alamos, New Mexico, in 1945. Soon after, a new element was introduced to apocalyptic scenarios: UFOs. On June 24, 1947, a pilot named Kenneth Arnold spotted nine disk-like objects flying at high speed near Mount Rainier in Washington State. The media dubbed the objects "flying saucers."

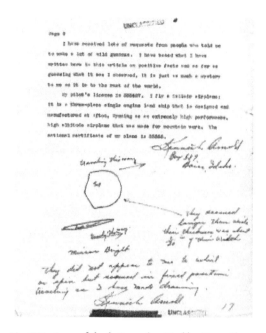

Fig. 20.1. Copy of the letter submitted by Kenneth Arnold to Army Air Force intelligence on July 12, 1947, detailing the flying saucers he claimed to have seen. Commons.wikimedia.org.

Almost immediately, UFOs and nuclear weapons were seen as part of an apocalyptic mystery. Less than a month after the Arnold sighting, the Buchanan Brothers released a song about the Flying Saucers in which they sang:

When you see a saucer fly like a comet through the sky

You should realize the price you'll have to pay

You'd better pray to the Lord when you see those flying saucers

It may be the coming of the Judgment Day (Buchanan Brothers, 1947).

By the end of 1947, over 800 more sightings had occurred. The psychologist Carl Jung claimed that UFO sightings fulfilled a spiritual need and that the anxiety of the Cold War was causing people to see them.

Christian dispensationalists such as Hal Lindsey claimed that UFOs were demonic and a sign of the end times (for more on Lindsey, see the previous chapter). Others believed the UFOs were friendly. On November 20, 1952, George Adamski (1891–1965) claimed to have met a blonde man from Venus named Orthon in the California desert. Orthon had come because people on other planets were alarmed by the proliferation of nuclear weapons and wanted to help the people of Earth. Soon, other "contactees" stepped forward. Many of these claimed they were contacted through "channeling" or telepathic communication. In the 1950s, most contactees claimed that benevolent aliens or "space brothers" had come to rescue humanity from nuclear war. Daniel Wojcik describes this scenario as "techno-millenarianism" because alien technology, rather than God, will redeem the world.

Fig. 20.2. Cover of the October 1957 Amazing Stories, which focused on UFO sightings. Commons.wikimedia.org.

Soon, NRMs formed around contactees. In 1954, Ruth Norman (1900–93) and her husband Ernest (1904–71) founded The Unarian Academy of Science. Ernest would channel messages from extraterrestrials that Ruth would transcribe into books. When Ernest died, Ruth became the group's charismatic leader. She believed in reincarnation and that she and Ernest had lived before in ancient Egypt, in Atlantis, and on other planets. In 1973, she announced that Earth had been admitted into a coalition of planets called the Intergalactic Federation. She predicted that in 2001, a landing fleet would arrive, consisting of thirty-two flying saucers, one from each planet of the federation. The saucers would stack on top of each other to form a tower and each saucer would house scientists from a different planet that would help humanity solve its problems and transform its spiritual consciousness. The Unarians periodically gathered to welcome the extraterrestrials, often in costumes inspired by their previous lives on other planets.

2012 and the Mayan Calendar

As interest in space brothers began to wane, some people became fascinated with the end of the Mayan Calendar on December 21, 2012. The Mayan "Long Count" calendar consists of 1,872,000 days, divided into thirteen units (called *pik* or *bak'tun*) of 144,000 days. The calendar begins on a mythical date of creation on August 11, 3114 BCE, and ends on December 21, 2012. Archaeologists still do not know exactly what the purpose of these calendars was and only a few Mayan texts hint at the significance of the end of the calendar. In 1966, archaeologist Michael Coe speculated that, "There is a suggestion . . . that Armageddon would overtake the degenerate peoples of the world and all creation on the final day of the thirteenth *bak'tun*" (Quoted in Sitler 2012, 65). Mayan scholar Robert Sitler suggests that Coe's interpretation—like the interpretation of UFO sightings—was colored by Cold War fears of nuclear weapons.

Beginning in the 1970s, dozens of New Age theorists speculated about the calendar's significance. By 2012, over 1,900 books had been published dealing with the "Mayan apocalypse." Through *bricolage*, various groups and theorists incorporated the Mayan calendar with other apocalyptic elements. Some speculated that the Mayans had predicted catastrophic Earth changes such as a pole shift. Members of a New Age group called the American Ramtha School of Enlightenment fled to a village in Southern France and sought protection on a peak associated with UFOs. Others, such as UFO enthusiast Richard Boylan, announced that extraterrestrials would admit Earth into a galactic federation in 2012. Ronald Emerich's 2009 film *2012*, which grossed over $788 million worldwide, is a classic piece of apocalyptic *bricolage* combining the Mayan calendar, Earth changes, and a global conspiracy.

The pace of apocalyptic *bricolage* is accelerating as the Internet makes it easier to disseminate unconventional ideas. Political scientist Michael Barkun (1998) notes that anyone can now construct their own apocalyptic scenario by selecting elements from a milieu of "stigmatized knowledge" that includes Biblical prophecy, conspiracy theories, Ufology, and New Age ideas. The study of NRMs has traditionally focused on movements, but sociologists Rodney Stark and William Bainbridge note that new religious ideas can be spread without a movement through what they call "audience cults." Audience cults consist of people who share an interest in religious ideas promoted primarily through media such as mail-order courses, books, AM radio programs, and websites. Audience cults are not full-blown movements, but perform some of the functions of a religion—in some cases, providing an apocalyptic worldview.

Remembering the Cult Wars

In the United States, unpopular religious groups have been attacked as "cults" since the 1920s. But the 1970s saw a period of especially heightened controversy over cults sometimes called "the cult wars." Philip Jenkins identifies the years of 1976–1981 as the peak of this period when the anti-cult movement (**ACM**), a coalition of both Christian and secular groups, mobilized to portray cults as a monolithic threat to society. This claim was often taken for granted by the media.

Beginning in 1971, families of individuals who had joined NRMs formed counter movements to oppose particular NRMs. These groups were often aided by **apostates** or people who had converted to an NRM, and then, left. Some psychologists and medical professionals were highly active in the ACM, as were Christian groups who had theological objections to NRMs. The ACM frequently claimed that cults recruited people through "brainwashing" and regarded religious conversion as a sort of mental illness. At the height of the controversy, some of the anti-cult groups called for laws that would restrict or eliminate religious freedom. It can be argued that the ACM demonstrated its own apocalyptic ideology, insofar as some anti-cult activists portrayed cults as a diabolic threat poised to destroy civilization and their own activities as part of a final battle between good and evil.

Multiple factors contributed to the cults wars. One factor was the counter-culture of the 1960s, which created a marketplace of spiritual seekers. In the United States, the 1960s was a period in which many young American advocated progressive politics and experimented with new ideas of sexuality and spirituality. By the 1970s, there was a conservative backlash against the perceived excesses of the 1960s, including the spread of NRMs. A second factor was immigration reform in 1965 that allowed a new influx of Asian immigrants. This encouraged NRMs from Asia to missionize in the United States. The Unification Church (also known as "The Moonies"), which originated in South Korea, and The International Society for Krishna Consciousness (ISKON), also known as the Hare Krishnas, were two such "immigrant" NRMs. These were also two of the groups most frequently targeted by the ACM. Sociologist David Bromley (2002, 17) notes that another factor was a changing economic situation in which work relationships were encroaching on traditional family relationships. In many households, both parents worked and children spent more time in daycares and with other outside forces. This shift may have made NRMs more appealing as a source of caring, family-like relationships. However, NRMs were often blamed for the erosion of the traditional family. The ACM claimed cults were "anti-family" and subverted traditional values. Philip Jenkins notes that the most feared cults of the era were those whose converts were young, white, and middle-class, while movements that recruited other demographics were not as closely scrutinized. Finally, claims about cults were supported by the rise of right-wing Christian groups with a theology of spiritual warfare. These groups saw cults as heretical false religions arising in the last days.

Most NRMs have a high rate of turnover, losing converts almost as quickly as they gain them, which produced a large number of apostates, many of whom were dissatisfied with their experiences. Especially livid apostates worked closely with the ACM and the media. They described abuse and other unsavory elements they had encountered while in an NRM. These stories became an important part of the cult wars. Sociologists coined the term "atrocity tales" to describe stories used to mobilize resources against a particular group. Sometimes, the abuses described in atrocity tales really happened, while at other times, they were exaggerated or invented. But the function of these stories is always to brand *an entire group*, rather than just a few individual members, as dangerous. In many cases, the ACM and the media presented extreme stories involving specific individuals and specific NRMs as typical of all "cults."

For example, in 1984, police raided a fundamentalist Christian community in Vermont and took twelve children into protective custody. Apostates from the group claimed the children were spanked continuously for up to eight hours. Local media reported on the raid and referred to the group as a cult. But the descriptions of child abuse were part of a custody battle for control of the children and several of the apostates later recanted their claims. The actions of the police were declared unconstitutional and all of the children were returned. However, these details received nowhere near the media coverage of the original raid (Wright 1997: 107–8). Headlines about cults abusing children reinforced the idea that mainstream religion, which is "normal" and good, can be easily distinguished from deviant and evil cults.

In the 1970s, it was widely claimed that NRMs recruited new members through "brainwashing." The idea of brainwashing emerged during the Korean War. It was closely associated with the fear of communism and the idea that Asian countries possessed mysterious techniques of mind control. Brainwashing had already been introduced to American culture by Richard Condon's 1959 spy novel, *The Manchurian Candidate*, which was adapted into a film in 1962. The ACM argued that cults brainwashed converts through techniques such as chanting and dietary restrictions. As such, it was claimed that cult members did not choose to join cults, but were suffering from a mental disease that could be treated. Significantly, several NRMs made the exact opposite claim—that mainstream society was brainwashing everyone and that only members of their alternative community had the freedom to think for themselves.

By characterizing religious conversion as brainwashing, the ACM sought to circumvent the constitutional rights of NRM members. This led to the rise of cult **"deprogramming."** People would hire deprogrammers to locate family members who had joined NRMs and forcibly abduct them. The deprogrammer would then attempt to reverse the brainwashing using their own regimen of mental coercion—itself a kind of "brainwashing"!

The characterization of "cult" participants as brainwashed also led to proposed legislation restricting the religious freedom of NRM members. The ACM claimed that joining a cult demonstrated a loss of responsibility comparable to a serious mental illness, mental retardation, or extreme age. Therefore, it was argued that cult members be placed under a conservatorship by their family members: essentially, adults would revert to the legal status of a minor and a court-appointed "conservator" would make decisions on their behalf. In 1977, five conservatorships were granted in California, but overturned on appeal. In 1980, a carefully worded bill called the Lasher Amendment was proposed in New York, altering state law to grant conservatorships for cult members. The governor vetoed the bill before it could be signed into law. Today, such claims about NRMs are unlikely to persuade judges or legislators, but many people still find the idea of brainwashing plausible.

Mass Suicide and Doomsday Cults

Even though the media and the public often misunderstand NRMs and millennial movements, sometimes, these groups really *do* engage in mass suicide and other forms of violence. While extremely rare, incidents such as the massacre of The Peoples' Temple in Guyana have left the public with the impression that NRMs are naturally inclined toward mass suicide. However, religion scholars and sociologists have noted that these cases are complicated and come about due to numerous internal and external factors. The role of outside forces in these incidents is often overlooked. As the ACM, media, and government grow increasingly suspicious of millennial movements, the possibility of violent conflicts increases. Catherine Wessinger is a religion scholar who has consulted with federal agencies to de-escalate standoffs with millennial movements. She argues that the worst thing government agencies can do in such situations is to make the movement despair of accomplishing their millennial goal. The likelihood of violence increases when a group gives up on the possibility of salvation for those outside their group and focuses only on themselves. This shift often occurs when millennial groups feel very discouraged, persecuted, or attacked.

The People's Temple

In 1978, The People's Temple became the classic example of a "destructive cult." James "Jim" Warren Jones (1931–78) founded The Peoples' Temple Full Gospel Church in 1955 in Indianapolis. Jones was a *bricoleur* with diverse influences. He was inspired by Marxist ideology and deeply concerned about issues of racism and social justice. He visited a Seventh-day Adventist church where he discovered faith healing. Jones staged miraculous healings, possibly as a source of revenue. He believed in reincarnation and claimed he had been the biblical Moses and the Russian leader Lenin in previous lives. Jones predicted an apocalyptic scenario involving race war, genocide, and nuclear Armageddon. This catastrophe was necessary to destroy an irredeemable capitalist system. He came to present himself as a messiah who could lead his followers to safety, after which they would create a new Eden (itself a reference to the biblical book of Genesis).

In 1965, Jones moved his followers to California, and the Temple created urban ministries that recruited black followers from San Francisco and Los Angeles. Jones became established as a progressive activist. But in the 1970s, a group called "Concerned Relatives," who did not approve of family members participating in the Temple, organized a campaign against Jones. Apostates working with journalists led to sensationalized newspaper articles outlining Jones's many sexual relationships with his followers as well as financial misconduct. The articles inspired an investigation by the Treasury Department and the IRS. In 1973, the Temple's San Francisco church was fire-bombed, probably by white racists. All of this inspired Jones to lead his followers to purchase land in Guyana, where they established an agricultural colony called "Jonestown."

In 1977, Jones brought the bulk of his followers, over 1,000 people, to Guyana to wait out the coming nuclear Armageddon. But the majority of the community were either too old to work or children, making their hopes of an agricultural socialist utopia impossible. Jones grew increasingly paranoid and began abusing drugs. When dissatisfied members left, his paranoia grew worse. At the urging of Concerned Relatives, Congressman Leo J. Ryan visited Jonestown to confirm Temple members were safe. On November 18, 1978, Ryan and members of his entourage were murdered as they attempted to board an airplane home. That night, Jones ordered the entire community to commit "revolutionary suicide" by drinking Flavor-aid mixed with cyanide. In total, 918 people died that day as a result of the Temple's actions.

Fig. 20.3. Sign above the entrance to Jonestown, which reads
"Jonestown People's Temple Agricultural Project."
Commons.wikimedia.org.

Both internal and external factors led The People's Temple to believe
their millennial goal had become impossible and to resort to violence.
While Jones described a coming apocalypse, his work as an activist
suggests he also believed he could transform the world peacefully
through political means. This means The People's Temple had the
potential to become a progressive millennial movement. However,
opposition from the ACM convinced them that only a catastrophe
could redeem the world. The move to Jonestown was an attempt to
create a new world by escaping American society. When this failed,
"revolutionary suicide" became a final form of symbolic victory.

The Branch Davidians

By 1987, Vernon Howell (1959–93) had become the leader of a
millennial group in Mt. Carmel, Texas, called the Branch Davidians.
The Branch Davidians had emerged from the Seventh-day Adventists
through a series of schisms and prophetic leaders. Howell's charisma
came from his impressive command of the Bible. He also experienced
a vision while in Israel, in which God informed him that he was a
prophet destined to die in Armageddon, be resurrected, and establish

God's kingdom. He saw himself as a "messiah" (by which, he meant an anointed servant of God) sent to interpret the seven seals. In 1990, he took the name "David Koresh," referencing both the Israelite king David and the Hebrew name for the Persian King Cyrus (Koresh), who liberated the Jews from Babylon.

Fig. 20.4. David Koresh. Commons.wikimedia.org.

The Branch Davidian community practiced a strict lifestyle based on their interpretation of the Bible. Citing Bible passages, Koresh ordered that all the women in the community were his "wives," and that all men other than himself should be celibate. Koresh identified himself as the "Branch of David" described in Rev 5:5 and, citing Psalm 45, he stated that he must sleep with virgins to sire a dynasty of children to rule the new world. In at least one case, these practices involved sexual intercourse with an underage girl. Several apostates were alarmed over these practices and began working with anti-cult groups. The apostates claimed the Branch Davidians were planning "another Jonestown," in which they would commit mass suicide.

In May 1992, the Bureau of Alcohol, Tobacco, and Firearms (BATF) began investigating the Branch Davidians. The Davidians generated revenue by purchasing guns for resale at gun shows. It was unclear there was anything illegal about these gun sales and the BATF was initially denied a search warrant. To gather evidence, they turned to apostates and anti-cult experts, including Rick Ross, a former deprogrammer. When a warrant was granted, Ross and others claimed that the Davidians would commit mass suicide rather than submit to a search. On February 28, 1993, the BATF decided to "serve the warrant," in the form of a paramilitary raid. The Branch Davidians defended themselves, leading to a shootout in which four BATF agents and four Branch Davidians were killed.

The next day, the FBI took control of the site and a 51-day armed standoff ensued. The FBI used a variety of tactics to convince Koresh and his followers to come out. Often, these tactics were contradictory. The sound of dying rabbits and other disturbing noises were played at high volume throughout the night to increase mental stress for the Davidians. But negotiators would also attempt to reason with Koresh and gain his trust. Negotiators wrongly assumed that Koresh had brainwashed his followers and had complete control over them—an assertion Koresh denied.

Fig. 20.5. Picture of a tank destroying the back wall of a building at Mt. Carmel. Commons.wikimedia.org.

Ironically, the actions of federal agencies proved to the Branch Davidians that Koresh's apocalyptic predictions were coming true. The Branch Davidians saw the FBI and BATF as the army of Babylon from Biblical prophecy. After the BATF raid, Koresh interpreted the situation as the fulfillment of the fifth seal described in Rev 6:9–11. This passage describes the souls of dead martyrs crying out for justice. They must wait "a little longer" until more martyrs are killed, then God's judgment will come. The Branch Davidians who had survived the BATF raid did not want to die, but they were waiting "a little longer" to see if the forces of Babylon would martyr them. To do otherwise would be to forsake their roles in God's divine plan.

Because the ACM regarded Koresh's religious beliefs as a form of mental illness, when he attempted to explain himself, the FBI dismissed his communications as insane "Bible babble." Bible scholars James Tabor and Philip Arnold realized that the situation could only be de-escalated by someone who understood Koresh's apocalyptic worldview. The FBI allowed them to engage Koresh in dialogue to see if an alternate interpretation of Revelation might be possible. They discussed whether "a little longer" might mean a period of years instead of days, in which case, the Davidians could surrender without defying God's plan. Perhaps God wanted Koresh to be a messenger instead of martyr.

On April 14, Koresh released a letter through his lawyer, announcing that he was writing a new interpretation of the seven seals, and that when it was handed over to Arnold and Tabor, he would surrender. The FBI interpreted this announcement as another ploy to drag the siege out further and stepped up their pressure tactics. Nevertheless, on April 18, writing supplies were delivered so that Koresh could write his new interpretation. But on the morning of April 19, the FBI attempted a final resolution to the standoff using tanks and CS tear gas. The Davidians still refused to come out, and by noon, the residence had caught fire, which ultimately killed 53 adults and 23 children. One survivor, Ruth Riddle, escaped with a floppy disk containing Koresh's exposition of the first seal that he had been working on during the attack. This suggests Koresh was earnest about his terms of surrender.

The massacre of the Branch Davidians is remembered as a classic case of how law enforcement should *not* deal with armed millennial movements. David Bromley notes that just as the Branch Davidians saw the FBI as the army of Babylon, federal agencies regarded Koresh and his followers as demonic opponents. The FBI also sought a "final resolution" to the Branch Davidians's defiance by using overwhelming force. In 1996, a congressional report concluded that the FBI's use of CS gas failed to show proper concern for the young children, pregnant women, elderly, and infirm civilians sheltered in the Brach Davidian headquarters. The incident also caused other millennial groups, including Heaven's Gate, to conclude the government would use similar tactics against them. For extreme right wing groups who already shared an apocalyptic suspicion of the federal government, the events at Waco became a symbol of religious persecution.

Heaven's Gate

On March 26, 1997, the bodies of 39 members of the group Heaven's Gate were discovered in a mansion outside San Diego. The victims had killed themselves by consuming applesauce or pudding laced with phenobarbital, followed by vodka, and then, placing plastic bags over their heads. Messages left by the group described leaving their "physical containers" to ascend into a spaceship that was arriving in the wake of the Hale-Bopp comet. Like the other incidents described here, Heaven's Gate was a millennial movement that did not initially set out to engage in violence. Instead, the decision to commit suicide emerged as the result of a long series of external and internal developments.

Marshall "Herff" Applewhite (1931–97) and Bonnie Lu Nettles (1927–85) founded "Heaven's Gate." The pair were *bricoleurs* whose ideas combined a literalist interpretation of the Bible, New Age ideas, beliefs about UFOs, and tropes from *Star Trek* and other science fiction. They called themselves "the Two," believing they were the two witnesses described in Revelation 11. They also referred to themselves variously as "Do and Ti" and "Bo and Peep." Applewhite and Nettles interpreted the resurrection of Jesus to mean that Jesus has transformed his human body into a divinized body. When Jesus ascended to heaven, he was actually picked up by a UFO and transported to the "Kingdom of Heaven," which the pair called "The Evolutionary Level Above Human" (T.E.L.A.H.).

The pair taught that those who were spiritually evolved would be picked up by flying saucers in a kind of "technological rapture." Like Jesus, their earthly bodies would be transformed into extraterrestrial ones that would be genderless and eternal. They would then spend eternity traversing space and helping other planets to evolve. Applying a literal interpretation to Jesus's parables, they taught that extraterrestrials used Earth as a "garden" in which they had "planted" souls. When those souls were fully developed, they would return to "harvest" them for T.E.L.A.H. In 1975, they began to spread their ideas in New Age circles and attract followers. These early followers were to sever their worldly ties, including family, friends, and jobs. Heaven's Gate also placed tremendous importance on overcoming sexual urges. Beginning in 1993, some members elected to undergo chemical castration to help with this process.

Nettles and Applewhite first received media attention in September 1975 after they gave a lecture on UFOs in Waldport, Oregon, and more than thirty people suddenly disappeared to join their movement. The media ridiculed the movement and speculated that these converts had been brainwashed. Nettles and Applewhite took this criticism badly. They predicted that, like the two witnesses in Revelation, they would be assassinated, resurrected, and taken into heaven.

Nettles died of cancer in 1985, creating a serious challenge to the movement's ideology. They had assumed they would be taken physically into spaceships. Applewhite now taught that they would be taken into the spaceships spiritually and that the body is merely a container with no value. He also introduced the idea of "Luciferians," or evil aliens who control the world's governments. The Luciferians use religion and sexuality to hinder human evolution. When the extraterrestrials arrived, they would not only harvest the evolved souls, they would also destroy the world and its remaining inhabitants. Applewhite explained that the "garden" was going to be "spaded under" in order to destroy the "weeds" planted by the Luciferians.

In 1993, the group took out an ad in *USA Today*, announcing that this was the last chance for escape on a spaceship before the Earth was spaded under. By this time, the group had dwindled to a small core of long-term, aging followers who lived almost entirely separated from mainstream society. Applewhite's health was now ailing too. Someone outside the group speculated that a UFO was hiding behind the Hale-Bopp comet. The group discovered this idea online and decided the comet signaled the arrival of the harvest: they would shed their Earthly bodies so that their evolved souls could be taken into the ship. They left behind tapes explaining that this was not suicide and that they were excited for their voyage.

While outside ridicule and indifference was a factor, the greatest factor in Heaven's Gate's decision to commit mass suicide was the death of Nettles, which caused the movement to reinterpret their beliefs and shift toward catastrophic millennialism. Suicide came to be seen as the last hope for achieving their millennial goal.

Conclusion

It is certain that new millennial movements will continue to form, combining ancient prophecies with a diverse array of modern beliefs and concerns. The 1990s saw a swell of millennial conflicts as the year 2000 approached, but Catherine Wessinger has speculated that this trend may continue until 2033—two thousand years after the death of Jesus. In responding to these groups, it is crucial that scholars, media, and law enforcement learn from the mistakes of the past. We should pay more attention to why people join these movements and be suspicious of explanations that reduce religious conversion to "brainwashing" or simplistic medical explanations. Wessinger cautions that we can never know in advance what course of action individuals will choose, and so, experts should refrain from either predicting a millennial group will resort to violence or declaring that a group is incapable of violence. However, cases such as the siege in Waco demonstrate that outside forces are often a key factor in determining whether a catastrophic millennial group turns to violence.

Finally, we must be more critical of how terms such as "cult" can be misused. The tragic cases above are exceptions rather than the rule and the result of specific historical circumstances, but careless characterizations about "cults" reduce these complex situations to a label. The rhetoric of "doomsday cults" engages in what Craig Reinarman and Harry Levine (1997, 24) call the "routinization of caricature" in which the worst cases are framed as typical cases, and the episodic is framed as the epidemic (Reinarman and Levine 1997, 24). It is exactly this rhetoric, backed by forty years of panic over cults, which led authorities in Palmdale, California, to assume a prayer group was preparing to commit mass suicide.

Study Questions:

1. Why have religion scholars objected to the idea of "cults" as something that can be separated from "religions?" What is the problem with labeling certain groups as cults?

2. What are some of the different ideas that people have been incorporated into apocalyptic *bricolage*? Give at least three examples.

3. What is problematic about treating someone's decision to join an NRM as if it were a disease? What are some specific consequences that have resulted from framing membership in an NRM as a medical problem?

4. Choose one of the millennial movements described above: The People's Temple, The Branch Davidians, or Heaven's Gate. Explain how both external factors and internal factors played a role in

the movement's decision to commit violence. In your judgment, which set of factors (external or internal) was more important?

Bibliography and Further Reading:

Barkun, Michael. "Politics and Apocalypticism." In *The Encyclopedia of Apocalypticism*. Vol. 3. Edited by Stephen J. Stein. New York: Continuum, 1998, 442–60.

Bromley, David G., Anson D. Shupe, and J. C. Ventimiglia. "Atrocity Tales, The Unification Church, and the Social Construction of Evil." In *The Journal of Communication* 29:3 (Summer 1979): 42–53.

Bromley, David G., and J. Gordon Melton. *Cults, Religion, and Violence*. Cambridge: Cambridge University Press, 2002.

Buchanan Brothers. "(When You See) Those Flying Saucers." RCA, 1947.

Gallagher, Eugene V. "Compared to What? 'Cults' and 'New Religious Movements.'" In *History of Religions* 47:3 (2008): 205–20.

Jenkins, Philip. *Mystics and Messiahs: Cults and New Religions in American History*. Oxford: Oxford University Press, 2000.

Lanternari, Vittorio. *The Religions of the Oppressed; A Study of Modern Messianic Cults*. New York: Knopf, 1963.

Lewis, James R. *Doomsday Prophecies: A Complete Guide to the End of the World*. Amherst, NY: Prometheus Books, 2000.

NBC News. "Police Alert: 6 Adults, 8 Children Plan Mass Suicide." September 19, 2010. http://www.nbcnews.com/id/39251083/ns/us_news-life/t/police-alert-adults-children-plan-mass-suicide/#.VVEAztpViko. Accessed May 11, 2015.

Reinarman, Craig, and Harry G. Levine. *Crack in America: Demon Drugs and Social Justice*. Berkeley: University of California Press, 1997.

Sitler, Robert K. "The 2012 Phenomenon New Age Appropriation of an Ancient Mayan Calendar." In *Nova Religio* 9:3 (2006): 24–38.

____. "The 2012 Phenomenon Comes of Age." In *Nova Religio: The Journal of Alternative and Emergent Religions* 16:1 (2012): 61–87.

Stark, Rodney, and William Sims Bainbridge. *The Future of Religion: Secularization, Revival, and Cult Formation*. Berkeley: University of California Press, 1985.

Tabor, James D. and Eugene V. Gallagher. *Why Waco?: Cults and the Battle for Religious Freedom in America.* Berkeley: University of California Press, 1995.

Wessinger, Catherine. *How the Millennium Comes Violently From Jonestown to Heaven's Gate.* New York: Seven Bridges Press, 1999.

Wojcik, Daniel. *The End of the World As We Know It Faith, Fatalism, and Apocalypse in America.* New York: New York University Press, 1997.

Wright, Stuart A. "Media Coverage of Unconventional Religion: Any 'Good News' for Minority Faiths?" In *Review of Religious Research* 39:2 (1997): 101–15.

21

The End Is (Still) All Around

The Zombie and Contemporary Apocalyptic Thought

Kelly J. Murphy

GETTING PREPPED:

1. Can you give any examples of the "apocalypse" as it is viewed today, especially in pop culture?
2. What role do monsters play in contemporary apocalyptic stories?
3. Based on what you know about ancient apocalyptic literature and its many manifestations throughout time, what similar themes or ideas might you expect to find in contemporary pop culture references to the apocalypse? How might you expect contemporary (and especially secular) apocalyptic movies, television shows, or literature to be different than religious texts?

KEY WORDS:
VODOUN
ZOMBIES
OTHERING
GHOUL
HOPE

Here Be ... Brain-Eating Zombies?

According to popular lore, *hic sunt dracones*, "here be dragons," is a Latin phrase found frequently on ancient maps. Though, in fact, the phrase rarely occurs (the Hunt-Lenox Globe, dated to 1510 CE, is the one oft-cited example, but as scholars routinely note, it's on a globe rather than an ancient paper map), fearsome creatures *have* crowded our maps throughout history. For example, the warning *hic abundant leones*, "here lions abound," is found on the Cotton Tiberius map from 1025 CE, while a dragon appears among other wild animals on the Ebstorf Map (Fig. 21.1). Other old maps include drawings of strange looking animals, giant sea creatures, or warnings that "in these places scorpions are born" (found on the *Tabula Peutingeriana*, a medieval copy of a Roman map). Timothy Beal explains:

> Maps plot the lay of the land, making it known and knowable. In the process they also mark off what is unknown along their edges and within their deepest seas. On ancient maps, the *terra incognita*, or "unknown territory," was sometimes marked by images of fantastical monsters accompanied by textual warnings, the most famous being *hic sunt dracones*, "here be dragons." These monstrous figures indicate regions of dangerous uncertainty. They show where the limits of knowledge are. They dwell on the threshold between the known and unknown, this world and its otherworldly beyond (Beal, *Religion and Its Monsters* [2002], 194).

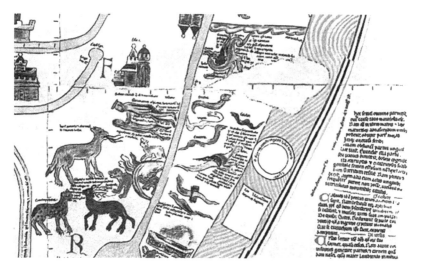

Fig. 21.1. Detail from a color facsimile of the thirteenth-century Ebstorf Map (the original was destroyed in World War II).

Monsters, then, are intricately connected to knowledge: to the world we know and the world we do not, to what we fear. (For more on monsters and religion more broadly, see Beal 2002.)

If you fast-forward from ancient maps to the contemporary world, you are more likely to see a sign that reads, "Zombie Apocalypse—Are You Ready?" than "Here Be Dragons" (Fig. 21.2). For example, on January 29, 2009, drivers entering Austin, TX encountered a hacked road sign that flashed the warning "Zombies Ahead"—there were, of course, no real zombies ahead. The prevalence of zombie warning signs in our lives provides a window into the apocalyptic monster that dwells on the borders of our contemporary collective imagination in much the same way that dragons or lions or strange beasts marked the unknown territory of ancient maps.

Fig. 21.2. "Zombie Apocalypse . . . Are You Ready?" Photo by
flickr user Stephen Dann via Creative Commons.

Zombies surround us. They moan, groan, and gnaw their way into
our daily lives—they are present in our cell phone commercials, our
disaster training plans, and our 5K Runs. Zombies multiply on our
television shows (*The Walking Dead; Fear the Walking Dead; iZombie*), we
destroy them in our video games (*Call of Duty; Plants vs. Zombies*), we
flip through hordes of them in our novels (*World War Z; The Girl With
All The Gifts*), and they shuffle or speed across our movie screens (*Shaun
of the Dead; 28 Days Later*). These monsters, whose origins are vastly
different from their modern-day manifestations, are so pervasive in
contemporary culture that even observations on the fact that our
world is zombie-crazed are everywhere we look.

Zombies function much in the same way that dragons, lions, or
otherwise fearsome beasts functioned on ancient maps, by "dwell[ing]
on the threshold between the known and unknown, this world and
its otherworldly beyond" (Beal, 194). They help us to grapple with the
space that often exists between our *expectations* of the world and the
way we actually *experience* the world. For instance, consider a scene
from AMC's *The Walking Dead:* A herd of "walkers" (read: zombies) has

just destroyed Hershel Greene's family farm, where Greene and his family, as well as the main character Rick Grimes and his people, had managed to establish a relatively safe space in the post-apocalyptic world of the television show. Standing on the highway, crowded by abandoned cars and rotting corpses, Hershel urges Rick to go, to find a safe place for his son Carl. But Rick turns to Hershel—a self-professed Christian—and responds, "You're a man of God. Have some faith." To this, Hershel replies, "I can't profess to understand God's plan. Christ promised the resurrection of the dead. I just thought he had something a little different in mind" (*Beside the Dying Fire*, Season 2, Episode 13). For Hershel—and likely for many viewers—the zombie stands between expectation and reality.

Both Hershel's reflections on resurrection and Beal's observation that monsters occupy the liminal space between this world and the otherworldly beyond reflect the surprising ways that zombies (and, more broadly, monsters) relate to the realm of the marvelous and the sacred. Yet, what place do zombies—one genre of many genres of contemporary, pop culture apocalyptic stories—have in a book that primarily focuses on the extrabiblical and biblical apocalyptic texts and their long afterlives? As James Lowder writes, "All zombies are created equal. All zombie stories are not. The best ones, like *The Walking Dead*, get into your head and make you think—make you fatten up the gray matter that the living dead lust after so ravenously" (Lowder 2011, xii). In short, the answer is in how these stories, both ancient and contemporary, make us *think*.

There are no zombies in the Bible. Sure, Ezekiel brings to life a valley of dried bones (Ezek 37), and the book of Daniel promises that "many of those who sleep in the dust of the earth shall awake, some to everlasting life, and some to shame and everlasting contempt" (12:2). Jesus revives his friend Lazarus from the dead (John 11), and upon Jesus's death in Matthew's Gospel, we read that the tombs opened up and "many bodies" rose and eventually entered Jerusalem (Matt 27:52–53). Most famously, all four Gospel accounts record that Jesus appeared in resurrected form following his death (Mark 16; Matt 28;

Luke 24; John 20). But none of these figures are zombies, a creature that derives from a historical context that is vastly different from the worlds that produced the ancient apocalypses. Yet, despite the fact that there are no zombies in the Bible, and despite that the original concept of the zombie has very little to do with contemporary conceptions of the zombie, both ancient and contemporary apocalyptic stories *reveal* our fears, our contexts, our critiques of the world around us, and, at times, our hopes.

Monsters as Revealers

The monsters we fantasize about (zombies or otherwise) reveal to us something about ourselves (Cohen 1996, 4; Beal 2002, 6–7). At first glance, there might not seem to be anything particularly religious about the zombies we see in our pop culture apocalyptic stories. Yet, though we often think of monsters as "demonic or 'evil,'" in fact, "the monster's religious import is rooted in the word itself: 'monster' derives from the Latin *monstrum*, which is related to the verbs *monstrare* ('show' or 'reveal') and *monere* ('warn' or 'portend'), and which sometimes refers to a divine portent that reveals the will or judgment of God or the gods" (Beal 2002, 6–7). Hence, etymologically, a "*monstrum* is a message that breaks into this world from the realm of the divine" (Beal 2002, 7). In short, it is not the monster itself that matters—rather it is what the monster reveals, its message or warning. As apocalypses *reveal*, so too do monsters.

In ancient apocalypses, one example of monsters-as-revealers is found in Daniel's recounting of his strange dream vision:

I, Daniel, saw in my vision by night the four winds of heaven stirring up the great sea, and four great beasts came up out of the sea, different from one another. The first was like a lion and had eagles' wings. Then, as I watched, its wings were plucked off, and it was lifted up from the ground and made to stand on two feet like a human being; and a human mind was given to it. Another beast appeared, a second one, which looked like a bear. It was raised up on one side, had three tusks in its mouth among its teeth and was told, "Arise, devour many bodies!" After this, as I watched, another appeared, like a leopard. The beast had four wings of a bird on its back and four heads; and dominion was given to it. After this I saw in the visions by night a fourth beast, terrifying and dreadful and exceedingly strong. It had great iron teeth and was devouring, breaking in pieces, and stamping what was left with its feet. It was different from all the beasts that preceded it, and it had ten horns. I was considering the horns, when another horn appeared, a little one coming up among them; to make room for it, three of the earlier horns were plucked up by the roots. There were eyes like human eyes in this horn, and a mouth speaking arrogantly. (Dan 7:1–8)

Of course, Daniel's vision is not of real beasts that will, in the far-off future, arise from the sea. Rather, as Christopher Hays and others have argued in this volume, the ten horns symbolize the various rulers who came to power after the death of Alexander the Great. The "little horn," which appears among the other horns, plucking them away, represents Antiochus IV, famous for his oppressive and despotic rule over the Jewish population under his control (see Hays, chapter 2). Any confusion over whether the beasts are real or symbolic is cleared up in the text of Daniel itself. When Daniel approaches one of the divine attendants and asks the attendant to interpret the dream, the attendant replies, "As for these four great beasts, four kings shall arise out of the earth" (Dan 7:17). In short, the monstrous beasts of Dan 7 reveal the fears and concerns of the author(s) of the book of Daniel—namely, the terrifying presence of the Seleucid Empire and its effect upon the land of Judea. The attendant assures Daniel that his God will crush these foreign kings and restore divine rule.

If the monstrous beasts in the book of Daniel are symbolic, then what is the message of the monsters we call zombies? Unlike many of the other monsters that have captured Western imagination (e.g., vampires or werewolves), the zombie is unique in that it did not develop in Europe (McIntosh 2008; Dendle 2010; Kee 2011). Rather, the history behind the (now often thoroughly Americanized) zombie begins with **vodoun**, a religious tradition of West Africa and Haiti. The earliest ideas of the zombie in American thought had nothing to do with the flesh-eating zombies who roam in hordes on *The Walking Dead*, which follows a now routine series of events found in zombie stories all across the contemporary world—some kind of infection (often unexplained) occurs, turning the recently dead into mindless creatures that roam about searching for human flesh (and, sometimes, specifically brains), and the bite of one of these infected human-but-not-quite-human creatures turns others into the same. Although the exact etymology of the English word *zombie* is unknown, zombie scholars largely agree that the word itself is West African in origin, and that it entered American English via Haiti, where many West Africans were enslaved and/or oppressed during French and subsequent US occupation of the island. According to Shawn McIntosh, "The word likely comes either from a tribe from Gabon called the Mitsogho, who have the term *ndzumbi*, cadaver of the dead, or from the Kongo *nzambi*, which means 'spirit of a dead person'" (McIntosh, "The Evolution of the Zombie" [2008], 2). The origins of the term are related to the dead, but not to the cannibalistic walking dead of contemporary American television and movie screens.

Fig. 21.3. *Zonbi*, by Haitian artist Wilson
Bigaud, 1939. En.wikipedia.org.

As they developed within Haitian folklore, zombies looked much different than what we know today. First, according to the legends, only sorcerers (known as *bokors*) could create zombies (McIntosh 2008, 2). Second, there were more than one type of *zombi* that Haitians feared: "spirit zombies (*zombie jardin*), and the type that made its way into poplar culture, the body raised from the dead (*zombie corps cadaver*)" (McIntosh 2008, 2). Both types could be controlled by the *bokor*, though McIntosh claims that "spirit zombies are much more powerful and frightening than physical zombies, because a bokor controls the spirit of a dead person and can inject that spirit into a variety of living creatures to do the bokor's bidding" (McIntosh 2008, 2–3). Third, per McIntosh, "In Haitian society, being turned into a zombie is a form of social sanction"; it was the "just rewards" for a person who had transgressed some social norm (McIntosh 2008, 3). Thus, it was less a fear of the zombie, and more a fear of becoming a zombie that worried people; "Haitian peasants greatly fear being removed from 'the many' and becoming 'the one.' This is the exact opposite of what causes fear among modern audiences in industrialized society, who are afraid of losing their individuality and becoming one among 'the many'" (McIntosh 2008, 3). Zombie scholars largely agree that, initially set within its Haitian context, folklore and stories about the *zombi* reflected fears of enslavement and being controlled by another person, but never of a flesh-eating monster.

The path from Haitian folktales about zombies to the zombies of the Western world is well-rehearsed by zombie aficionados. The first and earliest appearances of a "zombie" in Western culture look much more like the Haitian creatures described above than the tattered, decaying, flesh-hungry monster of *The Walking Dead*, *WWZ*, or *Warm Bodies*. One of the earliest literary references in English to a "zombie" is found, famously, in William Seabrock's 1929 novel, *The Magic Island*. In a chapter called "Dead Men Working in Cane Fields," Seabrock writes:

> I recalled one creature I had been hearing about in Haiti, which sounded exclusively local—the zombie . . . while the zombie came from the grave, it was neither a ghost nor yet a person who had been raised like Lazarus from the grave. The zombie, they say, is a soulless human corpse, still dead, but taken from the grave and endowed by sorcery with a mechanical

semblance of life—it is a dead body which is made to walk and act and move as if it were alive. (Seabrock [1929] 2016.)

Already Seabrock, though describing what he claims to be a Haitian phenomenon, connects zombies and the Bible via Lazarus. More importantly, Seabrock set the stage for the zombie to bite its way into the popular imagination of Americans.

Following *The Magic Island*, zombies continued to stumble into American culture, but the depiction of zombies begin to change (slowly). The most often-cited example of how this occurred is the 1932 film, *White Zombie*. While the film stays close to the original Haitian concept, where people are forced to work for another with no will of their own, and seems to borrow from Seabrock's descriptions, the film also radically changes why the zombie is to be feared. Most significantly, *White Zombie* begins to think about the walking dead in relation to questions of race and gender, while adding concerns that were very different from the original Haitian stories. This trend continues into contemporary zombie novels, television shows, and films.

The plot of the film is simple: a wealthy plantation owner in Haiti becomes obsessed with a white woman named Madeline, and hires an evil sorcerer named Murder Legendre (played by Bela Lugosi of *Dracula* fame) to turn her into a zombie so that he can force her to stay with him. She manages to break out of her zombified spell and is rescued by her fiancé, Neil. Two quotations from the film help to illustrate how *White Zombie* reflects concerns over race and gender in the US during the 1930's. In the opening scenes, a carriage driver sees figures shuffling toward the road; he later explains these figures to Neil as he and Madeline disembark from the carriage, "They are not men, monsieur! They are dead bodies. Zombies! Corpses taken from their graves and made to work in the sugar mills and fields at night." Later, when Madeline's fiancé Neil discovers that she is not dead (as he'd believed), he exclaims, "Surely you don't think she's alive, in the hands of natives! Oh no! Better dead than that!" As many scholars have noted, these scenes are examples of **othering**: portraying those whom one sees as different from oneself as "Other," somehow fundamentally separate, and thereby reinforcing the belief that these "Other" people are somehow less important or less human (Kee 2011; see also DeGoul 2011). Both the zombies—and so too, the "natives" in the film who have been turned into zombies through "black magic"—are portrayed as essentially Other (see Kee 2011). As is regularly observed, this is doubtless because the white colonizers of Haiti feared the black Haitians they had enslaved and/or oppressed. In the eyes of both the filmmakers who created *White Zombie* and the viewers who watched the film, the zombie was a vehicle to express their fears—namely, people different, or Other, from them.

Fig. 21.4. Poster for the film *White Zombie*.
En.wikipedia.org.

The title *White Zombie* betrays these fears. The "white zombie" in the film is none other than Madeline, the young white fiancé who is turned into a zombie. No longer is becoming a zombie something that happens to Haitians, as described in Seabrock's novel, but something that could happen to non-Haitians as well. Moreover, as Madeline is turned into a mind-controlled shell of who she once was, she too becomes Other. When Neil proclaims, "Surely you don't think she's alive, in the hands of natives! Oh no! Better dead than that!" the film makes it clear, as Kee notes, that "it is better for a white woman to be destroyed than to intermix with the 'natives'" (Kee 2011, 16). Madeline's change into a zombie reflected fears not only of the Other, but also reveals fears and insecurities about women; specifically, that women might somehow be subject to the Other, weak enough to be taken over by them and willing to mix with those who were different than they were (Kee 2011, 16). So one of the movie posters advertising the film reads, "With these zombie eyes, he rendered her powerless. With this zombie grip, he made her perform his every desire!" In order to be saved, women like Madeline would need (white) men like Neil to save them (Kee 2011, 16–17).

As is often noted, at the heart of *White Zombie* are numerous questions and concerns simmering in then-contemporary American culture: issues surrounding colonialism and imperialism, coupled with fears that white (especially male) Americans might be losing power, both nationally and abroad (see Kee 2011). Additionally, the film promotes American stereotypes about gender, race, and the (profoundly misunderstood) **Vodoun** religion. Through careful analysis, the "monsters" of *White Zombie* reveal to us the fears and worries of the people who produced and watched the film. These fears and worries are closely related to the context that produced the film.

Notoriously, George Romero's films—beginning with *Night of the Living Dead* in 1968—radically transformed the zombie into the monster that slouches insatiably throughout American culture in the twenty-first century. Romero combined the Haitian notion of a human who lacks will power and the ability to think for themselves with the idea of a **ghoul**, a flesh-eating monster (Dendle 2010, 6). Romero's transformation, as Peter Dendle writes, "liberated the zombie from the shackles of a master, and invested his zombies not with a function (a job or a task such as zombies were standardly given by voodoo priests), but rather a drive (eating flesh)" (Dendle 2010, 6). The result: the birth of the moaning, decaying, slow moving, flesh-eating monsters that are scary because they cannot be stopped and because everyone human has the potential to become one. Such a creature is known among zombie fans as the "Romero zombie" (although the creatures are never called zombies in *Night of the Living Dead*). All subsequent zombie apocalypses are based, in part, on this creature from Romero's films (e.g., *World War Z, Sean of the Dead, Pontypool, iZombie*, etc.). Yet, zombies would continue to change, depending on when and where they appeared. This was especially the case in a post-9/11 world, which with fears of terrorism would give rise to the "fast zombie," like the rage-monsters of *28 Days Later* or the wall-scaling zombies of the film *WWZ*. More recently, zombies have taken a turn to the self-reflective, partial humanity-retaining creatures of *Warm Bodies* and *iZombie*.

The first zombies in America illustrated Americans' fear of the Other and concerns about race and gender in the 1930s. Romero continues this theme, yet with *Night of the Living Dead*, also creates a "new" monster. In many ways, he created an entirely *American* monster, whose name might derive from a West African word, but who would embody entirely Western (and often exclusively North American) concerns. The zombie continues to be one of our favorite monsters, from Romero's films, the many cannibalistic zombies movies inspired by Romero, to novels such as Max Brook's *World War Z* or Colin Whitehead's *Zone One*, and the comics and AMC television series *The Walking Dead*. In each case, zombies are (then and now) intricately connected to the context in which they were produced.

Context

In earlier chapters, you saw how closely connected apocalyptic texts are to the contexts in which they were produced. So, for instance, in the book of Revelation, the dragon that appears in Rev 12–13 and the two beasts found in Rev 13:1–18 are intricately connected to both other biblical texts and the larger ancient Near Eastern world. The first beast found in Rev 13:2 is apparently some kind of leopard, bear, and lion amalgamation ("And the beast that I saw was like a leopard, its feet were like a bear's, and its mouth was like a lion's mouth"), which closely resembles the strange beasts described in Daniel 7, where the descriptions of the beasts function as symbols for various oppressive empires, especially Antiochus Epiphanes IV (e.g., Dan 7:25). The authors of Revelation also utilize ancient Near Eastern imagery in their depiction of the monsters, especially for the dragon found in Rev 12–13, which closely resembles the Canaanite god Baal's sea-monster enemy Lothan, upon which the biblical Leviathan seems to be based. Yet in the new context of the book of Revelation, the dragon and beasts mean something new, too. According to many scholars, the beasts become symbols for the larger Roman Empire and elements of the Roman imperial apparatus that early Christian communities feared, while the dragon represents Satan throughout the book of Revelation (see Jeffcoat Schedtler, chapter 8). In Daniel and Revelation, monstrous beasts and terrifying dragons are a reflection of the sociopolitical context(s) of the author(s) who created them.

The biblical Leviathan provides another example. This ancient sea monster is found, in varying forms, in Canaanite and Ugaritic texts that pre-date the Bible. Leviathan swims his way into the Bible precisely because the biblical writers lived in the ancient Levant, and thus, they knew stories of sea monsters from the cultures that surrounded them. Yet, when he appears in the biblical texts, Leviathan is also continually reshaped and reformed. In some texts, God fought and defeated Leviathan before God was able to create the world ("You crushed the heads of Leviathan; you gave him as food for the creatures of the wilderness" [Ps 74:14]). However, in other texts, writers instead depict Leviathan as a kind of divine pet ("Yonder is the sea, great and wide/ creeping things innumerable are there/living things both small and great/There go the ships/and Leviathan that you formed to sport in it" [Ps 104:25–26]). These different depictions and changing portraits of Leviathan reflect the context in which the texts were written and exemplify how monsters change according to context (Beal 2002, 25–30). For example, many scholars argue that Psalm 74 was written after the Babylonian destruction of Jerusalem in 587 BCE. Appropriately, it makes sense that they might remember a time when their God was able to destroy a primordial chaos monster—surely if God can do that, God can *also* destroy the Babylonians who have wreaked such havoc on God's people (Beal 2002, 25–28, 80). By contrast, insofar as Psalm 104 appears to reflect a confidence in and praise of God's creation, it was perhaps written in a time that reflects more political stability or calm, and in which the threat of primordial chaos was not perceived (Beal 2002, 25–28). Later, when echoes of Leviathan appear in the book of Revelation's dragon, the sea monster transforms into a "new battle-red monster of destruction and persecution, namely, late first-century Rome, its emperors and its armies" (Beal 2002, 80; for more on Leviathan and a host of other biblical monsters, see Beal, *Religion and Its Monsters*). Leviathan, like the zombies of the nineteenth, twentieth, and twenty-first centuries, was continually changed and adapted to new contexts and situations.

Romero's *Night of the Living Dead* provides a contemporary analogue to how monsters change and reflect their context as they do so. For the first time, an evil sorcerer does not control the living dead and, for the first time, the living dead desires human flesh. Romero's creature in *Night of the Living* Dead is radically changed from Seabrock's depiction of zombies or the toiling field workers of *White Zombie*. Nearly the entire movie takes place inside a farmhouse in the United States; the living dead remain outside, only rarely directly threatening the main characters. When Ben (an African American male) and Barbra (a young white female who spends most of the film catatonic) make their way to the farmhouse, they discover a group of people hiding in the cellar, including Harry, a middle-aged white man, often described by film viewers as self-righteous and hot-tempered, who (among other things) locks Ben out of the house when Ben attempts to rescue some of the fellow survivors. In the end, Ben alone survives the night, only to be killed by a group of (all white) men who see him in the window of the farmhouse from afar as they are roaming the countryside and shooting any and all living dead that they might find. The movie ends with flashes of various photos, including one of Ben being placed onto a burning pile of wood among a pile of bodies of the living dead. The new context in which the zombie finds itself is radically different from earlier contexts, and the monster changes to reveal something new.

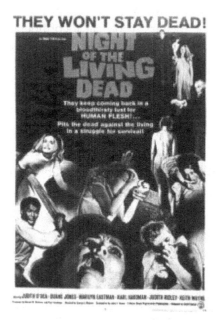

Fig. 21.5. Poster for Romero's *Night of the Living Dead*, the film that introduced the zombie into popular culture. En.wikipedia.org.

Zombie scholars regularly observe that however terrifying the zombie might be, it is routinely the case that the zombie threat usually pales in comparison to the threat of those still living after the epidemic has broken out. This can be seen in *Night of the Living Dead*, where Harry, and, later, the posse of men who show up to clear the countryside of the infected, pose more of a threat to Ben than the living dead ever do. Yet what does this reveal about the context that created this new monster? Scholars often note that *Night of the Living Dead* reflects the racial tensions of 1960s America. According to Romero, Ben was not originally slated to be played by an African American actor, but with the casting of the actor who played Ben, "Many audiences perceived the parallel between America's increasingly violent civil rights struggles—particularly the then-recent assassination of Martin Luther King by racist hitman James Earl Ray, with the suspected cooperation of the FBI—and Ben's execution at the guns of the redneck posse at film's end. Without a black actor in the lead, *Night* would still have been an innovative shocker but wouldn't have hit the cultural nerves it did" (Kane 2010, 36). In short, Romero's characters end up becoming intricately linked to the world in which they were created.

Like ancient apocalypses and their monsters, zombie films and narratives reflect the contexts in which they are created, and in so doing, often reveal the fears of those that write them. Originally, the fear of becoming a zombi in Haitian folklore revealed fears of slavery and loss of power, while *White Zombie* reveals the fear that white American colonizers had of those who were different from them. With Romero's introduction of the flesh-eating zombie into American culture, zombies would continue to reflect the contexts in which they were created. For example, Romero's *Dawn of the Dead* ruthlessly reflects American consumer culture in the 1970s, where hordes of the undead swarm to a shopping mall as if programmed to do so by their former selves. Max Brook's novel *World War Z* highlights American isolationist policies in an imagined global outbreak of a zombie virus. Isaac Marion's novel *Warm Bodies* has a self-aware zombie who reflects on American attitudes toward work, musing to himself, "I remember effort. I remember targets and deadlines, goals and ambitions. I remember being *purposeful*, always everywhere all the time" (Marion, 9). The template of the zombie as a vehicle for betraying the context in which it was created has been used outside of America as well, notably in *Shaun of the Dead*'s comedic take on the British slacker generation. Similarly, the British horror film *28 Days Later*, though not strictly about zombies proper, but rather concerned with people infected with a "rage virus," is often held up as reflecting post-9/11 concerns over terrorism, while also wrestling with human capability for cruelty and violence in the face of an apocalyptic event. Yet zombies, like ancient apocalypses, do more than simply reflect the culture they are produced in; they also serve to prophesy, in the biblical sense, against the perceived social ills of the contexts out of which they shuffle.

Prophecy

The word "prophecy" often invokes images of crystal balls and predicting far-off future events (cue Nostradamus or Professor Trelawney from *Harry Potter*). Yet, the original Greek meaning of the word *prophētēs* was not to predict the far-off future, but "to speak for another." In this way, biblical prophets such as Jeremiah or Ezekiel spoke for God to the ancient Israelites and warned them of their (perceived) wrongs, often giving the people a chance to turn back and repent. In general, biblical prophets were more interested in the *near* future than in the far off future. This, of course, is one of the distinctions between the genre of biblical apocalypse and the genre of biblical prophecy, though at times, the ancient apocalypses functioned prophetically, too—such as when John of Patmos warns of the dangers of the Roman Empire, its Emperor(s), and its socio-political machinations (see Rev 2:19–29; 17:1–18:24).

If it is routinely the case that the zombie threat usually pales in comparison to the threat of those still living after the epidemic has broken out, it is also the case that in zombie narratives, the zombie also pales in comparison to the ills of the society that produced the monster in the first place. Kim Paffenroth writes that although zombie films "depict the apocalypse in outwardly secular terms as a mass plague, usually with no explicit mention of God," they "nonetheless frequently use that apocalypse to pass judgment on current American society and sinfulness, often sounding much like Old Testament prophets in their decrying of sins and announcement of judgment" (Paffenroth 2012, 145). Paffenroth traces the way that Romero's films function prophetically, noting how from *Night of the Living Dead* forward, the films would assess—and find wanting—the society they portrayed (Paffenroth 2012, 149). For Paffenroth and others, *Night of the Living Dead* provides one example of how zombie films, like stories that feature monsters—biblical or otherwise—function to reveal to society perceived imminent dangers. Despite the fact that the main character in *Night of the Living Dead* is Ben, an African American male, the film itself never makes note of the race of Ben or any of the other characters (Paffenroth 2012, 150). Romero, according to his own words, cast the actor who played Ben because of his acting skills and not because of his skin color (Kane 2010, 31–36). Yet, as noted above, though Ben survives the night, he is immediately killed by a group of (all white) men who see him from afar in the window of the farmhouse as they are eliminating the infected population. Paffenroth writes, "Romero seems to go out of his way to surround the posse with imagery that makes it nearly impossible to overlook their similarity to an American lynch mob—a crowd of exclusively white men, only loosely governed by governmental authorities, with guns and barking dogs, killing everything in their path" (Paffenroth 2012, 150). He continues, "Moreover, in their roles as protectors and re-establishers of societal order—which is to say, white, American, capitalist order—against the zombies' chaos, the posse's killing of a black man may be meant to equate him with the zombies as a perceived threat to that order" (Paffenroth 2012, 150). Accordingly, Romero's film functions prophetically, warning of the dangers posed by the racism and social tensions of 1960s America. Like the biblical prophets, Romero seems to be calling on Americans to turn and change their ways.

Fig. 21.6. Ben and others contemplate their next steps in Night
of the Living Dead, © Image Ten, 1968.

At face value, comparison between Romero's film (and many other
zombie narratives or movies) and the prophets seems to highlight the
former's bleakness, at best. After all, what hope for the world is there
in *28 Days Later*, where soldiers attempt to rape women even after the
breakout of virus that causes the infected people to act violently? Or
in Brooks's *World War Z*, where a survivor reflects on the end of the
human war with the zombies, "We'd just gotten the word, it was VA
Day. There was no cheering, no celebration. It just didn't seem real.
Peace? What the hell did that mean? I'd been afraid of so long, fighting
and killing, and waiting to die, that I guess I just accepted it as normal
for the rest of my life. I thought it was a dream, sometimes it still
feels like one . . ." (Brooks, 338). Often, the zombie apocalypse seems
anything but hopeful.

In the biblical prophetic books, those who had erred heard the
prophet's message and (usually) had a chance to turn from their
wrongdoings. In the zombie apocalypse, the presence of zombies
sometimes means that it is too late to right whatever might have gone
wrong. It is only in retrospect that whatever led to the destruction of
human society, as we know it, is revealed (if it ever is). Even when
Night of the Living Dead ends with the apparent destruction of all the

zombie-esque creatures that killed everyone in the farmhouse except Ben, Ben himself dies at the hands of his apparent rescuers. There's not much **hope** in such a scenario—and this strongly contrasts with the cathartic message of the books of Daniel or Revelation, which assure their audiences that soon, the world will be righted and the divine balance of good restored.

Hope

Unlike some zombie stories, one of the recurring themes in ancient apocalyptic texts is that of hope. Daniel ends with the promise of eschatological salvation ("you shall rise for your reward at the end of the days" [Dan 12:13]). So too in Revelation, with its raging beasts and looming dragons at the beginning, one still finds hope in the book's end, when residents live peacefully in the holy city, replete with streets of gold and the radiance of a rare jewel (Rev 21:9–27). At the end of the day, no matter how desolate or terrifying the ancient apocalypses might seem at first, they are ultimately meant to be read as hopeful and cathartic for their intended audiences.

At first glance, there does not seem to be much that is hopeful in zombie narratives or films. This is particularly the case in the story of Ben outlined above. Though Ben survives the horrors of the *Night of the Living Dead*, in the morning he is immediately shot by the posse of men who (perhaps?) mistake him for one of the flesh-eating creatures. Romero's films are often starkly desolate: in the original script of Romero's 1979 *Dawn of the Dead*, the two protagonists, Peter and Francine, were going to kill themselves after the shopping mall in which they had briefly found refuge was attacked by a biker gang and swarmed by the undead. In the released version, things do not end much more positively—the pair manages to fly away in a helicopter, but it's only partially fueled and leaves the viewer with an ominous sense regarding their ultimate survival. Even when a Romero ending is more positive—as when a trio of survivors makes it to a zombie-free island in the 1985 *Day of the Dead*—it is still portentously marked by a final scene when one of the survivors wakes up from a nightmare in which she was being attacked by a zombie and then subsequently gets a calendar out of her bag, crossing off the number of days since they managed to escape to the safe island. How many days of safety and island-living tranquility do they have left, before the undead find their way to the island?

Yet, in contrast to the often-bleak narratives found in Romero's films, other zombie stories do include a striking element of hope. Though it might not at first glance seem to be the case, the television series *The Walking Dead* has, in some ways, always been about hope: from the outset, Rick hopes he would find his family, that he would find them a safe place to thrive in the aftermath of the apocalypse, and that some kind of just and merciful society might be rebuilt out of the wreckage of the post-apocalyptic world. This is the impetus that drives Rick from his hospital bed and into the streets of Atlanta, searching for his missing wife and child. In the fourth season, hope in the face of a zombie apocalypse is at the forefront of the show, especially as the group experiences one devastating loss after another. Some of these losses consist of deaths of favorite characters: Bob, Beth, Tyrese, and Noah. Other moments explore characters' loss of hope. After Beth's death, as the group makes their way toward Washington D.C., Maggie asks Sasha, "How much longer do we have?" Though Sasha responds in terms of miles to their destination, Maggie simply notes, "That's not what I meant." Her hope—like many others in the group—wanes as each opportunity for rebuilding eludes the group. By the end of the fifth and most recent season, the hope of the walled neighborhood called Alexandria falls alongside the memories of other dashed hopes: the CDC, the prison, Terminus. Once again, viewers are confronted with the characters' devastating loss in the face of the zombie apocalypse—what remains to be seen is how the characters will regroup and recuperate, and thereby, return them to the (however subtle) theme of hope that has marked the series since its opening episode.

For the survivors on *The Walking Dead*, hope keeps them going. This is not the hope that God will intervene and destroy the Roman Imperial system, the Walkers, or the equally frightening human enemies such as the Governor, the community at Terminus, or The Saviors, with Negan as leader. But it is, nonetheless, *hope*. Constantly echoing in the background are Rick's words from the first episode of season two. There, Rick stood alone on a hilltop, reflecting on the revelation that the CDC held no answers or help for the survivors. Though Rick was speaking into a two-way radio as part of a promise to reunite with Morgan, a post-apocalyptic friend he had left behind in the first season, the words became prayer-like when he spoke them into the silence: "We're facing a long, hard journey. . . . That's what lies ahead, and I'm trying hard not to lose faith. I can't, if I do the others––my family, my wife, my son . . . there's just a few of us now. . . . So we've got to stick together" (Season Two, Episode 1). Community has been what has provided the survivors in *The Walking Dead* with hope in the face of a world that is otherwise bleak and full of anguish (see Moyse 2012, 124–44). *The Walking Dead* reveals to contemporary audiences the roles that hope can play, not only in the fictional imaginings of a horribly violent, post-apocalyptic life, but also in everyday life—much as apocalypses did for the audiences of the early Jewish and Christian apocalyptic tales. In *The Walking Dead*, the zombie apocalypse is rooted, ultimately, in the hope that *humanity* might turn to good, to rebuilding, to restoring—even in the face of evil.

At first glance, the themes of bleak despair and/or hope that run like a thread through both ancient apocalyptic stories and contemporary ones such as *Night of the Living Dead* or The *Walking Dead* may seem fundamentally different. Both *Night of the Living Dead* and The *Walking Dead* are largely secular narratives; God is sometimes invoked, but religion takes a back seat to survival. Yet, even as hope takes on different forms in different contexts, the literary worlds of the ancient Jews and Christians and the on-screen world of Ben or Rick are strikingly similar: there are sometimes only small differences between ancient and contemporary apocalyptic thought. In particular, the difference between the often ultimately hopeful stories of *The Walking Dead* and the often desolate, uninviting world of the Romero films returns us once more to ancient apocalyptic texts. There, too, is a significant tension. In books such as Daniel and Revelation, *this* world is repeatedly portrayed as hopeless, awful, bleak, and controlled by the powers of evil. After all, these books proclaim time and time again, you only have to look around to see that this is the case. The tension then is with the counter-intuitive promise that the texts hold for their audiences: that despite how the world seems, God—and not humans—is ultimately in control of history. The oppressed and downtrodden audiences will, the books proclaim, prevail in the end (even though this seems highly unlikely using the logic of the world in which the audiences live, where figures such as Antiochus IV or Nero dominate and oppress). Much like the tension between the bleak outlook of Romero and the (however muted) hope of *The Walking Dead*, ancient apocalyptic narratives sit on the threshold between the bleakness of this world and the hope of the divine. Of course, in the world of the *The Walking Dead*, hope ultimately resides in *humans*—that, at the end of the day, there is enough good in humanity to overcome the evil that is also present. In the ancient apocalypses, hope resides in God's divine intervention into history, and with the handful of the faithful who will eventually prevail.

Conclusion

Like biblical monsters, the monster we now call "zombie" has changed—and doubtless, will continue to change—with time. With each change—from the original Haitian concept of the zombi as an enslaved and possessed individual to the xenophobic themes present in *White Zombie,* to the shuffling, flesh-hungry figures from *Night of the Living Dead*—the creatures we call zombies reveal to us our fears: fear of the Other, fear of women, fear of terrorism or ecological destruction or death. Zombies, too, reveal much about the context and situations of their creators as well as their audiences—from the real life effects of colonization, the ways in which racism renders survival hopeless, or the fact that we might live in a world that we see only through the screens of our computers and smartphones. Good zombie stories also reveal the concerns of their makers, who prophesy against the dangers of ignoring the social injustices that surround us or turning a blind eye or living a life that destines us all for destruction. And often, even the most hopeless zombie tales nevertheless provide us with something cathartic, something to hold onto or hope for in the face of the world around us, which might not be quite what we want it to be. Zombies, in their many forms, *reveal*—they cross the threshold from the mundane to the marvelous, they show us what we otherwise miss in our banal, workaday lives. In the stories we tell, zombies, like all monsters, are good to think with.

Faced with the shambling, stumbling zombie hordes—or, perhaps more terrifyingly, with the rage-filled zombie-esque monsters of *28 Days Later* or the wall-scaling zombies of the film *WWZ*—people often ask, "But what do zombies mean?" There have been many attempts to categorize the zombie, to say, "*This* is what zombies signify." Yet, like Leviathan and the monstrous beasts found in apocalypses, the zombie signifies many things at once (even if, in a particular narrative, we can narrow down their meaning potential to fear of the Other or concerns over death or worries about terrorism). The multifaceted emotion the zombie provokes ultimately goes beyond any literalistic referent. In this way, the zombie helps us to think, to understand our contexts, to critique social ills, and exemplify the resilience of hope in the face of a world that argues that all is lost. Zombies mean all this and more, just as ancient apocalyptic texts and their monsters did and continue to do.

Finally, as scholars have long noted, apocalyptic texts—sacred or secular, ancient or modern—all ask the same profound questions humans have long wrestled with: what does it mean to be human? What separates "us" from the "Other"? Why do we exist? How do we avoid the mistakes made by those who came before us? Where we are going—not just today, tomorrow, or according to our five-year plan, but where is history headed and what is our place in that narrative arc? Perhaps most importantly, how can we make things better *here and now* when it seems like this world is at its worst?

Study Questions:

1. Where did the contemporary idea of zombies come from? How is it different than the original conception of the *zombi* in West African and Haitian thought?
2. "Monsters" often change over time. In what ways does this reflect the fears/concerns of their contexts? Give at least one ancient and one contemporary example of such a change.
3. Why are the categories of violence, gender, and race useful for analyzing contemporary pop culture imaginings of the apocalypse? What similarities and differences do you see between these themes in contemporary apocalypses and in ancient apocalyptic thought and its afterlives?
4. What role do both fear and hope play in contemporary apocalypses in pop culture? What similarities and differences do you see between these themes in contemporary apocalypses and in ancient apocalyptic thought and its afterlives?

Bibliography and Further Reading:

Beal, Timothy K. *Religion and Its Monsters*. New York: Routledge, 2002.

Brooks, Max. *World War Z: An Oral History of the Zombie War*. New York: Three Rivers Press, 2007.

Christie, Deborah, and Sarah Juliet Lauro, eds. *Better Off Dead: The Evolution of the Zombie as Post-Human*. New York: Fordham University Press, 2011.

Cohen, Jeffrey, ed. *Monster Theory: Reading Culture*. Minneapolis, MN: University of Minnesota Press, 1996.

DeGoul, Franck. "'We are the mirror of your fears': Haitian Identity and Zombification." In *Better Off Dead: The Evolution of the Zombie as Post-Human*. Edited by Deborah Christie and Sarah Juliet Lauro. New York: Fordham University Press, 2011.

Dendle, Peter. *The Zombie Movie Encyclopedia*. Jefferson, NC: McFarland, 2010.

Kane, Joe. *Night of the Living Dead: Behind the Scenes of the Most Terrifying Zombie Movie Ever.* Kensington: Citadel Press, 2010.

Kee, Chera. "'They are not men . . . they are dead bodies': From Cannibal to Zombie and Back Again." In *Better Off Dead: The Evolution of the Zombie as Post-Human.* Edited by Deborah Christie and Sarah Juliet Lauro. New York: Fordham University Press, 2011.

Lowder, James, ed. *Triumph of the Walking Dead: Robert Kirkman's Zombie Epic on Page and Screen.* Dallas, TX: BenBella Books, 2011.

Marion, Isaac. *Warm Bodies.* New York: Atira, 2011.

McIntosh, Shawn. "The Evolution of the Zombie: The Monster That Keeps Coming Back." In *Zombie Culture: Autopsies of the Living Dead.* Edited by Shawn McIntosh and Marc Leverette. Lanham, MD: Scarecrow, 2008.

Moyse, Ashley John. "When All is Lost, Gather 'Round: Solidarity as Hope Resisting Despair in the Walking Dead." In *The Undead and Theology.* Edited by Kim Paffenroth and John W. Morehead. Eugene, OR: Wipf and Stock, 2012.

Paffenroth, Kim. "Apocalyptic Images and Prophetic Function in Zombie Films." In *The Undead and Theology.* Edited by Kim Paffenroth and John W. Morehead. Eugene, OR: Wipf and Stock, 2012.

_____. *Gospel of the Living Dead: George Romero's Visions of Hell on Earth.* Waco, TX: Baylor University Press, 2006.

Pagano, David. "The Space of Apocalypse in Zombie Cinema." In *Zombie Culture: Autopsies of the Living Dead.* Edited by Shawn McIntosh and Marc Leverette. Lanham, MD: Scarecrow, 2008.

Poole, W. Scott. *Monsters in America: Our Historical Obsession with the Hideous and the Haunting.* Waco, TX: Baylor University Press, 2011.

Seabrock, William. *The Magic Island.* New York: Dover Publications, 2016. (1929).

Contributors

Travis E. Ables studies Christology and anthropology in the Augustinian tradition, and has a special interest in medieval apocalyptic and mystical traditions. He is the author of *Incarnational Realism: Trinity and the Spirit in Augustine and Barth* (Bloomsbury, 2013), and is writing *The Body of the Cross: A Theological History of the Atonement* (Fortress). He is currently an independent scholar and in the discernment process for the priesthood in the Episcopal Diocese of Colorado.

Brennan Breed is Assistant Professor of Old Testament at Columbia Theological Seminary. He is author of *Nomadic Text: A Theory of Biblical Reception History* (Indiana University Press, 2014), and contributed to Carol Newsom, *Daniel: A Commentary* (Westminster John Knox, 2014). He has published research on art history in the volume *Ut Pictura Meditatio: Meditative Image in Northern Art 1500-1700*. Brennan regularly teaches courses on the book of Daniel, reception history, and the history of visual art. He was awarded the Manfred Lautenschlaeger Award for Theological Promise in 2016.

Greg Carey is Professor of New Testament at Lancaster Theological Seminary. His publications include *Ultimate Things: An Introduction to Jewish and Christian Apocalyptic Literature* (co-edited with L. Gregory Bloomquist) and *Vision and Persuasion: Rhetorical Dimensions of Apocalyptic Discourse*.

Thomas Fabisiak focuses on ancient apocalyptic literature and its modern reception history, as well as on literary theory, social theory, and the history of the critical study of religion and the Bible. He is the author of *The "Nocturnal Side of Science" in David Friedrich Strauss's Life of Jesus Critically Examined* (SBL Press, 2015). Fabisiak serves as Co-Director of Candler School of Theology's Certificate in Theological Studies Program at Lee Arrendale State Prison in north Georgia. He is working with Life University and the Georgia Department of Corrections to launch an Associate of Arts degree program at the facility in Summer 2016.

Christopher B. Hays is D. Wilson Moore Associate Professor of Ancient Near Eastern Studies at Fuller Theological Seminary. His publications include *Death in the Iron Age II and in First Isaiah* (Tübingen: Mohr Siebeck, 2011), for which he was awarded the Manfred Lautenschlaeger Award for Theological Promise in 2013, and an upcoming article, "From Propaganda to Apocalypse: An Empirical Model for the Formation of Isaiah 24-27," to be published in *Hebrew Bible and Ancient Israel*.

Justin Jeffcoat Schedtler is Visiting Assistant Professor of Religion at Macalester College. He has taught courses on "The Book of Revelation: Then and Now" and "The End Times: Apocalypticism in the Bible and Beyond." His publications on the book of Revelation include *A Heavenly Chorus: The Dramatic Function of Revelation's Hymns* (Mohr Siebeck, 2014) and *The Last King: Royal Ideology in the Book of Revelation* (forthcoming).

Joshua Jipp is Assistant Professor of New Testament at Trinity Evangelical Divinity School. He has recently published *Christ is King: Paul's Royal Ideology* with Fortress Press (2015) and a review article of one of the most prominent apocalyptic interpreters of Paul, "Douglas Campbell's Apocalyptic, Rhetorical Paul: Review Article," *Horizons in Biblical Theology* 32 (2010): 183–97.

Joseph Laycock is Assistant Professor of Religious Studies at Texas State University. He is on the editorial board for the journal*Nova*

Religio and his books include *The Seer of Bayside: Veronica Lueken and the Struggle to Define Catholicism* (Oxford University Press, 2014) and *Dangerous Games: What the Moral Panic over Role-Playing Games Says About Play, Religion, and Imagined Worlds* (University of California Press, 2015).

Ingrid E. Lilly is a visiting scholar at the Pacific School of Religion (Berkeley, Calif). She has taught at Western Kentucky University, San Francisco Theological Seminary, the Graduate Theological Union, Candler School of Theology, and Georgia State. She is currently writing a book on the cultural history of spirit and the ANE combat mythos. This topic intersects with her work on environment, climate, natural disasters, and religion. Other projects include her first book, *Two Books of Ezekiel: Papyrus 967 and the Masoretic Text as Variant Literary Editions* (Brill, 2010) and the educational web-publication FLOODofNOAH.com, which led to an interview appearance on On Point (NPR).

Mohamed A. Mohamed is Assistant Professor of Sociology at Northern Arizona University, where he specializes in Globalization, Sociology of Religion, Politics, Social Movements, Sociology of the Internet, and Contemporary Social Theory.

Kelly J. Murphy is Assistant Professor in the Department of Philosophy and Religion at Central Michigan University, where she teaches "From Revelation to 'The Walking Dead': Apocalypse Then and Now," along with other classes on the Hebrew Bible and the New Testament. She is the author of *Gideon The Man* (Oxford University Press, 2017), and has written for Ugarit-Forschungen, The Journal of the Bible and Its Reception, the Fortress Commentary on the Bible: Old Testament and Apocrypha, and the Women's Bible Commentary, Third Edition. Her work on zombies and the apocalypse has appeared in online publications like The Washington Post and Religion Dispatches. She also serves on the steering committees for the Society of Biblical

Literature's Poverty in the Biblical World section and the Ideological Criticism section.

James W. Perkinson is a long-time activist/educator/artist from inner city Detroit, currently teaching as Professor of Social Ethics at the Ecumenical Theological Seminary and lecturing in Intercultural Communication Studies at the University of Oakland (Michigan). He holds a PhD in theology (but focused broadly on history of religions) from the University of Chicago, is the author of *White Theology: Outing Supremacy in Modernity*; *Shamanism, Racism, and Hip-Hop Culture: Essays on White Supremacy and Black Subversion*; *Messianism Against Christology: Resistance Movements, Folk Arts, and Empire*; and *Political Spirituality in an Age of Eco-Apocalypse: Essays in Communication and Struggle Across Species, Cultures, and Religions*; as well as a book of poetry entitled *Dreaming Moorish*. He has written extensively on questions of race, indigenous struggle and colonialism in connection with religion and urban culture and is a recognized artist on the spoken-word poetry scene in the inner city.

Matthew S. Rindge is Associate Professor of Religious Studies at Gonzaga University, where he teaches "Bible and Film" and "Life and Teachings of Jesus." He is the author of two books: *Jesus's Parable of the Rich Fool: Luke 12:13-34 among Ancient Conversations on Death and Possessions* (SBL, 2011) and *Profane Parables: Film and the American Dream* (Baylor University Press, 2016). His articles and essays have appeared in scholarly journals (*Journal of Biblical Literature, Catholic Biblical Quarterly, Teaching Theology and Religion, Interpretation*), edited volumes (*Bible and Cinema, The Bible in Motion*), and media outlets (The Washington Post). He chairs the Bible and Film section in the Society of Biblical Literature, and serves on the steering committee for SBL's Bible and Popular Culture section. In 2011 he received the Paul J. Achtemeier Award for New Testament Scholarship.

Shayna Sheinfeld is Visiting Assistant Professor of Religion at Centre College in Danville, Kentucky. She has published articles on the pseudepigrapha, on apocalypses, and on the reception of Jewish scripture in Second Temple, Rabbinic, and early Christian circles. In addition to teaching about biblical texts and Judaism, Dr. Sheinfeld teaches upper-division courses on apocalypses in the ancient and modern periods, as well as courses about women in antiquity and about suffering, pain, and martyrdom in Jewish and Christian texts. She also writes extensively on pedagogical practices in the classroom.

Karl Shuve is Assistant Professor of Religious Studies at The University of Virginia, where he covers apocalyptic trends in courses on "The Rise of Christianity" and "The Nag Hammadi Library and Gnosticism." He is the author of *The Song of Songs and the Fashioning of Identity in Early Latin Christianity* (Oxford: 2016).

Michael J. Thate is a Post-Doctoral Research Associate at Princeton University as well as an Alexander von Humboldt Fellow at Tübingen University. He is the author of,*Remembrance of Things Past?* (Mohr Siebeck, 2013). In addition to several journal articles he is also the editor of two projects: one on participation themes in antiquity and Paul (Mohr Siebeck, 2014); the other on the philosophical ethics of Albert Schweitzer (Syracuse University Press, 2016). His current research revolves around material messianisms during the early twentieth century, measurements of time, and the temporal effects of technology.

Robert H. von Thaden Jr. is Associate Professor and Chair of Religious Studies at Mercyhurst University in Erie, PA. An active member of the Society of Biblical Literature, he serves as chair of the Cognitive Linguistics in Biblical Studies section. He is also serving as the current president of the Eastern Great Lakes Biblical Society. He is the author of *Sex, Christ, and Embodied Cognition: Paul's Wisdom for Corinth* (Deo, 2012) and a number of essays and articles.

Robert Williamson Jr. is Margaret Berry Hutton Odyssey Associate Professor of Religious Studies and Director of the Miller Center for

Vocation, Ethics, and Calling at Hendrix College in Conway, Arkansas. His course "Revelation and Resistance" explores apocalyptic literature as resistance to Empire in both ancient and modern contexts. He is the author of *The Forgotten Books of the Bible*, forthcoming from Fortress Press in 2017.

Jackie Wyse-Rhodes is Assistant Professor of Religion at Bluffton University in Bluffton, OH and aPhD candidate at Emory University, currently writing a dissertation that explores depictions of the natural world in early Jewish apocalyptic literature. At Bluffton, Jackie teaches exegetical seminars for undergraduates on ancient apocalyptic literature and the book of Daniel. She has published an essay on violence and peace in the Book of the Watchers in the collection *Struggles for Shalom: Peace and Violence Across the Testaments* (Pickwick Publications, 2014).

Index